ECONOMICS OF RACISM II: The Roots
of Inequality, USA

ECONOMICS OF RACISM II

The Roots of Inequality, USA

Victor Perlo

International Publishers / New York

Dedication
This one is for Joelle,
valiant fighter for equality

Library of Congress Cataloging-in-Publication Data

Perlo, Victor
    Economics of Racism II: the roots of inequality, USA /
    Victor Perlo
    p. cm.
Includes bibliographical references and index.
ISBN 0–7178–0697–9 : $18.50 (alk. paper).
ISBN 0–7178–0698–7 pbk. : $9.75 (alk. paper)
1. Racism--Economic aspects--United States. 2. Afro-Americans-
-Economic conditions. 3. Hispanic Americans--Economic condi-
tions. 4. United States--Race relations. I. Title.
E185.8.P417 1996   96–7304
331.6'396073--dc20   CIP

CONTENTS

ACKNOWLEDGEMENTS

My thanks to:

Eugene and Beulah Link for their encouragement and assistance

Professor David Eisenhower for his contribution of the chapter on Education

Professor Lawrence Weiss for his contribution of the chapter on Health Care

Betty Smith, whose role as publisher was much exceeded with her technical skill, editorial suggestions, and continuing attention to details

My Ellen, whose editorial and consultative participation was essential to completion of the manuscript and its preparation for publication, and for her significant contribution to the quality of the book.

CREDITS

Cover and cartoon on page 125 by Norman Goldberg

Charts by Ellen Perlo

LIST OF TABLES

vii

LIST OF CHARTS

GLOSSARY

AFL–CIO	American Federation of Labor–Congress of Industrial Organizations
BLS	Bureau of Labor Statistics of U.S. Dept. of Labor
CBTU	Coalition of Black Trade Unionists
CEA	Council of Economic Advisers (President's)
CPI	Consumer Price Index
CPI-U	Consumer Price Index-Urban
CPR	Current Population Reports, Census Bureau
E&E	*Employment & Earnings*
EEOC	Equal Employment Opportunity Commission
EROP	*Economic Report of the President*
FDIC	Federal Deposit Insurance Company
FRB	Federal Reserve Board
GDP	Gross Domestic Product
GNP	Gross National Product
HEW	Department of Health, Education and Welfare
Hist. Stat.	*Historical Statistics of the U.S.*
INS	Immigration and Naturalization Service
IRS	Internal Revenue Service
IWW	Industrial Workers of the World
NAACP	National Association for the Advancement of Colored People
NAFTA	North American Free Trade Agreement
NCES	National Center for Educational Statistics
NLRB	National Labor Relations Board
NYT	*New York Times*
SBA	Small Business Administration
Stat. Abst.	*Statistical Abstract of the United States*
WSJ	*Wall Street Journal*

ECONOMICS OF RACISM II: The Roots
of Inequality, USA

1. Introduction

Racism and the struggles swirling around it have taken center stage in the political life of the United States. Of course racism has been virulent throughout U.S. history, a country built on the labor of African slaves, as well as on the exploitation of other immigrant workers. The Civil War in the 1860s ended legal slavery, but after the defeat of postwar Reconstruction, plantation owners and capitalists subjected Black people to a semi-slave "Jim Crow" regime in the South until the mass struggles of African Americans erupted in the mid-1950s.

That Civil Rights Movement, involving millions of Black people and their white supporters, reached its climax during the mid-1960s. The mass struggles led to laws passed by Congress that compelled the retreat of racist ruling cliques in southern states. Some essential goals were partly won: the right to enter public places and to purchase all services offered to the general public without being segregated or otherwise discriminated against; the right to vote and to be elected to office.

Those victories remain far from complete. Many eating places evaded the law by establishing themselves as "whites only" private clubs. School desegregation was fractionally accomplished, and in many northern cities has decreased. Gerrymandering and other ploys still reduce the effectiveness of minorities' votes. There are still many cities, suburbs, sections of towns that are out-of-bounds to Black homeowners. Police brutality and murder of Blacks and all racial minorities continues on a critical scale.

In fact, in the 1980s and the 1990s, there has been a serious escalation in the racist offensive. It embraces all aspects of life—economic, cultural, social, political—even to so basic a feature as the right to exist. Slavery, with its crude inhumanity, meant vast profits for the slave owners. The current racist offensive is also motivated by greed. Huge profits are realized from the underpaid labor and inflated living costs charged the rapidly growing minority population. Moreover, increasingly, the living standards of white workers are pulled down by the extra exploitation imposed on the victims of racism.

The right-wing political offensive against elected Black officials has a similar impact, as in the U.S. system, elected incumbents are key to appointing their constituents to government jobs and access to government contracts. In addition, the right-biased judicial system strikes one blow after another against affirmative action, the principal mechanism designed to reduce discrimination against African Americans.

Then, too, racist prejudices are inflamed by cultural attacks that, on the one

1

hand overemphasize the few instances where Blacks have "made it"and live in harmony with whites and, on the other hand, give wide publicity and credence to the ugly, fraudulent, scientifically discredited theory of Black "genetic inferiority."

A very important factor: rapidly escalating in numbers and power, police forces and their political allies make criminal assaults on Black and Latino communities, killing indiscriminately and, without due process, imprisoning a large percentage of Black males. While falsely accusing African Americans and Latinos of being the main perpetrators of crime, the police, themselves, have become infested with large-scale corruption and have become a well-paid haven for racist thugs and hoodlums.

All these factors deal devastating blows against the victimized minorities. This is the frightening environment in which we consider all aspects of life, in the context of the economics of racism.

Economic equality is a necessary condition for furthering and safeguarding the gains of the Civil Rights movement; for making real the formal political and social equality inscribed in law.

The primacy of economic struggle is unquestionable. It is certain to grow; bound to become central to any upsurge of large-scale public activity that aims to deal with the country's economic problems. Sixty years ago Franklin D. Roosevelt, then President of the United States, referred to the South as our nation's number one economic problem. And so it was, largely because the Black population was then concentrated in the South, and their special oppression, economic and otherwise, was most extreme there. Now this oppression has been modified somewhat, but certainly not ended. It has spread out geographically and has, to some extent, become more uniform in its severity throughout the country.

Today we have to say that economic discrimination against African Americans is the nation's number one problem within the overall context of a decaying capitalist system and the corresponding sharpening of the class struggle between capital and labor. No economic problem affecting the majority of the population can be solved or significantly eased unless the solution includes a vast improvement in the economic situation of Black people and substantial reduction of discrimination against them. As the African American people, along with the growing Latino population, have provided increasing superprofits to their exploiters, reactionaries have continually sought to roll back all earlier, hard-won gains.

Since about 1980, right-wing forces centered in the Republican Party have used racism as their decisive political weapon to win victories at the polls and in economic policy. This does not mean that the majority of workers condone such policies but that the majority of voters were persuaded to support those candidates. The majority of white Americans are not conscious racists. Yet, unfortunately it is true that millions of white Americans are infected with racist prejudices to varying degrees, derived from the racist propaganda fostered by those who profit from discrimination. The reactionary trend intensified in the 1990s with the rise of neofascist groups and their strong links with the Republican Party. As a result, there has been an increase in the exploitation and impoverishment of the Black and Latino peoples, with negligible opposition from the other capitalist party, the Democrats.

This book examines the ideological weapons of the racist economic offensive. It exposes and counters a number of apologetic explanations for white/Black inequality, mainly those that "blame the victim." There is the fashionable rationale that white males are victims of "reverse discrimination" due to gains by minorities and women—an argument readily refuted by objective facts, but still influential among sections of the white population. It feeds on the insecurity that all workers feel in this age of mass downsizing, plant closing, and overall instability of employment. Especially sinister is the reanimated propaganda of genetic inferiority, popularized in the pseudo-scientific "Bell Curve" of Herrnstein and Murray.

The linkage between the fate of the entire working class and that of the minority peoples—especially Black and Latino—is explored, along with a discussion of the actual and potential role of trade unions. Also analyzed in detail is the all-out campaign, intensified in the mid-1990s, against "affirmative action."

In economic terms the goal is not "equal opportunity" but equality in practice. This requires special measures to overcome the inequality built into the existing structure, to systematically and deliberately raise the relative economic status of masses of African Americans to a level of equality with white workers in a short period of time. It requires an effective, enforced program of affirmative action.

Since the 1940s, the economic gains that Black people have achieved absolutely and relatively were not due mainly to affirmative action but to a spillover from the vast expansion of the economic size and power of U.S. imperialism, and to the huge demand for labor as a result of its wars: World War II, Korea, Vietnam.

Analyses of the economics of racism have a long history, going back to the works of Karl Marx and W.E.B. Du Bois. In recent years, such studies have proliferated, with contributions by scholars, Black and white; research departments of African American organizations; and economists of all persuasions. Noteworthy are the outstanding works by Massey and Denton on housing and segregation;[1] Kozol on education;[2] and Horne on affirmative action;[3] as well as more general works by Hacker[4] and Tidwell.[5] But there are also rationalizations for racism by African Americans that are widely circulated and quoted by the Establishment media as justification for blaming the victim. Discrimination against Hispanic people of Latin American origin (Latinos) is also severe, as brought out in many chapters of this book. The victims, and their supporters, regard this as a manifestation of racism. There is no officially recognized "Hispanic race," and most Latinos, ethnically, are a mixture of white European, indigenous and African stock. From the viewpoint of their oppressors and exploiters, they are regarded as conquered peoples.

There are two roots of this particular racist ideology: (1) the invasion and seizure of their homelands in the Southwest of the United States in the 1830s and 1840s; and (2) the appropriation of the resources and the brutal exploitation of the peoples of Latin America by U.S. monopoly capital over the past century. Most "Hispanics" in the United States are immigrants—or their descendants—from these countries.

In official U.S. classifications, most Latinos are counted as "white." Will they gradually be merged into the dominant white sector, as were earlier immigrants from Europe? So far there is little sign of it. The difference in historical background and, to some extent, the class composition of the immigrants—plus, to varying degrees, color—impede such a resolution. The overall trend for several decades has been toward rising discrimination against, and impoverishment of, "Hispanics" in the United States.

Struggles to correct this, along with discrimination against and impoverishment of other racially oppressed peoples, is now on the agenda.

The intensification of racism in the 1990s has been accompanied by a renewal of active anti-Semitism. In Europe for a thousand years, ruling classes used anti-Semitism as a weapon to divide exploited peasants and workers. Anti-Semitism accompanied the European capitalists when they came to America. Many Jewish people, of all social classes, emigrated to America to escape the horrors of European persecution, even before it reached its climax in Nazi Germany. Today, more Jews live in the United States than in any other country, and they play a disproportionately large part in the economic, cultural and political life of the country. The latest intensification of anti-Semitic incitations is very serious.

There is another aspect to this problem.

Friction between the Jewish and Black communities has focused on the issue of Zionism, and solidarity with oppressed Arab peoples by African American groups. However, while the existence of Israel has strong support in the U.S. Jewish communities, its imperialist stance does not. Those who depict Jews as the main exploiters of Black people are provocateurs, exponents of the divide-and-rule tactics of racists. Sure, Jewish capitalists have racist prejudices, as do Christian capitalists; and Jewish capitalists participate in superexploitation of Black people, as do all capitalists. But a significant proportion of Jewish people among workers and professionals—and even some capitalists—understand the links between racism and anti-Semitism and have participated in the civil rights struggles of the African American people.

However, because of the different class composition and economic status of the Jewish population, the anti-Semitism against them differs in character from the racism directed against African Americans and other oppressed peoples. Hence it is not a subject for further inclusion in this study.

The oppression of Native Americans is undeniably a very important factor in any analysis of the economics of racism. But statistical data are very limited and, further, there are special features also beyond the scope of this volume.

Taking all factors into consideration, it is clear that African Americans remain the prime victims of racism, and their struggles are the key to the overall fight for equality of all peoples. Therefore most attention is devoted to the economic status and trends among African Americans and the struggles against the racism they experience.

Racism is a specific product of capitalism, a universal feature of capitalism. Racism, national oppression and discrimination will be completely eliminated only under a democratic socialism. But major gains can be made, beginning right now. What is necessary in this hostile capitalist environment, however, is persistent and organized struggle for full equality. The interlock between the situation of the working class as a whole and that of the African American people has become especially decisive since World War II. The regional distributions of Black and white workers is less diverse; the industrial and occupational scope of Black workers has drawn closer to that of white workers; and the weight of Black workers in the entire working class has increased, along with that of Latino workers. Hence the use of racism as a lever to split the working class, for simultaneously clobbering the conditions of labor as a whole, and super-exploiting its Black and Latino components, is magnified.

Consequently, the interest of the entire working class, notably that of its white contingent, in aiding the Black and Latino struggles for equality has sharpened. The necessity for all workers to realize this and to act accordingly in a united way is essential to turn back the offensive of capital, and to resume a renewed people's offensive for a better life.

It cannot be overemphasized that the fortunes of African Americans are inextricably linked with those of the whole working class. White workers must be brought to understand that their best interests, their jobs and their security, can be assured only when all workers have equality. Black people are overwhelmingly members of the working class, as are the majority of white people. Concepts of solidarity, of unity in struggle against employers, of cooperation on the job, all foster anti-racist tendencies among white workers, and especially among the more conscious and active trade unionists. At the same time, Blacks cannot solve the problems of racism in isolation from the working class as a whole, with its large white majority, and the struggles of all labor against exploitation.

Whites must realize that Black leadership has come to the fore in the struggle for Black liberation, and that Black leadership is necessary for its success. This must increasingly be a leadership rooted in the working class, which alone can pursue the cause of equality without inner contradictions—such as those confronting Black capitalists, who are simultaneously victims of discrimination by white capitalists and themselves the exploiters of workers.

It is no accident that overall gains in the relative and absolute economic conditions of the African American people coincided with a period of an upward trend in real wages and in union membership, which peaked in the early 1970s. The subsequent decline in real wages and union membership has coincided with, and had disproportionate impact upon, the situation of Black workers, which in turn has led to a drop in the real incomes of the African American people and in their relative economic position.

Gains are possible under capitalism, but not inevitable. Matters can go in the opposite direction, towards a fascist apartheid system. Powerful forces push in that direction. And if unrestrained racism, all-out fascism, prevailed in such a powerful country as the United States, the danger of nuclear war, with its threat to existence of humanity, would become most acute. The decisive defeat of racism requires supplanting a decaying system of capitalism with a more advanced socialist system.

The final chapter outlines a program for the struggle against racism. Much of this program has been projected by African American political figures—notably the Congressional Black Caucus. To some extent the program coincides with that of the more advanced and progressive trade unions.

I hope that my suggestions will help in the development of a program for renewed, more powerful mass actions against racism by a decisive section of American workers and people. Aspects of social life have taken on increasing prominence in the fate of peoples, and also involve huge and rising costs, interacting with economic life on a new level.

Two chapters in this work have been contributed by specialists in their fields; Professor Lawrence Weiss on health and Professor David Eisenhower on education.

2. Population

In 1994 there were about 75 million people of racial minorities in the United States, representing 28% of the total population of 267 million. This is our estimate, approximately 7 million higher in total population, with 5 million more as minority people than the official Census figures. The increases are consistent with responsible estimates of the undercount in the 1990 Census of Population, and with subsequent rates of increase as estimated by the Census Bureau. The minority population has increased by as much 25 million since 1980, accounting for more than half the total increase in population. A breakdown of the minority population, as of 1991:

TABLE 2:1. U.S. POPULATION, 1991

	Millions	% of Total
Non-Hispanic White	190.0	73.4
Black	34.5	13.3
Hispanic	24.0	9.3
Asian	7.5	2.9
Native American	3.0	1.1
TOTAL	259.0	100.0

These figures are linked to the 1991 estimates of the U.S. Census Bureau and are, in turn, closely aligned with decennial official Census reports. But our data are more accurate than official Census reports, which for decades have been disputed by many city officials, and Black and Latino leaders, as being systematic undercounts. When the Census Bureau finally conducted a special survey to determine the shortfall in the 1990 survey—an exercise that showed an undercount of more than 5 million—Secretary of Commerce Robert Mosbacher forbade Census Director Barbara Everitt Bryant to publish the results. However, Ms. Bryant publicly upheld the survey in defiance of her boss, a plutocrat friend and close political associate of George Bush. [1]

The Census fails to cover: (1) a significant proportion of the more than 6 million people in prisons, jails, nursing homes, dormitories and other group quarters; (2) many of the millions of undocumented immigrants, and (3) it covers only a fraction of the escalating number of homeless people.

Table 2:1 shows our estimate of the 1991 population, roughly 6 million more than the amended Census estimate for that year. About half of the additional uncounted were African Americans; somewhat less were Latinos; the rest were "others," including non-Hispanic whites.

The population of all oppressed peoples is growing more rapidly than that of the non-Hispanic whites. In fact, according to Census projections, the non-Hispanic white population will begin to decline after the year 2030. By about 2010, minority peoples will constitute about one-third of the total, and by the year 2050, half the U.S. population.

In the 1980s decade, the non-Hispanic white population increased by only 4%; the Black population by 15%; Native Americans by 43%; Hispanics by 50%; and peoples of Asian origin by 90%. About half the rapid rise in the Hispanic population is attributable to immigration; of Asians, mainly to immigration; and as for Native Americans, partly because more people so identify themselves.

U.S. policy has favored immigration of Asian peoples, in large measure to procure the skills of Asian professionals, especially from India; partly as a source of cheap labor—from Indochina and its neighbors—and to some extent for political reasons, to encourage defection of anti-Communist "refugees" in order to fuel the propaganda mill and to strengthen right-wing anti-labor forces within the United States. This last factor also applies to Latinos who emigrate from Cuba. But even more, in regard to Hispanics, there is the ignoble manipulation of government rules in order to obtain an endless supply of undocumented workers—who have no legal rights—as well as "legal" immigrants to work for minimum and sub-minimum wages under appalling conditions in agriculture, service industries, and sweatshop manufacturing.

U.S. capitalism's inherent racism, directed most imperiously against the African American people, holds down immigration of Africans. This policy is fueled by fears of the militancy of African Americans, such as that shown in dramatic Civil Rights struggles of the '60s and widespread local actions since. During the 10-year period 1981-1990, of 7.3 million immigrants, 3.5 million came from North and South America; 2.8 million from Asia; 0.7 million from Europe; and fewer than 0.2 million from Africa. Also, approximately 0.4 million came from predominantly Black-populated islands of the Caribbean.[2]

According to official projections, the number of Latino people will surpass the number of African Americans by 2010, and by 2050, the population distribution would be that as shown in Table 2:2.

In this calculation, the overall projection has been increased from 383 million to 391 million to avoid undercounting the numbers of Latinos, Blacks, Native Americans and Asians, since about 8 million of these peoples are projected only as Hispanic. Although this method has flaws, too, it seems more reasonable than that used by the Census, which classifies all Hispanic

Blacks—as well as Hispanic Asians, etc.—only as Hispanic, but not as Black, Asian, etc. The estimated 8 million increase is trivial in relation to the accepted wide range in the projected total population, and in the projected population for each of the races.

TABLE 2:2. PROJECTED POPULATION, 2050[3]

	Millions	% of Total
Non-Hispanic White	202	51.7
Black	62	15.9
Hispanic	81	20.7
Asian	41	10.4
Native American	5	1.3
TOTAL	391	100.0

Undercounting minorities is not an accident, but a result of and an expression of deliberate racist discrimination, especially against African Americans. It is a political and economic weapon, connected with the sinister design to hold down and/or reduce the Black population.

Their class and racial prejudices lead many Census takers to omit counting people in some of the poorest areas, especially those inhabited by Blacks and Hispanics. Simultaneously, many of the most oppressed people fear all government representatives, in view of their life experience in which official representatives appear only as persecutors—as police to harass and arrest; as bailiffs to evict; as FBI and immigration agents to deport; as tax and bill collectors; and as welfare investigators who withhold funds to a whole family if a man is found living in the house.

It is difficult to obtain a complete count of minorities and to a lesser extent of poor whites, unless decisive steps are taken to end discrimination, segregation, and poverty generally. Even short of that, realistic approximations of the total minority population, and their economic characteristics, can be procured and officially certified by standard statistical methods. (Nowadays, most Census totals are "blown up" small samples. Moreover, totals of many measured categories are further increased above the amounts reported to allow for systematic underreporting by respondents. There are valid techniques for correcting for population undercounting; Census statisticians have applied these techniques and, in some cases, published their results.)

When the Census Bureau made the minor adjustments in response to vigorous pressure, the New York tally was adjusted to reduce the undercount to 235,000, according to some calculations. The estimate of a total U.S. undercount of 5.25 million apparently applies after allowing for these minor adjustments. The main undercount is concentrated in cities and, according to local political leaders, is largest in California, by about one million.

The immediate political impact was the reduction of representation in Congress (New York City lost one Representative) and in state legislatures. It means a substantial loss in the share of federal aid allocations to the cities, where the need is greatest. Overall, it is a manifestation of the gross governmental discrimination against minority peoples.

As a spokesman for Mexican-American groups put it, "The Bush Administration is saying that minorities don't count as much as other Americans."[4] In 1991, Mayor Raymond Flynn of Boston, President of the U.S. Conference of Mayors, put it this way: "The message to the American people is the poor don't count, so don't count the poor." Then-mayor David N. Dinkins of New York City was even sharper: "There was a time when folks who looked like me were counted as three-fifths of a person. This is not far removed from that."[5]

African Americans and Other Minorities

In 1780 African Americans—90% of them slaves—numbered 800,000, 19.3% of the total population. The number of slaves multiplied rapidly, from 700,000 in 1790 to 4 million in 1860, on the eve of the Civil War. For a period, the number of free Blacks grew even faster, reaching 14% of all African Americans by 1830. After 1830 there was a slowdown, presumably because of the intensified efforts of slave owners to prevent runaways. Nevertheless, by 1860 there were nearly a half million free Black people.

Even so, throughout most of U.S. history, the proportion of African Americans in the population declined as the tide of European immigrants increased the white population faster than the importation of slaves and, after 1860, the natural growth rate of African Americans. Later, however, with the imposition of immigration restrictions, the decline in the relative share of the Black population ended and, in fact, rose, especially after World War II. According to official Census figures, the growth was from 9.7% in 1930 to 12.1% in 1990 (13.5% by our adjusted figures, Chart 2A).

In recent decades, the overall percentage of minority or oppressed people has increased rapidly, from one sixth of the population in 1970 to one quarter of the population in 1990. The increase in the Black population has been outpaced by the rapid increases in Latino and Asian populations, spurred by large-scale immigration, so that by 1990 the total of "other" minorities approximated that of Blacks (Chart 2B).

Official projections assume continued large scale immigration from Mexico and other Central American countries, as well as from Asia, with some

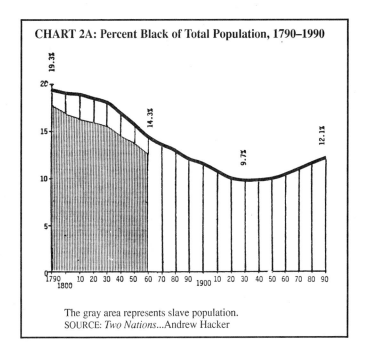

CHART 2A: Percent Black of Total Population, 1790–1990

The gray area represents slave population.
SOURCE: *Two Nations*...Andrew Hacker

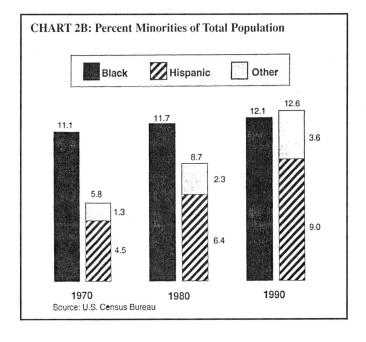

CHART 2B: Percent Minorities of Total Population

Black   Hispanic   Other

Source: U.S. Census Bureau

arrivals—mainly of Blacks—from the Caribbean, but virtually no immigration from Africa. This immigration pattern reveals the political motivation of the U.S. government. It welcomes trained professionals and capitalists from Asia; it encourages and, to some extent cannot prevent, a large scale influx of low-wage workers from Mexico; a strictly limited number of Blacks from the Caribbean countries, also as low-wage laborers. There are some other categories as well; Indochinese opposed to socialism; anti-Communist Cubans; and professionals from former socialist countries in Europe, especially from the former Soviet Union.

On the whole, projections are for a continued rise in the proportion of African Americans in the total population, with an accelerated increase of Hispanics and Asians. Government estimates foresee that by the year 2010 minorities will total about 85 million, about one third of the total population.[6]

There are significant qualitative differences between these groups of non-Native American, non-white peoples. The Black and Hispanic peoples are overwhelmingly working class, with a partial exception of a significant number of Cuban capitalists and professionals. The Asians are mainly petty bourgeois—small proprietors, professionals—and, especially in the case of the Japanese, capitalists. The recent wave of immigrants from Indochina, mainly workers, is an exception. All of these people are subject to racial prejudice, in varying degrees. Among the main sectors of Asians, their *economic* status is equal, or superior, to that of average white Americans.

The racist discrimination and oppression against African Americans is most severe in almost every respect. Economic discrimination against Hispanics is nearly as bad, but their segregation from the majority white society is less rigid. Roughly 95% of the Mexican Americans regard themselves as white and have more opportunities than African Americans for social and residential acceptance among whites. The status of Puerto Ricans, particularly numerous in the Northeast, is closest to that of Blacks.

Regional Distribution of Minorities

At the close of the Civil War, over 90% of African Americans lived in the South, mainly in the countryside. During the next 30 years, migration northward was matched by a higher birthrate in the South, so that by 1880, 90% of all Blacks still lived there. Then the northward movement picked up tempo: the South had 77% of the Black population in 1940 but 53% in 1970. Since then, the North/South regional distribution of Blacks has largely stabilized: the net reverse migration reported in recent years has been balanced by other factors so that the Southern share of the African American population has been constant.

TABLE 2:3. REGIONAL DISTRIBUTION OF BLACK POPULATION, 1920-1990

| | Total Black Population (thousands) | | | |
	Total	North & West	South	% of Total in South
1920	10,463	1,557	8,912	85
1940	12,866	2,961	9,905	77
1960	18,872	7,560	11,312	60
1970	22,581	10,611	11,970	53
1980	26,495	12,447	14,048	53
1990	29,986	14,157	15,829	53

SOURCES: Stat. Abst.,1993, T 32, p.30; Ibid., 1982-83, T 36, p.32; Hist. Stat., Vol. 1, Series 176, p.2

When slavery was abolished, 36% of the population in the South was Black. In the large 'Black Belt" within the South, Blacks were a majority, but they lacked political power and elementary civil rights. The partial revolutionary gains at the end of the Civil War were reversed by the ensuing racist offensive of the landowners, whose former holdings were restored by their northern capitalist allies in the superexploitation of the Black population.

The slowest growth in Black population was between 1920 and 1940, at 1.04% per year. The great economic crisis of the 1930s created conditions for lowered birth rates, higher infant mortality and lowered life expectancy. Compare the 2.4 million increase in Black population from 1920-1940 to the 6 million rise in the next 20 years (1.93% per year)! The more favorable conditions for growth were brought about during World War II and the rapid growth of the U.S. economy after that war; by the Korean and Vietnam War production upsurges; and by the civil rights gains of the 1960s. The alarmed ruling circles launched a propaganda campaign and took measures to temper the growth of Black population. In the 20 years from 1970-1990, the rate of growth slowed to 1.43% per year. The racist offensive, combined with the overall worsening of workers' conditions, especially of oppressed peoples—basically accounted for this downtrend.

The stability of the southern share of the Black population at 53% from 1970-1990 is associated with the marked deterioration of conditions for African Americans in the northern industrial states, with widening Black/white differentials in the North, along with industrial expansion in the South. As a result there was a certain drawing together of the anti-Black economic differentials in the main regions of the country (see Chapter 3). Although 53% of African Americans still live in the South, the periodic northward migration, together with the rapid increase in the white and Latino southern population, has led to a steady reduction in the proportion of Blacks in the South—to 18.5% of the population in 1990. Elsewhere, the percentage of Blacks in the population has gone up over the past 50 years, even during the 1980s—despite the decline of basic industry—partly due to significant white migration to the South.

Geographic Segregation and Exclusion

Minority peoples are subjected to double segregation and exclusion: they are concentrated in cities, which are a relatively small part of the total U.S. land area, and they are essentially excluded from the vast expanses that comprise most of the area of the United States. Secondly, within the cities, they are segregated in the most inhospitable areas—in terms of quality of housing, public services, environment, access to jobs and recreation—and are excluded from the most desirable sections, which in some cases constitute the larger part of the cities.

The wide geographic distribution of African Americans is considerably different from that of Latinos, Asians, and Native Americans: with 53% of African Americans in the South, 20% in each of the Northeast and Midwest, and about 10% in the Western states.

Roughly two-thirds of the Latino people live in the western states and Texas. More than half live in two states, California and Texas. One sixth (16.6%) of the Latino people live in the northeastern states, with Puerto Rican immigration a major factor; 10% live in the southern states outside Texas, mainly in Florida, where immigration from Cuba is important. Just 8% of the Hispanic population live in the midwestern states.

Distribution of Asian peoples is similar to that of Hispanic, with a majority living in the West but with a substantial number in the Northeast.

By 1990 there were also 12 large cities with a majority Latino population. Miami and Hialeah, Florida, where the Cuban emigres are concentrated; 3 Texas cities on the Mexican border; and 7 cities in California. Latinos, mainly from Mexico, were 40% of the population of the City of Los Angeles, but 95% of the population of East Los Angeles.

Whatever their geographic location, African Americans bear the brunt of exclusion and segregation. In the metropolitan areas, especially in the Northeast, 72% of the African Americans live in central cities; 27% in metropolitan communities outside the central cities; and less than 1% in the countryside. The distribution of Latinos is similar. But only 22% of whites live in the central cities while 63% are in the suburbs and 15% in the countryside. In the Midwest, the distribution of all races was similar to that in the Northeast.

Generally, Black people who live outside the central cities live in satellite communities under conditions similar to those in the central city. Thus, while 39% of the population of Chicago was Black in 1990, in Gary, Indiana (which is within the same metropolitan area), 81% of the population was Black. But in the other suburban communities of the Chicago-Gary metropolitan area, only 7% of the population was Black. Only 20% of the white population lived in the two large cities; 80% in the surrounding suburbs.

Most of the 366,000 Blacks (24%) living in Illinois outside of Chicago and Gary were concentrated in a few communities and virtually excluded from the rest.

In 1970, only three cities with populations over 100,000 had a majority of African Americans, but by 1980 there were 13 such cities. The total population of all but one of the cities with majority Black populations was lower in 1990 than in 1980, and in 11, lower than in 1970 (see Table 2:4).

TABLE 2:4. LARGE CITIES WITH MAJORITY BLACK POPULATION
(Numbers in Thousands)

City	%Black Pop.	Total Pop.		Black Pop.			Non-Black Pop.		
	1990	1970	1990	1970	1990	% Change	1970	1990	% Change
Gary, In.	80.6%	175	117	92	94	+2%	83	23	-72%
Detroit Mi.	75.7	1514	1028	662	778	+18	852	250	-71
Atlanta Ga.	67.1	495	394	254	264	+4	241	130	-46
Washington D.C.	65.9	757	607	538	400	-26	219	207	-5
Birmingham Al.	63.3	301	266	126	168	+33	175	98	-44
New Orleans La.	61.9	593	497	267	308	+15	326	189	-42
Baltimore Md.	59.2	905	736	420	436	+4	485	300	-38
Jackson Miss.	55.7	154	197	61	110	+80	93	87	-6
Richmond Va.	55.2	249	203	105	112	+7	144	91	-37
Memphis, Tn.	54.6	624	610	243	334	+37	381	276	-28
Macon Ga.	52.2	122	107	46	56	+22	66	51	-23
Inglewood Ca.	51.9	90	110	10	57	+470	80	53	-34
Savannah Ga.	51.3	118	138	53	70	+32	65	68	+5

SOURCE: Census of Population, 1990; cities over 100,000 and more than 50% Black.

The population decline in the predominantly Black central cities has been accompanied by an uptrend in the population of the greater metropolitan areas and suburbs of these cities. In only one of the 13 cities, Savannah, was there a rise in the white population within the city. In 7 of the cities, the white population was down more than one-third. In both Gary and Detroit, the white population declined more than 70%.

Physical ghettoization is accompanied by financial ghettoization. The U.S. financial structure is anti-working class as well as racist. It permits capitalists and those in the upper middle class to arrange financial enclaves that enable them to obtain adequate—and even more than adequate—tax revenues to finance their educational, medical, and other public services. The major financing is provided by the economic enterprises drawn into their areas, and by the taxes paid by the workers in the community.

The central cities, denuded of industry, populated by a large percentage of impoverished people, and with little outside sources of revenue, are in chronic crises. Inevitably there is not only deterioration of municipal services, but also cutbacks in municipal employment. The white people who remain in the central cities are almost exclusively workers and are victims, although less oppressed, along with the Black people.

In the four largest U.S. cities, the combined Black and Hispanic population accounts for more than 50% of the total, with a substantial addition of Asian and Native American peoples. This was true of only one city, Chicago, in 1980, and of none of them 20 years ago (see Table 2:5).

TABLE 2:5. FOUR LARGEST U.S. CITIES, 1990

		Percent Distribution				
City	Total Pop. (000)	Non-Hispanic White	Black	Hispanic	Asian	Native American
New York	7,323	39.5	28.7	24.4	7.0	0.4
Los Angeles	3,485	35.7	14.0	39.9	9.8	0.6
Chicago	2,784	37.9	39.1	19.6	3.1	0.3
Houston	1,631	39.9	28.1	27.6	4.1	0.3

SOURCE: *Stat. Abst.*, 1993, Table 46, pp.42-44.
NOTE: The percentage of non-Hispanic whites is calculated by subtracting from 100 the sum of the four given percentages for other races. There are minor distortions in offsetting directions in this process.

The fastest growing groups are the Hispanics and the Asians.

New York City and New York State have the largest African American populations of U.S. cities and states. New York City, only 0.6% of the land area of the state, has 2.1 million Black people, 74% of the State's total. New York City, plus five other large cities which, combined, have 0.8% of the state's area, have 83% of New York State's Black population.

But in most of the state, as in most of the country, there are large—mostly rural—areas with no, or virtually no, African American residents. They are almost completely excluded from 34 of New York State's 60 counties. These 34 counties constitute considerably more than half the state's land area. In each of these counties, African Americans constitute less than 2% of the population—other than prison inmates or those stationed on military bases. They are almost wholly excluded from the entire northern quadrant of the state, and from the southern tier along the Pennsylvania border. There isn't a single African American household in Hamilton County, in the heart of the Adirondack Mountains. The 12 Black individuals in the county may be in-house service workers on large estates or in camps and resorts, of which there are many. Putnam County, regarded as part of the New York Consolidated Metropolitan Area, has less than 1% Black households.

In most of the United States, zoning of African Americans' homes is even more restricted: Take Illinois. Chicago has the second largest Black population among U.S. cities, more than a million. There are also significant clusters of African Americans in Peoria. In East St. Louis, at the southwestern corner of the state, 98% of the fewer than 50,000 inhabitants are Black. But between the Chicago Metropolitan area and East St. Louis, except for a few communities along the Mississippi River, Illinois is another example of U.S. apartheid: there are 22 counties without a single African American household.

In most parts of the United States, African Americans are similarly restricted! In the entire quadrant west of the Mississippi River and north of the 40th parallel, Black people number roughly 500,000—about 2%—of the 25 million population. But these half million are overwhelmingly concentrated in the handful of cities from Minnesota's Minneapolis and St. Paul to Seattle, Washington. Throughout most of Iowa, the Dakotas, Wyoming, Montana, Idaho and Utah, there are no Black residents; none or a mere handful in most of the rest of the states in that vast region, which comprises about 30% of the contiguous land area of the United States.

The 53% of African Americans who still live in the South are more scattered. While they are concentrated in the large cities, significant but declining numbers remain in the countryside, their historic location. Deprived of their former base as sharecroppers, farm laborers and to a small extent, farm owners, today the southern rural Black population lives in extreme poverty, more severe than that of the area's rural whites. Even in the South, African Americans have been excluded from many areas. There are no Black households in four Georgia counties or in six Arkansas counties, while in other large areas there are mere handfuls of Black residents.

The *Wall Street Journal* identified "America's 20 Hottest White-Collar Addresses"—fast-growing rural counties to which corporations are moving their headquarters, setting up factories, and subsidizing top-quality schools, encouraging managers and professionals to move there. [Technological links, such as computer links between manufacturing plants, suppliers and distributors, have given corporations freedom to move out of traditional business centers.]

Separating professionals, technicians and administrators from the bulk of the workers, this trend not only creates bastions of political support for the corporate bureaucracy and ruling elite, but also is a means of further intensifying racial separatism and discrimination against African Americans and Latinos. The article admits:

> One thing hasn't changed...Fast-growing pockets of wealth and affluence are still almost entirely white; in most of these counties, the Black population is less than 1%... [7]

Exclusion of African Americans from large, and small, areas—whether in the North, South, East, West or Middle America—has significant sociological consequences. It means that tens of millions of white Americans have no economic connections with Black people, either as fellow workers or in trade; have no social contacts in schools, cultural or religious centers. In fact, doubtless millions of white Americans go through life without ever meeting any African Americans, or even seeing one except in the movies or on TV. These millions are vulnerable to the racist slanders that have become a major tool of the capitalist profiteers, especially their most extreme anti-labor, reactionary sector and its political representatives. The hatred, racism (and anti-Semitism) that spew forth unchecked, 'round the clock, on the radio and TV stations throughout America's heartland incite KKK-like violence and prevent cooperation and understanding among people with different ethnic and racial backgrounds.

Thus the two dimensions—segregation and exclusion—are compounded; they affect every aspect of life. The impact is borne most heavily by the oppressed peoples, but it also has pronounced negative impact on the entire working class, including white workers.

As the number and importance of minority workers increase, their segregation and exclusion make unification of the whole working class more difficult. This, in turn, abets capitalist attempts to create divisions and foster discord among workers of different ethnic and racial backgrounds—politically and in economic and social struggles against employers and the Establishment brass.

U.S. workers are acutely aware that companies use poverty-wage labor in Latin America and Asia, especially, to pull down conditions and intensify exploitation in the United States. U.S. workers support struggles of Mexican workers, and workers in other low-wage countries, to catch up to U.S. levels rather than to be used to pull down U.S. wages.

It is equally important to recognize that the substandard conditions of segregated minority workers in the United States are also used to lower the standards of white workers. Hence white workers, in their own interest and in the collective interest of all labor, need to support actions of African Americans,

Latinos and other minorities for equality, for desegregation, for the breakdown of invisible walls barring these workers from their rightful status.

The inner cities of the country's metropolises, while suffering economic decline, have more than ever become centers of cultural and social life, of political activism of all kinds. Public transportation facilities and the streets of the cities reflect the diversity of racial and ethnic groups. Those who use subways and buses are mostly wage and salary workers. Cities have the real potential for building a unified working class and peoples' movement. Unity of peoples of all races, nationalities and ethnic groups can resist the financial and political pressures of monopoly capital and can win the struggle to reduce exploitation, raise living standards and eliminate the acute social problems that threaten the cities, and the people who live in them, with disaster.

In building that unity, a special responsibility falls on white people. Their participation in actions to end these evils is essential for success.

Occupation

African Americans are overwhelmingly members of the working class. A 1991 Census report on the occupational distribution of full-time workers age 25 or over shows that nearly 85% of the African Americans in the labor force are workers. About 15% hold positions as managers, executives, etc., or are professionals. And contrary to the norm for whites, 63% of employed Black males are blue-collar workers.

TABLE 2:6. CLASS DISTRIBUTION OF EMPLOYED PERSONS, 1990,
          AGE 25 OR OVER

Occupation	White	Black
Capitalist class	13.3%	7.1%
Middle class	13.8	8.9
Working class	72.9	84.0
higher paid	27.8	19.4
average wage	26.0	33.7
low paid	19.2	30.9

SOURCE: BLS *Employment & Earnings*, 1/91, T 21, p.184

Among Black workers, about one-third receive low or poverty wages as laborers or service workers (Table 2:7).

The class distribution of white males is very different: about 18% are capitalists, or tied to the capitalist class by their managerial/executive positions;

14% are middle-class professionals; and the remaining 68% are workers. However, only about 15% are in low-wage jobs.

TABLE 2:7. CLASSIFICATION OF MALES WITH FULL-TIME JOBS, 1990,
          AGE 25 OR OVER

	White	Black
Executives, managers, etc.	17.8%	7.9%
Professionals	13.8	7.4
Technicians	3.3	2.6
Sales persons	12.3	5.1
Clerical, etc.	5.1	9.1
Skilled crafts	19.2	17.9
Operatives	13.4	21.8
Laborers	7.0	10.0
Service workers	4.5	15.5
Not specified	3.6	2.7
TOTAL	100.0	100.0

SOURCE: U.S. Census Report on the Black Population, 3/91, p-20, No. 164; T 13, pp.68-69; T 12, pp.59-64
NOTE: In this table, figures for whites are not corrected for the distortion that results from inclusion of 95% of Hispanics.

Further, Table 2:7 needs considerable revision. By omitting young workers (16-24), it reduces the proportion of lower-category blue-collar and white-collar workers. Second, the data for whites includes Hispanics. As a result, it substantially underreports the percentage of non-Hispanic whites who are executives and professionals. Finally, it does not take into account the large number of Black workers who are employed only part-time, nor does it consider those part-timers whose job classifications are less favorable than that of the fully employed workers.

A comparison with 1980 data shows that there has been no significant change in the classification pattern, although there have been some gains by African Americans in professional-technical categories. But these have been more than balanced by the rising concentration of Black workers in low-end service jobs.

The occupational categorization of African American women is quite different than that of African American men. Perhaps the most significant difference is that the numbers of Black women "executives, managers, and professionals, etc." *exceeds* those of Black males in these categories and by a wide margin! In these classifications, as in others, the earnings of Black women are far less than the earnings of Black men, but little less than those of white women, and in some cases are even higher than of white women.

Taking all these factors together, the departure from the structure of U.S. occupational life among whites has serious repercussions on the life of African American households, with far-reaching social and political consequences. This problem is more fully analyzed in Chapter 7.

Despite changes in methods of classification over the years, analysis of official reports since 1980 indicates a widening of class differentiation among the African American population. In particular, the share of Black capitalists, executives and managers has increased, as has the share of professional people—not capitalists and not workers, but in-between. As a result, the influence of Black capitalists and of those sharing their ideology upon the political life of the African American population has been strengthened.

At the same time, however, within the working class the proportion pushed down to the lowest category—service jobs—and to the ranks of the chronically unemployed has gone way up.

These trends are equally valid in respect to the Hispanic population, though less dramatically.

There is another indicator of the class differential among whites, Blacks and Hispanics—the sources of their incomes. Table 2:8 shows, for each major category, the percentage of Black and Hispanic incomes to those of whites, in 1991.

TABLE 2:8. SOURCES OF INCOMES OF AFRICAN AMERICANS AND HISPANICS AS PERCENTAGE OF INCOMES OF WHITES (AGE 15 AND OLDER), 1991.

	Blacks	Hispanics
	(percentage of white)	
Black and Hispanic population, 15 years and up	13.6%	9.4%
Income Total	8.8	5.9
Property income	2.8	2.0
Non-farm proprietors income	3.8	4.4
Farm proprietors income	1.1	0.9
Wages and salaries	9.5	6.5
Government transfer payments	11.6	5.6

SOURCE: U.S. Census, P-60, No.180, T 34, p.174; T 31, pp.148-51.
NOTE: This table not corrected to eliminate Hispanics from the white total.

The data show that in 1991 Blacks 15 years of age and older numbered 13.6% of whites and Hispanics 9.4% of whites, while the shares of income were considerably less. Property income, which may be taken as a proxy for capitalist class income, was only 2.8% of white property income for Blacks and 2.0% for Latinos. Although wage and salary incomes were higher, they were still meager relative to whites'—reflecting the higher proportions of the working class among oppressed peoples.

It is also politically important to analyze government transfer income— i.e., Black and Hispanic as a percentage of white. The relative Black share, 11.6%, while larger than their 8.8% overall income share, is still less than the numerical percentage of African Americans in the population (13.6%). The Hispanic share of government transfer funds is also less than their share in overall income and in percent of population.

These disparities affect a whole series of entitlements—payments to which workers are entitled when they reach old age or are hit by unemployment, disability or poverty. They have won the right to these payments as a result of long struggles for legislation and for recognition of the responsibility of the government and society. Those (capitalists) who dictate government policy are constantly exerting pressure to reduce payments of these entitlements, dubbing them "mandatory" payments. Their special focus of attack has been on welfare payments—aid to dependent children, food stamps, medicaid, etc. (see also Chapter 5).

The Drive to Halt Black Population Growth

The deliberate undercounting of the African American population is in accord with the sinister design of the ruling class to hold down, or even reduce, the future Black population. So long as there was a growing need for manual labor, first in agriculture and later in industry and service, more Blacks were wanted, slave or free. But for several decades the demand for unskilled manual labor has stagnated and even declined. New jobs are centered in white collar, technical, professional, managerial, clerical and, most recently, in health service occupations. Automation of kitchens and laundries, and the availability of cleaning appliances, has reduced the demand for domestic help.

The entrenched ruling class, protective of its privileged position, is reluctant to provide minority children with the education they need to develop the knowledge and skills requisite for high-tech jobs. And even when African Americans do have the skill, they are passed over in favor of whites or Asians—including new immigrants.

So there is a permanent large-scale surplus of potential labor among the Black population. A concomitant is that millions of African Americans live in a state of permanent deep poverty, only partly relieved when their bodies are needed in time of war.

The genocidal precept at the root of this campaign became global in the 1940s.

After World War II, as U.S. power spread to Asia and the Far East, it confronted social upheavals which threatened the stability of regimes that welcomed U.S. investments and military bases. Wealthy U.S. families, headed by the Rockefellers, formed the Population Council, with the aim of persuading the peoples of Asia to curtail their population so that there would be fewer mouths to feed, instead of taking radical measures to alleviate poverty and to increase the supply of goods available to the masses.

Through its propaganda and subsidies, the Population Council boasted of stimulating hundreds of thousands of abortions in Japan at a time when abortions were still illegal in the United States. Later the focus shifted to India, where U.S. private and governmental monies were used to finance large-scale sterilization.

Along with continued global practical application of this Malthusian doctrine, in recent years it has been brought home to the United States.

In the 1970s the *New York Times* carried a two-page advertisement signed by 17 key individuals, urging population stabilization. Playing on the popular concern with pollution and the deteriorating environment, it blamed these evils on too many people: "For, let's face it, *people pollute!*" exclaimed the ad. Of course, people pollute, but people also clean up dirt, and can prevent and reverse the worst forms of pollution. Whether they do so depends not on how many people there are, but on how well society organizes the disposal of waste, how well it acts to preserve and improve the environment.

The fact is that the main polluters are the factories and power plants of the corporate conglomerates—especially the defense plants with their nuclear waste—which stubbornly ignore laws and regulations intended to force an end to pollution of the environment. Not to mention the thousands who suffer, many fatally, from industrial poisons, toxic chemicals to which they are exposed on the job, in drinking water, from landfill, toxic rain, contaminated food, etc.

Zero-population advocates equate the "population bomb" and the "atom bomb" as twin clouds threatening humanity. But the real threat to humanity, the atom/nuclear bomb, is still with us.

In 1975 the federal budget allocated $284 million for family planning to "serve" 7 million people: "Efforts will be concentrated on providing services to low-income persons.";[8] The main "service" was sterilization of the poor, mainly Black welfare mothers; women in jail; even Black youngsters and teenagers to prevent future childbearing. The Department of Health, Education and Welfare paid for 100,000 to 150,000 sterilizations per year, often coerced by the threat to end welfare payments. There were doctors who refused to deliver African American babies unless the mothers consented to simultaneous sterilization operations. This was after 1970, when it was estimated that one out of every six married partners between the ages of 20 and

29 included at least one sterilized partner. Then, as a result of a suit brought by the National Welfare Rights Organization, District Judge Gerhard A. Gesell ordered limitations to federal financing of sterilization.[9]

During the 1980s, the sterilization campaign died down. But its long-term impact on slowing the growth of the Black population is obvious. Contributing to the same end are discriminatory, poorer medical care for African Americans, reflected in the high infant mortality rate, and the inordinately high death rate of young Black males—as well as the high rate of their imprisonment.

The Population Council has recently resumed and intensified its well-financed activities, with the backing of many Congressional members and governors.

George Bush, while still President, signed a declaration designating the last week in October 1992 as "Population Awareness Week," and a ten-page mailing on population control was sent out to tens of millions of Americans. Did George Bush see a contradiction between his advocacy of population "awareness" and his espousal of the "right to life," right-wing anti-abortionist movement?

As yet, these frightening practices only point in the direction of genocide. But there is a sinister parallel with the beginnings of Hitler's policy of reducing the population of "undesirables," which began with 56,000 sterilizations a year and ended with the mass murder of millions in the gas chambers.[10]

With the accessibility of contraceptives and the legalization of abortion, irreversible sterilization operations should be limited to cases of medical necessity. More fundamentally, it is time to defeat the use of population control as a socioeconomic weapon against selected sectors of the population.

3. Incomes of African Americans and Latinos

Personal income is the primary indicator of economic well-being. African Americans and Hispanics, the two main minority peoples, are subjected to extreme income differentials. Currently Black people have decidedly less than half the incomes of whites, when certain necessary adjustments are taken into consideration. The situation of Hispanic people is only marginally better, and for some sections of the Latino peoples, even worse. Furthermore, for the past generation these enormous gaps have increased and the number of victims has grown. At the same time, the absolute real income levels of Black and Hispanic peoples have been declining, along with, but even faster than, that of the working class as a whole.

Income and other economic indicators for white people in this volume generally represent those of *non-Hispanic whites*. This is necessary because in the main Census Bureau annual reports used as sources, 95% of the Latino peoples are also classified as white, and their low incomes artificially pull down the reported averages for the category, white people. In the 1975 edition of *Economics of Racism*, I made this adjustment, as in subsequent publications. Recently the Census Bureau itself has begun publishing some statistics for non-Hispanic whites.

The latest Census figures, for 1992 and 1993, show Black *median* family incomes at 52.5% of white, and Hispanic at 58.5% of white. However, moderate but realistic adjustments lower *effective* Black median incomes to 40-45% that of white, and *effective* Latino family incomes to about half that of white.

For most comparisons I use family income; not household income, which combines the incomes of families and single individuals. Also, I use *median* income, which represents the income of the family "in the middle"—with as many family incomes above the median as below it—rather than "mean" (average) income, which gives excessive weight to those with very high incomes.

Trends in Income Differentials

Since the Great Depression of the 1930s, there have been two periods of notable improvement in the relative and absolute status of the African American population.

1. The first was the World War II period. The crucial need for the armed forces and for production enabled millions of Black workers to obtain industrial jobs, at wages considerably higher than their previous incomes as southern sharecroppers, or laborers and servants—although still at less than the wages of their white co-workers. Also, there was significant migration out of the still semi-feudal South to the partial freedom of the northern states. The determination of African Americans to achieve dignity and decent living and working conditions was an important factor, encouraged by efforts of progressive working class forces.

Notable was the activity and influence of the U.S. Communist Party, which achieved an unprecedented breakthrough with the election of the African American Communist, Benjamin J. Davis, to the New York City Council in 1943. Pete Cacchione had been elected in Brooklyn as a Communist in 1941. The Party was also important to the successful unionization campaigns in the country's basic industries, through the Congress of Industrial Organizations (CIO), which had a major impact. Where union contracts were won and African Americans participated in the leadership of some locals, the overt relegation of Black workers to the most underpaid, dirty and dangerous jobs could not be fully maintained.

2. The next period of important gain was the decade of the 1960s and into the early 1970s. Decisive were the civil right struggles of the African American people in the South, which won them the right to vote and gradually ended many of the most disgraceful, overt segregationist practices. Progressive forces from among white workers and youth, students and professionals gave active assistance.

The civil rights legislation of the 1960s formally outlawed discrimination and called for enactment of effective affirmative action measures toward achieving equality. While never more than marginally enforced by successive racist administrations—national, state and local—these laws have provided a platform for continuing struggle.

Also significant in its direct economic impact was the substantial mobilization of manpower and industry for the outrageous U.S. aggression against Vietnam. As during World War II, although on a smaller scale, this war opened many new opportunities for African Americans. Then-President Lyndon Johnson used the civil rights legislation and other social reform measures—dubbed the "Great Society"—to try to defuse mass resistance to the war.

3. The U.S. defeat in Vietnam ushered in a period of all-out capitalist offensive against the U.S. working class, an offensive that gathered momentum during the reactionary administrations of the 1980s and has become part of U.S. standard operating procedure. The anti-labor drive is linked to the racist offensive against the African American and Latino peoples, so that these workers have lost more than has the working class as a whole. It's almost as if the American ruling class has been seeking revenge at the expense of the U.S. working people for its defeat in Vietnam.

In this same period the struggle against racism merged somewhat with militant struggles against sexism, which won relative gains for working women—including Black women—who are a more-than-average proportion of the Black labor force. The fight against racism was increasingly conducted in the electoral arena, resulting in political gains—which did not, however, bring about the economic power necessary to improve the overall economic plight of the African American people. (Appendix Table 3A, and Chart 3A below, show the relative gains and losses of Black families.)

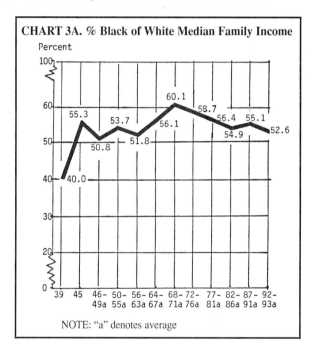

CHART 3A. % Black of White Median Family Income

NOTE: "a" denotes average

Data on Latino peoples are available only since 1972. Except for cyclical fluctuations, their relative position has deteriorated ever since, most sharply during the 1980s and '90s. Overall, during the past 20 years, their relative family incomes declined from about 70% to 59% of the white family median. The Black/white ratio declined from a peak of 60.7% in 1969-70 to 55% during the 1980s, with a further sharp drop to 52.5% in 1992-93. As a result, all of the gains of Black people since World War II towards reducing gross economic discrimination have now been wiped out.

At all times, the median family income of Hispanic families was higher than that of Black families. Still, this partly reflected the larger size of most Latino families. Per capita incomes of Hispanics are lower than those of Black people.

Overall, however, the family income figures do reflect the reality that discrimination against Latino peoples, in a number of respects, is slightly less severe than against African American people. But this varies regionally. In the Northeast, where the Hispanic people are mainly from Puerto Rico, the median incomes of Latinos are somewhat lower than those of Blacks. However, the differences are minor when related to the similarity. There is danger, however, that whatever differences exist can be used by demagogues and racist political manipulators to create hostility between Hispanic and African American peoples so as to hinder their unity in struggle.

Because of a technical factor in Census Bureau procedures, it is likely that the relative decline in the Black/white median income ratio has been steeper than shown in Chart 3A and Appendix Table 3A. (Changes in Census methods in 1974, 1983 and 1987 had the combined effect of raising Black incomes nearly 5%, while leaving white (and Hispanic) incomes virtually unchanged.)

Intensity of Discrimination

The average Black/white income ratio of less than 55% for the late 1980s and early 1990s understates the real degree of economic discrimination against African Americans in at least two important ways:

1. There is marked differential in living costs against African American families. Blacks do not have access to the same range and quality of goods and services as do white families, and are forced to pay more for what they do buy. Rev. Martin Luther King, Jr., who lived in the Chicago ghetto area of North Lawndale, said there was a "10 to 20 percent 'color tax'" on produce there. Prize-winning specialist on problems of education Jonathon Kozol wrote that this is "an estimate that still holds true today."[1]

This factor applies not only to food, clothing, appliances, etc. Recent studies, including official surveys, have revealed that the discrimination against Black people in housing is even more extreme, and extends to their virtual exclusion from living in the most desirable areas. I asked an African American professor residing in a suburban town whether he considered the 10-20% estimate of Rev. King valid. "No," he responded, "it's 30%." This was the subjective response of a man sensitive to problems of discrimination affecting him and his children. Doubtless many African Americans would agree.

The chapter on housing presents evidence that almost all financial institutions discriminate against African Americans in granting home mortgages:

two of the country's largest banks—in Atlanta and in New York—charged Black families usurious interest rates for home mortgages, more than double the standard rates. Inner-city Blacks are four times less likely to obtain mortgages for home purchase than whites in general, as well as their white neighbors.

Living costs are significantly higher in the central cities where 58% of Black, and 54% of Hispanic households were located in 1992. A rapidly declining 25% of white households lived in these cities (see Chapter 4 for greater detail).

In the central cities, Black/white income ratios are usually in the 40-50% range (Chart 3D, p. 39), but the absolute levels of incomes are higher than in other areas. This does not reflect higher living standards in the central cities, but higher living costs. But, because of the concentration of Blacks in the central cities, it results in the overall averages of Black/white income ratios being above 50%, even in metropolitan areas where Black/white ratios are well below 50% in both the central cities and the suburbs.

In addition, a special study of automobile insurance rates in Connecticut was made for this book. It found that car insurance for statistically identical borrowers, on the same vehicle, was markedly higher in the central city of New Haven, with its minority population of more than 50%, than in the suburbs, with small Black populations, and 50% higher than in the exurbs, where incomes are much higher and only a few Black families live (details in Appendix).

2. Further distortion results from differences in kinds of income. Black and Hispanic incomes consist overwhelmingly of wages and salaries. Their shares of property income are very small. The annual Census reports on peoples' incomes (CPRs) are based on surveys of samples of households, which report nearly all their wage and salary income, but omit large parts of their property income. In order to adjust the CPR-reported figures to more comprehensive totals compiled by other agencies, it is necessary to increase the CPR-reported wage and salary income by 3.1%, social security income by 3.2%, but property income and other capitalist income by 75.6%. Making these adjustments for Black, Latino and white separately reduces the 1992 Black/white median family income ratio from 52.4% to 49.1%; and the Hispanic/white ratio from 58.4% to 56.2%.[2]

Considering the overall impact of the effects of higher living costs and more complete survey reporting of income on the reported figures of personal incomes, it is reasonable to conclude that a more fully adjusted Black/white family income ratio would be in the 40-45% range, and the Hispanic/white ratio in the 50-55% range.

Additional factors that intensify economic discrimination are dealt with more fully in chapters on education, on health care, etc.

Trends in Real Family Incomes

Here we examine the trends in family incomes of white, Black, and Latino families separately. The period 1967-93 is covered for white and Black families, 1972-1993 for Hispanic families, no earlier figures being available. Real median incomes are used. Money incomes are adjusted by the regular consumer price index (CPI-U) to obtain real median incomes in 1992 prices. The results are presented as index numbers, with a 1972 base, in Chart 3B. Real incomes of both white and Black families increased rather sharply between 1967 and 1972, when real wages of workers were still rising. However the period 1972-73 represented the peak in real family incomes as it did, until now, in real wages. The trends are affected by sharp cyclical fluctuations, notably in the 1980-82 crisis, and again in 1990-1992.

Over the two decades, 1973-1993, while real median incomes of white families remained unchanged, those of Black families declined 11%, and of

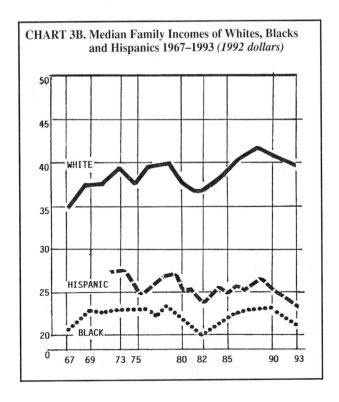

CHART 3B. Median Family Incomes of Whites, Blacks and Hispanics 1967–1993 *(1992 dollars)*

Hispanic families 17%. (Full data are in Appendix Table 3B.) Thus there was a marked widening of gaps far too wide to begin with.

Statistics of per capita incomes show more positive trends, partly because the average size of families has declined, but mainly due to the sharp increases in high incomes, pulling up per capita incomes even while most people were losing ground (see Appendix to Chapter 3).

Regional Differentials

Table 3:1 and Chart 3C show the changes over the past several decades in relative Black/white family income differentials in each of the four major regions of the country. In the period 1959-70, African American families in the South made the sharpest gains, 11 percent, in relative income. But even with the gains, by 1970 the relative status of Black people remained behind

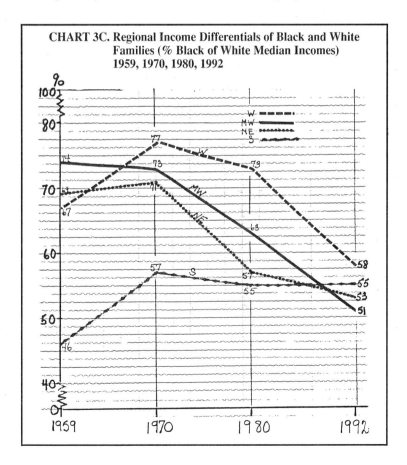

CHART 3C. Regional Income Differentials of Black and White Families (% Black of White Median Incomes) 1959, 1970, 1980, 1992

that in other regions. During this period there were only minor changes in the Black/white income ratios in the Northeast and the Midwest, but substantial gains in the West, where a much larger and faster growing Mexican American population was the prime victim of super-exploitation and discrimination.

After 1970 the structural crisis of U.S. capitalism featured a relative decline in basic industry, including conversion of much of the middle west into a "rust bowl." Black workers felt the brunt of the losses, and relatively few obtained substitute jobs in the escalating high-tech industries or in the bloated financial activity in the metropolitan centers. In the West, Blacks lost most of the relative gains of the previous period. In the Northeast and Midwest, earlier gains and more were lost, so that by the early 1990s, the relative position of Black people was far worse than in 1959. The most extreme losses were in the Midwest, with Black/white median income ratios falling from close to 75% to not much more than 50%, and by 1992, definitely lower than the ratio in the South. In the Northeast, also, the ratio fell. Since Black workers made no further gains in the South, the tendency was towards regional equalization at a low level.

TABLE 3:1. REGIONAL INCOME DIFFERENTIALS
OF BLACK AND WHITE FAMILIES

Region	Percent Black of White Median Incomes			
	1959	1970	1980*	1992*
Northeast	69%	71%	57%	53%
Midwest	74	73	63	51
South	46	57	55	55
West	67	77	73	58

SOURCES: 1959 and 1979, Economics of Racism Table 12, p.59; 1980, calculated from P-60-132, Table 14, pp 40-42; 1992 calculated from P-60-184, Table 13, pp 40-43;
* Data for 1980 and 1992 represent percent of Black to Non-Hispanic white median family income.

The tragedy and crime of these decades has been the equalization of discrimination, not in progress, but in regress: the reversion of nationwide differentials to those in the South.

The fact that in the South, Black to white median family income was maintained at close to its peak 1970 level may be attributed to two factors:

• Continuing gains in local, as well as national, Black political representation, and the step-by-step reduction or elimination of the crudest forms of southern apartheid.

• More favorable economic trends due to the relocation of many corporate production facilities to the South to take advantage of the lower wages and, even more, of the "right-to-work" laws and other anti-union regulations. With the increasing demand for labor there, jobs were more available for African Americans than in the North.

However, even with the overall decline in workers' incomes in the North, the South as a whole remained the poorest section of the country. The fact that by 1992 the Black/white income ratio in the South was approximately equal to that in the North doesn't obscure the fact that incomes of both Blacks and whites were generally lower in the South.

Moreover, sharp differences in income and economic status developed within the South. The Capital area—Delaware, Maryland, District of Columbia and northern Virginia—has median white and Black family incomes well above the national average. This area is considered part of the southern region. Right next to it, West Virginia is one of the poorest states. And the nadir of Black poverty and racist victimization is in the Mississippi Delta states: Mississippi, Louisiana and Arkansas (see Table 3:2). In these states, even white per capita incomes are furthest below the national average for whites, but Black per capita incomes are still lower.

TABLE 3:2. BLACK AND WHITE PER CAPITA INCOMES—U.S. AND MISSISSIPPI DELTA STATES, 1989

State	White	Black	Black % of White
United States	*$16,074	$8,859	55.1%
Mississippi	12,183	5,194	42.6
Louisiana	12,596	5,697	45.2
Arkansas	11,472	5,729	49.9

SOURCE: Stat. Abst., 1993, T.734, p. 468.
* The U.S. figure for whites represents non-Hispanic whites, as adjusted from data supplied by U.S. Census of Population, 1990. This adjustment was not necessary in the three states because their Hispanic populations are minimal.

Education and Income

Racism erects major roadblocks to prevent oppressed peoples from getting adequate education. Moreover, for the most part, a college degree or advanced technical training is necessary now to get a job that pays an adequate wage or salary. The obstacles that African American and Latino people must hurdle in order to obtain advanced education are greater than ever. This issue is discussed in detail in Chapter 12.

However, we comment here to put into the income framework the ideological offensive that charges: (a) African Americans inherently do not have the ability of whites to achieve educational success: and (b) they do not make the necessary effort. The "ability" argument is crude racism—the concept that Black people are genetically inferior mentally. The second charge is a cruel and hypocritical reversal of the truth: African Americans and Latinos make extraordinary efforts to obtain education, even at the cost of combining long hours of hard, low-paid labor with academic work. Even so, the economic payoff when they reach their educational goals is much less than for whites.

Destruction of the Black Family Base

The destruction of economic security for a large part of the Black population has seriously weakened the African American family structure. By 1991, less than one-half of all African American families were headed by a married couple. Women who never married, or else divorced or widowed, headed most of the remainder. Poverty is most acute among the families of single women bringing up children. The median income of Black families headed by single women is not only far below the poverty line, but is also just one-third the median income for Black families headed by married couples. And the median income for families headed by Black women, in 1991, was just 55% that of non-Hispanic white families headed by women. Black families with both husband and wife working had 83% the median income of similar white families.

Although only 22% of all Black households were in this category—with 83% of white family median income—this figure is often cited by itself to give the false impression that there has been important progress towards equality, and to justify the argument that Black people can "make it" if only they get their act together. But the fact is that the institutionalized racism of capitalism ensures that only a small percentage of Black families will "make it," even to the 83% figure.

Use of selected statistics to deceptively portray African American progress is another example of "blaming the victim"; however, such pronouncements continue, including by some African Americans who have gained recognition and/or fame—e.g., Clarence Thomas, Bush's right-wing appointee to the Supreme Court.

Perhaps the most widely used racist canard is that which blames the African American people, and especially Black men, for the large number of single-mother Black families. Propaganda to the effect that single mothers are mainly Black is misleading. Let's analyze the data:

In 1991 the number of white single-women family heads was nearly double that of similarly situated Black women and five times the number of such Latino women. But the proportion of Black families headed by a single parent is three times the corresponding proportion of white families—and has been for the past half century. However the magnitude of this situation is new among whites as well as Blacks.

In 1950, five-sixths of Black families were headed by married couples, the same proportion applicable to white families today. The percentage of Black families headed by a single parent—male or female—went up from 17% in 1950 to 52% in 1990; among white families, from 5.3% in 1950 to 17.3% in 1990—about the same rate of increase for both groups.[3]

Andrew Hacker writes:

> During the past generation, single-parent households...have become increasingly common in America and the rest of the world. That this arrangement now accounts for over half the black families has aroused great concern. For one thing, the loss of male breadwinners has done much to perpetuate poverty....
>
> On the whole, these changes are relatively recent. In 1950 only 17 percent of black households were headed by women, equal to today's white rate. So within living memory, homes with two parents present were very much the black norm. This makes it difficult to describe the matrifocal families that preponderate today as being a "legacy" of slavery....[an argument used by racists].

Slave owners, Hacker points out, generally prevented normal family life among the slaves, often exercising the prerogative they assumed to rape "their" Black female slaves.

> Yet it is now apparent that arrangements imposed by the owners were never accepted by the slaves themselves. Once freed, blacks sought the durable unions they had been denied. For almost a century following the Civil War, black families remained remarkably stable. Despite low incomes and uncertain employment, recent increases in homes headed by single parents cannot be attributed to a plantation past. Not only have other developments been at work, but they cut across racial lines.[4]

Economic Insecurity: Causes and Effects

The global changes in family structure are a consequence of the overall decay of capitalist society and increased exploitation, combined with aspects of women's liberation—itself a positive development that has had some paradoxical effects. Hacker stresses social factors such as the irresponsibility of many fathers toward their children and the easing of censure against women bearing children out of wedlock.

More basic, in my view, is the stress created by intensified economic insecurity: rising unemployment; the 100% increase, over two decades, in the number of people counted as living in poverty; the unprecedented 20% decline in private-sector real earnings since the early 1970s.

In the 1980s and 1990s, there has been a new factor: a majority of the largest U.S. corporations have sharply cut their work force in the United States and have projected further reductions, running into the hundreds of thousands at IBM and General Motors. This is accompanied by expansion of U.S. corporate facilities abroad.

In addition, there is a growing trend to replace regularly employed workers with temporary part-time, or contract, workers. Now numbering up to one-third of the work force, these employees have no pension or health benefits, no assurance of work from one week to the next, and are prey to mulcting of as much as one-third of their earnings by employment intermediaries. Along with this is the extension of the work-week imposed on the dwindling regularly employed work force.

In a recent study, Harvard professor Richard Freeman found that while the official unemployment rate in Great Britain was far higher than in the United States, the percentage of workers losing their jobs in any given month was five times as high in the United States as in Great Britain.[5] Such irregularity of employment and the consequent economic insecurity afflicts African Americans much more than whites.

How do these economic factors break up homes? A recent interview of a Michigan GM worker and his wife by a journalist is indicative. His job will end in 1995 when the plant closes. He is tempted to go to Texas, where he might find employment in an operative GM plant. But his wife, with a good job outside the auto industry, does not want to give it up and move. He does not want to stay in Michigan, work at McDonald's for poverty wages and become financially dependent on his wife. This is a white family whose marriage is threatened by the economic crisis. But this kind of situation is multiplied many times for African American families.

Special Discrimination Against Black Men

This is a key feature of American racism. The capitalist class, with the collaboration of the media, have fostered a fear and hatred of Black men to justify their practice of a new, higher level of job discrimination—last hired, first fired, or laid off. When jobs were somewhat more available to Black men, in the late 1930s and '40s, and again in the '60s, unity of white and Black workers on the job led to some real gains for all workers. A lesson thoroughly absorbed by the employers.

A new level of employer refusal to hire African American men in the private sector and the constant attacks on affirmative action, plus corporate downsizing, closed industrial plants, and cutbacks in the public sector have caused the percentage of Black men holding full-time jobs to plunge drastically and alarmingly. In 1972, 53.5% of white men (age 15 and over) held full-time jobs, 43.3% of Hispanic, and 42.1% for Black men. Over the past 20 years, the full-time job picture for white men was virtually unchanged at 53%.

Hispanic men had improved their situation modestly to 47%, but only 39.9% of Black men had full-time jobs. More dramatic still are the comparisons of full-time male workers per family and per household in 1992:

TABLE 3:3. % FULL-TIME MALE WORKERS, 1992

	Per Family	Per Household
White	73.2%	51.6%
Black	52.8	37.2
Hispanic	70.8	50.9

SOURCE: P 60-184, Table 31, pp. 148-49, Table A, p. xii

Per family, full-time male Black workers are 28% fewer than male white full-time workers and 25% fewer than Hispanic, Per household, the disemployment of Black workers is again 28% in relation to whites, and 27% in relation to Hispanics.

There are other important consequences from the major discrimination against employment of Black men. The police raids, arrests and imprisonment of young Black men are so widespread that over 25% of them are either in jail or subject to probationary and parole restrictions. The imprisonment rate for Black men is higher in the U.S. than in South Africa. Yet politicians still compete in demanding more police, prisons, and executions.

A disproportionate number of young African American men join the armed forces to get food, shelter and some kind of training and education. They are thereby taken out of social circulation, but are also apt to be among the first killed in the various U.S. military adventures around the world.

Statistics do not show how many African American families are forced to maintain their marital relationships secretly because of the policies of the U.S. government. Aid to dependent children, medicaid, food stamps, etc. may be stopped if a working husband is discovered, even if his income is insufficient to bring the family above the poverty level. For government watchdogs, the family has to be headed by woman, with no man present. In fact, a father has to sneak home, as if he were living underground in a dictatorship. True, this also applies to all families—white, Latino, Native Americans, Asian, etc.—but the U.S. system's main pressure is directed against African American families.

Thus racists rationalize their ideology and discrimination, in part, by charging that the high percentage of African American families headed by a woman is the result of unique moral, cultural and/or genetic factors of the African peoples. These lies are exposed by the fact that, until recent decades, a different family structure was prevalent among African Americans—the two-parent family. The partial breakup of the two-parent Black family is a result of the effective assault by the racist capitalist class, and is used as a weapon to further oppress the Black people and to divide and weaken the working class as a whole.

Central Cities Foci of Most Extreme Discrimination

Nationally, in 1993, per capita income of Black people was 55.7%, and of Hispanics, 49.8% of that of whites. The latest year for which data for cities is available is 1989—from the decennial Census taken in 1990. In that year, nationally, the per capita income of Blacks was 55%, of Latin Americans 52%, and of Asian origin people 85% that of whites.

However, conditions were much worse in the central cities, where up to 75% of the African Americans and Latinos are segregated. In the two largest cities, New York and Los Angeles, the per capita incomes of Blacks were 40% that of whites; of Asians 50% that of whites; of Hispanics, 32% of whites in New York and 25% in Los Angeles. The ratio for Native Americans was between those of Blacks and Asians.

It is difficult to comprehend the depth of the social gulf implied by such data. Chart 3D shows the relevant figures for whites and Blacks in seven cities: the northern cities of New York, Chicago, and Detroit; the Western City of Los Angeles, and southern cities of Birmingham, New Orleans and Houston—the latter sharing some characteristics of Western cities.

Most of the cities are poor—only New York and Los Angeles, of the seven, have overall per capita incomes above the national average. Note the depth of poverty in Houston, the core city of the great oil and petrochemical industry; in Chicago, hub of the country's industrial heartland; in New Orleans and Birmingham, the largest cultural and heavy industry centers of the South; and, most conspicuously, Detroit, the automotive capital of the world, which had less than two-thirds of the national per capita income. But even New York and Los Angeles, with per capita incomes 12% above the national average, are really poor in comparison with most of the country.

How does that figure?

• The cities have to provide transport and other services to the suburban commuters who come into the city to work but contribute little or nothing to its finances.

• While the cities have a larger than average share of resident rich people, the tax systems are regressive. In most cases there is no income tax, or only a flat rate income tax, so that the wealthy pay only a little toward the city's income. Further, the cities' finances are generally hobbled by state and banker control, with unreasonably low limits imposed on city spending.

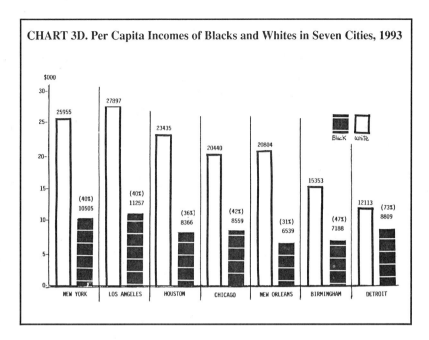

CHART 3D. Per Capita Incomes of Blacks and Whites in Seven Cities, 1993

• Public services cost more because of the physical problems of keeping up transport, sanitation, public facilities; because of the added costs of police, education, etc.; because stronger unions are able to win justly higher wages than prevail in many smaller cities.

• Living costs are certainly higher in the central cities than in most suburbs and rural areas, especially housing costs.

There is the salient fact that white per capita incomes are far above what is the national average for most central cities. Black per capita incomes are moderately above the national average in New York and Los Angeles, and below in the other five cities. In four of the five, Latino per capita incomes are below the national average; in two, New Orleans and Birmingham, they are well above the national average for Hispanics—in Birmingham, close to the per capita income of whites. The Hispanic population in these cities is very small and, in varying degrees, Latinos are here subjected to a lesser degree of economic discrimination.

Detroit is a special case: there urban decay has become extreme. The Big Three auto companies deserted the city, and even its near suburbs. Population declined from 1.5 million to one million in 20 years, mainly from the flight of whites.

Detroit changed from a city of neat one-family homes—whole blocks of

Black and white families, back to back, with no visible exterior differences—to one of run-down dwellings, where Blacks and poor whites still live. (The majority of whites moved to suburbs.) Obviously this widened housing gap weakened the Black-white unity among workers who had built some of the strongest unions and best working conditions in the country.

Thus the 1990 census shows that Detroit had a per capita income one-third below the national average. Even white per capita income was one-fourth below the national average for whites. Thus, in comparison with other cities, the relatively high ratios of Black and Hispanic incomes to those of whites doesn't mean that the minorities are better off than in other cities, merely that the remaining whites are also, for the most part, living in near poverty or outright poverty conditions.

There are only 95,000 white households in Detroit city. But there are 1,096,000 white households in the main suburbs—Macomb, Oakland, Washtenaw and Wayne counties—that, together with the city, make up the Detroit metropolitan area. Among African Americans, 270,000 households are still in the city; 66,000 in the suburbs—6% of the total suburban households. And although the incomes of the suburban Blacks are considerably higher than those in the city of Detroit, they are still only 70% of those of the better-off suburban whites.

Averaging these factors for the area as a whole, the median Black household income is $19,800, barely half that of the $38,700 median of white households. (For more complete analysis, see Appendix Table 3C.)

Or consider the example of Buffalo, New York, a working class city with weakening industry. The per capita income of Buffalo city's 205,073 whites—$12,025—is only about half that of New York City's whites; the per capita income of the 98,801 African Americans is $7,727 compared with $10,505 for New York City Black people. Both Blacks and whites do better in Buffalo's suburbs—whites by about $2,700 per capita and Blacks by about $2,200 per capita. But only 19,122 African Americans live in the suburbs as compared with 809,965 whites—80% of the Buffalo metropolitan area of a little over a million.

Then there's Hewlett Harbor Village, in Nassau County, Long Island, N.Y., with a 1989 per capita income of $89,402. Of its 1,193 population, 14 are Black. And there's just one Black in Plandome Manor Village—presumably a household servant—where the per capita income is $65,948. Then there's Roosevelt—a Census Designated Place (CDP), a small area in the town of Hempstead. Of Roosevelt's 15,030 residents, 13,331 are Black. The per capita income of the CDP is $12,955, barely half the county average of $25,584.[6] (Housing discrimination and its effects are further discussed in Chapter 11. The even more extreme conditions in the rural South are dealt with in Chapter 5.)

4. More on Income and Wealth

Widening Income Dispersion

The United States has lost significant ground in economic rivalry with its imperialist competitors, most notably Germany and Japan—and its East Asian satellites. However, these losses are moderated by the overwhelming U.S. military superiority, including its bases on the territory of its rivals. This puts a certain limitation on the intensity of competition, so that the losses of U.S. influence are only relative within a framework of the inflated profits of imperialism: the loss in global economic status has not ended the ongoing personal gains of the U.S. capitalist class as a whole and, especially, of its power elite.

Rising labor productivity, combined with the steady reduction in real wages and the undermining of labor's bargaining power, has led to a jump in the rate of exploitation of labor, accelerated by greater extra profits from racism. There are also added extra profits from a rising tide of direct foreign investments, especially in neocolonial countries with wage levels one-tenth those in the United States, but where the most modern technology is being used.

Japanese and German foreign investments may grow faster, but those of the United States continue to dominate decisive fields, such as petroleum and natural gas, and their exploitation. The monopolization of industry and finance has skyrocketed so that the incomes of the most powerful tycoons—the billionaires and centimillionaires who dominate the transnational corporations—have multiplied many times, far exceeding the growth rate of capitalist profits as a whole.

Consider this fact: In 1970 about 640 persons reported incomes of more than a million dollars on their income tax returns. In 1990, 64,000 such reports were filed. Even adjusting for higher prices, the number of people with exorbitant incomes multiplied more than tenfold. The phrase, "the rich get richer, the poor get poorer," has become common in recent years, but it has been true in the United States for decades as exploitation and oppression of the working class by the capitalist class has intensified.

One way of examining this scientifically is to trace the changing relationships between medians and means in measurements of income distribution. The "median" is the income of the person in the middle—with as many having higher as lower incomes. The "mean" is the arithmetic average of all persons, including that of the millionaire and that of the pauper. Consider three individuals, with respective incomes of $10,000, $20,000, and $30,000. The median is $20,000. The mean in this case is also $20,000, the sum of the three incomes divided by three. But in real life, the incomes of the three are apt to be $10,000, $20,000, and $60,000 respectively. The median is still $20,000, but the mean has increased to $30,000. The increasing inequality of income in the United States is revealed by the rising excess of mean over median in averaging income distributions. This is shown in Table 4:1.

TABLE 4:1. PERCENT EXCESS OF MEAN OVER MEDIAN IN INCOME
           DISTRIBUTIONS 1967-1993

Year	Households	Families	Males 15 & over
1967	11.8%	10.9%	9.0%
1970	14.5	12.6	13.0
1980	18.9	14.0	22.4
1990	24.9	20.5	28.3
1992	26.7	20.8	31.0

Source: P60-188, Tables D-1, D-2, D-3; pp. D2, D5, D8

Most social analysis focuses on use of medians as representative of the majority of people, and that is the correct procedure. But the inordinate rise in inequality, if not taken into consideration, leads to false conclusions. Over the past 25 years, the percentage excess of mean over median incomes went up 2.5 to 3 times in the case of households and families, and more than 4 times among males. Surely that represents an unacceptable, far-reaching rise in the inequality of incomes.

The situation of *white* males must also be taken into consideration in this analysis. They, it is claimed by racists, are victimized by affirmative action. The increase in the excess of means over medians among white males, like that of all males, was more than 4 times. Between 1980 and 1983, the real mean income of white males rose 10% while the real median income declined 4%. This signifies a rapid increase in the incomes of *upper-income* white men but a decline sustained by the *majority* of white men.

Inequality of incomes has increased among Blacks and Hispanics as well as among whites. Class differentiation among African Americans has sharpened: the number of very rich Black people is rising along with a growing number of poor and the deepening of their poverty. One consequence is an increasing influence of Black capitalists in organizations of the African American people, leading to critical situations in traditional Black organizations, historically rooted in the militant struggles of an oppressed people.

However, there is a decisive difference in these trends concerning white people, and Black and Latino peoples. Among whites the amount by which the rich are getting richer exceeds that by which the poor are getting poorer. Among Blacks and Hispanics, the opposite prevails: the number of poor getting poorer vastly exceeds the number of rich getting richer.

Chart 4A shows the changes in the proportions of very rich and very poor between 1974 and 1991.

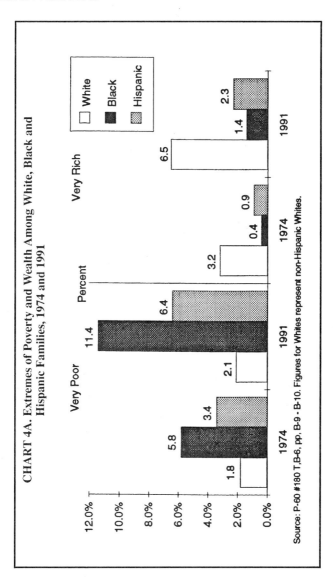

CHART 4A. Extremes of Poverty and Wealth Among White, Black and Hispanic Families, 1974 and 1991

Source: P-60 #180 T,B-6, pp. B-9 - B-10. Figures for Whites represent non-Hispanic Whites.

In 1974, among whites, 1.8% of all families were "very poor," with incomes under $5,000. By 1991, 2.1% of white families had incomes under $5,000 (all dollar figures are adjusted to 1991 price levels). In 1974, 3.2% of white families were "very rich"—with incomes above $100,000. But by 1991 the number of wealthy white families had doubled to 6.5%, more than three times the number of very poor families. [Data for white families adjusted to non-Hispanic white basis and, for 1974, to correct CPI.]

In 1974, 5.8% of Black families were very poor, and only 0.4% were very rich. By 1991 the number of very poor families had doubled, proportionately, to 11.8% of the total. The number of very rich Black families had also multiplied, but still amounted to only 1.4% of all Black families.

By 1991, there were 3.5 million white families with incomes of more than $100,000, a truly formidable number in terms of an economic and political power bloc. That was 32 times the 108,000 Black families in that elite income bracket.[1]

However the dollar incomes of individual rich African Americans do not approach the excessive millions and billions that white plutocrats have. The political and economic weight of the handful of super-rich Black performers, athletes, etc., is trivial compared with the clout of the Perots, Waltons, and other new billionaires, or with those who control the vast institutional conglomerations of wealth—the Rockefellers, Morgan group, du Ponts, Fords, etc.

Yet, even this lesser degree of rich African Americans has contributed to a significant rise in capitalist influence on the direction and agendas of Black conferences and organizations—which all too often are focused on improving opportunities for Black-owned business rather than on achieving equality for the masses of Black working people. The demands for Black business are legitimate, but their priority over the needs of Black labor has a negative influence on the mass movement for full equality.

These comparisons do not minimize the extent of poverty among white people. The number of non-Hispanic white families in deep poverty in 1991 exceeded the combined total of Black and Latino families in that dire circumstance. However, poverty among whites is more widely disbursed geographically, and mixed in among better-off white people, in contrast to the concentrations of poverty among the African American people and Latino peoples.

(Appendix Table 4A gives Census data for households with very low and very high incomes.)

Chart 4A understates the domination of whites in the capitalist class. Many of those shown as having household incomes above $100,000 consist of two earners, with more than $100,000 between them, plus what they may get in pension benefits, investment income, etc. A much sharper picture emerges when data are limited to individuals who "earn" more than $100,000—either through wages, salaries, or self-employment, or some combination thereof.

As of 1991 there were 1,353,000 white males with incomes of $100,000 or more; but only 12,000 Black, and 27,000 Hispanic. Among whites, the largest grouping with incomes above $100,000 were executives and managers; i.e., capitalists in the most basic sense. Besides the 576,000 highly paid executives, there were 456,000 highly paid white male professionals, and 231,000 salesmen with incomes above $100,000.

Among Blacks, the figure of zero in the printed tabulation means that the actual number was less than 500 executives and managers. Of the 12,000 with incomes above $100,000, ten thousand were doctors, lawyers or judges.

There were 143,000 white women with earnings above $100,000, barely one-tenth as many as white men. But there were 11,000 Black women with earnings above $100,000—virtually equal to the small number of Black men in the highest earning category; another 2,000 Black women had earnings just below $100,000 ($97,500-$99,000). Of course, this is not a sign that African Americans have made special progress in overcoming sexual discrimination, but is another of the many aspects of special discrimination against Black men. There were only 1,000 Hispanic women reported with earnings above $100,000.[2]

The first year of significant recovery from the depression of 1990-1992 failed to show any improvement in household incomes: the overall median fell another 1%, bringing the total decline since 1989 to 7%. Declines for all minority peoples were more drastic than those for whites, reflecting continued intensification of racism.

Incomes of Native Americans

Current data on incomes of Native American families are not published in the annual Census Bureau reports. However, data for Native American households for 1989 are available from the decennial Census of 1990. These and other data indicate that the overall incomes of Native Americans are somewhere between those of African Americans and Hispanic peoples. However, there are vast differences between the status of Indians living on and off reservations. More Native Americans live in California than in any other state, almost all of them off reservations. The 1990 median income of California's native American families was $27,818, which was higher than the medians for African Americans and Latinos.

However in nearby New Mexico and Arizona, where most Native Americans live on the Navajo, Hopi, and other reservations, median incomes were abysmally low, $13,909 in Arizona and $14,917 in New Mexico.

These miserable conditions were matched, or worse, among the Black populations of the delta states of Mississippi, Louisiana and Arkansas, with median household incomes of $11,625, $12,029 and $12,128 respectively.[3]

Economic and Social Status of Asian Americans

Asian people are the most rapidly growing sector of the U.S. population, increasing from about 2 million in 1970 to about 10 million in 1995. In the 1975 edition of *Economics of Racism*, Asian Americans were still included among "oppressed races," although significant differences from others were noted. Thus 1969 per capita incomes of the Japanese were already above those of whites, while incomes of the Chinese were only slightly lower—and of Philippine-origin people moderately lower—than those of whites. Already the Japanese and Chinese share in managerial and professional employment exceeded their share in total employment. Analysis of 1966-67 EEOC data revealed no economic discrimination against Asians that could be reflected statistically.[4]

Reasons for this difference—discussed therein—included the influence of the Communist-led Longshoremen's and Warehousemen's Union (ILWU) centered in California and Hawaii, which won big gains for its members, as well as diplomatic-political concerns of the U.S. government in its relations with Japan, South Korea and other Asian governments.

Considering further developments, it is no longer appropriate to regard Asian people as a whole as an oppressed minority economically, although a relatively small section can be so categorized. By and large, the economic status of Asians is roughly comparable to that of whites.

The majority of Asians may be regarded as members of the working class, with significant representation in all major occupation groups, including a substantial majority in white collar occupations. More than one-third have college degrees, a far larger proportion than any other racial group. More than one-quarter are in professional categories, in addition to those who are self-employed. Representation of Asians among capitalists, including small proprietors as well as high-ranking executives and investors in corporations, is well above average.

Roughly two-thirds of the growth in the Asian population over the past recent decades has been through immigration. Thus it is heavily, if not decisively, influenced by U.S. government policy, which actively seeks out and grants immigration visas to professionals and capitalists. Also, to limited groups of impoverished Asians wanted as service and sweatshop laborers.

More Asians live in suburbs than in central cities. Unlike African Americans and Latinos, the majority of Asians own their homes.

Over the three years 1990-1992, the average rate of immigration, as a percentage of the population at the beginning of the year, was as follows: Blacks, 0.29%; Hispanics, 1.30%; but Asians, 3.67%.[5]

This is the main factor accounting for the explosive growth of the Asian population, a trend encouraged by the U.S. government, which finds political, economic and social advantages in the specific Asians permitted as immigrants. Hispanics are also encouraged to immigrate but mainly to promote competition for low-wage jobs. Moreover, the data on Latinos do not reflect "illegal"—undocumented—immigration, which is large, but numerically unmeasured. The big furor over efforts to reduce illegal immigration, and the cruel treatment of those caught, is partly for show and partly to intimidate and control those who succeed in entering illegally.

The relatively low immigration rate of Black people certainly reflects the racist policies of U.S. imperialism, which regards the Black people as the most militant section of the oppressed immigrant groups and fears an increase in their numbers. The barriers to the immigration of Haitians during 1994, in direct contravention of U.S. official policy of welcoming refugees from political terror, was a striking example. A contributing, but not major, factor is the lack of highly trained professionals, wealthy capitalists, etc., from Black African countries, and the Caribbean, who want to immigrate. Sections of Asian people do remain highly exploited. Examples are Filipino, Vietnamese, and other Asian workers employed in sweatshop and service industries; non-family members employed in Chinese and other Asian restaurants. As of 1993, approximately 15% of Asians, as compared with 10% of whites, were classified as living in poverty. As of 1989, 6.7% of Asian households had very low incomes, as compared with 4.7% of white families.

At the other extreme, Asians are very well represented among capitalists and high-income professional and managerial personnel: 7.5% of Asian households—as compared with 4.9% of white households—had 1989 incomes above $100,000. In absolute numbers the 151,000 high-income Asian families exceeded corresponding numbers of either Black or Latino households.

In larger private establishments reporting to the EEOC for 1992, 26.5% of Asian employees were in professional categories, as compared with 16.1% of white employees, 6.3% of Black, and 5.4% Hispanic. On the other hand, the 35.9% of Asian employees in blue collar occupations was smaller than that of whites or of any other minority group.[6]

The relatively favorable position of many Asian households in accumulation of wealth is also noteworthy. Among Asians 25 years or older, 36.6% held a bachelor's degree or higher, as compared with 21.5% of whites, 11.4% of Blacks and less than 10% of Latinos or Native Americans. The relative position of Asians among those with higher academic degrees was even more outstanding.[7]

But national average statistics do not present an adequate picture of the socio-economic status of Asians. The situation of those living in large cities, such as New York and Los Angeles, is quite different from that of suburbanites. In New York City, among the more than half a million Asians, there are both impoverished, poorly educated people with low incomes—including recent immigrants, and there are highly paid, highly educated professionals and executives. And there are many white and blue collar workers in various categories in between. In 1989 in New York City, the per capita income of Asians was 42% lower than that of whites (not adjusted to exclude Hispanics); but 22% higher than that of African Americans and 53% higher than that of Latinos. Sixteen percent of Asians were classified as living in poverty, a considerably higher percentage than among non-Hispanic whites, but far lower than the rate of poverty among Blacks, Latinos and Native Americans. In Westchester County, on the other hand, fewer than 5% of Asians were under the official poverty level—about the same percentage as whites. Asians' mean household income exceeded $81,000, compared to $74,000 for white households—but was probably no higher than the average for non-Hispanic white households.[8]

There is a large and growing concentration of Asian people in the Los Angeles area. Within the city, they are a mix of workers—many in low-wage industrial and service occupations—and professionals, along with Korean and Chinese small merchants in mainly Black and Latino residential areas. Chinese people, mainly in upper income brackets, have become the largest group in the suburban cities of Monterey Park (already 58% of the population in 1990) and Alhambra (up from 2% Asian in 1970 to 38% in 1990). The suburb of Westminster, southeast of Los Angeles, is referred to as "Little Saigon," including among the large Asian population wealthy Vietnamese businessmen and large real property owners.[9]

The heavy inflow of immigrants into California—mainly from Latin America, plus Asia—has combined with the serious decline in employment in the military industries. As no public or private civilian industries have replaced them in the depressed economy of the early 1990s, the result is mass impoverishment of hundreds of thousands, along with intensified competition for the declining number of jobs. This situation was made to order for reactionaries and neo-fascists to divert the victims to fighting each other along racial lines instead of fighting the capitalist class and government responsible for the critical economic conditions. This took on a particularly noxious form of anti-immigrant propaganda, culminating in the overwhelmingly favorable vote in 1994 for the infamous and certainly unconstitutional "Proposition 187" denying social services, including education and non-emergency medical care, to undocumented immigrants. While mainly directed against Mexicans and Salvadorans, Vietnamese and other Asians are also targets.

As the Asian immigrants have not been tabulated by academic and government bodies, as have African Americans and Latinos, these data should be regarded as preliminary and subject of change in the rapid development of this fastest growing segment of the U.S. population.

U.S. Immigration Policy: Imperialist and Racist

The U.S. government, whenever it fits anti-Communist cold war policies, makes a big issue over the "right" of anyone to leave a country, but has never affirmed the right of anyone to enter a country. It made political capital over the "Berlin Wall," erected by the former GDR government to control transborder movements under cold war conditions, surrounded by hostile NATO and German forces determined to undermine and destroy it. But the United States has hundreds of miles of wall, fences and snake-infested ravines as its border barriers with Mexico.

Only 44 out of 4,000 border officers within the Immigration and Naturalization Service (INS) are Black, and only one of 42 patrol chiefs and deputy patrol chiefs. In 1991 a suit by 19 Black agents in Los Angeles grew into a class action suit on behalf of 850, reportedly the largest discrimination action ever brought against a government agency. A hearing conducted by Rep. John Conyers, Jr., uncovered details of the shocking, crude discrimination against African Americans in the INS. With such virulent racism among the bureaucracy, how can people of color expect anything but the cruelest treatment when trying to enter the United States?[10]

Certainly many times more Latinos have been killed crossing the U.S. borders than Germans—including CIA agents of various nationalities—killed while attempting to violate the former GDR borders. Yet the focus and the fuss was always on the former GDR. And let us not forget that U.S. naval forces engage in outright illegal piracy on the high seas, kidnapping thousands attempting to move from one country to another, including to the United States.

Immigration has always provided a large part of U.S. population growth. In recent decades it has followed specific U.S. imperialist objectives:

1. The importation of highly trained technicians and professionals for U.S. military and civilian industries, especially as they can usually be paid lower salaries than U.S. trained specialists.

The largest potential source has been Asia, where millions were professionally trained without the possibility of employment at high salaries in their home countries—India, Pakistan, the Philippines, Hong Kong, China, etc. Thus the relatively higher immigration from Asia, accounting for two-thirds of the growth in U.S. Asian population, and the high proportion of Asian professionals.

2. The importation of millions of undocumented workers, often without legal residence rights, for hard labor at negligible wages, and with terrible conditions of work, housing, education and health. This has applied mainly to Hispanics from Mexico, Central America and some South American and Caribbean countries where U.S. capitalists, in collaboration with reactionary landowners and industrial and financial combines, have forced conditions of labor and life way below those in the United States two centuries ago.

To avoid starvation and brutal repression, masses emigrate to the United States, where conditions—even for rightless refugees—offer better opportunities for survival than those prevailing in their home countries. Some Asians fit into this category as well, but on a relatively small scale.

3. The open door to anti-Communists, "dissidents," opponents of socialist and other anti-imperialist regimes for the dual purpose of weakening their homelands and for providing support for reaction within the United States. In the case of Eastern Europe and the former USSR, there was an additional purpose: getting many thousands of the world's best-trained, most experienced scientific and technical personnel.

4. A welcome mat to capitalists from all countries, including financial finaglers seeking safe havens in the United States from crimes committed in their own countries. U.S. policy has been more favorable to Cubans than to other Latino immigrants, because of their anti-Communist sentiments. As a reward for their defection, they often get better jobs and have a somewhat higher standard of living than other immigrants from Latin America.

There was a period, however, when the policy of welcoming Cuban "refugees" was interrupted because of a temporary flood of such emigres, which seemed beyond the capacity of the United States to handle comfortably. The United States, which for decades had castigated Cuba for restricting emigration, now castigated the Cuban government for permitting unrestricted exodus. An agreement with Cuba was finally negotiated to limit emigration, and the United States "relented," agreeing in November 1994 to admit Cubans on Guantanamo.

U.S. Racism Internationally

Attitudes towards Asians provides a clear example of how the U.S. ruling class, with its control of the media and of propaganda and disinformation, turns racist incitement on and off as its requirements change.

When the principal Asian residents in the United States were Chinese—brought here as farm and railroad laborers, mine workers, etc., with no citizenship rights—they were subjected to fierce racist abuse. Reactionary ideologists propagated fears of the "yellow menace." And during World War II, the treatment of Japanese Americans was vastly different from that of Americans of German or Italian origin, although the United States was at war with all three countries. Japanese—even those born in the United States—were segregated in concentration camps. Germans and Italians were not displaced, although there is reason to believe that some Germans, especially, were able to assist the Hitler regime by reporting shipping convoys for attack by German submarines, etc.

The racism involved in selecting Japanese cities as the targets for atomic bombs is all too apparent. In later years, racism helped justify the vicious destruction rained upon North Korea and Vietnam. Remnants of anti-Asian racism are still seen in the anti-Communist campaigns against North Korea and in the allegations of "human rights" violations in China, Singapore, etc. The Chinese have publicized the determined and systematic violations of human rights in the United States.

However, in general, racism against Asians has been reduced. The Japanese and South Korean rivals of U.S. capitalists are also associates in profitable joint ventures, expanding in scale. These partners completely support the political-military forays of the U.S. Incidents of racist violence against Asians have decreased as has racist propaganda against them.

Shifts in public attitudes toward minorities are consciously directed by the capitalist class through control of the media, of educational institutions and curricula, and the politicians. Thus, the forces that manipulate a selective easing of prejudice against Asians intensify propaganda against African Americans and Hispanics.

It isn't only that politicians in one campaign after another use racism as an electoral weapon,with candidates of both party's calling for the death penalty, more prisons, and elimination of the social safety net that is the lifeline of the rising number of African Americans excluded from economic life. On the ideological front they are also active. They give maximum exposure to the racist "scholarly" work, *The Bell Curve*, a book that purports to prove the inferiority of African Americans. Pages of "expert" reviews differ only on the extent to which it is "valid" or "invalid"—as if Hitlerite racist ideology has its "good points"and "bad points." The book rapidly made the "best seller" list.

On the practical side, the mass emigration of professionals from Asia and Eastern Europe makes it easier for Washington to slash the funds required to enable U.S. minorities to obtain professional training, on the grounds that they are no longer needed.

The hypocrisy of Proposition 187, designed to magnify discrimination against Latin Americans, is emphasized by a contradiction: the immigrants are illegalized, subject to deprivations and deportation—even back to death squads in El Salvador—while the employers who hire them are exempt from punishment. This incongruity became apparent when it turned out that it is an accepted practice for the well-to-do to hire "undocumented"servants and not pay social security taxes on their account. After one potential appointee's name was removed from consideration because of the publicity, other cases were ignored. Now a new ruling formally exempts wages to undocumented aliens from any tax deductions, thereby ruling out future social security benefits to them.

Differing attitudes and applications of discrimination and racism serve the capitalists' aim to turn persecuted peoples against one another instead of against their joint oppressors; frictions between African Americans and Latinos over jobs; Blacks and Latinos against Korean merchants; between Jews—still subject to anti-Semitism—and African Americans.

Obviously to achieve equality and liberation, high priority must be placed on mass, united anti-racist actions by all of its victims, along with the white working class majority—also losers, but also having a special responsibility in overcoming these evils.

Personal Wealth

Wealth is of major importance for economic well-being. It provides economic security and stability beyond current income, which for a worker is subject to sharp changes with shifts in employment status. Substantial wealth provides a backstop when jobs are terminated, as well as when a family is faced with major health expenditures, or losses due to natural disasters—e.g., fire, flood, etc. Through savings accounts and investments, wealth provides a source of income that may fluctuate, but averts the crises faced by workers when adversity hits.

Substantial wealth offers the opportunity to "escape," or, as expressed in capitalist ideology, to "rise above" the working class and become a part of the middle class. Of course, very large accumulations of capital are essential to gain full capitalist class status, to reap full benefit from the system of "free enterprise."

But even moderate accumulations of wealth provide for a more comfortable lifestyle, whereas lack of net worth may impose many of the hardships of poverty, even for those with current incomes above the official—or unofficial—poverty levels.

Discrimination against Blacks and Latinos with respect to wealth is more extreme than discrimination with respect to income. In 1991, the latest year for which Census data are available, the median net worth of white families was $44,408; of African American families, $4,604; and of Hispanic families, $6,345 (Chart 4B).[11]

An FRB study, using somewhat different methods of estimating net worth, indicates even more disparity in wealth, and a significant intensification of discrimination during the 1980s. While the mean levels of wealth rose signifi-

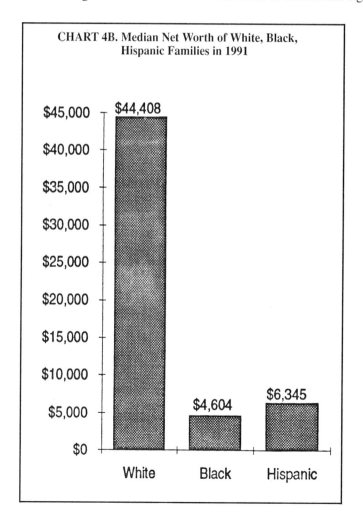

CHART 4B. Median Net Worth of White, Black, Hispanic Families in 1991

cantly between 1983 and 1989, the median wealth level dropped, even during a period of relative prosperity, reflecting the sharpening class differentiation and further impoverishment of working class Black and Hispanic people.

TABLE 4:2. MEAN AND MEDIAN NET WORTH OF HOUSEHOLDS
           1983 and 1989, in 1989 dollars

	1983		1989	
	Mean	Median	Mean	Median
	thousands		thousands	
White	$173.0	$54.3	$203.8	$58.5
Non-white and Hispanic	37.6	6.9	45.9	4.0

Source: Arthur Kennickell and Janice Shack-Marquez: "Changes in Family Finances from 1983-1989", FRB, Jan. 1992, T 2, p.3

Considering the wide margin of error in these statistics, it can be stated that the *average* net worth of Black and Hispanic families—which over-weight the wealthy and well-off families—was approximately one-fifth that of white families, while the median wealth, which essentially reflects the situation of working class families, was only one-tenth that of white families. These differentials are incomparably worse than the two to one differentials in income.

Also important is the kind of property owned. Nearly three-fourths (73.5%) of Black net worth consisted of equity in homes and cars, forms of personal property from which little accumulation of income or wealth could be expected. Hispanic households also had 64.7% of their net worth in ownership of homes and cars. The figure for white families was 47.3% of their total net worth, which while high enough, still meant that more than half of the average white family's net worth could produce some additional income or wealth.[12]

Not that home or car ownership implied much monetary value. The median equity in a Black homeowner's home was $27,000, and in the car, only $3,200. That means that for the most part, the homes and cars were held in escrow for the real owners, the holders of mortgages and car loans. Similar data applied to Hispanic owners' equities, while those of white home and car owners ran considerable higher.[13]

Even on that level, home ownership by Blacks and Latinos was inadequate in relation to the standard American "norm." This is more than a psychological factor. While ownership of a mortgaged home hardly provides absolute security, the insecurity faced by a tenant is much greater. In addition to the landlord's prerogative to refuse to renew a lease, there are very few limits on the power to raise rents beyond the tenant's income, whereas mortgage rates are fixed—except for those based on changes in interest rates.

Under U.S. conditions, lack of home ownership, combined with insecurity of employment, make African Americans the main victims of evictions and homelessness.

A critical component of American life, outside large cities, is the private car or "light truck," the high-powered vehicle suitable for larger families who can afford them. Public transit systems have not kept up with growing populations and the escalating complexity of travel requirements. Many areas are totally without public transit systems.

A worker without a car is severely handicapped in finding a job, and getting to the job once it is secured. This especially affects ghetto residents in metropolitan areas, as more and more production and trade enterprises move out of central cities. Factories and shopping facilities are miles away, too distant to manage without good public transport. Although factories have large parking lots for cars , there are long and difficult traverses from public transportation for those who have no car. As of 1991, while 90% of white households owned a vehicle, only 63% of African American households and 76% of Hispanic households did.[14]

A checking account is another important convenience. Most employers pay wages and salaries by check, not cash. The same applies to social security and other government payments. With a bank account, a check can readily be cashed, and other payments made by check. Between 1983 and 1989, according to FRB data, there was a decline in the percentage of households with checking accounts. In 1989, 80% of white households had checking accounts, but only 45% of minority households. Those without bank accounts are forced to stand in line and pay usurious amounts at check-cashing depots.[15]

According to the FRB study, the decline in checking accounts was partly because funds were shifted to other forms of assets, especially by people with higher incomes, e.g., payments made by credit card. Another factor has been the rising bank charges on checking accounts, charges that are unduly high for small accounts. Poor people without checking accounts are often unable to obtain credit cards, or have to pay exorbitant fees. These charges, as well as the ripoffs by check-cashing establishments, are part of the extra profits gained from exploitation of African Americans, Hispanics, Native Americans—and some Asians.

Changes in net worth were closely associated with changes in income The Federal Reserve article summarized overall changes:

Although the aggregate median family income did not change, a breakdown of the population by demographic groups shows mixed changes. The median income for families headed by persons with at least some college experience rose, but this increase was offset by declines in all other education categories. A moderate increase for white families was offset by a decline for nonwhite and Hispanic families.... Mean net worth rose more than 23 percent, whereas median real net worth rose only 11 percent.... As with income, the contrast between the mean and median suggests an increase in the concentration of net worth among wealthy families. While small increases in median net worth were widespread, some marked declines also occurred. The decline was especially sharp for single parents and for nonwhites and Hispanics.[16]

Bearing in mind that the Federal Reserve study covered a period of rising employment and economic activity, not including the pre-1983 or post-1989 cyclical crises, these results give emphasis to the intensified impoverishment of large sections of the working class, but especially of the Black and Hispanic peoples—at the same time as class differentiation increased among Black and Hispanic peoples as well as among whites.

The Commerce Department report showed a serious drop in the average household's net worth during the crisis period 1988-1991, amounting to 12% for white households; 5% for Black households, and 17% for Hispanic households.[17]

Concentration Of Wealth

Nearly 3.5 million households reported net worth of $500,000 or more in 1991. Amounting to 3.64% of all households, they may be regarded as the affluent section of the population—roughly defining the size of the capitalist class. Many more with very high incomes, who spend lavishly but have not accumulated wealth, are for most practical purposes also in the capitalist class category.

TABLE 4:3 NUMBER AND PERCENT OF HOUSEHOLDS WITH NET WORTH EXCEEDING $500,000, 1991.

	Households *(thousands)* Total	Net Worth Over $500,000	
		Number	% of Total
Total	94,692	3,447	3.64%
White*	75,322	3,268	4.34
Black	10,766	29	0.27
Hispanic	6,407	56	0.87
Asian	2,094	93	4.44
Native Amer. and other	423	4	0.87

*Data for non-Hispanic whites partly estimated.
SOURCE: P70-34, Table 4, p.7

These data indicate that only among white and Asian peoples are the capitalists an important sector of the population. Black, Latino, and Native American households, constituting 20.8% of all households—and about 25% of total population—account for only 5.3% of the wealthy households.

The exclusion of Black people from the ranks of the wealthy and the capitalist class is particularly notable. Some African American publications have emphasized the increasing Black share of capital and celebrate the individual capitalists of African origin.

Between 1988 and 1991 the number of Black households reporting net worth of more than $500,000 doubled. This may be due, in part, to the fact that more attention was given the matter, with a resulting rise in the number of African Americans to report their wealth. At any rate, this does not change the lack of financial power of the Black community relative to that of the white capitalists. Even after the increase, the number of rich African Americans is less than 1% that of wealthy whites, and their average wealth is far less.

From some points of view, the definition of those with net worth of more than $500,000 as wealthy is too broad. The popular concept of "rich" is defined by the term "millionaire." As of 1989, Barry Johnson and Marvin Schwartz, of the Treasury Department's Income Tax Division, estimated 3,417,000 top wealth-holders—close to the number shown in table 4:3. Of these, 1,260,000 had a net worth of more than $1 million—that is were millionaires, properly speaking; and 109,000 had a net worth of $5 million or more. This small group of about 100,000 people actually make up the dominant sector of the capitalist class. Obviously almost all of these 109,000 are white. And their combined net worth of approximately $1.4 trillion dollars[18] is more than double the entire net worth of all Black and Hispanic households in the United States ($568 billion).

The dramatic disparity is sharpened when we consider the combined net worth of all white families, $9 trillion—or $9,000 billion—and compare it with the combined net worth of all Black households, $300 billion, and Hispanic households, $268 billion.[19]

That means that the combined net worth of all African American and Latino households came to only one-sixteenth that of white households—a difference highlighted by the fact that most Black and Hispanic "wealth" consists of the slim equity in homes and cars.

The other side of great wealth is bankruptcy, debts that cannot be repaid. Those who suffer thus far exceed the number of the wealthy. As of 1991, 10% of white households; 30% of Black households; and 23% of Hispanic households had zero or negative net worth.[20] These are the 10-15 million households of all races, but mostly concentrated among Black and Latino households, living precariously, in danger of repossession of car, home and furniture, and of being forced into the growing ranks of the homeless. The status quo highlights the need for a change, not only for Blacks and Latinos, but for the working class as a whole—independent political coalition based on mass action rather than on capitalist politicians.

5. Poverty

President Franklin D. Roosevelt said in 1937: "I see one-third of a nation ill-housed, ill-clad, ill-nourished." Since then the productivity of American workers has multiplied many times. The wealth and power of United States capitalism and imperialism has reached awesome—and to the world's peoples—mortally dangerous heights.

FDR spoke during the world's most prolonged, severe cyclical crisis in the history of capitalism. Yet how little has been gained since by the multitudes! And how many more people than in 1937 are ill-housed, ill-clad, ill-nourished! For many millions now these terms must be sharpened—to homeless, freezing, hungry, even starving.

Poverty is a fully logical feature of capitalism, more completely than in earlier exploitative societies. The slave owners had a self-interest to at least minimally feed and house their slaves. The feudal lords had a responsibility, and a self-interest, in their serfs retaining a share of the crop they raised.

But the capitalist has the requirement to feed only those workers whose labor he is directly exploiting, and only for so long as that exploitation is profitable to the capitalist. The ideology of capitalism is that of extreme individualism. The code words—"freedom," "enterprise," "risk-taking"—signify a system that rewards victors in an "every one for himself" competition, with the stakes of the victors potentially limitless and the leavings for the losers potentially zero.

But there is a contradiction. Capitalism has attained a high degree of civilization in material and some cultural spheres. The existence of poverty in the midst of the soaring luxury of the capitalist class is universally recognized as an evil. Poverty has been a conspicuous factor throughout the existence of the capitalist system.

Among the advanced industrial countries, that is, the imperialist countries, the United States stands out as both the most powerful and wealthy and the most afflicted with poverty; and the one where poverty is most decidedly spreading. Now, by official acknowledgment it is felt by about 40 million in the United States, and by realistic measurement, double that.

Poverty is not a genteel state of having a lower-than-average income, of not being able to afford luxuries. It means hunger. It means evictions, and increasingly, homelessness. It means humiliating appeals, sometimes successful, sometimes not, for reluctant official or private assistance in order to survive. It means illness, lack of adequate medical care and, for millions, premature death.

The scourge of poverty is magnified by racism. In 1993, nearly half of all poor people—19 million—were white, representing nearly ten percent of the white population. But 11 million were Black, one-third of the African American population, and 8 million Hispanics, over 30% of the total, were counted as poor. A similar percentage applied to Native Americans. Moreover, generally, poor Blacks, poor Hispanics and poor Native Americans were poorer than poor whites.

Despite the fact that worker productivity has escalated, the gap has widened between the income of the workers who produce more and the bosses who profit more from the increased production. As result, with the rise of unemployment and the all around downtrend of workers' wages and benefits, there are tens of millions, conservatively, who lack nourishing food, decent housing, access to health care and other components of a standard of living necessary for even minimum decent survival. That lifestyle is far removed from the "middle class" standard touted by the media as typical of the "average" American family.

Not only are tens of millions of Americans without adequate income, but the meager government support measures won from the 1930s through the 1960s have been ruthlessly reduced. The approach of the government, the special-interest lobbies, the rich, their churches and foundations is to depend on "private charity." And ever since the time of Charles Dickens in England, this device has been used by the wealthy for their own ends. In fact, the philanthropic donations succor only a few selected recipients and have only miniscule impact on the overall wretched conditions. But the donors garner heaps of favorable publicity and public honor—and huge tax write-offs.

New York State's Westchester County is one of the country's "wealthiest" in terms of per capita income. Many rich people live there. But, "Westchester County must address a growing problem that is forcing thousands of county children to go to bed hungry.... Together, the county's pantries and kitchens served 2.5 million meals in 1990—up from 1.5 million in 1988," according to the Reverend John Duffell, a food bank administrator.

He said: "It is the human face of hunger in Westchester that we need to see.... The face of children who line up with their parents at 5 a.m., even in the rain, to ensure that they will receive a bag of groceries before they run out."[1]

According to a survey, in Long Island's Suffolk county,

...one-quarter of low-income families experienced hunger. Hunger keeps children from paying attention in class, leaves them three times more likely to suffer...illness, and forces them to miss more school days than children who eat enough.

Almost half of those families said they ran out of money for food an average of five days a month. In half the households, adults did without food or skimped on portions when money was low. In 22 percent of the households, adults said they cut back on their children's meals by eliminating food or cutting portions.[2]

The sharp decline in the economy of New York City during the late 1980s and early 1990s has caused mass homelessness and hunger. A *New York Times* editorial headed "Hunger, a Growth Industry" tells of one non-profit outfit, City Harvest, that expanded by 30% in 1992. With eight vehicles operating around the clock seven days a week, it distributed 6 million pounds of food to soup kitchens, food pantries, etc. in the city—up from 4.6 million pounds in 1991. Even so, it covered only 130 of the 750 distribution points in the city.

At a Mexican resort in 1991, young Kismayu Indian children, noses pressed to the dining room windows, watched guests at mealtimes. The inn manager explained that they were waiting for the leftovers from diners' plates. I was appalled.

But conditions in New York City are no better! City Harvest collects the leftovers from banquets, weddings, bar mitzvahs, holiday parties, corporate feasts, movie shoots and charity balls. The difference is that the hungry New York children do not look through the windows at the fortunate celebrants who are leaving them scraps.

Comments the *Times* about City Harvest's operations: "There's no short-fall in supply or, unfortunately, in demand."

It calls for a $2 million federal grant so that the company can double its provision of garbage to the hungry. There are 120 similar operations extant in 38 states.[3] All this at a time when the U.S. government subsidizes the destruction of billions of dollars worth of oranges, milk, grains and other farm products so monopoly cartels can raise prices!

Far out of proportion to their numbers, the African American, Latino and Native American people are the victims of this bestial "charity," which substitutes for the most elementary public social programs.

Homelessness, along with hunger, has become a major cause of suffering for the first time since the 1930s. Estimates of those without any home—sleeping on the streets and in alleys, in cardboard tents, in subways or in public shelters—run into the millions. Many more are forced to live "doubled up": the official figure is about 7 million, but the actuality is certainly much more. Families hide their predicament to avoid evictions. With rents high and rising and rental housing in short supply, with banks quick to foreclose on mortgage delinquencies, the unemployed and those working at poverty wages are all too often forced to choose between food and shelter—a choice no one should ever have to make.

In urban centers, smaller cities as well as metropolitan spreads, the majority of the hungry and homeless are African Americans and Latinos. In many of the rural poverty areas, whites are often the majority. But overall, racism has intensified the poverty, the inhumane and unnecessary suffering of the oppressed peoples of the United States.

Official counts of poverty began with the year 1959. The number decreased from just under 40 million in 1960 to a low of 23 million in 1973.

But that marked the peak of improvement. By 1993 the official total exceeded 39 million and, considering social and political trends, probably exceeded 40 million by 1995. Within these broad trends, there were cyclical fluctuations. The number of poverty-stricken people increased in every downturn of the business cycle, and decreased in every upturn, with the exception of the upturn officially measured as beginning in 1992, during the first two years of which poverty continued to increase, and at a significant pace.

The percentage of people suffering poverty decreased from 22.2% in 1960 to 11.1% in 1973, then increased to 15.1% in 1993. Naturally the overall increase in the *percentage* was less than the increase in *numbers*, considering the rise in the total population (see Chart 5A).[4]

The period 1960-73 was one of rising real wages, rising median family income. It was influenced by the increasing impact of major gains in social legislation and trade union organization won during the course of struggles of

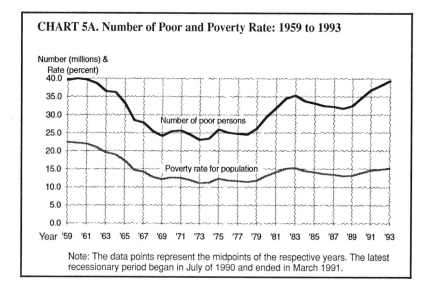

CHART 5A. Number of Poor and Poverty Rate: 1959 to 1993

Number (millions) &
Rate (percent)

Number of poor persons

Poverty rate for population

Year '59 '61 '63 '65 '67 '69 '71 '73 '75 '77 '79 '81 '83 '85 '87 '89 '91 '93

Note: The data points represent the midpoints of the respective years. The latest recessionary period began in July of 1990 and ended in March 1991.

the 1930s and 1940s, and reinforced by the reform legislation (dubbed "The Great Society") and civil rights legislation of the 1960s. These were the results of major mass struggles—the historic struggle against the apartheid conditions of extreme discrimination and segregation of Black people in the South, and the struggles to end the Vietnam War.

The subsequent period has been characterized by declining real wages and union representation, stagnant or declining median family income, a capitalist offensive against labor and its unions and, during the 1980s, brazen racism spearheaded by the executive and judicial branches of the U.S. Government.

Moreover, there has been a qualitative worsening of poverty in recent decades that is not measured statistically. Notably, as indicated, homelessness and hunger. The dominant reactionary political power of the 1980s sharply curtailed previously won programs to reduce and relieve poverty—the so-called "social safety net"—even as the need for such measures has risen. And racism has become an increasingly important, in some respects decisive factor in causing and maintaining large-scale poverty.

Between 1973 and 1993 there was an officially acknowledged increase of 16 million, or 70%, in the number of people surviving in poverty. Considering the substantial increase in productivity per person, no matter how measured, the ability of the United States to provide a good living, not to speak of a barely adequate living, has increased significantly during this period, yet it has fallen short of this requirement by a widening margin. While the lowest income strata have suffered the most severe losses, real wages and salaries have also declined virtually across the board. Nearly all the accretion of income produced during this period was seized by the big capitalists, their executive and managerial staffs, and their high ranking political representatives, as reflected in income distribution statistics showing that the top 5-10% made huge gains, and the lowest income contingents suffered serious losses, while those in the middle either lost some or stagnated.

Thus the accumulation of wealth by so many billionaires and centi-millionaires, the salaries and bonuses of top corporation executives and bond and stock salesmen in the tens and even hundreds of millions of dollars, have been appropriated directly out of the misery and super-exploitation sustained by these tens of millions of people existing in conditions of poverty.

Table 5:1 shows the latest numbers and increases in poverty, with the several times higher rates of poverty among African American, Latino and Native American peoples, than among white people (see also Charts 5B, 5C, 5D).

The increase of nearly 7 million in the number counted as living in poverty over four years embracing both the downside and part of the upside of a cycle is noteworthy. The number and percentage of people living in poverty increased for every racial group. Also significant is the fact, not shown in

TABLE 5:1. PERSONS IN POVERTY, 1989-1993, NUMBER AND PERCENT

	Number *(thousands)*			Percent	
	1993	1989	Increase	1993	1989
Total	39,265	32,415	6,850	15.1%	13.1%
White*	18,883	15,499	3,384	9.9	8.3
Black	10,877	9,525	1,352	33.1	30.8
Hispanic	8,126	6,086	2,040	30.6	26.3
Asian	1,134	1,032	149	15.3	14.2
Native American** and Other	1,028	564	464	25.1	22.2

* Refers to non-Hispanic White
** These figures have exceptionally wide margins of error because of the lumping together of Native Americans and "Others," which covers a variety of self-identification by surveyed people. The sum of the numbers shown for the separate races slightly exceeds the total because of several hundred thousand Hispanic people also classified as being in other non-white races. The very large increase shown for "Native American and Other" is partly due to a sharp increase in the number of Hispanic people also classified as "other."
SOURCE: Census Bureau, P60-188, Table C, p.xvi

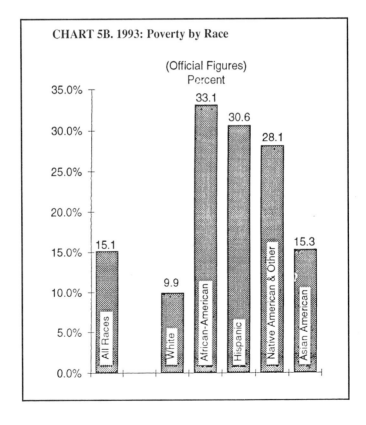

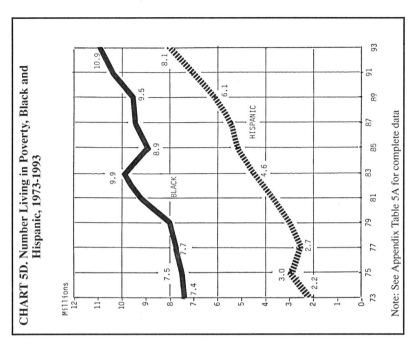

CHART 5D. Number Living in Poverty, Black and Hispanic, 1973-1993

Note: See Appendix Table 5A for complete data

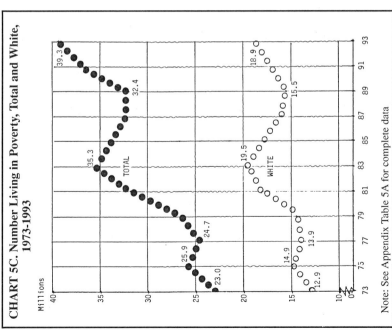

CHART 5C. Number Living in Poverty, Total and White, 1973-1993

Note: See Appendix Table 5A for complete data

table 5:1, that the total number and the number of each group living in poverty increased between 1992 and 1993, although the latter year was the first year of really substantial economic revival. Whites account for nearly half of those living in poverty, and nearly half of the numerical increase. On the one hand, this disproves propaganda implying that poverty is a concern only of minorities. On the other hand, whites are nearly three-fourths of the counted population. Minorities, with not much more than one-fourth of the counted population, account for at least one-half of the poverty-stricken, and generally tend to be more deeply in poverty.

Appendix Table 5A reveals a special intensification of poverty, during economic expansion as well as decline, in the 1990s. In the official designation of the business cycle, 1992 and 1993 were wholly years of economic recovery. Yet in each of these years the number counted as living in poverty increased by 1.3 million, or about 3.5%. The economic expansion became broader in 1994, and it remains to be seen whether the poverty numbers turned downward. There is severe danger that any reduction will be limited and temporary, in view of the special emphasis of the right-wing offensive against the most exploited, poorest sections of the population.

Class and Racial Patterns of Poverty

Poverty is an affliction of the working class. A substantial majority of the 18-54 year olds classified as living in poverty had jobs at some time during 1992, but most of these did not have full-time jobs. Obviously, in many cases, that was why they fell into the poverty classification.

A majority of men in the prime working ages who remained out of the labor force for a whole year, other than housekeepers and students, suffered from work disabilities.[5]

Still, why did so many of those living in poverty work only part of the year? This relates to the instability of employment in the United States (data are supplied in Chapter 6). International comparisons show that unstable employment, interspersed with periods of unemployment, is a several times more serious factor in the United States than in Western Europe. Correspondingly, the economic status of many workers fluctuates between above poverty and below poverty levels. Such instability is serious enough among white workers, but is an extreme affliction against the African American contingent of the working class.

These facts are important to counter the propaganda barrage branding the poverty-ridden as an "underclass" to be differentiated from the working class. Establishment media, following the pronouncements of reactionary ideologues, encourage the spread of this lie among workers, accompanied by the equally misleading designation of workers with steady jobs at average wages or better as members of the "middle class." Unfortunately, all too many trade union officials have adopted these fictional categories, confusing their members and inhibiting labor solidarity in struggles with particular employers or over legislation.

The true facts are also needed to deal with reactionary propaganda attributing poverty, especially among African Americans and Latinos, to subjective character "flaws."

The Census Bureau, in its annual report on poverty, fuels such propaganda by its choice of data to be emphasized. The summary section of the 1992 report shows only 40% of poor people as having worked at any time during the year, and just 9% full-time, year around. However, the data selected cover all people aged 16 or over, including full-time students. It also includes 31 million workers aged 65 and over, mainly retired. Men and women are combined in the table, including the considerable number of women who are full-time homemakers.

Details are provided in the main portion of the report, but the summary table is widely cited by journalists and other government publications. In fact, among poverty-stricken people *below* retirement age, 64% of the men and 45% of the women worked. Among men in the prime working age range, 25-54, 21% had full-time, year-round jobs.

A particularly vicious form of propaganda is denunciation of poverty-stricken single mothers as "welfare queens." Among wives in married couple families below retirement age, *36% of those below the poverty line worked*, including 33% of those with children under six years old. But among single mother heads of household living in poverty, *44% worked, including 43% with children under six years*. In short, despite the difficulties of caring for young children without decent child-care, and other handicaps associated with low-income and head-of-household responsibilities while working, nearly half of these poverty-stricken women managed to find jobs and work at least part of the year, a larger proportion than among poor married women.[6]

The *New York Times* editorialized in 1994:

> Demonizing welfare mothers has become political sport, with politicians everywhere blaming them for moral decline, budget deficits and even poverty itself. A report...by New York's Citizen's Budget Commission challenges this stereotype in useful and enlightening ways. It shows that women on welfare make up a far smaller percentage of the poor than popular wisdom would have it. It also confirms (that) Medicaid, not welfare, is the prime source of runaway spending on poverty.

Welfare mothers are routinely portrayed as slackers who make up the bulk of the poor and soak up more money every year. The fact is that only one in four poor households in New York City is headed by a single parent; welfare payments, when adjusted for inflation, have actually declined by 30 percent since 1972.

The poor in New York are also more ethnically diverse than commonly supposed. Among the elderly, for example, nearly half of all households in poverty are headed by whites. Like earlier studies, the commission's report suggests that the failure of welfare payments to keep pace with inflation contributes to homelessness.[7]

But it isn't that Medicaid payments are too high, but rather that the need for them is so great because U.S. law does not provide free medical coverage as a right, especially to those who cannot afford it privately. Medicaid spending, under present conditions, is grossly inadequate, partly because the amount is left to the mercy of the separate states, which provide most of the financing for Medicaid.

Transfer Payments

Programs lumped together under the designation "welfare," such as aid to dependent children and food stamps, are part of government transfer payments, which include all payments by federal, state and local governments to individuals other than wages and salaries, purchases of goods and services. Medicaid benefits for poor people are about equal in dollars to what is generally called "welfare." Total government transfer payments for poor people in 1993 came to $270 billion, equal to just 27% of all transfer payments, and only 4.3% of the gross national product.[8]

Most of these transfer payments do not provide cash to the poor, but are payments by the government to hospitals, doctors, drug companies, insurance companies, HMOs, etc. Therefore, they include large amounts of profit and overhead to these providers. The largest part of transfer payments are linked to what workers earned while working, including social security benefits, civilian and military government retirement and disability benefits.

The historical development of these transfer payments was to provide a social safety net against old age and disability, and unemployment. They amounted to a begrudging and inadequate recognition by the ruling class that their capitalist social system, if left to the "free market," resulted in intolerable suffering to increasing portions of the population. Thus, directly or indirectly, they were all aimed at providing protection against people falling into poverty, hunger and homelessness, or relief from poverty for those who had been thrust into that situation by the blows of the capitalist economy.

The social safety net was not established as a unified structure, but as the result of mass struggles for each web of the net, against the opposition of the capitalist class. These were concessions to the working people, aimed at preventing or moderating social unrest and rebellion, rather than at improving conditions. There remain huge gaps in the U.S. "safety net," especially insofar as it concerns the poor and oppressed who have had, historically, the least political clout.

The Census Bureau, in its consumer income reports, provides information on receipt of cash transfer payments, by race. These reports show that minority peoples, instead of being favored in this respect, are discriminated against. On a per capita basis, Black people receive about 20% less than white, while Latino and other minority people receive about 40% less than white.

TABLE 5:2. RECEIPTS OF TRANSFER PAYMENTS, PER CAPITA, 1992

	Amount
White (non-Hispanic)	$2,200
Black	1,772
Hispanic	1,298
Asian, Native American	1,284

SOURCE: Calculated from P60-184, Table 34, p.174; Table B-14, pp B-27-B-31

Family Breakup and Poverty

Poverty in the United States is highly aggravated by the breakdown of traditional two-parent family structures. More than 60 percent of poor people are either members of single-parent families or are living as single individuals. By 1992 the number of impoverished people living in female-headed single parent families slightly exceeded the number of those living in two-parent families; with a comparative poverty rate five times as high in the single-mother headed families as in those with two parents. More white people live in families headed by a single female than the combined total of Black and Hispanic people living under these conditions.

Racial differences in poverty are extreme for all kinds of families. Among two-parent families, the 1992 rates are 5.2% for whites; for Blacks, 14.3%; for Hispanics, 21.4%. Among single-female-headed families, the respective rates are: white, 25.6%, Black 53.7%, Latino, 51.2%.[9] Especially noteworthy is the fact that the poverty rate for white single-mother-headed families is considerably higher than the rate for Black and Hispanic two-parent families.

Poverty rates, of course, are significantly affected by cyclical fluctuations in the economy. During the cyclical downturn 1978-82, the overall poverty rate increased by 3.8 percentage points. During the ensuing 7 years of recovery and expansion, it receded by 3.4 percentage points; while in the three years of downturn and depression 1989-1992, the poverty rate increased by

1.7 percentage points. The directions of change were identical for whites, Blacks and Hispanics, and in each case the changes were substantial.[10]

Correspondingly, there is a close correlation between unemployment rates and poverty rates. Campaigns for jobs at adequate wages are the key element in political action to reduce poverty, especially in the minority communities where joblessness and poverty are most severe. Of course, this has nothing in common with the drive to impose forced labor on welfare recipients, while doing nothing to relieve their poverty—indeed worsening it by imposing essentially unpaid labor on top of other burdens.

The Tragedy of Poverty Among Children

Children of all ages are the most acute victims of poverty, and relatively, the most numerous. While serious in scale and depth throughout the working class, regardless of race, it is by far most acute among minority, and especially African American children. A Washington research organization, in a 1990 report, asserts:

> Among Blacks in poverty, no group more fully dramatizes the depth of the problem before us than their children. They are not only the most vulnerable victims of poverty; they are also, literally, the future. If current trends hold, these children will be increasingly hard pressed to overcome the burdens imposed by poverty. Growing numbers of them will not succeed.

An important, well-documented conclusion of the study is that the increase in female-headed families is

> not enough to account for the growing numbers of Black children living in poverty. In fact, declining economic opportunity has played at least as great a part in increasing the prevalence of childhood poverty.
>
> Of particular importance are findings regarding the deepening of poverty, with the slide of many Black families from the working poor category to the ranks of the dependent poor. Families caught in this downward shift are not only subject to greater economic deprivation; but without employment they also have less opportunity to enter the economic mainstream.[11]

The report was based on statistical data up to 1984. In the previous 11 years poverty among children had become much more acute, increasing by about 50% in numbers and as a percent of all children. Deterioration has continued since 1984, especially among Black and Hispanic children. By the early 1990s minority children constituted a substantial and increasing majority of all children living in poverty. About 22% of all children were classified as under the official poverty level, including 13% of white children, 47% of Black children and 40% of Latino children.

Poverty reaches overwhelming proportions and severity among the children of single mothers. The official poverty rates by 1992 for children under 6 years was 66%, including 57% among white children, 73% among African American children, and 72% among Latino children. Altogether, regardless of family structure, there were close to 6 million children and babies, one out of every four, who were deprived of adequate nourishment, health care, protection against harm from drugs, violence, and accidents—6 million who lack the requirements for strength and health throughout life, if they survive.[12]

Racist Impact on Poverty Even Sharper

The differential impact of poverty against Black and Latino peoples is even sharper than the three or four times higher rates shown in official statistics. The poverty thresholds used by the U.S. government are identical for all races, classes and locations. But, as shown in Chapter 3, living costs for Black families, especially, as well as for Latino families, are significantly higher than for white families, even when living in the same city.

Also, living costs are much higher in central cities than in many suburbs and in the countryside. The *New York Times* complained editorially:

> The cost of food, rent and other consumer goods can be twice as high in Manhattan as in Little Rock, Arkansas. Yet the income cutoff for poverty programs is the same in both places, $14,764 for a family of four. That produces the ridiculous and unfair result that a Manhattan family earning $15,000 does not qualify for Federal nutrition or education programs while on Arkansas family earning $14,500—the equivalent of $29,000 in Manhattan—does.[13]

The *New York Times* probably exaggerates the actual difference in living costs between New York and Little Rock, but it is certainly substantial. However comparisons are available between living costs in the Los Angeles Metropolitan Area and the Little Rock area. Los Angeles is the second largest city (in terms of population). For the second quarter of 1993, with an average of 100 representing the U.S. cost of living, that for Little Rock was 90.7, and for Los Angeles, 130.5, or 44% higher. The index for the New Haven metropolitan area, in the general region of New York, was 130.2 in the 3rd quarter of 1992 (not available for 1993).[14] (While the indexes are calculated for a "mid-management" standard of living, there is good reason to believe that the differences between metropolitan areas are similar for a working class standard of living.)

Overall, in 1993, 56% of Black families, and 51% of Hispanics but only 21% of white families, lived in central cities, and the minorities were especially concentrated in very large central cities.[15]

Actual Poverty Rate Double the Official Figure

This is a bold statement, and calls for full documentation.

To begin with, the method used to define poverty thresholds has a built-in bias which systematically understates the increase in the income required to escape poverty, and correspondingly understates the rise in poverty. The basis of all official poverty thresholds was an Agriculture Department 1955 "economy food budget," the least expensive of four "nutritionally adequate food plans"—which implied adequate calories, but apt to be overweighted by starchy, fatty items. It was further determined at that time that the "average" family spent one-third of its income on food. Consequently the poverty threshold was estimated at three times this "economy food budget." Year after year, starting with 1959, the poverty thresholds are increased exactly in proportion to the consumer price index.[16]

In the decades since 1959, the consumer price index for food has increased by virtually the same percentage as the overall index. Consequently the current poverty thresholds, in effect, assume that working class people are still getting by while spending one-third of their incomes for food, and still have enough left for all other necessities. Fat chance!

Non-food Costs Have Expanded

The Bureau of Labor Statistics calculated that in 1991 all consumer units spent 14.1% of their outlays on food, including 9.0% of their total on food at home. Semi-skilled blue collar workers spent 15.6% of their total outlays on food. Service workers, the lowest paid group, 16.5% of the total. The lowest fifth of population, by income, spent 17.7% of their total on food; the highest 20%, "only" 12.2%—even though their dollar food outlays were three times those of the lowest fifth—at least part of which represented more and better food.[17] In 1992 Black families spent 16.0% of their total on food, not so much more than the 14.2% of their much larger total spent by white and other consumers.[18]

These facts conclusively establish that to be consistent with poverty thresholds adopted 40 years ago, the actual current minimums should be doubled. That would not automatically, necessarily, double the number of people included. But in fact, it would more than double the number. The Census Bureau estimated that in 1993 there were 91 million people with less than 200% of the official poverty threshold, 2.3 times those officially counted as living in poverty.[19]

Government officials, in allotting various types of poverty relief, implicitly recognize the inadequacy of the official poverty thresholds, and use much higher cut-offs ("e.g., children in families with income below 185 percent of the appropriate poverty guidelines may be eligible for the reduced-price school lunch program").[20]

Different percentages are used for various types of benefits, ranging from the guidelines themselves to double the guidelines. In most places officials skimp on providing these benefits, miserly as they are, and those receiving them must be regarded as a minimum of people actually living in poverty, and deserving of assistance.

In 1992, 61 million people lived in households receiving one or more types of "means-related assistance." An additional 10 million people lived below the official poverty level but received no form of assistance.[21] That makes a total of 71 million, almost double the 37 million then officially counted as living in poverty. Making allowance for the millions living in poverty but never counted as even existing in official surveys easily raises the total to more than double the official count. Such an adjustment would raise the total to the 73.5 million people living below 175 percent of the official poverty threshold in 1992. Raising this to the same relation to preliminary figures for 1993 brings the total to 78.7 million.[22] By 1996, a realistic measure of people suffering from poverty is 80 million, roughly 30% of the population. I emphasize that this is a *reasonable, not a far-out, radical estimate*. Table 5:3 shows the number and percentage of people below 175% of the official poverty threshold as of 1993.

TABLE 5:3. PEOPLE BELOW 175% OF OFFICIAL POVERTY THRESHOLD, 1993

	Number in thousands	Percent of population
Total	78,665	30.3
White	42,867	22.6
Black	17,706	53.8
Hispanic	14,751	55.5

SOURCE: P60-188, Table 6, pp.22-24

Thus more than one-fifth of the white population, and more than half the Black and Hispanic population, suffer severe deprivation. It is *certainly a notable fact that by this broader definition, more than half of the deprived are white*; the other that more than half of the two largest oppressed groups are below the adjusted boundary. With the insecurity of economic life afflicting workers, farmers and small business in the United States today, many of those now living under reasonably comfortable conditions may find themselves thrown into the ranks of the more than 40 million white people already suffering poverty or severe deprivation.

On the other hand, the shocking percentage of more than 50% of African

Americans and Latinos suffering poverty by this broader definition emphasizes the racist features involved in U.S. poverty, and should caution those ideologues, both white and Black, who tend to exaggerate the extent to which
Black people have obtained so-called "middle-class" status.

The two features taken together gives emphasis to the elementary truth
that racism offers no means of escape from poverty; that a general war on
poverty cannot succeed unless it is accompanied, prominently, with very specific measures to eliminate the racist features of poverty. The struggle against
racism may well prove the decisive key factor in finally making the vaunted
"American standard of living" a reality for the entire population.

Poverty and Health

Soaring costs of medical care have brought the issue of health insurance
to the fore in the political life of the country. Focus has centered around the
15 percent of the population—37 million people—without any health insurance. Here again, African American and Latino people are proportionately
the most deprived, along with all people at or below poverty levels. As of
1992, 11.5% of whites, 20.1 % of Blacks, and 32.6% of Hispanics were without any coverage. Among people below the official poverty level, 28.5% were
completely without coverage, including 27.4% among whites, 22.6% among
Blacks, and 41.2% among Hispanics.[23]

The apparent slightly better coverage of below poverty Blacks than below
poverty whites is due to greater use of Medicaid coverage, which applies to
60% of the Black population. In practice, treatment under Medicaid may often
be inferior to that under private, more expensive insurance. The disadvantage
of Latino people in health coverage is a shocking fact, partly due to language
difficulties in obtaining government benefits, and partly due to fears of deportation on the part of undocumented immigrants from Spanish-speaking countries.

The Clinton campaign promise of universal health coverage was shattered
by the Administration's backing away from its promise with a prolonged plan-
ning period. Meanwhile, its bureaucracy attempted to satisfy the demands
from all the profiteers in a private medical system, and from a furious assault
by pharmaceutical manufactures, insurance companies, health maintenance
organizations, and medical practitioners' organizations—all of whose extortionate profits would be threatened by a practical system of universal coverage. The Clinton Administration refused to consider the single payer system,
which would wipe out 30% or more of overhead costs at all stages of the present system as well as huge private profits. Examples of existing government
financed systems show that the single payer system would involve overhead

costs of not more than 10 percent. Minority peoples would be the main gainers from a genuine system guaranteeing universal coverage, with lower costs to all, and no costs to the poverty-stricken.

This problem is more fully examined in Chapter 12.

Significance of Poverty in the United States

It's a truism that poverty is, within certain limits, a relative concept. It verbalizes the suffering of those whose conditions of life are qualitatively far inferior to what has become achievable and more or less standard for a given society in a given historical epoch. Poverty in the United States has seriously intensified over the past two decades absolutely, and most decisively, relatively. The absolute deterioration is in a decline in the living standard of people living in poverty, as that is classified. The more severe relative decline is in the contrast between the absolute decline in conditions of the poor, and the increase in luxury and conspicuous consumption of those at the top, as well as the stagnation but less acute decline of those in the middle.

Poverty in the United States also stands out as more severe than in most other industrially developed—e.g., imperialist, states: states ruled by modern corporate tycoons, with various internationally interlocked interests. Income differentials in Western continental Europe and in Japan, for example, are half as extreme—by some measurements, as in the United States. The difference, of course, is not that German or Japanese capital is more generous than American capital. It results from a relatively much stronger and better organized working class, from far-reaching concessions wrested from governments and, so far, retained against the global offensive of big capital.

There is yet another special feature of U.S. poverty. To an extent not approached in most other industrially advanced countries, racism is a major feature here. People of color are a very large percentage of the population in the United States, and the poverty differential against them—a three to one higher poverty rate—is exceptionally high. Only in South Africa, among industrially developed countries, is poverty still far more extreme and prevalent among Blacks than in the United States. Recent major political gains in South Africa offer promise of improvement there. In Germany, England, France, etc., the immigrant populations subject to severe discrimination and a high degree of poverty are a much smaller part of the population than are oppressed people in the United States, and to some extent benefit from protections won for all workers.

Establishment spokespersons formally bewail poverty, but tend to blame it on its victims. Their "solution" is for poor people to "pull themselves up by their own bootstraps," and under current maximum emphasis, to mend their allegedly "immoral" style of life, to restore "family values," etc. The hypocrisy of this whole approach is so glaring with the current proliferation of the grossest crimes and corruption among the ruling circles, their smashing of all bounds in defiance of decent standards of personal life. Such decadence is so prevalent that there is no real attempt to cover it up. Repeatedly the prominent politicians, and radio publicists, most vehement in their racist diatribes against Blacks and Latinos, are exposed for involvement in extreme abuses of civilized personal behavior, including financial corruption as well as sexism and racism.

Such politicians and other propagandists will never urge the exploiters to yield the superprofits they derive from poverty in order to relieve it. Quite the opposite, they demand ever more concessions as "incentives" for them to "help the economy."

Yes, poverty must be combatted by efforts of its victims, but not through each poor person's solo struggle within the obstacles imposed by the system. Nor by the exclusive efforts of those trapped in poverty this year. But by the united, collective effort of the entire working population, including the many who went through periods of poverty, the larger number threatened with being thrown into poverty through prolonged unemployment and reduction of labor standards, as well as those currently with apparently secure higher wages, falsely classified as "middle class," but whose long-term interests are definitely not with those of the capitalist rulers.

End of the Century War Against the Poor

Political writer Kevin Phillips, in his book *The Arrogant Capital* (1994), describes the '90s of the last several centuries as decades of major revolutionary changes. His history is arguable, to say the least, and in its application to the end of the 20th Century a gross misuse of terminology. However, the 1990s might well be regarded as the decade of world capitalism's ominous, disastrous global counterrevolution against the working class and the peoples of the whole world. In the United States that counterrevolution is in full swing, embracing the full range of attacks on the civil, social, and economic rights of the masses of the population, including the plundering of public property and the liquidation of social services (privatization); the reactionary reversion of tax and budget systems; the increasingly brazen purchasing of elections by groups of the top multimillionaires and billionaires.

A special target of the far-right campaign are the scores of millions of the poor, and the additional millions designated for impoverishment. Some of the impact of that campaign is shown in the chart and table showing the rise of poverty over the past two decades, and most notably during the early part of the 1990s. The Republican Party most avidly has made the racist campaign against the poor the featured component of its propaganda and political program. The Democratic Party, under domination of its rightwing "Leadership Council," with even the one-time populist demagogy of the Democrats muted, has connived in the far-right assault.

The campaign became conspicuous during the 12 years of Republican Presidency, 1980-1992, and did not abate during the ensuing two years of a weak Democratic Administration. It reached a new peak in the elections of 1994, with stridently rightwing Republicans gaining control over both branches of Congress, the governorships of the largest states, the judiciary, and a more powerful semi-governmental instrument of finance capital—the Federal Reserve system.

The *New York Times* editorialized:

THE G.O.P. ASSAULT ON WELFARE
The welfare reform proposal drafted by House Republicans would violate good sense by turning welfare programs over to the states. It would violate common decency by victimizing millions of children, including legal immigrants. It would even violate the reasonable notion that Government should help needy Americans willing to work.

What the House Republicans have in mind is not reform but a grotesque assault on the poor for the sake of honoring their ideological war on Government. Its punitive measures go way beyond what conservative Democrats and Republicans, let alone President Clinton, have recently proposed.[24]

The *Wall Street Journal* headlined:

HUNGER AMONG ELDERLY SURGES; MEAL PROGRAMS JUST CAN'T KEEP UP
WAITING LISTS ARE GROWING
More than two decades after the creation of a federal law aimed at providing free meals to anyone over 60, several million older Americans are growing hungry— and their numbers are growing steadily.

In Detroit:

Carlos Castillo, 71, applied for the meals in February, writing on his application: "Please help me. I just got out of the hospital. Please. I need the meals now and every day. I will appreciate it. " He died in September before his turn came on the waiting list. Over his handwriting, the application now has two words: "Cancel. Deceased."

In Florida:

Central Florida's Osceola County, where nearly a quarter of the population is 60 or older, offers a glimpse of what the rest of the country faces. In the past year, the Osceola County aging department has had to jump hurdle after hurdle just to keep from axing any of the 400 people, averaging 87 years of age, who rely on it for cooked and delivered meals.

But all meals failed to reach the many on waiting lists.

So the agency found a dirt-cheap caterer to take over meal-preparation: the Osceola County Jail. Using prisoners to fill food boxes for the elderly, and with the warden not charging for labor, the county cut expenses by more than half, to 58 cents a meal...

Beverly Houghland, the agency council's executive director, says: "The hardest thing you'll ever have to do is tell someone that you can't give them meals."

Yet it happens all over the country.[25]

In the immediate wake of right-wing victory in the 1994 election:

NEW JERSEY PLANS TO CUT PAYMENTS FOR MEDICAID 20%...REIMBURSEMENTS TO HOSPITALS TO BE CUT BY $135 MILLION A YEAR STARTING IN MARCH.[26]

Nationally, the attack on medicaid, the only source of medical assistance for most poor people, and especially important for ghettoized African Americans—is a special target in the anti-people campaign.

Headline in *People's Weekly World*:

CHICAGO AUTHORITIES TEAR DOWN LOW INCOME HOUSING
    Police here swooped down on a tent city Oct. 7 and arrested three of a group of several hundred community residents who have been protesting city plans for the destruction of nine units of low-cost housing in the Westtown area on Chicago's Northwest side.

The housing was finally built after a long community struggle, but was targeted for destruction by Mayor Richard M. Daley:

The area, which is mostly Mexican immigrant and has smaller concentrations of Puerto Ricans, African Americans and working class whites, has been heavily targeted by real estate speculators for gentrification. A block and a half away is the home of former House Ways and Means Committee Chairman, Dan Rostenkowski.[27]

6. Employment and Unemployment, Part I

How can one account for the wide, and growing, gap in incomes between African Americans and whites, and between Latinos and whites? Academic researchers commonly "factor out" these differences: so much due to inferior education; so much to lower skills; so much to broken families; so much to location, etc. This tends to leave a tiny balance attributed to racism. Worse, these categories reflect the researchers' own racial prejudices, or at least their minimal understanding of U.S. racism and its penetration into all aspects of life.

Inferior education is due to racism; lower skills to less access to training and to employers' prejudiced judgments of comparative skills. Broken families, too, are often the result of the racist job and housing discrimination forced upon minorities. Location is a result of planned housing segregation in areas away from economic opportunities.

Therefore, one must conclude that the economic gap against African Americans and other minorities is entirely due to racism. The main components of the economic differential are:

* The possibility of getting any kind of job.
* The kinds of jobs available to whites, and to Blacks or Latinos.
* The gap in pay for the same or equivalent kind of work.
* Differences in ownership of capital (see Chapter 9).
* Differences in education and training resources (see Chapter 12).
* Comparative lack of physical freedom due to racist court and police functioning, imprisonment or the threat thereof (see Chapter 14).

Analysis based on the latest available data will also reflect the changes in the situation over the past 30 years—since the Civil Rights laws were supposed to significantly remove the differences.

Sylvia Nasar, combining the findings of several researchers, has reported a serious deterioration in the employment prospects of American men of prime working age. It applies to men of different educational and income levels, and of different races. But not equally.[1]

The hit taken by African American men is a dramatic indictment of worsening racism. In the 1970s, 78% of white men worked regularly full time. By 1994, 63% of white men held full-time jobs. But regularly full-time employed Black men fell from 73% in the '70s to 47% in 1994![2]

The prison population, not included, has risen faster than any other sector.

Ms. Nasar points out that by 1993 there were 4.6 million men in prison, on parole or on probation. Among the 9 million Black men, 2 million were imprisoned, on parole or on probation, or more than 20% of the adult Black male population. With the million actually imprisoned added to the population base, besides the substantial number on parole or probation who avoid Census counters, the proportion with full-time jobs falls to 40% or less.[3]

To some extent the decline in full time employment is accounted for by an increased proportion of retirees and full-time students; a factor affecting relatively more whites than Blacks, who do not live as long, and among whom fewer have rights to retire at earlier than 65 years of age.

Following the widening gap, the differentials in employment as of 1992 are shown in Chart 6A. The percentage of Black men with jobs was 12 percentage points below that of white men, and 11 percentage points below that of Hispanic men. In the case of women, the differentials are more moderate. The percentage of Black women with jobs was more than 4 points less than that of white women, and nearly as much above Hispanic women.

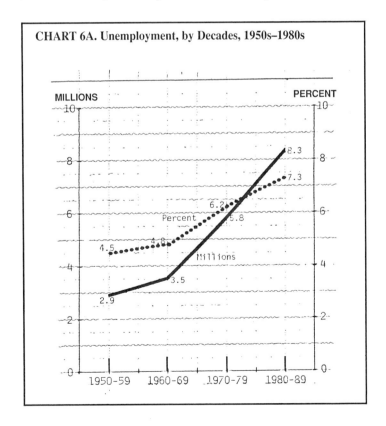

CHART 6A. Unemployment, by Decades, 1950s–1980s

The combination of relatively more full-time jobs and the higher pay has gulled all too many white male workers into thinking they are a superior sector of the work force. Racist ideologists use these differentials to help them convince white male workers that their "superiority" is threatened by affirmative action. In fact, these differentials represent the super-exploitation of African American and Latino men (and of all women)—super-exploitation that strengthens the employers and inexorably drags down the working standards for white male workers, too.

There is an additional factor regarding discrimination against African Americans: a major and increasing bias against Black men that is having terrible social and economic consequences.

Over the years there has been considerable advance in the relative employment and wage situation of women, and in this development there has been continuous, although far from adequate, affirmative action. But with respect to Black and Hispanic men, the opposite has been and is the case: the full weight of the capitalists' anti-labor offensive is directed against them.

Although there has been minimal improvement in some kinds of jobs available to minority peoples, it has not been in crucial areas, and there has been little change in the discriminatory pay for the same or equivalent work. The overall wage and salary differential has not been reduced.

Growth of Multi-Racial Working Class

Racially and nationally oppressed peoples accounted for one-sixth of the total work force in the early 1970s, and one-fourth by 1993. The increase in the minority work force between 1972 and 1993 was 105%, with Black employment going up 55%, Hispanic 151%, Asian and Native American 300%.

The 119 million reported as employed in 1993 includes about 10 million self-employed. The distribution of non-self employed, the wage and salary workers aged 16-64, is more relevant, as it indicates sources of surplus value and profits from exploitation. Table 6:1 summarizes the data for 1993:

TABLE 6:1. EMPLOYED WAGE AND SALARY WORKERS, 1993.

	Number *(thousands)*	Percent of Total
Total	108,648	100.00%
White	84,757	78.01
Black	11,673	10.74
Hispanic	8,717	8.02
Asians, Native Americans	3,511	3.23

(SOURCE: *Employment & Earnings*, Jan., 1994, Table 41, p.230)

Official statistics have always underreported the extent to which Black and Hispanic workers are barred from jobs, and their high unemployment rate. In January 1994 the BLS changed its method of estimating employment so as to partly redress that bias: the number of Blacks and Latinos counted as jobless was significantly raised. Overall unemployment, officially, rose by 10%, with the increase disproportionately concentrated among Black and Latino workers. Also, by allowing in part for the undercounting of the population in the 1990 Census, the BLS reported a higher percentage and number of employed workers. This increase was concentrated on Latinos, who thereby moved closer to white workers in the percentage with jobs. But it showed a further deterioration in the ratio of Black workers with jobs. If the same proportion of African Americans were employed, relative to their population, as whites, they would have 17% more jobs.

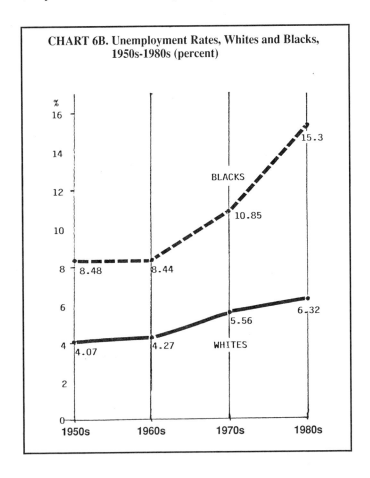

CHART 6B. Unemployment Rates, Whites and Blacks, 1950s-1980s (percent)

The job gains of Latino workers are welcome, but call for full evaluation. It is evident that employers often prefer male Latino workers to male Black workers because Latinos, many of them recent immigrants and some without documents, can be forced to work for lower wages and offer less organized resistance. The political and economic advantage to capitalists of splitting the Black and Latino workers is obvious. Workers' unity is possible, and crucial, as shown by Black-Hispanic cooperation in important recent struggles.

Access to a Job

The potential wage and salary work force consists of those between ages 16 and 64 who are not self-employed. For example, Blacks had 12.0% of the population in the working age range in 1992, but 12.5% of those not self-employed, because self-employment among Blacks is less, proportional to population, than that of other racial groups. This 12.5%, then, represents the potential share of Black workers in total employment, but they held only 10.7% of the actual wage and salary jobs. It would require a roughly 17% increase in Black employment to establish job parity. On the other hand, white wage and salary employment exceeded the white share in the potential wage earning population by 4%. Similarly, to bring Hispanic employment up to parity would require an increase of nearly 13%, and Asian and Native American employment by over 9% (see Table 6:2). However, to avoid balancing those increases with a decrease in white employment, it would be necessary to increase total employment by 4%. Then, with white employment unchanged, Black employment would increase 21.7%, Hispanic employment by 17.4% and that of other minorities by 14.0%. In numbers, it would mean 2.5 million additional jobs for Blacks, 1.5 million for Hispanics, and 0.5 million for others (see Appendix Table 6A).

However, just leaving white employment unchanged would be unsatisfactory, in view of the increasing number of white workers downsized out of jobs. Therefore, a program to overcome racism in employment would have to add many more jobs than the 4.4 million. This is discussed in the Program, Chapter 18.

The required increase in Black employment shown is a minimum for these reasons:

1. Fewer Black workers than white, relatively, can afford not to work—as full-time students, as full-time homemakers, or as well-pensioned early retirees from police forces, the military, etc.

2. The data concern the *non-institutional* population. However, the million Blacks in prison or jail also need jobs. Indeed, their joblessness contributed significantly to their imprisonment.

TABLE 6:2. DISTRIBUTION OF WAGE AND SALARY WORKERS FOR
EACH CATEGORY OF EMPLOYER, Percent of Total 1992

Category	White	Black	Hispanic	Other	TOTAL
Government	75.9%	15.1%	5.7%	3.3%	100.0%
Large Private	77.0	12.5	7.0	3.5	100.0
Small Private	80.3	7.4	9.5	2.8	100.0
TOTAL Actual	78.3	10.7	7.9	3.2	100.0
Potential Wage and Salary Workers	75.2	12.5	8.9	3.4	100.0
Percent Potential Over or Under Actual Potential Share	-4.0%	+16.8%	+12.7%	+9.4%	100.0%

SOURCES: See Appendix Table 6A

TABLE 6:3. DISTRIBUTION OF WAGE AND SALARY WORKERS IN EACH
CATEGORY OF EMPLOYER, Percent of Total 1992

Category	White	Black	Hispanic	Other	All Workers
Government	16	24	12	17	17
Large Private	39	46	35	44	39
Small Private	45	30	53	39	44
TOTAL	100	100	100	100	100

SOURCES: See Appendix Table 6A

Where Minorities Are Employed

Employers can be divided into three categories: government, large private, and small private: 17% of all workers are employed by federal, state or local governments, 39% are employed by large private employers, generally those with over 100 employees, and 44% are employed by small private employers (Tables 6:2 and 6:3).

Of employed Blacks, 24% work for government, twice the proportion of Hispanics, and far higher than whites or other minorities (Table 6:3). Latinos, with 5.7% of government jobs, Table 6:2, are obviously underrepresented.

The relatively better situation of Blacks in government employment somewhat offsets their worsening situation in private employment. The main areas of Black government employment are in the public school system, public transportation, the postal service, and in clerical, technical, and laborer jobs in the administrative apparatus.

Government, in effect, has provided employment to many Black workers rejected by the private sector. Several factors may enter into this:

1. In government, overt racism of profit-seeking employers is not so decisive; the racism of many government supervisors is moderated by the political character of their positions.

2. Barred from many types of private employment, Black workers turn to government jobs that whites may deem inferior in status, pay, and potential for promotion.

3. Practical affirmative action programs are relatively more frequent in government than in private companies.

4. The increasing number of elected African American officials make an obvious contribution to employment of more Blacks, although they are still seriously underrepresented in elected positions at all levels.

It's obvious that the privatization campaigns aggressively pushed by right-wing forces—indeed by the entire capitalist class in this country and much of the rest of the world—has a sharp racist edge. When schools, post offices, many other government enterprises and services are privatized, the new owners will be free to exercise their racist prejudices, and many Black workers' jobs will be lost.

Hispanic workers, on the other hand, are seriously underrepresented in Government. A large proportion of Latino people have immigrated in the last ten years, and many of them are not yet proficient in the English language. Further, the Hispanic community does not have as organized a struggle for government jobs as does the African American community.

Blacks had, in 1992, 12.5% of the jobs in large private enterprises, the same as their percentage of the potential working class. Hitherto, pressure from the EEOC has contributed to hiring of Black workers by large corporations. Further, companies selling consumer goods and services like to advertise their increased employment of minorities, considering the now substantial consumer base provided by non-white peoples. Many Blacks are employed at minimum or near minimum wages in the fast-food industry, poultry processing, and some others by large employers.

More than half of all Hispanic workers are employed by small private bosses; less than one-third of Black workers (Table 6:3).

Discrimination in Kinds of Employment in Government and Large Private Enterprises

However, in the federal, state, and local governments, the relatively high representation of African Americans is due more to their availability for jobs that scarcely pay a living wage than to some sort of triumph for affirmative action.

In 1992, of the nearly 10,000 highest ranking executive jobs in the federal sector, African Americans and Hispanics, between them, held only 500.

Blacks held about 15% of the "general schedule" white collar jobs; only 5% of those in the top grades with salaries of $42,601 to $76,982; but 23% of the lowest grade jobs paying $10,581 to $18,947. They also held 20% of the low-ranking wage-paying jobs.[4]

The discriminatory pattern of employment of Blacks and Hispanics in state and local government is shown in Table 6:4.

TABLE 6:4. BLACK AND HISPANIC SHARE OF JOBS, STATE AND LOCAL
           GOVERNMENTS, 1991, BY MAJOR OCCUPATION GROUPS

Occupation Group	Percentage Share	
	Blacks	Hispanics
Officials, Administrators	9.2%	3.3%
Professionals	13.4	4.3
Technicians	14.8	6.0
Protective service	16.2	6.1
Paraprofessionals	31.3	5.7
Administrative support	19.5	7.7
Skilled crafts	14.4	6.5
Service/maintenance	31.4	9.1

SOURCE: *Stat. Abst.* of the U.S., 1993, T. 501, p.318

Discrimination shows up in local government job placement; it is over-whelmingly white police officers who brutalize inner cities, perpetrate many murders, cause crippling injuries, make baseless arrests, violate all legal norms; while Blacks, to a relatively greater extent, may be employed as guards, parking ticket dispensers, etc. This pattern, as developed in Chapter 14, has particularly devastating effects on the African American community.

Nor is that all. Here is an example of racism that continued unchecked in New York City even while an African American was mayor:

The job of school custodian is a service job, listed under "cleaning and building service occupations." A college education is not requisite. In 1993 nationally, 22.6% of such jobs were held by African Americans; 16.4% by Latinos. But in New York City the school administration and the union bar-gained for school custodians separately from service workers generally, get-ting better wages and conditions for this small group. However, using tests irrelevant to the job, the school administration, without union veto, has kept most Black and Hispanic workers out of these positions.

Of 865 school custodians in the New York City school system in 1993, "...only 4.2 percent were Black, 3.4 percent Hispanic and 0.5 percent Asian, while Blacks make up 22.4 percent of the work force, Hispanic people, 18.8 percent, and Asians, 7 percent."

Typical of the snail's pace at which government agencies operate, it took the U.S. Justice Department's Civil Rights Division two years to investigate this well-known situation before calling for correction.

Scores of new custodians are hired or promoted every year. A simple ruling, supported by the union, to the effect that until minority employment is brought up to par, Blacks and Hispanics are to have absolute priority in hiring for these jobs—regardless of "loaded" tests—could soon have put an end to this specific racist discrimination.

Instead, the union actively opposed an affirmative action solution, claiming that any preference to Blacks would discriminate against white workers who obtained all the higher marks in the tests. Indeed, the persistence with which whites get all the top marks raises questions about manipulation. The argument of "reverse discrimination" is discussed in Chapter 8; and the relation of unions to affirmative action in Chapter 15.

A policy creating unity between Black, Brown and white workers would have strengthened the union to prevent the blow which hit all custodians shortly after the partial resolution of the particular issue.

Finally, under Justice Department pressure, a new contract was actually worked out between the school chancellor and the union. It provide for at least a certain degree of affirmative action. But enter the new New York City mayor, Rudy Giuliani. He immediately moved to prevent the agreement from being carried out by privatizing the custodian jobs, thereby smashing the union and turning the operation over to racist cronies. The union attorney warned, "...if we do away with all the [public] jobs, there will be no jobs for minorities."[5]

The fact remains that despite the very real racism that exists in the public sector, its practice has had to be restrained in comparison with that in the private sector. Consequently, the drive for privatization of government operation, combined with the budget "economies" at the federal, state and city levels, is an ominous threat to African American and Hispanic workers.

EEOC Reports

Yearly the Equal Employment Opportunity Commission (EEOC) tabulates the employment patterns of the large companies* that report to it. These corporations are supposedly subject to affirmative action programs. Their reports are an important source of information about the kinds of employment African American and Latino workers have access to in large corporations. Although these accounts are not definitive—not all companies send in reports and not all requested data are given—this EEOC analysis is more accurate,

---

* With 100 or more workers; if holding government contracts, 50 or more.

more specific in its classifications, than the Census Bureau's, which depends on workers' subjective descriptions of their occupations.

The Black share of total employment in the large firms that report to the EEOC is approximately in line with their share in the working class population base—12.5% in 1992. However, as the EEOC warned in the foreword of its 1975 report:

> Each year we have found inequities in the employment of minorities and women...these groups are underrepresented in the better-paying job categories and industries, and are instead concentrated in the less desirable positions. Minorities and women have improved their employment status over the years, but progress has been slow.[6]

And progress since 1975 has been even slower, if not infinitesimal, with respect to the minorities. There are several reasons to think that the shares reported to the EEOC in 1992 exaggerate the actual share: 12.5% for Blacks; 7.0% for Hispanics; and 3.5% for other minorities.

> ...The EEO-1 reporting program, like the income tax, is a self-assessment system. The employer is "on his honor" to make his best judgment in identifying his employees and in classifying them within the job categories.[7]

Furthermore, the EEOC has trivial resources—compared with the IRS— to check on accuracy. Obviously reporting companies are interested in trying to make each report on employment of minorities and women look as good as they can get away with.

Also, for 1967 more than one-fourth of employers of over 100 workers, hiring a total of up to one-seventh of all private workers, did not submit a report.[8] It is reasonable to assume that their employment of minorities and women was below that of the reporting companies.

Since 1967 the reporting trend has been consistently downward, so that in every major industrial sector, coverage was less in 1992. Furthermore, race and sex distribution were not tabulated in 1992 for 15% of the workers in submitted reports.

The EEOC report classifies workers into nine categories, five white collar and four blue collar. We have computed indexes of job pattern discrimination (see Appendix Table 6B and explanation) based on the relative number of workers in the two highest and the two lowest-ranking occupation groups. Among white males, approximately three times as many are employed in the two highest ranking job categories—officials and managers, and professionals—as in the two lowest; while among Black males, the opposite prevails, with more than three times as many employed in the two lowest, laborers and service workers, as in the two highest. Together these four groups account for between 40% and 50% of all workers covered by the EEOC reports. It is obvious from the data that there was an inordinate degree of discrimination in 1967 in all cases, but especially for Black males (28.72). That degree was halved by 1975, but the index was still an excessive 12.8.

An index of 1 signifies no discrimination. In 1992, the index for Black males was 7.70, for Hispanic males 8.68; for Black women 4.24, for Hispanic women 5.35. The indexes of discrimination against Latino workers have been increasing since 1980, largely because of their increasing employment in very low wage service jobs. The indexes declined sharply between 1967 and 1975, the period of initial impact of major civil rights legislation; but little improvement has been registered since. (Details are provided in Appendix Table 6B.)

Racist discrimination against Latino men and against Black and Latino women was moderated during the years when many large companies, fearing mass fightback or legal duress from workers and government, made token concessions toward compliance with official goals of equality.

By 1975 the pressure to conform to the spirit of civil rights laws had relaxed, and after 1980 virtually ended. It was in essence reversed by the political tenets of the Administrations in power, by the right-wing, anti-labor racist majority on the Supreme Court, and in the federal court system generally.

1992 indexes for people of Asian origin are close to 1, suggesting very little discrimination in the larger companies covered by EEOC. The severe discrimination against recent immigrants from Vietnam, Cambodia, China, and other Asian countries is not reflected, because for the most part they are employed in smaller establishments not covered by EEOC. There was an index of 4.22 against Native American men and 2.72 against Native American women. However, these cover very few reservation Indians, whose economic conditions are much worse.

A separate index was calculated showing the degree of discrimination against minority workers in craft jobs. Here an index of 100 indicates equality. For both African American and Latino males the indexes were close to 50, indicating that they had about half the appropriate number of craft jobs in the larger establishments covered by EEOC reports. (The overall pattern of employment by occupational group, for whites and minority peoples is analyzed in Chapter 7.)

The most extreme discrimination against African Americans is practiced by smaller employers, who account for 44% of all wage and salary jobs. Here Black employment was only 7.4% of the total in 1992. And it is among these employers that sociologists report the most overt bias against African Americans—slander, belittling of ability and, with respect to Black men, fear. Moreover, small employers are apt to give jobs to their relatives, social con-

tacts and people of their own ethnic group in preference to "outsiders."
African American employers are relatively few, and the total number of workers they employ is small. [Small employers do not report racial distribution of
workers. This is determined by subtracting the reported breakdown by government and large employers from official reports of total Black, Hispanic,
etc. employment. Obviously the margin of error is substantial, yet the overall
picture of low Black employment by small employers is valid.]

Hispanic and African Americans

Job distribution of Hispanic workers differs radically from that of Black
workers. Only 12% of Hispanic workers have government jobs—compared
with 24% of African Americans—and much smaller percentage of Hispanics
than Blacks are employed by large companies. However, employment of Hispanics by small employers is relatively large—more than half of all Hispanic
workers, and the absolute number in small firms exceeds that of Black workers by a wide margin.

In my estimation, a factor contributing to the relatively low share of Hispanic jobs in government and large corporations goes back to the timing of the
civil rights struggles of the 1950s and 1960s. Then, it was the African Americans, overwhelmingly, who led and participated in the militant actions. The
number of Latinos was then still less than half that of Blacks, and they did not
benefit as much from the hard-won affirmative action measures of that time.
Thus, by the early 1970s Latinos were already underrepresented in government and large enterprises relative to Blacks as well as to whites.

Thereafter, however, Latino employment in government and large companies rose more rapidly than African American. For example, the Hispanic
share of federal employment went up from 3.1% of the total in 1972-1974 to
5.4% in 1980-1982; in state and local, from 3.3% to 6.2%—increases consistent with the uptrend in overall Hispanic employment, from 4.5% to 7.6%. But
their employment rate in government and large companies never caught up to
or surpassed the rapid rise in Latino population, mainly due to immigration.

To a considerable extent the relatively large employment of Latinos by
small employers results from the victimization of immigrants, who have no
legal or organizational rights, no access to assistance. They are preferred for
minimum and sub-minimum wage service jobs—busboys and dishwashers in
restaurants; lawn and garden workers in the suburbs; operators in the small
sweatshops. Many find jobs as migratory farm workers from Florida to Maine
and from the Mexican border to Canada. These jobs provide no pensions, no
health care, no benefits at all.

The EEOC reports provide data to analyze the employment of minority workers over an extended period of time, with broader coverage than is available from other sources. But since only employment by larger firms is covered, neither government agencies nor small firms are included (see Appendix, Table 6C).

Over the 17 years 1975-1992, the share of minorities' jobs rose from 16.2% to 23.0%, a relative rise of 42.0%, corresponding approximately to the percentage rise in the minority population over that period. The rate of increase varied greatly from group to group: it was most rapid among Asians and slowest among Blacks. But in each case the rate of increase tallied with that of the group's total population. Generally, women's employment rose more rapidly than men's, as was also true for whites. But one comparison is striking: the share of Black men declined from 6.2% in 1975 to 5.9% in 1992.

Women in the Labor Market

While it is true that women's abilities are being recognized more and more in the U.S. economy, as is their status vs. men, it seems unlikely that numerical equality between the sexes will be realized in the foreseeable future, although wives who, traditionally "kept house" while their husbands worked and supported the family have become a distinct minority. Despite improved household appliances, child care facilities for those who can afford it, and women's campaigns for equal rights, there are a number of negative factors: maternity leave requirements; lack of affordable child care facilities; the desire of many better-off men to be the sole support of their families; continuing prejudices against hiring women in certain industries and occupations. Although in many instances, employers substitute women for men—at lower wages.

Thus while the proportion of women working went up from 33% to 50%, the proportion of men working fell from 82% to 71%. The increase of women overbalanced the decrease of men, so that overall there was a modest rise in the proportion of all adults working.

But that was not true of the African American population. Black women were not able to break into the labor force as readily as white women, so the rise in the percentage of Black women working was moderate. As a result, while the proportion of Black working women exceeded the proportion of white working women by a wide margin in the 1950s and 1960s, by the 1990s the proportion of white women with jobs was higher.

Thus, there remains considerable discrimination against Black women. However, because of the extreme discrimination against Black men, by 1992 the absolute number of Black women employed exceeded that of Black men. Considering the low wages received by so many African Americans, this

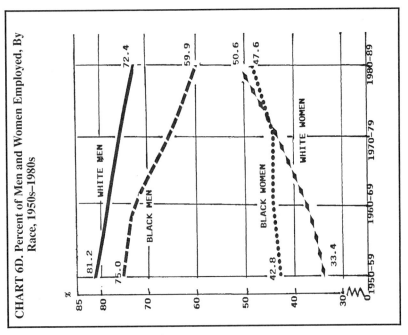

CHART 6D. Percent of Men and Women Employed, By Race, 1950s–1980s

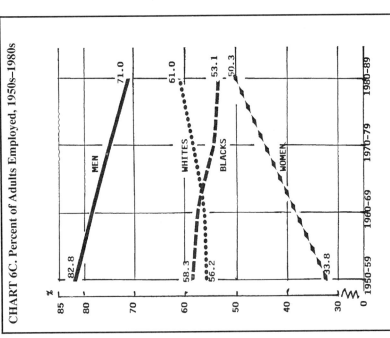

CHART 6C. Percent of Adults Employed, 1950s–1980s

development has seriously weakened "normal" family structures among the Black population. There was corresponding demoralization among whites, but the extent of single parent families was much higher among African Americans, making them a target of racist propaganda.

Regional Differences

Discrimination rates vary considerably in different areas—even in different parts of the same state. In California, the state with the largest Latino population—including an unusual percentage of immigrants—the 1992 discrimination index against Hispanic males was 16.28 and against Hispanic females, 9.41 compared with 6.43 and 2.59 against Black men and women, respectively. The African American population was much smaller.

On the other hand, extreme bias indexes prevailed against African Americans in many southern states, such as Mississippi where the rate against Black men was 13.31 and against Black women, 8.70 compared with Hispanic men, 2.31, and Hispanic women, 5.95. There the Hispanic population is quite small.

An important study of employer racism in Chicago was made in 1988-89 by Joleen Kirschenman and Kathryn M. Neckerman. (Their study, originally presented at a conference in 1989, is included in a volume containing all the essays prepared for that conference, which was funded by the Rockefeller and Ford Foundations, among other prestigious sponsors. Views expressed were heavily influenced by the teachings of William Julius Wilson, who contributed much to the study of what he and bourgeois society call the "urban underclass.")

They state:

> Despite blacks' disproportionate representation in the urban underclass, however defined, analyses of inner-city joblessness seldom consider racism or discrimination as a significant cause. In "The Truly Disadvantaged," for example, William Julius Wilson explains increased rates of inner-city unemployment as a consequence of other social or economic developments.

Wilson's thesis: Black unemployment and poverty are due to a combination of objective developments from which they just happen to be on the receiving end. Kirschenman and Neckerman disagree. They consider that race is one of a complex of motives influencing employers' hiring practices. They interviewed 185 Chicago and Cook County employers, asking a standard set of questions and presenting situations designed to bring out the bosses' attitudes. The employers didn't beat around the bush; they felt no shame at their racism.

Thus we were overwhelmed by the degree to which Chicago employers felt comfortable talking with us—in a situation where the temptation would be to conceal
rather than reveal—in a negative manner about Blacks.

While generally bad-mouthing the working class as a whole, the bosses
were blunt in their criminalization of Black workers:

common among the traits listed were that workers were unskilled, uneducated,
illiterate, dishonest, lacking initiative, unmotivated, involved with drugs and
gangs, did not understand work, had no personal charm, were unstable, lacked
work ethic, and had no family life or role models.

The authors noted that employers used gross discrimination against Blacks
in employment practices:

Far more widespread were the use of recruiting and screening techniques to help
select "good" workers. For instance, employers relied more heavily on referrals
from employees, which tend to reproduce the traits and characteristics of the current work force...a dramatic increase in the use of referral bonuses in the past few
years, or employers targeted newspaper ads to particular neighborhoods or ethnic
groups.[9]

Overall, the prejudices against Hispanics were less extreme than against
Blacks, with the scourge of racism sharpest against Black men.

...East European whites were repeatedly praised for really knowing how to work
and caring about their work... In the skilled occupations, East European men were
sought. One company advertised for its skilled workers in Polish- and German-lan-
guage newspapers, but hired all its unskilled workers, 97 percent of whom were
Hispanic, through an employee network.
    When asked directly whether they thought there were any differences in the
work ethics of whites, blacks, and Hispanics, 37.7 percent of the employers ranked
blacks last, 1.4 percent ranked Hispanics last, and no one ranked whites there.
Another 7.6 percent placed blacks and Hispanics together on the lowest level; 51.4
percent either saw no difference or refused to categorize in a straightforward
way...[10]

There were other ways in which employers indicated deeper racism
against Blacks than against Latinos. For example, they reacted negatively to
areas and projects where Blacks lived, but not to the sections where Mexicans
and Puerto Ricans lived.[11] Be that as it may, the preference for Hispanic workers, however, was clearly focussed on the most unskilled, low-paid jobs.

The researchers concluded:

Chicago's employers did not hesitate to generalize about race or ethnic differences in the quality of the labor force. Most associated images with inner city workers, and particularly with black men...

...And black job applicants, unlike their white counterparts, must indicate to employers that the stereotypes do not apply to them. Inner-city and lower-class workers were seen as undesirable, and black applicants had to try to signal to employers that they did not fall into these categories, either by demonstrating their

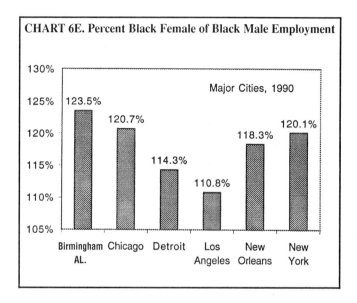

CHART 6E. Percent Black Female of Black Male Employment

Major Cities, 1990

Birmingham AL. 123.5%, Chicago 120.7%, Detroit 114.3%, Los Angeles 110.8%, New Orleans 118.3%, New York 120.1%

skills or adopting a middle-class style of dress...or perhaps (as we were told some did) by lying about their address or work history.[12]

Employment of more Black women than Black men is especially marked in large cities. Examples are shown in Table 6:5 and Chart 6E.

TABLE 6:5. PERCENT BLACK FEMALE OF BLACK MALE EMPLOYMENT

Large Cities, 1990		Large Cities, 1990	
Birmingham, AL	123.5%	Los Angeles, CA	110.8
Chicago, IL	120.7	New Orleans, LA	118.3
Detroit, MI	114.3	New York, NY	120.1

(Data Supplied by the Census Bureau from Tape File 3C. These figures include self-employment. If limited to wage and salary employment, the differentials would be wider.)

Nor does a move to the suburbs necessarily change this situation. Westchester County, a major suburb of New York City, has a large population of African Americans. The excess of employed Black women over Black men with jobs was a whopping 28.8%.

A further example of the special prejudice against Black workers: in health service occupations in 1993, Black workers were far more prominent than Latino workers—with one exception. Among dental assistants, 3.4% were Black; 10.4% were Hispanic.[13]

However, we emphasize that where the employment situation of Latino workers seems superior to that of Blacks, it is not to be interpreted as any relaxation of overall discrimination against Latino peoples. It simply reflects cases where Blacks are so much worse off, or their position has deteriorated. In other cases, seeming advantages of Hispanic workers may be illusory, and not only in employment in minimum or sub-minimum sweatshop jobs; but even in skilled craft jobs where wages are far below the standard rates paid to white workers. Also, situations differ among the national groups of Latino workers: the plight of Puerto Ricans is worse than that of Mexican Americans, and that of recent immigrants from Mexico and Central America is worse than for long-time residents of Mexican origin. At the same time, the relatively small Cuban population has been favored because of its usefulness to U.S. imperialism in its anti-Cuba campaigns.

"Especially Black Men"

Racist prejudices against hiring Black men have been intensifying in recent decades. There are some geographical areas and spheres of employment where discrimination against Latinos, Native Americans and Asian immigrants is as severe—or even sharper—than that against African Americans, but overall the racism against Blacks, and especially Black men, is of special importance socially and politically, as well as economically.

Chart 6A and Appendix Table 6D show the widening gap between the percentage of employed white and Black males. The number of Black men with jobs is 12 percentage points below that of white men, and 11 percentage points below that of Hispanic men—in relation to the adult male population of each group. In the case of women, the differentials are more moderate: Black women have 4 percentage points fewer jobs than white women, and almost that above Hispanic women.

Appendix Table 6D further sharpens the disparity between whites and minorities. While white women outnumber white men by 6.8%—normal considering the longer life span of women—there are 23% more Black women than Black men! The number of Hispanic women is slightly less than that of Hispanic men, readily explicable considering the fact that many male Latino men immigrate alone, hoping to send for their families later. As these data concern the non-institutional population, the 600,000 Black men held in jails and prisons are omitted. If they were added, there would still be 16% more Black women than Black men, and the percentage of Black men employed would be further reduced to 57.5%. Since many Black men—in addition to those in prison—are on parole, probation, or live in areas of severe police harassment, it is understandable that many of them avoid encounters with Census takers.

It is noteworthy that as recently as 1992, 8.5% more Black than Hispanic men had jobs, whereas by 1994, 6% more Hispanic men than Black men had jobs. This reflects, in part, the rapid increase in Hispanic immigration; and in part, the preference of employers for Hispanic men in a number of very low wage service jobs. Still, this, combined with the significantly lower employment of Black men than Black women, serves to emphasize the special, extreme, growing discrimination against Black men.

White women with jobs exceed Black women with jobs by approximately 4 percentage points, because of a higher percentage of unemployment among African American women. The proportions of white and Black women in the labor force are about equal.

The proportion of working women of all races has been growing (Charts 6C, 6D). And for at least the past third of a century—probably much longer— the relative share of African American working women has been significantly higher than among whites.

In addition, a qualitative change became apparent in 1988, the first year in which employed Black women numerically exceeded employed Black men.

Among Blacks, female employment increased from 77% of male employment in 1970 to 94% in 1980 and 102% in 1990. Among whites, the corresponding increase was from 59% in 1970 to 81% in 1990.[14]

Of course the scarcity of jobs fuels competition between African Americans and Hispanics—to the detriment of both. But usually there is no choice: employers or labor contractors deliberately bring in immigrants to take substandard jobs, under conditions that resident workers, Black or white, would refuse to accept. As a result the social problems of the cities are deepened, adding to the sufferings of both men and women. Bear in mind that the average wage or salary of women—Black, white and Hispanic—is considerably lower than that of males.

All too often jobless Black men, whether counted as unemployed or not, can't live with their families (whether or not they are formally married) because women cannot collect the federal aid for dependent children and/or the food stamps needed to eke out meager wages if a man is living with them. Although this government policy applies to all the needy, it afflicts a disproportionate number of African American families. It is one more facet of the overall racist pattern for breaking up Black families, destroying the social fabric and elementary security of life in the segregated Black communities.

Sociologists who attribute deteriorating social conditions to cultural factors—drugs, crime, morality, etc.—ignore the root cause: the combination of segregation/economic discrimination, and the special burden of racist hiring practiced against Black men. It must be emphasized that this discrimination does not imply preference for Black women workers; it does emphasize the ultra-discrimination against Black men.

The largest concentration of Black women workers is not, as once was the case, as private household domestics, laundry workers, etc., but as white collar employees, principally in clerical and related jobs.

As is true in many other spheres, it is likely that African American women exceed African American men in government employment by a wide margin In the private companies reporting to the EEOC, employed Black women exceed Black men by 13.4%, with 54% of them in white collar jobs—more than 25% as office and clerical workers.

The downsizing of jobs for African Americans is part of the extended structural crisis of U.S. capitalism, with its major decline—at first relative and then absolute—in manufacturing employment. The number of production workers in manufacturing reached 15 million during World War II, and that was again achieved or approached several times since, most recently in 1979. Since then the downtrend seems irreversible, with cyclical recoveries falling short of cyclical declines. The slide to slightly over 12 million in 1993 was followed by only snail-like recovery during 1994. By the unprecedented peacetime use of overtime and, especially, through transfer of more and more manufacturing facilities out of the United States, the corporate giants have been able to "downsize" their domestic operations. Thus millions of workers are being permanently thrust out of jobs.

The wholesale closing and scrapping of industrial plants, especially in the Midwest, created the "rust belt" in that traditional heartland of American basic industry. While overall economic activity has revived somewhat in the Midwest, the pattern is different, with manufacturing playing a lesser role than formerly.

Thus midwestern areas that were among the most depressed in the early 1980s were among the better-off areas of the country a decade later, enabling previously laid-off whites to get new jobs. Also, white youths entering the labor force were able to get jobs, but not Black males—not even as "last to be hired." Too many are doomed never to be hired.

The effect has been disastrous for African Americans. After leaving the southern countryside in periods of industrial expansion, they became blue-collar industrial workers. These more desirable jobs led to an improvement in living conditions and to a lesser degree of economic discrimination—especially in the highly organized industries of the North.

The income gap between Black and white has been sharpest in the Midwest, where the ratio of Black to white median family income fell from 73% in 1970 to 51% in 1993, a differential even slightly wider than that in the traditional area of Black oppression, the South (see Chart 3C).

In fact, many African Americans have been forced to migrate to other parts of the country, notably to the South, where industry is booming. Although social and economic discrimination is extreme there, too, Blacks may find some employment, even though in the worst jobs.

Milwaukee, a city one-third Black, is "hypersegregated" according to a University of Chicago study. In 1980, a year marking the beginning of an economic crisis, the white unemployment rate was 5.3%; the Black rate, 17.0%. In 1989, the peak of the Reagan-Bush boomlet, white unemployment in Milwaukee was 3.8%—as close to full employment as capitalism ever gets, except in all-out wartime. But the Black unemployment rate was up to 20.1%. While the Black population was half that of whites, there were three times as many African Americans as whites who were jobless.

Part of the reason was the shift in economic structure. According to a *New York Times* report, Milwaukee was flourishing. During the 1960s and 1970s Blacks got jobs in the expanding manufacturing base, helped by Civil Rights legislation and strong unions, which helped to reduce discrimination. Since 1979, although Milwaukee lost 47,000 manufacturing jobs, it gained 130,000 non-manufacturing jobs. But Black workers, just as able as white to adapt to and be trained for the new types of jobs, were never given that chance.

An ex-Army sergeant, 28-year old Anthony Hoskins, is an example :

He has applied at businesses around the city...K Mart, McDonalds, Wisconsin Bell, Harley Davidson. Usually he never hears from them. And if he does, he is told that he does not have the skills they are looking for.

These companies were hiring, but only white workers. Said Hoskins:

I'm in an endless cycle. How am I going to get qualifications if I never get a chance. You got 16, 17 year old white kids working and here I am, a grown man, an Army veteran, and I can't get a damn job.

Capitalist society regards veteran status as a legitimate basis for priority in hiring, reduction of real estate taxes, and other forms of affirmative action, of the much maligned "quotas." But not for African Americans.

The reporter, Isabel Wilkerson, writes that white manufacturing workers who were laid off can usually get other jobs when new businesses spring up. Such jobs have generally not appeared in Black sections...

> Black men stand idle on street corners blocks from the breweries and factories that used to employ them, while well-dressed white-collar workers sell insurance or computers out of some of those same factories, now converted into office parks.[15]

Most of the jobs that were filled during the Milwaukee upsurge required no more than a high school education. And most of the African American men who could not get jobs, the story indicated, did have a high school diploma. It is clear that the overwhelming reason for the appalling Milwaukee situation was/is crude employer racism.

Further, since most of the unemployed Black men live in the hyper-segregated ghettos of the city, their lack of a job deprives those areas of their purchasing power in the shops; ends their ability to pay rent or to pay the taxes needed to fund schools. Thus the cumulative deterioration of the housing, education, and health conditions of African Americans is directly connected with their racist exclusion from employment.

Part of the problem for the critical unemployment situation is the decline in unionization, and part is the racism that has kept unions from effective affirmative action programs as well as for refusing to modify seniority systems to guarantee against disproportionate layoffs of Black workers.

7. Employment and Unemployment Part II

By the 1970s the United States had lost its unchallenged supremacy in the capitalist world. It was afflicted by a long-lasting, complex structural crisis featuring, successively, the shattering of the basic industrial core of the Midwest; financial crises, most dramatically expressed in the $500 billion S & L debacle; and currently, the major "downsizing" of almost all major U.S. corporations, involving the permanent layoff of millions of workers.

This structural, systemic crisis continued through several of the cyclical crises and recoveries that are "normal" features of the capitalist economic system, each devastating the lives of many workers, farmers and small business people.

By the mid-1990s, however, the structural crisis was essentially resolved as far as U.S. monopoly capital was concerned. Industry was stabilized on a new basis, led by "high-tech" industries. The most serious financial problems were overcome. And the transnational corporations were reaping unprecedented profits from superexploitation of low-paid workers in less developed countries. U.S. capitalism, especially, was strengthened by the destruction of the USSR. Not that world capitalism was free of crises. Far from it. Or that material was not accumulating for new crises of U.S. capitalism. Parasitic and decadent features were becoming very prominent, and crisis conditions were afflicting broadening sections of the working class and oppressed peoples. Given the political balance of forces in the country, the capitalist class has been able to put the entire burden of the structural crisis onto the working class, and that burden grows heavier. A major burden is unemployment.

In many ways unemployment is far worse than revealed by the crude official statistics. So long as the U.S. economy was on a long-term uptrend, there was some opportunity for unemployed workers to get their jobs back after a certain period—longer or shorter—depending, among other factors, on the stage of the business cycle. It is true, however, that even in the best of times millions of lives were disrupted or devastated by unemployment and the resultant woes: going hungry, getting into debt, losing homes, etc. But in general, most unemployed workers would get back their old jobs or another in roughly the same line of work.

Now that is no longer true. Even at best, unemployment lasts longer than in earlier decades. The Economic Report of the President's Council of Economic Advisors, issued in January 1993—Bush's swansong—explained:

...the effect of the 1990-91 recession and subsequent slow growth period on labor markets was more severe than the absolute change in employment or the unemployment rate indicated. The unemployment rate peaked at 7.7 percent...15 months after the end of the recession. Typically, the unemployment rate hits its peak an average of only 3 months after the end of a recession...

In addition, the percentage of unemployed who lost their job permanently rather than being temporarily laid off, reached its highest point on record eroding workers' long-term job security and limiting prospects for the quick rebound in employment that usually occurs during a recovery.[1]

This crisis of the system has meant a long-term increase in the level and the rate of unemployment. The number of officially counted unemployed increased from 2.9 million in the 1950s to 8.3 million in the 1980s and the first half of the 1990s. The rate of unemployment increased from 4.5% during the 1950s to 7.3% during the 1980s, before receding to 6.5% for the first half of the 1990s (Table 7:1 and Chart 7A).

Further, official figures of unemployment are seriously understated. Alternative measures supplied by the Labor Department and calculations of leading trade unions set actual unemployment at 1-1/2 times the official figure.

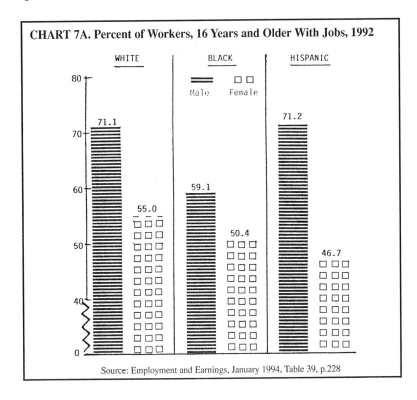

CHART 7A. Percent of Workers, 16 Years and Older With Jobs, 1992

Source: Employment and Earnings, January 1994, Table 39, p.228

Progressive researchers have provided evidence that 2 times the official figure would be more accuratê.

The impact of unemployment hits several times more people than the average number of unemployed. In 1990, when nearly 7 million were counted as unemployed on the average, a total of nearly 20 million—roughly three times as many—were jobless sometime during the year, using the restrictive official definition of unemployment. Thus 15% of the working class suffered unemployment, universally conceded as a dangerously high figure.[2]

These data attest to a high degree of labor turnover, great instability of employment. Comparative statistics show that loss of jobs in the United States averages 4 times that in Europe, even when the average rate of unemployment is lower than in many European countries.

During the three years 1991-1993, about 9 million workers were displaced by plant closing, relocation etc., of which 4.5 million had been on the job more than 3 years. Large corporations frequently announce plans to reduce employment by thousands or tens of thousands in order to reduce costs and raise profits. The workers live in uncertainty, not knowing just where the axe will fall: 60% of displaced workers did not receive advance notice of their impending layoff.

Racism is a factor here as in all facets of life. About 30% of displaced white workers had not found another job by February 1994, but 44% of displaced Black workers and 41% of displaced Latino workers remained jobless.[3]

By 1995, so inexorable was the downsizing of employment that workers generally no longer expected that, if laid off, they would sooner or later land other jobs. Impoverishment is the stark danger facing American workers, particularly serious for Black and Latino workers, whose lower wages rarely permit accumulating reserves "for a rainy day."

TABLE 7:1. NUMBER AND PERCENT OF UNEMPLOYED, BY DECADES 1950S TO 1990S (FIRST HALF)

Decade	Unemployment	
	Number *(millions)*	percent
1950s	2.9	4.5%
1960s	3.5	4.8
1970s	5.8	6.2
1980s	8.3	7.3
1990s (first half)	8.3	6.5

SOURCE: *Economic Report of the President*, Feb., 1995, T. B-33, p.312.

British millionaire economist John Maynard Keynes, whose influence continues to this day, led that school of Establishment theoreticians who considered government intervention to alleviate the evils of capitalism necessary to save it. He recognized:

> The outstanding faults of the economic society in which we live are its failure to provide for full employment and its arbitrary and inequitable distribution of wealth and income.[4]

However his position was contradictory: he also warned that reforms were desirable only to the extent that they did not disturb the capitalists' "incentive" to invest and produce, with due regard for the "nerves and hysteria and even the digestion" of the capitalist class.

Thirty years later, rightist opposition to Keynesianism was formulated by Milton Friedman, the American professor and presidential advisor, who wrote:

> What kind of society isn't structured on greed? The problem of social organization is how to set up an arrangement under which greed will do the least harm.[5]

But in a period of workingclass militancy, President Franklin D. Roosevelt approved measures of a Keynesian variety, broadly speaking, including social security, minimum wages, and the right to organize. After World War II, he promised the American people a better life, and in his 1944 "Economic Bill of Rights," his first declaration was that every person who is able and willing to work has the right to a job at decent wages, regardless of race, color or religion. However, after his death Congress failed to implement FDR's pledge. In deference to public opinion, however, it enacted a vague "Full Employment Act," which had no operative substance.

Under this Act, it was considered desirable to keep unemployment down to 4%, which politicians and Establishment economists defined as "full employment."

But by the 1980s, the boundary was raised to 6%. No longer was this considered full employment, but a desirable minimum level of unemployment. During the 1990s Federal Reserve Board chairman Alan Greenspan became a major propagandist for government policies to keep the unemployment rate above 6%. He specified no upper limit. When the rate of unemployment threatened to fall below 6%, he raised short-term interest rates repeatedly in order to brake economic activity and thus increase unemployment.

His argument was that a lower rate would be inflationary, a wholly spurious argument. The real objective was to hold down and reduce real wages, in order to hike profits of the capitalists. The fallacy of this position was shown during a period in 1995 when the rate of unemployment fell below 6% but the decline in real wages actually accelerated.

One of the reasons some economists say they support higher rates of unemployment is that the proportion of minorities in the labor force is rising, and their unemployment rate is higher than that of white workers. Thus racial discrimination is simultaneously approved *and* used as a weapon to impose high rates of unemployment on the entire working class.

Racism and Unemployment

In Roosevelt's time, 75% of the African American population lived in the Jim Crow South, largely as rightless sharecroppers and farm laborers. The Hispanic population in the United States was still small.

Thus struggles for progressive labor policies were posed in overall terms—with little or no emphasis on the extent of unemployment among Black workers. But by the 1970s—after the decisive activities of African Americans in the two previous decades—this pervasive evil could no longer be ignored, or treated as a minor issue. And with the expansion of the Latino population, subject to many of the ills of African Americans, everyone involved—politicians, academia, trade union officials, capitalists—has had to acknowledge that the super-unemployment of oppressed peoples is a major, cruel feature of U.S. capitalism.

Black workers have always been victims of the "last to be hired; first to be fired" practice. Employers, permeated with racist ideology, are reluctant to hire African Americans, especially males. To survive, Black men are often forced to take jobs at lower wages, doing dangerous or unhealthy work. And employers reap vast superprofits.

The unemployment rate among Black workers until the 1980s has typically been double that of white workers. In recent years, it has more often been 2.5 times that of white workers.

The same racist motivation imposes especially high rates of unemployment on Hispanics, Native Americans, and some sections of Asian Americans.

Moreover, the rate for non-Hispanic white workers is roughly one-half of a percentage point less than that for all whites, including Hispanic whites, for recent years. This effect has been going up with the rise in the Hispanic population.

There was a dramatic widening of the unemployment gap between African American and white workers during the 1980s, when the Reagan-Bush administrations added an overt racist offensive against the African Americans to their all-out offensive against the entire working class. Between 1970 and 1980 the unemployment rate of white workers rose a little less than 1 percentage point—serious enough—but it went up 4.5 percentage points (about 40%) for Black workers, reaching depression proportions with an average of 15.3% (Table 7:2).

TABLE 7:2. UNEMPLOYMENT, 1993

	Number *(thousands)*	Percent of Labor Force
Total	8,734	6.8%
White	6,547	6.0
Non-Hispanic White	5,498	5.5
Black	1,796	12.9
Hispanics	1,104	10.8
Asians & Native Americans	381	8.0

SOURCE: U.S. Department of Labor.

The decline in the proportion of African Americans, especially Black men, in the labor force and some of the reasons were discussed in Chapter 6. Particularly important in aiding the unemployment and imprisonment of Black

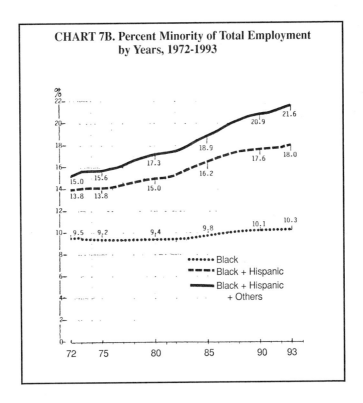

CHART 7B. Percent Minority of Total Employment by Years, 1972-1993

men have been the racist media campaigns and slogans, raised to a high pitch during the Presidential elections of Reagan and Bush in the 1980s. This has continued in the 1990s, in key state and municipal elections, as well as on radio talk shows.

Rudolf Giuliani used crime-scare tactics and personal slanders against incumbent African American Mayor Dinkins to win the New York City mayoral election in 1993. The racist Pete Wilson was reelected Governor of California by a plurality of votes in 1990. He directs an especially outrageous campaign against Hispanic immigrants and has eliminated affirmative action policies in University of California admission procedures. Wilson, by the way, presents an extreme case of the utter lack of principle of capitalist politicians. For many years he built a reputation as a strong supporter of affirmative action. Then, overnight, he changed direction 180 degrees, seeing the appeal to prejudice as the best way of winning election as a Republican in the State of California.

Jobless Men

Obviously, the most complete measure of joblessness is the count of those of working age who do not have jobs. Few men do not want to work. Today a substantial majority of college students either work or seek jobs to pay tuition and living costs; and disabled men are struggling for the facilities necessary to make employment possible and for affirmative action to aid them in getting jobs.

Detailed analysis reveals how enormous is the gap between Black and white joblessness. According to the minimal, official, account of unemployment, in 1992, 7% of white men and 15% of Black men (16 years and over) were unemployed—a gap of eight percentage points (Chart 7C).

But if a full count of joblessness is made—considering as unemployed all jobless males 16 and over—it turns out that 29% of white men and 41% of Black men are jobless.[6] The gap has widened to 12 percentage points.

However there is a distortion here: retirees constitute the major group of men who no longer want or need jobs. Hence it is more realistic to consider unemployment among males aged 16-64. Exclusion of older men from the population base affects whites much more than Blacks, simply because the overall impact of racism so seriously shortens the lives of African Americans, and especially Black men. So it turns out that the proportion of jobless white men aged 16-64 is 19%, against 35% of Black men. By now the gap is 16 percentage points, double that reported in the official BLS count of unemployment.

Nor does this tell the whole story! Government employment statistics are

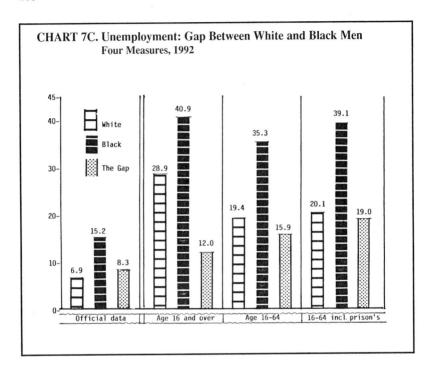

CHART 7C. Unemployment: Gap Between White and Black Men
Four Measures, 1992

based on the civilian *non-institutional* population. But with the jail and prison populations having doubled over the past decade, this factor has become a significant omission, especially with respect to Black men, who constitute close to one-half of all male prisoners. (Female prisoners are relatively few.) Prisoners, of course, are jobless in the most basic sense, even though many work at virtually unpaid forced labor.

Including prisoners, 20.1% of white men between 16 and 64 are without jobs, while 39.1% of Black men below 65 are without jobs.

All the figures cited above, and shown in Chart 7C exaggerate joblessness. There are some men who do not want jobs, because of early retirement or full-time scholarship, or disabilities. If this could be measured, it would reduce the figures cited and shown by a few percentage points, but not decisively.

Youth Unemployment

A particularly tragic feature of modern American life is the joblessness and overall economic insecurity afflicting the youth. The impact on African American and Latino youth is greatest by a wide margin, destroying lives and preventing millions from ever realizing their potential.

Chart 7D shows youth unemployment by percentage—understated

because BLS estimates are lower than the actual number of jobless youth who want and need jobs.

Among teenage youth in 1992, white males had an unemployment rate of about 19%; African American males, 42%; and Hispanic, 27%. Rates for teenage women were slightly lower. Among males in their early 20s, the white unemployment rate was a bit over 10%; the Black rate, 25%; and the Latino, 14%. Again rates for women were a bit less.

Looking at it another way, 46% of white male teenagers had jobs but only 24% of Black teenagers—relatively half as many. Among youth in their early 20s (20-24), 77% of the white as compared with 57% of the African American had jobs. That is, 43% of young Black men in their early 20s were not employed, whether counted as jobless or not.

Today the importance of education for employment is a fact of life. Of white youth 16-24, 21.8% were enrolled in college in 1992 compared with 16.4% of Black youth—a significant gap but not as great as it was some decades ago. But when it comes to getting a degree, 9% of the white youth compared with only 3% of the Black youth actually graduated from college—

CHART 7D. Youth Unemployment Rates, Age and Sex, 1992 (percent)

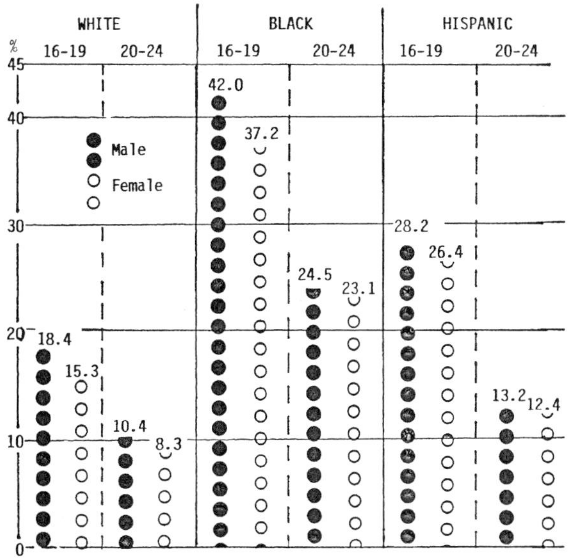

and a college degree has proven essential for obtaining a good job, with adequate salary and potential for advancement.[7]

Among youth who dropped out of college without getting a degree, the disparity is also vast: for white youth the unemployment rate was 7.4%, not much lower than that for white college graduates, although the jobs were not as good. But for Black youth who did not complete college, the unemployment rate jumped to 20.4%.[8]

Most students who come from working class and middle income families cannot afford the costs of a college education without part-time jobs. In fact, 60% of white college students were counted as being in the labor force, and of them, 7.5% were among the unemployed. But among Black college students, who certainly need the income more, only 44% were included in the labor force and of them, 19% were without jobs.

These data confirm the urgency for affirmative action measures that guarantee access to full scholarship funds for Black college students, along with a vast increase in the availability of such funds for all students, regardless of race or sex. Special consideration is required to guarantee access to jobs for Black youth who are just entering the job market—along with provision for protection against arbitrary firing by bosses after brief periods of token employment.

Data for 1994 show only trifling cyclical improvement in the youth employment/unemployment picture.

Discrimination in Kinds of Employment

There has been only trivial improvement in the employment pattern of African American workers over the past decade.

TABLE 7:3. COMPARISON OF BLACK AND WHITE EMPLOYMENT, BY SEX, AND OF BLACK WOMEN TO BLACK MEN FOR MOST PRESTIGIOUS OCCUPATIONS, 1993 (PERCENT)

Occupational Group	**Percent Black of White**		Percent Black Women of Black Men
	Men	Women	
Total population 16 & over	12.7%	14.4%	121.6%
Total employment	10.6	13.3	103.9
Executives	5.6	8.8	109.3
Professionals	5.8	9.7	186.7
Technicians	9.2	13.0	138.5
Sales persons	5.3	9.3	165.8
Skilled crafts	7.5	16.7	17.6

SOURCE: E & E, Jan., 1994, T. 3, pp.175-77 Annual Data; T. 21, p.204, Annual Data

Black males lose out—to both white men and to Black women—with employment of Black women closer to that of white women. I.e., the share of Black men in professional and executive jobs is less than half their relative share of the population, while the relative share of Black women in these categories is closer to two-thirds of their share in the population.

To get their fair share of work in relation to their percentage in the population, Black males would need 20% more jobs than they had in 1993! That is a far greater number than the official unemployment figures indicate.

Black women also fall short in total employment and are below par in all of the four favored white-collar groups, although they have made more progress than white women in penetrating the skilled crafts.

Although there are more Black women than Black men not only in total employment but also among executives and professionals, as well as among technicians and sales persons, this does not in any way mean that the status of African American women is satisfactory. Black women, more than ever, are the victims of triple discrimination: as women, as African Americans, as workers.

Table 7:3 again stresses the sharp discrimination against African Americans, especially Black men. But the extreme degree of discrimination is revealed by analysis of personnel in specific jobs rather than in broad occupation groups.

It cannot be overemphasized that the status of African Americans within such important categories as executives and professionals is clearly inferior. Even within particular occupations, they are often relegated to jobs without real financial incentives and without real executive power or important connections to the wealthy core in their specific spheres.

Consider two kinds of executive jobs: public administrators—the Black share was 11.5% in 1992; and financial managers—the Black share, 3.0%. Public administrators are appointed by elected officials, and African Americans got more of these jobs partly because there were many more Black elected officials. But further, white elected officials are subject to political pressure: they are obliged to have African Americans conspicuously in their entourage if they want to avoid uncomfortable accusations and even lawsuits, and, in order to entice the crucial Black vote when re-election comes up.

These jobs, while representing an opportunity for many African Americans to attain more consequential positions, are usually low-grade bureaucratic handouts. In no way can they be compared with the high-powered white government appointees who talk of the "sacrifice" they make to enter public service. What they mean is that the generous salaries they get do not compare with the pelf they are able to garner from their place in the corporate hierarchy, and they do not mention the unlimited opportunities they are offered—and accept—to supplement their incomes.

In public administration, the State Department and the CIA are the most prestigious. These are the bastions of the top ruling circles of finance capital, the strongholds of Ivy League members of multimillionaire families, the denizens of the Harvard and Yale Clubs, of the exclusive country clubs that still shamelessly exclude Blacks. And these appointed—not elected—administrators have the influence, the power, and the international connections to globalize the domination of U.S. imperialism. The fact that their efforts escalate the profits of the corporations from which they draw their opulent sustenance—held in trust for them while they are in government service—gives impetus to their actions. Needless to say, there are very few African American appointees in these agencies, and none in decision-making positions.

As an illustration, there was the tragi-farce of Clinton's appointment of Clifton R. Wharton, an African American, to the Number Two post in the State Department. After being assigned to paper-shuffling, he was then fired because he was shuffling paper!

However, financial managers exert real power in the business world, and have opportunities for realizing huge incomes. There are very few Blacks among them.

Professionals

In the category of professionals, the contrasts are even sharper. With a mere 7% of all professional jobs in 1993, African Americans were only 3.0% of the doctors and dentists, whose services are so vital for the health and well-being of the population. Not only do many white doctors and dentists discriminate against African Americans as patients, but their offices are not where Black people live, so emergency and life-saving care just aren't available (see Chapter 11).

Likewise, only 2.7% of lawyers were African American, a decisive factor in the high rate of convictions and jailing of Blacks, as well as in unfavorable outcomes in disputes with employers, landlords, and in business contacts generally.

There has been no improvement in the Black share of these occupations over the past 30 years. However, under a new system of counting, the Labor Department showed, for 1994, among physicians 4.2% Blacks and 5.1% Hispanics; among lawyers, 3.3% Blacks and 3.1% Hispanics. But be alert to the fact that these figures do NOT mean an increase of Blacks and Latinos: the 1994 data are a result of a new method of statistical manipulation.

On the other hand, 17.5% of dieticians—90% of them women—were

Black. Dieticians not only rate far down on the professional pay scale, but their role in health maintenance is, arguably, not decisive.

The share of African Americans is revealing in teaching positions: kindergarten, 11.7%; elementary school, 9.3%; secondary school, 6.9%; college and university, 4.8% (see Chapter 12).

There is one area where the unremitting battle for civil rights and job equality has had broad and highly visible results—albeit for only a tiny fraction of the Black people. In the U.S. sports/entertainment/media professions many of the outstanding stars, performers, athletes, etc., are Black; TV anchors, announcers, and newscasters are frequently teams of Black and white—as well as male and female. In baseball, football and basketball, especially, Black players are outstanding, although there are still too few as officials and managers. Hockey, tennis and water/snow sports, on the other hand, remain almost wholly white. Movie and television scripts increasingly portray African Americans in key roles—not always as positive role models!—and sitcoms tend to optimize average Black living conditions: the influence of Black capitalists is strongly evident. There are some—not many—Black musicians with symphony orchestras. In this area, there has been a prolonged and bitter struggle that has still a long way to go. But the breakthroughs in sports, media and the arts—visual and performing—show that concerted continuous pressure can effect a change in the white-dominated spheres.

Racism still dominates in the construction trades, with Blacks holding only 3.9% of supervisory positions, and 4.5% and 6.1%, respectively, in the key craft trades of carpentry and electrician.

As for agriculture, the remnants of Black farm owners and renter-operators continue to be pushed off the land, and by 1993 African Americans constituted less than 1% of all farm operators and managers, but 7% of farm workers.[9]

Unequal Pay for Equal Work

African Americans and Hispanics are systematically paid less than whites for the same general kind of work. Table 7:4 compares 1991 earnings of males for major occupation groups.

Black and Hispanic men, overall, receive about two-thirds the wages or salaries of white men; about three quarters in the high-ranking jobs—executives, professionals and skilled blue-collar jobs—and about 85% in the lower-paid white-collar and blue-collar jobs.

A considered conclusion is that part of the differential can be attributed to discriminatory assessment as to the kind of jobs Black and Hispanic men are able to get, but a major part to racism on the same kind of job.

TABLE 7:4. MEDIAN EARNINGS OF MALES BY MAJOR OCCUPATION:
BLACK AND HISPANIC AS A PERCENT OF WHITE, 1991

Occupation Group	Percent Black and Hispanic of White	
	Black	Hispanic
ALL OCCUPATIONS	68%	64%
Executives, Managers	75	77
Professionals	70	82
Technologists	79	75
Sales	53	70
Administrative support (Clerical)	90	76
Service Occupations	89	102
Farming, Forestry	46	101
Precision production	75	79
Operatives and laborers	85	76
Armed forces	98	85

SOURCE: Unpublished Data, Current Population Survey, Bureau of the Census. See also p. 297.

The data in Table 7:4 are based on relatively small samples, so may have wide margins of error. But while a given figure may not be precise, the overall picture is valid. The statistics show median incomes—those of the middle person in each group. Thus, among executives, while the Black median was 75% of white, the Black mean was 69%. *There were 1,353,000 white men with earnings over $100,000 yearly and only 12,000 African American men— 6,000 of whom were doctors—in that high income bracket.* These are people who, for the most part, may be considered part of the capitalist class; and emphasizes how that class is virtually exclusively white.

Why the Wage and Salary Differentials?

To repeat: racism is the decisive factor, basically the exclusive factor, behind racial earnings differentials. This is illustrated by analyzing the differentials within specific occupation groups.

E.g., African American public administrators and officials had median earnings 83% those of whites, while in the private sector, the median for Blacks was only 63% of white. Black/white differentials in averages are even wider because so many more white executives receive extremely high salaries and bonuses. In 1991, 478,000 white private-sector executives had earnings above $100,000 but *less than 500 Black executives. One Black capitalist for 1,000 white capitalists!*

A narrower differential among public executives is consistent with the previously cited data showing that the public sector creates a more favorable arena for struggle for equality than does the private economy.

There is another factor that is relevant to the wide salary gap in positions such as manager, administrator, etc. in private industry. In the upper echelons, to a considerable degree success depends on personal connections: it's not what you know, it's whom you know. In that respect, the top white executives—with their university, social and political contacts—have a decisive advantage over African American administrators. Their connections enable them to make deals at home and abroad, to arrange favors from politicians, to determine hiring and firing so as to step up the rate of profit. They are undeniably very good at exploiting labor and accumulating profits, a talent that fuels the power of the financial oligarchy, the top circles of monopoly capital. And this power is intrinsic to the racism of capitalism at its zenith.

The data for Black sales personnel—a median income only 53% that of whites—has similar roots, primarily in the area of high-cost purchases: real estate, insurance, stocks and bonds, automobiles, etc. The best sales are to contacts or to people who are "like you": i.e., whites have an advantage selling to whites; Blacks an advantage selling to Blacks. But more whites are richer, more prosperous, so more of them are able to make larger purchases. Also, most African American salespersons are employed in retail establishments: department and cut-rate emporiums, fast food and chain eateries and restaurants, shops in malls, etc., all low-wage enterprises.

Then there is also the 46% Black/white earnings ratio for farming. The ratio for the few remaining Black farm operators is a miserly 23%, but it is 91% for farm workers. The fact is that the wages for all farm workers are so low that it isn't possible to pay Black workers much less than Latino or white.

Company-provided training is valuable for gaining promotion and for holding a job in the event of layoffs. But employers discriminate against African Americans and Latinos in this regard, too. Over a five-year period, among young workers, 21.3% of white employees received company training; 17.4% of Blacks; 15.4% of Hispanics. The differentials were similar among males and females. Workers with more education were favored in training, as were those with higher scores on a standardized test. In general Black and Hispanic workers get less education and get lower scores on standardized tests, partly because of the cultural biases in these tests.[10]

To comply with the principles of the Fair Employment Act, and to effect affirmative action in compensation for past discrimination, a larger percentage of Black and Hispanic workers must receive company training.

Working class literature abounds with stories of veteran Black workers training white workers who are then promoted while the Black teachers are left behind. That's just one expression of the reluctance of employers to advance African Americans.

Trends in Wages

Since 1973 real wages have declined, hitting the entire working class. The overall downtrend has accelerated for men since 1979: median real wages of both white and Black males lost 8%, while Hispanics lost 16%. But women's real wages have gone up: year-round, full-time white women gained 10%; Black women, 9%; and Hispanic women workers, 5%. In 1992 among men, the Black median was 72.1% of the white median; the Hispanic median, 64.6% of the white median. But among women, the Black median was 91.5% of the white; the Hispanic, 79.1%.

During this entire period, there was a marked rise in the ratio of female to male median earnings. By 1992, the ratio among white workers was 70%, but among Blacks, 89%, and among Hispanics, 85%.[11]

Summarizing the data, including the impact of the uptrend in part-time work, the wage differential against African American workers narrowed moderately between 1973 and 1979, but lost part of the gains by 1992. There was no overall change in the differentials against Latino workers during the 1970s, and it has widened sharply since then.

The important relationship between unionization and Black/Latino wages is analyzed in chapter 15.

The Law and Reality

For nearly four decades equal employment opportunity laws have been on the books, calling for affirmative action programs as well as for compensating victims of discrimination because of race, sex, disabilities, etc. The EEOC has had key responsibilities in this respect, along with the Civil Rights Division of the Justice Department and assorted other agencies of federal and some state and local governments. In this and other chapters, much use is made of detailed statistical reports provided by the EEOC. By the mid 1990s, a major right-wing campaign was underway to remove legal impediments to racist discrimination.

Throughout the entire period, employer resistance has been persistent, enforcement weak, and criminal punishment of responsible individuals completely lacking—not provided for in law.

If the EEOC's record on enforcement was as good as its record on reporting employment patterns, this would be a much better country for working people. But its actual contribution to law enforcement has been trivial.

To begin with, its powers are limited. Where it finds discrimination, it can call for the guilty party to make restitution—or more often a "compromise" settlement, which falls far short of righting the wrong. If such a deal cannot be made, the Commission can turn the matter over to the courts to handle—

which means throwing the ball into the hands of the Justice Department, whose lawyers would have to prosecute the case. With this procedural rigmarole, including appeals to various levels of courts—which the employer defendants can readily afford—the whole process can take years. And the victims? At best they have gone through years of suffering before their grievance is even heard.

To the limited powers, add the limitation of will. Government officials in charge of such agencies are characteristically political appointees with the ideology of and prejudices of the capitalist class. During the Reagan-Bush years the majority of the five commissioners were philosophically opposed to affirmative action. Finally, President Clinton in 1994 appointed as Chairman Gilbert A. Casellas, who purports to wish to seriously enforce the law.

Staff and financial resources are wholly inadequate to handle the vast volume of cases of alleged discrimination—now approaching 100,000 cases a year. The current staff cannot cope with that number: there are 97,000 unresolved cases, more than double the number in 1990. When investigators finally get to a case, their tendency is to throw it out on any excuse. Only 3% are considered valid for court action or conciliation. Many investigators "...made light of employers' sexual and racial slights...were crude, abrupt, and ill-informed, and never returned telephone calls."[12]

The original basis of EEOC actions, Title 7 of the Civil Rights Act of 1964, aimed at discrimination in employment on account of race, color, sex, national origin, or religion. The whole history of the mass struggles and legal battles made correction of racial discrimination the main object. But the emphasis, at best, was on correcting proven cases of discrimination, rather than the pursuit of active measures to improve racial balance—i.e., affirmative action.

The whole tendency of the bureaucracy is to avoid strong action: 60% of cases are thrown out as not supplying sufficient evidence of discrimination. Others are thrown out because the complaining worker has moved, died, withdrawn the complaint, or some trivial agreed relief is given. Only 3% of the cases "...are deemed to show solid enough evidence of discrimination to deserve legal intervention, in court or through conciliation."

Emphasis is on getting cash payments for past discrimination. And the cash payments are rare and trivial in relation to the overall costs to victims. Subsequently additional laws were passed against discrimination on account of age and on account of disabilities, as well as strengthening provisions against sex discrimination.

The range of issues covered has been increased while budgetary allowances and personnel were slashed. Cases involving disabled persons, "unlawful retaliation," age discrimination, and sex discrimination run into less determined political opposition than against racism, which thereby gets shuffled to the back of the line.

Among cases filed in 1992, 26.1% dealt with sex discrimination, 21.1% discrimination against older workers, 19.3% against unlawful retaliation, and only 19.9% against discrimination on account of race—mainly against Blacks. In 1991, race discrimination cases were only 17.5% of the total.[13]

During fiscal year 1992 the largest settlement, $35 million—one third of all settlements of $96 million—were payments to 32 management level employees who were discharged on account of age.

The largest settlement in the agency's history, $66 million, was against AT&T for discrimination against pregnant women. That was more than two-thirds of all the settlements in that year.[14]

These settlements were deserved, but the implication of very little being done against racial discrimination is glaring.

The large 1992 settlement, for 32 executives, was by the Milwaukee office. Milwaukee is notorious as the city in Wisconsin where conditions of the Black population have shown no improvement, while over the state as a whole there has been a strong economic recovery. The contrast between the inner city and the rest of the state is exceptionally sharp, and the official line of opening up inner-city jobs to Black employers and employees is mocked by the reality.

> The Milwaukee district director, Chester V. Bailey, grew up amid civil rights struggles in Birmingham, Ala. "I have a mission here," said Mr. Bailey, who is Black. "We're doing things that people fought and died for in the '60s."
>
> But Mr. Bailey's hands are tied today. He speaks of a University of Wisconsin-Milwaukee study showing that Black and Hispanic workers hold just 1.2 percent of the management jobs in all the new businesses that have opened in downtown Milwaukee since 1982. "There," he said, "lie the seeds of a huge class action suit. But I can't do it. I don't have the resources."
>
> In four years...his investigation staff has grown from 15 to 20. But the number of new case filings has doubled.[15]

The basic terms of the original Title 7 have features that are in ideological conflict with its basic premise and can be used to wreck any case, as well as to justify the most outrageous cases of discrimination.

Even more broadly, discrimination is legal whenever the "national security of the United States" is involved. In a country where a large proportion of all employers have some military or "intelligence" contracts, this is a broad net to excuse any action and can be used against militant workers. Thereby discrimination can be used to weaken labor unity and labor organization.

Also legal is discrimination in accord with "bona fide" seniority or merit systems, or tests of ability. Thus the conflict between departmental and other seniority systems, which tend to perpetuate last-to-be-hired and first-to-be-fired fates of Black workers, can be settled in favor of the rigid seniority pattern. Also approved are the racially charged intelligence and other tests used to effectually knock out a large proportion of Black and Latino job applicants.

Another provision prohibits actions to correct imbalance in employment—i.e., affirmative action measures—except when racial motivation of the imbalance is proved.[16]

Despite these shortcomings, the EEOC is worthy of support and of much more intensive use by unions, political groups concerned with civil rights, the CBTU and other specialized working class organizations. But it remains clear that correction of employment discrimination has to be mainly through mass struggle. The greater the scale and intensity of these struggles, the more white workers will get off the sidelines and assist in overcoming discrimination against Blacks, and the more effective the EEOC and other legal remedies will be.

And isn't it time that the fascistic anti-Communist laws and rules, which permeate so much of U.S. society—including the constitutions of major trade unions, such as the nominally progressive United Auto Workers—be thrown out, as the most extreme and persistent form of anti-working class political discrimination in the United States, and many other countries?

Human Cost of Racism

No way can this outrage be dismissed as solely an "objective factor," not involving racism! [my emphasis--V.P.] In a frank expose, a *Wall Street Journal* headline admitted: IN LATEST RECESSION, ONLY BLACKS SUFFERED NET EMPLOYMENT LOSS. Analyzing EEOC data, the article found Black workers lost 50,000 jobs in 1990 and 1991, while overall employment of whites, Hispanics and Asians rose. The *WSJ* reporter obtained figures for major industrial companies. For example:

Sears Roebuck had 425,000 employees in 1990, of whom 16% were Black. But Blacks absorbed 54% of the job losses.

General Motors had 412,000 workers in 1990, including 17% Blacks. But Blacks were hit with 21% of the layoffs.

Not all the listed companies showed disproportionate layoffs of Black workers, but that was the general trend.[17]

AT&T, before its breakup into regional companies, was the country's largest employer, with more than a million workers. It was conspicuous for its racist policies. Before World War II, fewer than 1% of its employees were Black, and those were exclusively in cleanup positions. Even with the huge World War II labor demand and the postwar activity, Black employment at

AT&T reached only 1.3% by 1950. Civil Rights struggles forced a certain change, so that by 1990, 10% of its workers were African American.

A special, detailed report by the EEOC in 1972 revealed the limited, special character of AT&T's employment practices at that time. Blacks were almost totally excluded from the top craft jobs of switchman, cable splicer, PBX installer-repairman, etc.

> The exclusion of blacks from skilled craft employment is more complete in the telephone industry than in industry generally. In the New York area, the percentage of blacks in telephone company craft jobs was less than one-third the percentage of blacks in craft jobs in all industries. In Jacksonville, Florida, in 1967 there was not a single black in a telephone company craft job...[18]

But for low-end jobs, the telephone company hired mainly Black women so that 79% of its Black employees were women, overwhelmingly in operator jobs (as against 53% of white employees). The operator job was "horrendous," and the terrible conditions were "converting the Traffic Department (where operators worked) from simply a 'nunnery' into a 'ghetto nunnery,'" the EEOC reported.

The personnel vice-president of the Bell companies, Walter Staley, explained:

> What a telephone company needs to know about its labor market [is] who is available for work paying as little as $4,000 to $5,000 a year...It is just a plain fact that in today's world, telephone company wages are more in line with Black expectations—and the tighter the labor market the more this is true.[19]

What Staley left out, of course, is that the "need" for workers at such low wages reflected the company's successful drive for ever-higher monopoly superprofits.

As a result of the breakup of AT&T into regional companies, hiring discrimination in that particular branch of communications has become less acute. But nationwide, discrimination and racist attitudes remain intense, so that the differential unemployment rate against Black workers has increased. In fact, telephone company unemployment is rising rapidly. NYNEX, operating in the New York Metropolitan Area, having slashed employment from near 100,000 in 1988 to 75,000 in 1993, announced its intention to cut jobs a further 22%, to under 60,000.[20] Similar cuts were announced by other telephone companies. And, as in other industries, the African American workers losing these jobs will have the hardest time finding alternative employment.

Conclusion

Joblessness is a crime perpetuated by the U.S. capitalist class against the American working class. And the trend has been markedly upward since the end of World War II.

The burden on the African Americans, especially, but also on Latinos, Native Americans and on some sections of the Asian population severely reflects the inordinate racism of U.S. capitalism. The facts should dispel any illusions that white workers profit from, or are exempt from, the super-unemployment inflicted on minority workers. When 17 million white males—including 10.5 million, or 17% of all white males—sustain unemployment during a single year, this has to be recognized as an outrage borne by the entire population, not only by minorities.

The legislation enacted by Congress as a result of the civil rights struggles of the 1950s and 1960s was primarily intended to encourage employers to implement "affirmative action" programs. But actual effectiveness was limited by:

a) Constant lawsuits challenging the principal of affirmative action, with conflicting court decisions varying with the political winds;

b) Trivial appropriation of funds and—in the case of the EEOC—no enforcement powers so that influence has been limited to exhortation;

c) Since 1980, the use of racism as a major, and at times decisive, political weapon of right-wing politicians, with virtually no white Establishment politicians publicly defending effective affirmative action.

The initiatives of supporters, such as the Progressive Caucus in Congress and, increasingly, numerous independent local officials, are valuable. But in the last analysis the solution must be forced by the mass mobilization of Americans on a scale vastly greater than that of the powerful civil rights movement of the 1950s and 1960s—a united mass mobilization of white, African American, Latino, Native American, Asian-origin peoples; men and women, youth and seniors, disabled and hale, employed and jobless.

8. Affirmative Action

All U.S. inhabitants other than Native Americans are descendants of—or are themselves—immigrants. U.S. racism against African Americans—descendants of slaves, and more recent arrivals—affects 15%-20% of its total population. Discrimination against successive waves of white ethnic immigrants has been largely eliminated, resulting in a relative equalization in their economic status, residential intermingling, cultural assimilation and intermarriage. Most white Americans now name more than one country as the homelands of their forefathers.

The iniquitous maltreatment of African Americans is in glaring contrast to the improvement in relations among white peoples. Racism violates the precepts of equality and justice guaranteed in our Constitution and called for in the United Nations Charter and resolutions on human rights. The details of those human rights resolutions might as well have been stamped "Top Secret," inasmuch as they remain unknown and scarcely accessible to most Americans.

The United States has no laws against verbal expressions of race hatred or anti-Semitism, and even those guilty of physical violence are rarely punished for crimes against humanity. Hypocritically, U.S. military aggressions are justified as being necessary to combat alleged violations of human rights by rulers unpopular in Washington. What human rights of citizens can be assured by American bombers and invading troops that slaughter multitudes of the civilians they are "protecting"?

Yet in one important respect, progress has been made. The majority of white Americans believe they oppose racism, even though most are imbued, in varying degrees, with racial prejudices. Thus there is a social basis for major improvement.

Racist discrimination is not a requisite for exploitation of labor, but it is essential for maximum profiteering. And that huge super-profit provides the incentive, the driving force, behind all-out efforts of the capitalists to maintain and intensify the evil. Racism is so deeply imbedded in the system of exploitation and plunder that its elimination within the bounds of capitalism is unlikely—any more than is the exploitation of labor. But racial discrimination can be substantially reduced, and in the process there will inevitably be a significant reduction in the exploitation of labor, thereby improving the lot of the entire working class.

Positive actions to redress inequalities suffered by sections of the population are generalized under the rubric *affirmative action*. Affirmative action laws have been enacted on behalf of "women and minorities," thus encompassing Hispanics, Asians and Native Americans as well as African Americans. Later legislation added the disabled to the list of beneficiaries. But these laws have been only marginally carried out. It is the African Americans who are in most urgent need for affirmative action, and it is against them that there is the strongest resistance to its application. Gertrude Ezorsky eloquently states:

> This book focuses on black persons as beneficiaries of affirmative action in employment. In adopting that focus I do not mean to deny the entitlement of other minorities, women, or groups such as handicapped to such benefits. Blacks, however, as descendants of slaves brought to this country against their will and as victims of the post-Reconstruction century of murderous racism, which was encouraged, practiced, and given legal sanction by our government, have a unique entitlement to special efforts to ensure their fair share of employment benefits.[1]

The same considerations also apply to wages and salaries, housing, education, health services, and access to capital.

When we refer to programs meeting the special requirements of Black people, we mean those that specify priority of benefits to Blacks, with quantitative and time targets for achieving equality in the given sector. Not that these programs and those for all the people are mutually exclusive. Special priorities for Blacks and other minorities, directly or indirectly, are beneficial to all working people.

Experience has proven conclusively that the absence of overt discrimination and the provision of formal equality of opportunity are insufficient. Generalized strictures against discrimination are of minimal significance. Such measures assume that discrimination and segregation are deviations from some norm of behavior. On the contrary, discrimination and segregation are the norm for those who control the country's economic and political life, a norm which they are determined to maintain. Thus far-reaching affirmative action measures, vigorously enforced, are central to progress against racism.

Historical Background

Following the Civil War, in response to the freedmen's struggles for land and basic political and civil rights, Congress passed a number of laws designed to put former slaves on a rough legal par with white people. The 14th Amendment to the Constitution further strengthened codification of equality. But following the defeat of Reconstruction reforms, engineered by the capitalist class, these paper gains were revoked, and the majority of Blacks were doomed to further generations of semi-feudal exploitation and racist humiliation, especially in the Jim-Crow South. World War II, the victories of socialism and the defeat of fascism, the participation of Black people in defense of the United States, the rise in influence and organization of the U.S. working class, and finally the Civil Rights campaigns of the 1950s and 1960s led to a substantive advance in the struggle against racism. A series of important executive orders and Congressional actions over the period 1961-72, under three presidents—Kennedy, Johnson and Nixon—codified this advance. In 1961 President Kennedy, by Executive Order, established a commission on equal opportunity, which mandated:

> ...federal contractors to take "affirmative action" to ensure that there be no discrimination by "race, creed, color, or national origin." For the first time, the government ordered its contractors not only to avoid discrimination, but to take positive steps to redress the effects of societal discrimination.[2]

Title 7 of the Civil Rights Act of 1964 created a permanent Equal Employment Opportunity Commission (EEOC) to enforce non-discrimination by employers, labor unions and governments. In 1971, following the initiative of Assistant Secretary of Labor Art Fletcher, a Black man, President Nixon strengthened previous orders "... by requiring annual affirmative action plans from major contractors, and including hiring goals and timetables. According to Fletcher, the Nixon Administration ordered what Congress had not: numerical goals and enforcement."[3]

Thus, the concept of *affirmative action* to reduce historical racial discrimination became the law of the land. It was a vital step forward from the thesis that all that was necessary was "a level playing field" on which Blacks could compete for advancement—a hypocritical concept in that the real playing field was hopelessly slanted against Blacks.

Large and medium-sized companies had to submit to the EEOC numerical goals, both short term and long term, with timetables for their accomplishment. Inevitably, this entailed allotment of numerical proportions in hiring and promotion of minority workers, generally encompassed by the term "quotas."

The early 1970s was a peak period of affirmative action, with significant victories. A 1972 act added the key provision that the EEOC was "empowered...to prevent any person from engaging in any unlawful employment practice." It could take cases to court, and the judge might "order affirmative action...which may include reinstating or hiring of employees." The new law had serious weaknesses, including an anti-Communist clause, but it provided a practical lever that for a certain period accomplished concrete results. An EEOC guide to employers warned:

> If a statistical survey shows that minorities and females are not participating in

your work force at all levels in reasonable relation to their presence in the population and the labor force, the burden of proof is on you to show that this is not the result of discrimination, however inadvertent.[4]

This expressed the positive approach to equal employment—that it is insufficient to avoid obvious manifestations of discrimination; it is necessary to eliminate it in practice.

Affirmative Action

Application of the 1972 law, under a 1973 court decision, benefited the 3,800 African American workers among the 13,000 total employed at U.S. Steel's Fairfield, Alabama plant. It ended the discriminatory departmental seniority system that blocked Black promotion to better jobs. More important, it required equal hiring of Black and white apprentices, and of Black and white clerical and technical employees, until African Americans held 25% and 20%, respectively, of positions in those categories.

It also required hiring one Black out of three supervisors until their share reached 20%. Implementation was entrusted to a committee of three: a company and a union representative and Black worker appointed by the court.

Unions played a positive role in some cases, a negative role in others. The Black Caucus of Detroit Edison Co.'s employees brought suit after the rele-

World cartoon by Norman Goldberg

THE BOYS' CLUB

Chadwick, all this affirmative action is just plain pandering. I didn't need it. By dint of hard work and dedication, I climbed the corporate ladder until my father appointed me vice-president.

vant union locals refused to file their grievances. A Black judge fined the company $34 million, and a local union $250,000, and set hiring requirements similar to those imposed on U.S. Steel.

The EEOC, the Civil Rights Division of the Justice Department, trade unions, groups of workers and civil rights organizations launched thousands of cases during this period. The Contract Compliance Division of the Labor Department offered hopes of 500,000 new hires and promotions to minority workers and women by employers holding federal contracts. Under these pressures, many large corporations set up equal employment offices and took limited positive measures, as did various government agencies. As a result, during the '70s, many African Americans were hired in skilled craft jobs, as police officers and in other government job categories. However, the gains were always partial, never coming close to equality. There was no guarantee that improvement would be generalized, would lead to a real, lasting reduction in the overall scale and severity of discrimination.

Under existing laws and procedures, each process takes years. Court orders, including appeals to higher bodies by racist defendants, can drag on for more than a decade. There is no enforcement machinery authorized to impose imprisonment or substantial personal fines on racist employers and corporate officials. The successful cases were carried through by progressive government officials in the administration of an overtly racist president, Richard Nixon. How was this possible? Only because Nixon, beleaguered by the threat of impeachment, found his control over various government agencies weakened:

> With White House officials busy defending the president and themselves against mounting Watergate and related scandals, lower-echelon officials were left to their own devices, and they thereby gave the Administration a stronger pro-civil rights record than it might have desired.[5]

But even before Nixon was removed, centralized racism was restored. The Reverend Theodore M. Hesburgh, activist Chairman of the Commission on Civil Rights, was removed, as was pro-Civil Rights Chairman William H. Brown of the EEOC.

Implementation of the Fairchild decision against U.S. Steel was frustrated by corporate, government, and union officials who won a court-determined consent agreement that substituted financial payments to Black workers for a genuine affirmative action promotion program.

My conclusion is contested by some politically advanced steel workers, who contend that it was the consent decree under which Black steelworkers made progress. However, the consent decree, over the opposition of African American organizations, abandoned the key element of the Fairfield decision—numerical quotas in hiring for better jobs in the industry. The impact of this failure is shown by EEOC reports revealing that only trivial progress has been made in the employment pattern, and none in the overall employment, of Black steelworkers. Appeals to higher courts by Detroit Edison and other companies weakened or reversed positive lower court decisions.

A decisive political balance in favor of equality was needed to bring earlier victories to fruition, and to generalize them into the economy as a whole. It did not exist in the 1970s, nor yet by the mid-'90s. Meanwhile, presidents Reagan and Bush had packed the Supreme Court with a racist reactionary majority, and appointments at lower levels moved in the same direction.

Bill Clinton, in his years as Governor of Arkansas, did not improve the state's sorry record of discrimination. As President, he sought the political support of African Americans by nominating and appointing Blacks to significant posts, including at the cabinet level. However, he readily yielded to racist pressure, which singled out these choices. He withdrew nominations and forced the resignation of cabinet members accused of corruption for minor offenses that are regularly ignored in the case of white appointees. In 1994 he used maximum influence to ensure passage of a crime bill sharply edged against Black people. And his speeches have featured "blame the victim" tirades about family and sexual matters.

He endorsed the anti-labor NAFTA agreement, violated his campaign promises to put over a jobs bill and raise minimum wages. Partly because of the Clinton Administration's rightward drift, the big business, anti-labor, racist offensive prevented the working class generally, and Blacks and Latinos in particular, from benefiting from the economic revival of 1993-94. This set the stage for the Republican Congressional gains in 1994, and a sharp offensive emanating from Congress against poor people, with "minorities," women, and children the main targets.

Yet the legal basis and enforcement machinery remain, limited as they are, and constitute a means of effecting affirmative action in the sphere of employment. Less than half of privately employed workers are covered, and the percentage has been declining. Many companies fail to submit required reports; there is no publication of affirmative action goals, timetables, or quotas, and no clear enforcement procedure. Specific affirmative action programs, including hiring quotas, have been set up by some local governments and some private companies. But these—often won by effective campaigns of public advocacy groups and union locals—cover only a trifling proportion of all workers. Racist opposition is almost universal, intense, and well financed. With the rightward direction of national politics, practical affirmative action programs remain marginal in scope and under siege.

The Campaign Against Quotas

Determined to preserve racist patterns, the capitalist class has centered its legal and ideological campaign against quotas; against any use of time limits and numerical requirements in hiring minority workers. In Establishment propaganda, "quotas," like "Communism," has become a term of opprobrium, and is applied to a wide range of affirmative action measures that need not involve specific quotas. Many advocates of affirmative action declare their opposition to "quotas," just as many liberals and progressives dissociate themselves from any measure or organization that might be labeled "Communist." Such retreats strengthen reaction in all areas.

Clinton nominated Lani Guinier, a progressive African American woman, to the post of Assistant Attorney General in charge of Civil Rights. She was clamorously denounced by racist forces and dubbed the "Quota Queen," although in her writings she had generally opposed the use of quotas. Clinton bowed to racist pressure and withdrew her nomination.

Widespread Use of Quotas in American Life

Attacks against quotas are almost exclusively limited to their use to combat racism. Quotas are generally accepted as desirable regulatory devices in many spheres.

Gerald Horne writes:

> One of the earliest forms of affirmative action could be considered the heralded "40 acres and a mule" that should have been allocated to former slaves upon their emancipation...Though often denounced in ritual fashion, affirmative action has actually been part of our society for decades. For example, in cities like New York there has traditionally been an effort by political parties to put forward a so-called "balanced ticket" that included an Irish-American, Italian-American, Jewish-American, et al. This was seen as part and parcel of democratic practice. There was no clamor about how such a process negated "merit." Curiously enough, it was only when African Americans began to demand inclusion on such "balanced tickets" that this kind of demagogy arose.[6]

Racism was so powerful in North Carolina that, despite the substantial share of Black people in the population, until 1990 no African Americans were elected to Congress. Under court order, two districts were fashioned with a Black majority, leading to the election of Black representatives. But by 1994 a major campaign was underway in North Carolina and other states, where similar affirmative action decisions finally led to election of Black representatives, to have Congressional district maps redrawn so as to restore the all-white composition of these states' delegations. This in a country where gerrymandering of electoral districts to suit all sorts of special interests is tra-ditional! Again, only when districts are drawn so as to redress the gross injus-tice against Black voters is the hue and cry raised.

The United States has all sorts of affirmative action programs—special benefits for veterans and for the physically handicapped, lower prices for senior citizens and children, special benefits for tens of thousands of anti-Communist "refugees"—while admission is refused African, Latino and Indigenous peoples from the Americas—who are refugees from real fascist terror, from countries where torturers and murderers are financed and trained by U.S. intelligence and military agencies.

Children of the upper-crust multi-millionaire "rulers of America," mainly of north European heritage, have what amounts to a 100% quota for admis-sion to Ivy League colleges, regardless of their academic attainments and/or undisciplined life styles.

American universities historically used quotas to limit entry of Jewish stu-dents, regardless of academic qualifications. Because of Jewish national tra-ditions of study, and specific factors in their geographic and occupational distribution, the proportion of Jewish students qualifying for college admis-sion exceeded their proportion in the population. These quotas exercised a real discrimination against Jews, based on anti-Semitism, and comparable to the racism directed against African Americans—who were actually subject to much more restrictive quotas, far below their proportion in the population or the numbers of academically qualified Blacks. While anti-Jewish quotas are less important than a generation ago, undoubtedly some of them still exist. Under such a system, for example, a Jewish youth might require a mark of 90 in a college entrance exam to qualify for admission, while a non-Jewish youth would require only 80.

But now, let's turn that around. And suppose, as a technique for bringing Black college attendance up to 15% of the total—corresponding to the Black proportion of the population of college age—Blacks are admitted with a mark of 70, whereas whites require a mark of 80. An exact counterpart in industry might be a requirement for Blacks to get a mark of 70 instead of a standard 80 in a plumber's exam.

Let's note that in present practice, priorities for college admission are much more far-reaching, and are granted to particular social classes and racial-ethnic groups. Harvard, one of the most prestigious colleges in the country, formally gives priority of admission to children of alumni, and to cer-tain other specified groups. All private colleges give priority of admission to offsprings of substantial contributors of endowments. A son of an alumnus, or of a donor of $100,000, is almost guaranteed admission, regardless of acade-mic or other past record. And admission to Harvard and other Ivy League colleges is virtually a ticket to employment in the upper corporate or government bureaucracy, in major law firms, and other such juicy slots, for students with the "right" social status.

This is a priority for the capitalist class, and in particular for the upper layers of the capitalist class. It is a priority for the Anglo-Saxon-Germanic origin section of the capitalist class, who historically comprised the overwhelming majority of students and others connected with the Ivy League colleges.

Clearly, by any standard of justice and equality, this kind of favorable discrimination, involving crude nepotism and ethnic/religious exclusiveness, should be abolished. But those groups denouncing priorities and targets for African Americans are silent about it. And it is the opposite in its real content to priorities for Blacks. Similarly, quotas limiting the admission of Jews are opposite to quotas guaranteeing the admission of Blacks.

The limiting quotas aim to and do bring about discrimination. So does the system of favoritism for members of the capitalist class, their relatives, etc. But positive quotas for Blacks aim to and do reduce discrimination, and can finally end it, if sufficiently generalized.

Does a positive quota for Blacks act as a limiting quota for whites? Technically perhaps, but to a trivial extent. Thus, an increase in Black admissions to law school from 5% to 15%—using hypothetical figures—represents an increase of 200%, while the corresponding reduction in admission of whites, from 95% to 85% of the total, represents a decline of only a little more than 10%. However, certainly after a brief interval, whites will suffer no decline in admissions, and total admissions will be increased to adjust for the increased number of Black law students. This is so because currently the Black people as a whole simply lack access to legal services of any quality. The large-scale training of Black lawyers will do much to correct this situation, rather than taking business away from white lawyers. But more fundamentally, the decline in the percentage of admissions accruing to whites will not be in any sense discrimination against whites, but merely the correction of historical discrimination in favor of whites.

The perspective is clearer when we discuss doctors and medical schools, employment of skilled workers and professional and specialized technical personnel in occupations suffering from a shortage of personnel. The preferential training and hiring of Blacks will not slow up the training and hiring of whites at all, but can be a spur to the establishment of sorely needed additional schools and other training facilities.

In a case that was expected to set a precedent, De Funis, a white applicant for admission to a law school, complained that he was not admitted, while Black applicants with lower marks were admitted under a program designed to ease the shortage of Black attorneys. De Funis did *not* attack the simultaneous admission of a number of whites with lower marks than himself, based on a variety of criteria. The Supreme Court ducked the issue by dismissing the case on a technicality.

The Chamber of Commerce, the National Association of Manufacturers, the AFL-CIO, and a number of Jewish organizations oppose preferential admissions. The United Automobile Workers, the National Council of Jewish Women, the NAACP Legal and Educational Fund, and Harvard College are among groups that support preferential admission of Blacks.

In other areas, the U.S. government and cartel-like groups of big farmers impose quotas on production of a broad variety of farm products, even requiring the destruction of vast quantities of fruits in order to raise high prices still higher.

A *New York Times* news account in December 1994 dramatically counterposes the negative and positive attitudes of racist politicians towards quotas: AFTER YEARS OF DESPAIR, TOBACCO FARMERS ENJOY PROSPECT OF BETTER TIMES, reads the headline over the picture of John Collett of Thomasville, North Carolina, "...who expects to get over $140,000 from the tobacco crop on his 150 acre farm. Mr. Collett says: 'It's a surprising turnaround and I'm on cloud nine.'"

Doubtless he owes much of his good fortune to Jesse Helms, senior Senator from North Carolina, a powerful advocate of the tobacco and cigarette industries and, following Republican victories in the 1994 elections, Chairman of the very important Senate Foreign Relations Committee.

Helms is one of the most extreme right-wingers in U.S. politics, an avid supporter of imperialist aggression abroad, and an outspoken, crude racist. Indeed, racist incitation and slander are his main political weapons. He is unalterably opposed to any reduction of discrimination against African Americans, and would blow a gasket at the very mention of affirmative action quotas for employment of Black workers, who constitute an important sector of his state's labor force.

But for his voting supporters, who grow tobacco, and for his close friends at Philip Morris and R.J. Reynolds, the leading cigarette manufacturers, quotas are just great—positive quotas as well as negative quotas. In keeping with "free trade" rhetoric from Washington, imports of tobacco were taking a rising share of the market. So in 1993 "lawmakers from tobacco-growing states pushed through legislation that required cigarette manufacturers to maintain a 75 percent United States tobacco content in their product."

That has caused cigarette companies to sharply increase their purchases of domestic tobacco. Each grower is assigned a "quota...which they accept in exchange for stabilized prices." The Agriculture Department was about to assign 1995 quotas 16 to 19 percent higher than the 1994 quotas. Collett, who had exceeded his 1994 quota of 75,000 pounds, was about to ride the gravy train.

In effect, tobacco farmers today are granted a monopoly of tobacco growing, and guaranteed high prices—not minimum prices, but monopoly prices far above world market levels. Needless to say, Helms is not ranting about "reverse discrimination" against small farmers effectively barred from the market. The *New York Times* article tells us nothing about the miserable conditions and low wages of hired laborers who toil on the tobacco farms. But it does mention the $20 per hour made by union members among the 1,800 employed at Philip Morris' nearby plant. They operate a highly automated line "that spits out about 85 billion cigarettes a year." These jobs are considered a kind of monopoly of the highly paid workers, many of them now working 12 hours a day, 7 days a week, to meet the demand, according to the local union president. But encouragement of excessive overtime contributes much to the employment decline of 12,000 since 1965 in jobs in the North Carolina cigarette industry. Here's where union refusal of overtime plus a program of affirmative action would open the doors for hiring many thousands more workers at good wages, with priority to the Black workers who hold very few of the high-paying jobs.[7]

Quotas are assigned to different countries for import of sugar into the United States—with Cuba's quota, zero. Quotas are imposed or negotiated on imports of cars, steel, textiles, etc.

Washington carries on tense debates with Japan over trade conflicts. U.S. negotiators demand broad concessions for U.S. corporations operating in Japan and threaten far-reaching sanctions if their demands are not met. During 1993-94 Mickey Kantor, the U.S. trade negotiator, with full presidential support, demanded a 50% share of the Japanese market for computer components for a U.S. company, Motorola. Kantor officially referred to this as a quota demand. But doubtless U.S. officials would reject out of hand a demand for a 20% quota for Black and Latino workers in Motorola factories. The Japanese negotiators, hypocritically, insisted that specific numerical quotas were contrary to "free trade" principles.

A key argument against affirmative action employment programs for minorities and women is that they constitute "reverse discrimination" against white males. However, affirmative action programs, whether or not they involve quotas, refer to hiring, not firing. No workers are replaced by Black workers, but the programs aim to overcome the historical discrimination in hiring against Blacks and women; discrimination which in effect constitutes "affirmative action" in favor of white males.

Discrimination against Black workers comes through many channels—through traditions of exclusion, through direct racist choices of employers, through Blacks lacking the connections with bosses that determine so much hiring and promotion, through Blacks getting lower marks on biased, and often irrelevant, tests.

Trade Unions and Affirmative Action

Black workers have contributed much to the U.S. trade union movement. They respond more readily to organizing campaigns; they tend to be among the more militant members. On the other hand, Blacks have gained significantly from union membership. Wage differentials against Black union members are half those against unorganized Black workers. But the fact that there do remain significant differentials against Blacks and Latinos —in shops with union contracts—in kinds of jobs and in earnings—shows that unions have a long way to go.

Unions have a mixed record with respect to affirmative action. Historically, unions combatted employer discrimination in promotions to better jobs and to departments with improved conditions and pay by fighting for and winning seniority systems, which theoretically democratized the choice of workers for promotion, and retention of jobs when layoffs occurred. But in many cases the seniority systems were marred by their application separately within each department, rather than on a plant-wide basis. This often became a device to retain favored departments as all-white enclaves.

However, some unions actively fought for affirmative acton measures. This was so in the landmark case of United Steelworkers vs. Weber, involving a Kaiser Corp. steel plant in Louisiana. Black workers had been virtually excluded from skilled craft jobs. The union negotiated an agreement that 50% of openings for such jobs (along with sizeable training programs) would be allotted to Black workers until their share of the craft jobs equalled their percentage in the local labor force.

Weber, a white worker, claimed he was unfairly deprived of promotion because of this agreement. Obviously Weber was backed by powerful and wealthy racists who could afford the prolonged and expensive legal battles that ensued. The Supreme court decided in favor of the affirmative action program in 1979, five years after the original suit was filed.

Unfortunately, such clear-cut victories are too rare, and too long delayed. Moreover, the rightward packing of courts during the 1980s and 1990s renders legal victories more and more difficult.

Emboldened by 1994 electoral victories, racist politicians have gone beyond attacks on "quotas" to open attacks on any kind of affirmative action. Propaganda in the media, often disguised as news reportage, strives to arouse mass opposition among white workers to affirmative action.

The long-term resolution of this argument requires combining affirmative action programs with radical, far-reaching programs that advance the well-being of all workers. It is a fact that the Congressional Black Caucus has been the most advanced group in the House of Representatives, promoting measures that would benefit the overwhelming majority of the population of all races, while a number of important trade unions go along with such an approach.

The response of the UAW, one of the two largest American unions, is of special importance. An issue of its monthly publication, "Solidarity," effectively rebuts the arguments of affirmative action opponents, along lines similar to those presented in this chapter. However, it weakens its own arguments by promoting a very limited vision of affirmative action:

> Typical programs range from helping disadvantaged students meet college admission standards to advertising jobs in minority media...Most affirmative action programs don't guarantee jobs or college enrollment and don't demand "preference" or "quotas," but simply correct the selection process where bias might otherwise distort decisions.

In fact, the UAW leadership has done little to promote affirmative action in the automobile industry: "The UAW's leading affirmative action tool is pre-apprenticeship training to prepare students to take apprenticeship exams."[8]

This program is trivial in scale and has not systematically been promoted as an affirmative action measure.

Still, "Solidarity" is important in combatting racist prejudices among auto workers and in others in industries where the UAW is prominent.

Affirmative action programs with scope and force are required across the board, not only in employment. Desegregation and measures to ensure access of African Americans to good housing in all areas, without their having to contend with neighborhood harassment, is essential and is necessary to make affirmative action employment programs fully effective.

Affirmative action in education is crucial in order to give Black and Latino youth access to full training and higher education in the high-tech, production, research and administrative areas where the better paying jobs are. Priority financing and other support should provide Blacks with advanced medical training and with legal training to ensure that there is an adequate number of competent doctors and lawyers to protect the health and legal requirements of African Americans.

Affirmative action programs are required to eliminate the discrimination against minorities in access to quality medical care, which has so much to do with the shocking disparity in life expectancy rates, and in access to professional lawyers in this period when there are so many Black victims of police brutality and police sweeps of inner-city communities, as well as outrageous verdicts by judges.

It becomes more and more apparent that a campaign to make the goals of affirmative action a reality is essential for the well being of all working people. Most affirmative action initiatives have been concerned with its application to employment. But the need for such protection in the areas of education, housing, health, etc. is also crucial. These areas are covered in relevant chapters of this volume.

9. Black Capitalism

For centuries Black slaves cultivated and harvested the rich southern farmlands. They fought against the slaveowners in the Civil War for "40 acres and a mule"; they had the right to be free, to own and farm the land they had worked so long as slaves. Legislation to meet part of their demands was introduced in Congress by the leading radical, Thaddeus Stevens. But it lacked sufficient popular support and the northern capitalists wanted to maintain their business ties with the defeated plantation owners, to get a larger share of the profits derived from the exploitation of the Black farm workers.

General Sherman, in his memoirs, tells of taking time out from a major campaign to have dinner with a plantation owner friend, and how, after the war, he arranged for the restoration of land to another plantation owner. This sort of policy was followed generally by the government of President Andrew Johnson; it led to the reversal of the political gains of the Reconstruction period and spawned the iniquitous injustices of the apartheid South.

In some areas regiments of Black soldiers and slaves did seize the lands of planters; some few union generals did turn over abandoned lands to former slaves; and the Freedman's Bureau, established during Reconstruction to assist the liberated people, did lease some land to the former slaves. Thus a limited number became small farmers in the South. They and their descendants clung to the land, but their hold was gradually destroyed by the racist offensive that continues to this day.

Gradually losing ownership of the land, the Black farmers were forced into sharecropping—a semi-feudal form of tenancy. The principal crop was cotton, and mechanization in the 1930s and 1940s destroyed even this level of relationship to the land. In 1960 there were still 2.6 million "Negro and other" people living on farms, 16.4% of the total farm population. But the number was more than halved each decade, so that by 1990 there were only 113,000 "Black and other races" living on farms, 2.5% of the total.[1] Of these, probably not more than half were African Americans. However, several million African Americans continue to live in rural southern, largely segregated, villages, with only occasional farm labor and little other work available.

The decline in farm *ownership* and operation was even more drastic. From 689,000 farms operated by Blacks and other minority people in 1945, at the end of World War II—the majority tenant farmers—the number fell to 104,000 by 1969 and to 23,000 by 1987, of whom only 4,000 were really full-time commercial farmers with sales of more than $10,000. The number was even slightly less than the largely dispossessed Latino farmers.[2]

The long-time ouster of African Americans from the land in the South has resulted in their translocation to inner city ghettos, North and South. It also prevented their accumulation of capital and formation of a substantial capitalist sector. Historically, in the United States as well as in other major capitalist countries, land ownership and the exploitation of farm labor has been a prime source of accumulation of capital.

The Origins of Black Capitalism

During the frightful post-Reconstruction decades of Jim Crow and lynch law, Black educator Booker T. Washington, backed by white capitalists, founded Tuskegee Institute in Alabama. There Black youth were taught craft skills and some business methods. Washington urged African Americans to accommodate to oppression, not to resist it; to be good workmen, and for some to seek advancement in the business world. Towards that end he organized the National Negro Business League in Boston. He became the Establishment-appointed spokesman for the Black people, and his institute was granted $600,000 by steel magnate Andrew Carnegie. Early in the 20th century he acted as go-between in the appointment of Blacks to federal jobs.

In the 1920s Marcus Garvey preached liberation with his plan for the African American masses to go back to Africa and set up businesses there. He raised millions of dollars from among the Black people to set up a steamship line to carry travelers to Africa. It went bankrupt and Garvey was imprisoned, then deported to his native Jamaica.

Washington and Garvey, however misguided, reflected the aspirations of Black people for *a means of escape* from their oppression. And white capitalists encouraged the concept of Black capitalism as a means of maintaining that oppression, while blocking off normal routes through which Blacks might become capitalists.

In 1969 the Nixon Administration and heads of leading corporations joined the campaign for "Black capitalism," urging African Americans to become capitalists in their own ghettos and propagandizing the opportunities for them to become bureaucrats in large companies.

All of these movements had a common theme, and all aimed to divert the Black people from mass struggle against their oppressors. It was futile to encourage efforts to obtain improvement for the masses via the elevation of a few African Americans to the capitalist class.

W.E.B. Du Bois, the most progressive and honored African American over a span of many decades, was basically oriented to a program of mass struggle. Although not always free of illusions, he clashed with Washington and Garvey and later, when he became oriented to the working class and socialism, he wrote:

> I saw clearly...that the solution of letting a few of our capitalists share with whites in the exploitation of our masses, would never be a solution of our problems, but the forging of eternal chains.[3]

If Washington and Garvey started movements on their own initiative, the recent Black capitalism campaign was hatched in the boardrooms of U.S. corporations and in the political power center. It was revived at the time of the upsurge of Black liberation struggles, and business and government leaders made a major propaganda campaign for it. The government appropriated hundreds of millions of dollars to support it and leaders of a number of the petty bourgeois radical Black organizations were won over to it and took on jobs within its framework—the Black Panthers, CORE, e.g. Other groups, such as the Rev. Jesse Jackson's PUSH, attempted to combine mass actions for jobs and other gains of workers with a focus on winning financial support for various aspects of Black capitalism.

An important aspect of the Black capitalism drive was the much vaunted program of financial assistance to Black enterprises. The projection of loans and subsidies, presented to the public as some sort of special benefit, as the acme of civil rights promotion, was nothing of the kind. *Far from representing a special benefit to minority business, the much-touted federal expenditures on their behalf cover up a continuation of gross discrimination against them.*

The total of government investment capital and procurement contracts awarded to U.S. business came to more than $100 billion in fiscal 1973. The share of all minority enterprises was less than 1%, and of Black business, less than 0.5%.[4] Even in order to bring the share of minorities up to their share in the population, the amount of federal orders, loans, and grants to them would have to be multiplied 20 times. And even more would be needed to start to overcome the discrimination within the private capitalist world so as to include actual "special assistance" for minority business.

The government's campaign to aid Black capitalism practically collapsed with the Nixon Administration, but the concept remained alive in Establishment propaganda. For example, the federal Small Business Administration (SBA) provides assistance to enterprises through loans and loan guarantees. It is not a large program, and the share going to minority businesses is very meager indeed, considering the fact that almost all Black and Latino businesses are small and their access to standard commercial credit is very limited. Moreover, the minority share of SBA loans has declined, and the amount of such loans, in real terms, has at best stagnated: from 23% in 1970 and 15% in 1973 their share fell to 11% in 1990 and 13% in 1992. The amount of the loans to minority firms has also had a downward trend: from $578 million in 1970 and $1,057 million 1973 to $508 million in 1980 and $808 million in 1992 (all expressed in 1992 dollars)—see Chart 9A.[5]

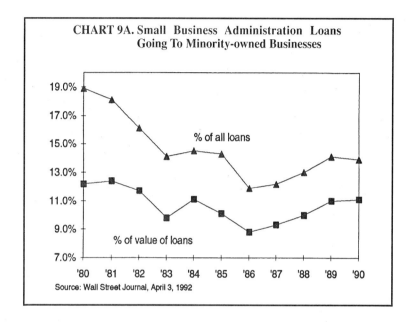

CHART 9A. Small Business Administration Loans Going To Minority-owned Businesses

% of all loans

% of value of loans

Source: Wall Street Journal, April 3, 1992

To interpret these figures, consider that the minority population went up sharply as a percentage of the total population in this period of more than two decades, so their share of loans should have increased. Further, since the Latino and Asian populations have risen and their small business position improved relative to that of African Americans, it follows that the downtrend of SBA loans to Black enterprises has continued. The minority share of SBA loans increased to 19% in 1994, in figures not completely comparable with those cited above.

Governments, state and local as well as federal, carry out diminishing portions of their activity through direct government investment and employment of personnel. Instead, private companies are awarded huge government contracts for various investments and services. In the case of the federal government, the largest and most expensive contracts are for military and related purposes.

Federal government contracts in 1991 came to $186 billion, of which only $6.7 billion—3.6%—went to minority contractors.[6]

African American contractors have never succeeded in obtaining more than a miniscule share of government contracts. In 1987 Black construction firms received only 1.04% of all contractor and sub-contractor revenues. Responding to public pressure, a number of local governments issued affirmative action set-asides for Black contractors. But even this inadequate concession has a dubious future in view of Supreme Court decisions against "quotas."

Evidence of judicial discrimination was blatant in the case of Richmond, Virginia. With a population of 50% African Americans, Black contractors got less than 1% of the contracts. In the landmark *City of Richmond vs. Croson* ruling, the U.S. Supreme Court ruled that the trivial share of contracts awarded to Black firms was no basis for claiming discrimination, and the Richmond set-aside program was thrown out. This decision was stark proof of the overt racism of the Supreme Court majority.

That decision, in 1989, had serious consequences:

> ...the record shows that after the Supreme Court decision, which terminated Richmond's set-aside program, many state and local jurisdictions have suspended or abolished their own programs on grounds of reverse discrimination. It also shows that after programs are suspended, the black share of public contracts drops drastically. Since discrimination against blacks continues, reinstituting or adopting race-conscious programs in the construction industry is justified.[7]

Even before the Supreme Court decision, the business of Black contractors had been stagnant over the previous decade. In 1977, their share of revenues, 1.03%, was virtually unchanged by 1987.

> To a large extent, the disparity in black participation is because of bias...documented in officially sponsored studies [in many areas] by Brimmer & Co., a Washington, D.C.-based economic consulting firm...
>
> ...evidence reinforced Brimmer & Co.'s conclusion: Racial bias is widespread and deeply rooted in the construction industry.
>
> The discrimination is facilitated by industry organization, policy and practice... Common threads, such as apprenticeship systems and trade unions, help connect the construction industry. Moreover, there is an old-boy network composed entirely of white males. The key link is the local contractors' association, but other trade associations and clubs also alert members about important information and early warnings of upcoming contracts.

The situation isn't quite as bad in public sector construction because of the prevalence of public bidding for jobs. But

Frequently the officials letting public contracts belong to the old-boy network. Once a contract has been awarded, the GC [general contractor] normally shares work with subcontractors who are part of their network.[8]

Extent of Black Capitalism

Since 1969 there have been periodic Census surveys of Black and other "minority" enterprises. These show Black business stuck in the same trivial, marginal role in U.S. capitalist enterprise, with sales at about one-fifth of one percent (.20%) and employment at one-fourth of one percent (.25%) of all private companies. Total employment by Black-owned firms amounted to between 1.5% and 2% of the number of African Americans in the labor force. Of course not all employees of Black-owned firms are Black, but even if they were, it would hardly make a significant contribution to the job problems of African Americans (see Tables 9:1 and 9:2). Note that data in the tables ends with 1987. No information from the 1992 Census of Minority Enterprises will be released until the second half of 1995. This is unfortunate in that it makes it difficult to assess the impact of the 1991-93 cyclical crisis and depression on Black companies.

* TABLE 9:1: COMPARISON OF SALES BLACK BUSINESSES AND ALL
  PRIVATE BUSINESSES, CENSUS YEARS, 1969-1987

Year	Sales ($billions)		% Black of Total
	Black Firms	All Private Firms	
1969	4.474	2,009	0.22
1972	5.861	2,557	0.23
1977	8.645	4,699	0.18
1982	12.444	7,755	0.19
1987	19.763	10,621	0.19

(Sources: Black firms: Respective Censuses of Minority Business. All private firms: *Stat. Abst.* 1993, Tables 850, 851,855 pp.532, 533, 535 for 1987; similar tables in earlier issues for earlier years.)
*See Appendix, p. 297.

Thus, between 1969 and 1987, sales of Black firms multiplied 4.5 times and of all private firms more than five times—not surprising considering the three-fold jump in prices and the growth in population. The table confirms the fact that Black business has made no gains—a decline, actually-in its overall position in the economy: from 0.22% of total sales in 1969 to 0.19% in 1987.

The Census Bureau, in a futile attempt to gild the lily, put out a release asserting that Black business sales were 1% of the total of all U.S. sales receipts, using a figure for the U.S. total of about $2 trillion instead of the actuality—more than $10 trillion. Their trick is to compare the total for *all* Black firms with that for all *small* firms.

TABLE 9:2. TOTAL EMPLOYMENT IN BLACK ENTERPRISES AND IN ALL
PRIVATE BUSINESS; BLACK EMPLOYMENT AS A PERCENT-
AGE OF BLACK-OWNED FIRMS AND ALL PRIVATE FIRMS

Year	Employment (thousands)		Labor Force (thousands)	Percentages Black Employment of total employment	
	Black Firms	All Private	Black	All Private	in Black firms, of Black labor force
1969	152	58,200	8,000	0.26%	1.9%
1972	147	60,300	8,708	0.24%	1.7%
1977	164	67,300	9,933	0.24%	1.7%
1982	166	73,700	11,331	0.23%	1.5%
1987	220	85,200	12,993	0.26%	1.7%

(SOURCES: Black employment: Census of Minority Business, respective years Private sector employment: BLS data contained in *Business Statistics*, 1961-88, p.46; Black labor force: BLS, various publications.)

Researchers Marcus Alexis and Geraldine R. Henderson comment on the inability of Black firms to supply African American consumers with their needs:

> African-Americans are a large market, about one-quarter of $1 trillion per year—more than most countries in the world. This market, for the most part, is not being served by African-American businesses, whose sales are less than one-tenth of African-American purchases ($19.7 billion for businesses versus $216 billion for households). Much of the income that enters African-American communities soon leaves them... Middle Eastern and Asian merchants have won significant market shares in the Bedford Stuyvesant section of Brooklyn and in South Central Los Angeles, despite large African-American populations there. African-American sellers cannot rely on race alone to attract patronage; the race-patronage link is not strong in African-American communities. Black consumers desire quality goods at reasonable prices, knowledgeable sales people, and respect. These should be readily available from motivated African-Americans.[9]

Comments such as these may be misused to fuel Black-Asian hostility, as previously white owners of local convenience stores were used to fuel Black-white (Jewish, Italian, etc.) hostility. The main plunderers of the African American people and the main exploiters of their labor are the large capitalists of all races—mainly white, of course—who rarely locate banks, well-stocked chain stores, or other well-equipped and efficient service establishments in ghetto communities. Also, few African Americans are employed in the communities where they live.

It is a fact, unfortunately, that Black capitalists cannot be considered particular friends of the Black working class—or workers of any race. Indeed, Black bosses exploit their workers, Black and white, as do all capitalists.

TABLE 9:3. AVERAGE ANNUAL WAGES AND SALARIES PAID
by Type of Ownership, 1987

All Industries:	All Owners	Women Owners	Black Owners	Black as % of Total
Total	$20,168	$13,176	$12,612	63.5%
With less than 20 employees	17,946	NA	(12,612)*	70.3
Manufacturing:				
Total	25,475	19,099	17,810	69.9
With less than 20 employees	20,746	NA	(17,810)*	85.8

* Estimated. Practically all Black-owned firms employ less than 20 workers
(Source: *Stat. Abst.*: 1991, Ts. 873,874,875, pp.532-33)

Table 9:3 shows that wages of workers in Black-owned establishments were less than two-thirds of the average for all firms, and 70% the average for small firms—and most Black-owned firms are small. Part of the shortfall in wages was due to the sectoral distribution of Black ownership, focusing on low-wage service and other industries. However, wages in Black manufacturing firms were also only 70% of wages paid by all manufacturing firms, and 86% of the wages in small manufacturing companies. Black owners also paid lower wages than women owners.

The increasing exploitation of labor by Black employers is indicated by the rising value of sales per employee, from $47,000 in 1982 to $64,000 in 1987. By comparison, average sales per employee in all firms in 1987 was $43,000. This may be qualified by considering that most Black firms are very small, in which the employer and members of his family may also work. But the same applies, although to a lesser degree, in small white-owned firms.

In fact, most of the more than 300,000 Black-owned companies are one-person, or one-family operations, without hired workers. Objectively, these are self-employed workers, mainly in blue-collar or service occupations, but also including a small number of professionals. Available data indicate that the average gross revenues of these self-employed persons have been dropping sharply in real terms and, as of 1987, were actually less than the average wages paid by the 70,000 Black-owned firms that hired workers. This indicates that many of the Black independents who file business returns may be among the large numbers of laid-off workers and employees who try to get by by setting up home businesses, or telemarketing, etc.

Only a few hundred Black-owned companies with hired workers have labor earnings of $10 million or more.

Women and Minorities

Not only has the growth of Black business been insignificant—stagnant in fact, in relation to the entire economy—but it has been substantially surpassed by the scale of Latino-owned business, and even more by Asian-owned business. Latino business is also small compared with the Latino population, and its growth has also been slow.

In referring to ownership of capital, the Census grouping "women and minorities" is especially deceptive. Women—overwhelmingly white women—have rapidly increased their ownership position in American business enterprises: their sales were 14 times those of Black-owned firms in 1987.

TABLE 9:4. SALES OF FIRMS OWNED BY WOMEN AND "MINORITIES," 1987 (BILLIONS OF DOLLARS)

Category of Owners	Sales and Receipts
Women	$278
Asians	33
Latinos	25
African Americans	20
Native Americans	1
All Firms	10,621

Obviously American big business is still decisively a "man's world." Women capitalists often inherit their ownership from deceased spouses, and it is white men who have the substantial interests and investments to bequeath.

Since 1987 Asian ownership of U.S. businesses has escalated. This category includes Koreans and others who emigrate with capital from their homeland, or who can borrow needed capital from Asian-owned banks in the United States. U.S. branches of the giant Japanese banks are prominent in financing Japanese-Americans, as well as people of other races and ethnic origin. But more important are the large stakes of major Japanese and other Asian corporations in the U.S economy: by 1991 Japanese-owned companies in the United States had an investment of $97 billion, sales of $320 billion, and paid $28 billion in compensation to 706,000 employees.[10]

Franchising and Unions

An increasing form of business operation in the United States is franchising. That is, small capitalists buy franchises to operate individual units (like branches) of the parent company—e.g., service stations, restaurants, outlets of national chains marketing shoes, sporting goods, etc. Through these franchises, giant corporations "leverage" their capital, raising their rate of profit. The franchise purchasers provide the basic capital plus up-front fees and they remit a percentage of their sales, keeping only a narrow margin themselves, which can only be realized by paying low wages. The U.S. Department of Commerce estimated that in the early 1990s there were 550,000 franchises with annual sales of $758 billion. As in other lines of enterprise, Black and Latino capitalists have a tough time getting the capital, including bank loans, to buy franchises. Altogether, the Commerce Department estimates that 2.5% of franchises are minority owned.

Fast food operations and cleaning establishment chains are significant here. As of 1991 Black franchisers had 509 of the 11,000 McDonald's units. But 500 of Coverall North America, a commercial cleaning firm with a total of 1,729 units, were franchised to African Americans. The substantial Black share in this category signifies the reorganization of janitorial work, to which Blacks were historically consigned, so that intensified exploitation is now imposed on the cleaning sector.

Frequently Black executives in corporations, laid off in the waves of downsizing, use their accumulated savings and severance pay to buy a franchise—some require "only" tens of thousands of dollars of initial capital. That's not so with Burger King, rated fifth in the magazine *Black Enterprise*'s list of the largest 50 Black franchise shops. Start-up costs for a Burger King franchise are $250,000-$350,000. African Americans in 1991 held only 150 of the more than 5,000 Burger King franchises.[11]

Shops of that kind are difficult for unions to organize: most workers are young and take the jobs to fill in until something better comes along; work is part-time; shifts are irregular, etc. In 1987-88, a Black capitalist bought three Burger King franchises in Detroit, with its predominantly Black population. A majority of the approximately 50 workers in the three units signed union cards for the Food and Commercial Workers Union, AFL-CIO, which asked for an NLRB election. To defeat the union, the employer raised wages a dollar an hour above the minimum, got rid of and replaced many workers, gave a few employees straw boss jobs. Black business organizations in Detroit supported the owner, and African Americans on the board of the Detroit branch of the Coalition of Black Trade Unionists (CBTU) were able to prevent a full

CBTU endorsement of the organizing campaign. The union lost the election by a 3 to 2 vote.

Needless to say, African American capitalists are no worse than white capitalists in their anti-union campaigns. Neither are they better: they are capitalists first and African Americans second when it comes to labor relations—even if all their workers are Black.

The Black Enterprise 100

Beginning in 1973, the magazine *Black Enterprise* has published the list of the 100 largest Black-owned industrial and service companies. The sales of the 100 have grown considerably faster than the sales of all Black-owned firms, just as the largest corporations have grown most rapidly in the overall economy. Sales of the top 100 went up from $2.3 billion in 1982 to $6.7 billion in 1994. However, $1.8 billion of the 1994 total reflected the sales of Beatrice International Holdings, Inc., consisting solely of the European operations of a splitoff from a larger United States corporation, and having no significant impact on the U.S. economy. The increase of 113% in the sales of the other 99 companies approximates the percentage rise in GNP (gross domestic product), over the same period.

In addition to the 100 largest Black-owned industrial and service companies, beginning in 1987 *Black Enterprise* has listed the 100 largest Black-owned auto dealerships. By 1994 the combined sales of these 200 companies totalled $11.7 billion, and their employment of 48,000 was about one-fifth the employment of all Black-owned firms.[12]

The $4,123 million sales of the 100 top automotive dealers in 1993 came to almost exactly 1% of all motor vehicle dealers that year. The 100 largest account for about one-half of total sales of all Black-owned automotive dealers, so the Black share of the market is about 2%.[13]

In the 1960s, when Civil Rights laws and public opinion called for affirmative action, the Big Three auto companies, led by Ford, decided to get some Black dealers with an eye to winning sales in African American communities, as well as to gain general approbation. That is why the share of Black business in autos, small as it is, stands out in comparison with the trivial share of Blacks in overall business activity.

Black and other "minority" auto dealers suffered severe losses, and many were driven out of business, during the 1990-92 economic crisis. All told, there are about 700 Black, Latino and Asian auto dealers in the United States, somewhat more than 3% of all dealers. African Americans account for more than half the minority dealers.

Many Blacks, Hispanics, and Asian-Americans were encouraged to buy dealerships, mainly because of special recruiting efforts by the Big Three U.S. auto makers. These programs were aimed, in part, at expanding the manufacturers' appeal in minority communities.

But now, some of the same dealers who benefitted from these programs say they're being swamped by the heavy debts they took on to foot the $1 million average cost of getting a dealership off the ground. And minority dealers say it doesn't help that many of them got franchises in economically depressed neighborhoods or thinly populated rural areas...

Judson Powell, for example,says it isn't slow sales that are pushing his dealership into the red, but high rent and high interest rates on loans from Ford... "It's sort of like being a sharecropper," contends Mr. Powell... "Everything I make I owe to Ford."

Mr. Powell says he isn't sure how much longer the dealerships will survive.[14]

As with capitalist firms generally, the larger Black-owned firms succeeded in getting more out of fewer workers. Between 1991 and 1992, their sales and receipts rose 14% while their employment dropped 2%.[15] All of the 200 top firms had sales of $10 million or more, but their combined sales—$9 billion— was less than the sales of each of more than 50 white-owned corporations, and the top white corporations sell more than ten times that. The listed Black-owned companies suffered extreme instability, with the impact of racial discrimination adding to the overall unpredictability of the system and the pressure of the largest monopolies on a small and medium-sized firms.

Only seven companies made the *BE* list of 100 every year during the first 20 years of its publication.

Black Finance

The situation of Blacks in finance is especially weak. As of 1992 only 77 Black-owned banks, savings and loans and insurance companies had come to the attention of *Black Enterprise*, six fewer than the year before. The reduction reflected the special vulnerability of Black-owned companies to the economic crisis of 1990-92.

As of 1994, *Business Week* listed the 25 largest Black banks and savings and loan companies, with combined assets of $3.2 billion, and employing 1,901 workers. Black banks participated only modestly in the business growth of that recovery year. They were largely, perforce, focused on a "niche" business, servicing the financial needs of inner-city residents and enterprises. But because of the poverty of the residents, and reduction in Government programs for "community redevelopment," African American banks were especially loaded with weaker loans, more likely to default than the average. One victim of the financial crisis of the early 1990s was the Freedom National Bank of Harlem, New York City, which had a certain symbolic significance

and served as a repository of the funds of a number of African American organizations, churches, etc. When Freedom National failed, the Federal Deposit
Insurance Company (FDIC) refused to pay off depositors of more than
$100,000 in the bank, although it waived the legal restriction and paid off
completely large depositors in most of the hundreds of failed white-owned
banks and insurance companies.

This treatment must be contrasted with the hundreds of billions of U.S,
taxpayers' money used to bail out depositors in the wave of savings-and-loan
failures a few years earlier.

As of 1994, *Black Enterprise* listed the 15 largest Black owned insurance
companies, with combined assets of only $0.7 billion, employing 3,026 work-
ers. Black insurance companies had a traditional role in the South, selling
burial insurance to poor people, for which small weekly premiums were collected; 13 of the 15 insurance companies listed are in the South. Fifteen Black
investment banks were also listed, participating in the distribution of government bond issues, made available through set-aside programs of one sort or
another. They were especially vulnerable to the Republican onslaught on set-
aside programs, and one Black investment bank, Daniels and Bell, folded,
thereby losing the only Black-owned seat on the New York Stock Exchange,
a strategic necessity for large-scale profitable business.

Government and Corporate Bureaucracies

Reports of the EEOC and the Commerce Department show that the
fastest-growing occupational category among Blacks is that of executives and
managers, even though Blacks are pitifully underrepresented in total higher-
level employment.

Increased elections of Black and Latino members of Congress, state legislatures, and as Mayors resulted, in turn, in these officials and representatives
increasing the hiring of minority personnel to top-ranking positions. On the
national level, also, even Republican administrations tend to increase their
promotion of minority officials, in consideration of their increased overall
role among the voting population. Perversely, Republicans, in their assault
against affirmative action, have given substantial publicity to the ideology of
Black conservatives who provide rationalizations for attacking affirmative
action. Their objective is to win away the upper layers, economically, of the
Black population from traditional support of the Democratic Party.

In turn, the weakened Democratic Party strives especially to maintain its
lead in this respect. President Clinton, in the mid-1990s, claimed to have
nearly doubled the number of appointments of Black officials, even though he
shamefully repudiated those of his nominees selected for special attack by the

Republicans. Indicative of the new significance of this factor, the African American who became chairman of the Joint Chief of Staffs, General Colin Powell, made prominent by his role in the war against Iraq, was widely discussed as a possible presidential contender.

Especially important is the growing participation of African Americans in the corporate bureaucracy. For giant transnational corporations, this is important in terms of relationships with many foreign countries and, even more for companies providing consumer goods and services, in obtaining the business of Black and Latino customers. Thus Sears Roebuck, in its 1992 annual report, stressed its increased employment of Blacks from 5.9% of the total in 1966 to 14.8% in 1992. But most striking was the increase in employment of officials and managers from 0.4% to 6.7% and of professionals from 0.8% to 7.9% of totals in these categories.[16]

True, both in government and in corporations, "minorities" are shunted off into non-strategic departments, and face discrimination in promotions.

However, the fact remains that there are now several hundred thousand African Americans in the upper reaches of the corporate structure. They have become part of the capitalist class—in their income level, their relationship with workers, and their ideology. As such, they have a significant political impact on the Black community, and it is an influence that attempts to limit the scope of movements of the African American people, to brake their militancy, and to control Black elected officials, who depend upon them for campaign funds.

The growing Black participation in the corporate bureaucracy and the widening income differentials in the African American community—along with the weakening of the trade union movement and of left progressive forces within the trade union movement—had a significant impact on the direction of civil rights movements and organizations during the 1980s and early 1990s. These movements, and the Black politicians and elected officials, focused on progressive issues such as higher minimum wages, the right to organize, government spending for jobs, etc., and played an important role in this respect. But the struggle for effective measures against discrimination, measures that require affirmative action programs—with quotas—in the spheres of employment, and education; large housing programs designed to desegregate; and other measures, were muted. Those specific affirmative action proposals put forth in organizational programs, conferences, etc., were often focused on aid to Black business, ghetto economic development, etc.

Dr. Andrew Brimmer, the first African American member of the Federal Reserve Board, now heads his own research firm. He is an insightful and objective observer of Black capitalism. What he said two decades ago is fully applicable today.

He told an NAACP audience in 1971 he was "afraid of a schism develop-ing" between "a handful of Black people" who are "doing a hell of a lot bet-ter than any of us thought they would do," and the "vast proportion" of Black people "who still do not have marketable skills." He was "particularly dis-tressed" by the declining emphasis on job opportunities, in contrast to a ris-ing demand for expanded opportunities for Blacks to own and manage their own businesses.

Brimmer went on to say:

> I must hasten to add that, while I personally have serious reservations about many of the numerous programs aimed, hopefully, at increasing business ownership by Blacks, I believe that those Black men and women who are convinced that they can succeed in business should have a chance to try their luck.[17]

Brimmer's ambivalent approach is justified. To see the fallacy of Black capitalism as the solution for mass Black inequality and oppression is one thing. But the demand for the *right* of Blacks to own businesses and to obtain high positions in the corporate and governmental bureaucracy is valid, through of limited economic impact. Part of the entire democratic struggle in the country requires that Black capitalists and would-be capitalists have all of the necessary access to credits, supplies, government subsidies and loans, technical aids, etc., that are necessary for their success. Given the historical pattern of discrimination and exclusion from business opportunity, this requirement means much more than the elimination of existing gross dis-crimination against Black businesses. It requires real, as distinguished from token, special government assistance and guarantees, on a very large scale, to provide the possibility of Black capitalists making definite headway in over-coming their past virtual exclusion from industry and finance, and from con-trolling positions generally in the national economy.

This issue, nonetheless, remains a *secondary* element in any progressive program for equality and liberation from racist oppression. The demands of the masses of oppressed minorities, connected with and part of the demands of the working class as a whole, must have priority, including the struggle against exploitation by all capitalists. Indeed, the programs advanced by pro-gressives all project a reduction in profits and a limit to the scope of capital. Objectively, this means moving in the direction of socialism, which would eliminate capitalists as a class, while utilizing the managerial and professional skills of all—African Americans, Latinos, whites and all others—in the inter-ests of all the people.

Right-Wing Assault Against Black Business

Black-owned businesses are prime targets in the right-wing campaign against affirmative action. Black capitalists have been especially dependent on clear-cut affirmative action programs, the preferences and "quotas" which are the key terms racists vilify in their major campaign of the 1990s against affirmative action. Percentage set-asides for Black contractors and subcontractors on government contracts at various levels have been relatively more significant to Black capital than preferences in employment have been to Black workers. A *Black Enterprise* article is headed: "An all out assault on minority preference contracts threatens to dismantle many Black-owned businesses." The article begins:

> When members of the Republican Party began to plan their assault on affirmative action earlier this year they needed a symbol in the tradition of Willie Horton and "welfare queens."

They selected a minority tax break for companies that sell media properties to minorities. Using an attempt of Black capitalists headed by Frank Washington to buy the Viacom cable system, which didn't go through, as a target,

> Washington and Viacom have become symbols of evrything conservatives say is wrong with minority set-asides: that as a policy, it is economically ineffective, administratively inefficient and ultimately unfair.

Black capitalists argue that set-asides of shares of government contracts for minorities merely help "level the playing field" against the tens of billions of subsidies and other advantages which are granted to giant multinational corporations.

Republicans like House Majority Leader Newt Gingrich "argue that race-and-gender based preference systems discriminate against others—read: white males."

At stake for Black entrepreneurs in this is the very existence of their businesses. According to a 1994 survey of 70 of the 100 largest Black-owned companies, "more than 58% noted that at least half of their business was in the public sector. According to Harriet Mitchell, president of the National Minority Supplier Development Council, 'Without direct mechanisms to ensure inclusion, African American business will decline precipitously.'"

As in other areas, the Democrats have retreated before, and effectively collaborated with, the Republican assault:

In April, President Bill Clinton signed legislation to eliminate the minority tax provision, surrendering the first battle in a major legislative fight to repeal set-asides and affirmative action laws in the United States."[18]

"Black banks and thrifts have found there ain't no hiding place from the onslaught of the new Republican Right on a roll." In 1994 the Treasury Department phased out for small banks the use of interest-free government loans, a standard practice remaining in effect for larger banks. Since all Black-owned banks are small, they are all hit by this provision.

Black capitalists have formed a PAC (Political Action Committee) to fight anti-affirmative action efforts.[19]

A conference of Black economists held in the spring of 1995 made the Republican "Contract With America" the centerpiece of its deliberations, considering it a major attack on the entire Black population, especially the working class and the poor. It's significant that the conference was sponsored by the magazine *Black Enterprise*. Groupings of Black capitalists have much better access to the media and to political leadership than do such working class groups as CBTU; but even the arguments of Black capitalists and economists in their corner obtain very little broad publicity, and are swamped by the massive propaganda of the right-wing racist offensive.

10. Who Gains and Who Loses From Racism?

There can be no doubt that cupidity—the unbridled drive for wealth—was the motive for the brutal capture and inhumane transport of Africans to enslavement in the United States. So, today, capitalists derive superprofits from the immoral discrimination imposed against minority peoples—especially African Americans, Latinos and Native Americans—in all aspects of life. That's one side of the story.

The other side is the material losses of those who are the victims of racism, especially the monetary losses. Direct superprofits from discrimination are not the only gains of the capitalist class from racism, nor do the wage/salary income losses of Blacks measure the total costs to them. While these direct extra profits are the basic material motive for racism, and the income differentials are the primary loss to those victimized; and while these basic factors can be measured with reasonable approximations, other material costs are more difficult—or impossible—to estimate.

These most serious effects of racism and discrimination, which do incalculable damage to all victims, include the attempts to undermine their racial pride, dignity and self respect; to deny them social acceptance, recognition of ability and, most important, equality of status. They are subjected to police brutality, criminalization of their youth, inadequate social facilities, etc.

Slavery was the most extreme manifestation of the despotism imposed on the captive Africans. And, just as those subjugated peoples rebelled against the slave owners, so today the oppressed minorities—especially the African Americans—are protesting against these chauvinistic credos, which are as onerous to their spirits as homelessness, hunger and joblessness are to their daily well-being.

What Minorities Lose

I estimate the material losses of oppressed peoples in 1992 at $522 billion, with more than half of the total—$275 billion—sustained by African Americans (see Table 10:1 and Chart 10A). Losses more than doubled in the 20-year period 1972-1992, with the rise in the population of oppressed accounting for 75% of the increase, and the decrease in real per capita income of minorities for 25%. Added losses of Latinos, Native Americans and Asians were highest because their populations rose most rapidly. However, Asians as a whole were not so badly hit relative to their population because so many of them are either middle to highly paid salaried personnel, professionals, or proprietors.

Going back to the mid-1950s, losses due to racism have multiplied 3.7 times! The 1955 *Economic Report of the President* estimated the loss at $20 billion for 1954.[1] The following year John Roosevelt, son of F.D.R., raised the ante to $30 billion.[2] So, splitting the difference to $25 billion as a consensus estimate for 1955, the amount would be $141 billion in 1995 prices. (These data refer to all minorities.)

But I have made estimates of African American losses for various years since 1972, and Billy J. Tidwell of the National Urban League has made estimates for Black losses for the years 1980 through 1988. (His method of calculation is consistent with mine.)

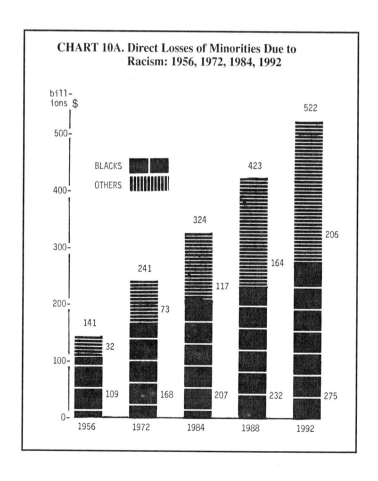

CHART 10A. Direct Losses of Minorities Due to Racism: 1956, 1972, 1984, 1992

TABLE 10:1. LOSSES OF MINORITIES DUE TO RACISM, SELECTED
YEARS, 1955-1992, Billions of 1995 Dollars

Year	Blacks	Hispanics	Others	Total
1955				141
1972	168	73*		241
1984	207	117*		324
1988	232	164	27	423
1992	275	206	41	522

* Includes Asians and Native Americans
(Amounts converted to 1992 dollars with use of CPI-U (consumer price index for urban consumers).
Sources: Data adjusted to 1995 prices by use of CPI
1955: Average of 1954 and 1956 estimates
1954: *EROP* 1955, quoted in Tidwell, p.59
1955: John Roosevelt, quoted in *Economics of Racism*, p.149
1972: Perlo, *Economics of Racism*, pp.150-151
1984: Perlo: *Superprofits and Crises*, p.94
1988: Blacks: Tidwell, p.63
Hispanics and Others: P-60, no. 172, T. B-15, p.377. Losses equal to difference in per capita
income from non-Hispanic white per capita income, multiplied by numbers of minority people:
5% added to allow for undercount of Hispanics and Others.
1992: Calculated from P-60, No. 184, T. B-19, p.B-38. Losses estimated as equal to differences
of mean per capita income from mean per capita income of non-Hispanic whites, multiplied by
number of minority people. 5% added to allow for undercount of minorities.
Data adjusted to 1995 prices by use of consumer price index (CPU).
The data for 1992 include a 5% addition to allow for the undercount of the Black and Latino
populations in the 1990 Census, which is consistent with published estimates. But this does not
allow for the income losses of prisoners—tripled in number on probation or parole, who are, naturally, reluctant to talk to Census takers. Also, many minority people lack telephones, by which
surveys are made, and the rising number of homeless people should also be considered.

By 1995, it is safe to say, losses of oppressed peoples due to racism
exceeded $600 billion, approximately 8% of the gross domestic product. And
this does not include the very substantial penalty they pay due to price discrimination for consumers goods and services, in receipt of health, educational and other services.

How Does Racism Affect the Labor Force?

Racist propaganda asserts that the Black workers' gains are the white
workers' loss, and vice versa. The arguments used to try to convince white
workers of this are:
  • If Black workers are hired, white workers will lose their jobs:
  • If Black workers are promoted and their wages are raised, it will be at
the expense of higher wages and promotions for white workers.
Unfortunately, many white workers are influenced by this propaganda that
portrays Black workers as their economic rivals. But there is fundamental fal-

lacy in the arguments—the implication that there is a fixed number of jobs, a fixed total of wages to be distributed among the working population as a whole so that the gains of one group of workers are at the expense of other workers. This goes back to the "wage fund" theory popularized at the start of the 19th Century by Thomas Malthus, John R. MacCulloch, James Mill, and other economists who provided the theoretical basis for the brutal exploitation of labor on which British industrial dominance of that period was built.

Malthus also included the concept that the earth could support only a certain fixed population, already reached at the time of his writing. The idiocy of the whole theory is proved by the many times multiplication of both population and total wages in the past two centuries.

But Malthusianism, in all its main variants, has been revived recently—with the particular purpose of spurring racism in both domestic and foreign affairs.

A modern version of Malthusian economics is the contention that any increase in wages causes a corresponding rise in prices, so that real wages do not advance. A more "reasonable" position is that the share of wages in the total product cannot increase, so that wages cannot go up more than the average productivity of labor.

But this is contrary to the basic principal of labor organization and labor struggle at the most elementary level of trade union consciousness. The workers' position, throughout the history of the labor movement, has been that workers' gains are at the expense of capital, that the total social product can increase and labor's share in it can increase as well. In this respect, workers have really followed the position pioneered by Karl Marx in his practical work with the British trade unionists. And this includes a majority of U.S. workers who are ignorant of Marx's work.

Under the Malthusian principle, it would appear that any gain of white workers would have to be at the expense of some other group of workers, most notably Black workers, and, on the other hand, that any gain of Black workers would be at the expense of white workers.

However, the main policies of the U.S. labor movement have been anti-Malthusian. For example, organized workers provided the momentum for enactment of minimum wage legislation, and led campaigns for raising and broadening the coverage of the minimum wages. Workers at all levels know that raising minimum wages helps improve their own wages and working conditions.

Workers often strike for the reinstatement of workers discharged by the arbitrary action of a supervisor, or as a penalty for militancy. They know that the security of their jobs will be enhanced, not reduced, by saving the jobs of those let go by the employer.

Trade unions lead the fight for more federal jobs for the unemployed, knowing that these jobs are not at the expense of existing jobs, but help to protect them from unemployment, and strengthen the bargaining position of privately employed workers.

And now there are more than 15 million Black workers who have been systematically discriminated against. Many have never been permitted to hold a steady job. The *majority* have never been promoted to jobs matching their capability, or given the special training required where that is necessary. They have been concentrated in special job categories with lower incomes, and discriminated against in a thousand different ways.

Will ending this discrimination injure the position of white workers as a whole, or of a majority of white workers, or of individual white workers? On the contrary, it can only contribute to improvement of the situation of white workers as a whole and need not injure the situation of a single white worker.

Logically, campaigns for equality for Black workers should be accompanied by campaigns providing gains for all workers. Usually groups struggling for equality do include both kinds of demands such as fair employment for Blacks in the skilled construction crafts, plus a big expansion in the housing program and construction employment overall. But it is only when whites and Blacks unite around both halves of such programs that, under the real conditions existing in the United States, major gains can be won. When trade unions and other organizations try to campaign *only* for the general goals of workers, without simultaneously taking up the special needs of Black workers, they lack the power to win, in view of the real alignment of political forces in the United States today.

Discrimination is a weapon of employers, an instrument for making greater profits at the expense of Black and white labor. That is why employers attempt to convince white workers that any reduction in discrimination is at their expense—as exemplified by a Wall Street Journal article under these headlines:

UP THE LADDER BLUES
  "White Males Complain They Are Now Victims of Job Discrimination
  They Say Companies Favor Women, Racial Minorities in Filling Manager Posts
  Prodding from Uncle Sam"
The story begins:

New England Telephone & Telegraph's top executives recently got a long letter from a young white male in middle management who complained that his future looked pretty dim because of the company's push to advance women and members of racial minorities into management slots. Are guys like him going to have "to pay for [this company's] discrimination practices during the past century?" he asked.

The top brass sent him a long-winded reply that boiled down to: Yes. Generalizing, the article stated that most complaints by whites to the EEOC charging "reverse discrimination" in promotion came from management personnel, not ordinary employees and workers.[3]

So far as the corporate bureaucracy is concerned, undoubtedly bitter competition for advancement will continue, and we cannot be upset about the ambitious ones who fail to get ahead in the already overblown management staffs.

But the propaganda is directed to all workers, not just managerial employees. And the issue is common at all levels—the issue of favoritism. Where workers succeeded in establishing unions they acted to end company favoritism. One instrument for this policy was the establishment of seniority systems. But racism and male supremacy have often permitted favoritism to continue in the form of seniority systems that keep minorities indefinitely in inferior departments, and women in lower-paying jobs.

Successful trade unionism requires an even more vigorous campaign against group favoritism than against individual favoritism. The steel industry presents a typical example of special relevancy.

A 1970s court decision required steel companies to end unit seniority systems that discriminated against Blacks and women. The national leadership of the United Steel Workers of America and some local leaders opposed these moves, sabotaged them and succeeded in watering them down.

They were promoting the superficial view that opening up the better departments to Black workers would take jobs away from white workers. But this is not a situation similar to the scramble for promotion among managers. Labor turnover, more adequate manning of stations, and curtailment of overtime can ensure against any white worker losing a current job. The ending of mainly separate Black and white departments will make it possible to unite all workers into a powerful force that can improve the economic, health and safety conditions of every worker throughout the plant.

Unfortunately, that 1970s decision still reflects the thinking of too many trade union leaders! Moreover, this type of discrimination directly backfires against white workers. In March 1974 the U.S. Steel Corporation closed the wheel mill at its Gary works. The 200 workers there were transferred to other sections of the plant. Using the unit seniority system, the company reduced the grade and pay of many of the workers. A white worker, Lee Lane, filed a complaint with the NLRB charging that his 10 years of experience had been ignored, and that he had been reduced to the rank of laborer with a radical reduction in pay. Lane said:

The Fairfield decision is one of the most important things steel workers have got.

Plantwide seniority is something we all need. They say its only for the blacks, but unit seniority hurts white workers too, and I don't see why we can't work together.[4]

General Posing of White Losses from Racism

Michael Reich succinctly explains how employers use racism as a social and psychological weapon to advance their profits at the expense of white workers:

Wages of white labor are lessened by racism because the fear of a cheaper and underemployed Black labor supply in the area is invoked by employers when labor presents its wage demands. Racial antagonisms on the shop floor deflect attention from labor grievances related to working conditions, permitting employers to cut costs. Racial divisions among labor prevent the development of united worker organizations both within the workplace and in the labor movement as a whole. As a result union strength and union militancy will be less the greater the extent of racism...the economic consequences of racism are not only lower incomes for Blacks but also higher incomes for the capitalist class and lower incomes for white workers.[5]

In a study of metropolitan areas, Reich found a quite significant correlation between the degree of income inequality between whites and Blacks and the degree of income inequality among whites. In those areas where the white/Black differential was greatest, the percentage share of white income received by the top 1% of the whites—that is, the top capitalists, was highest, and the general spread between wealth and poverty among whites—the so-called Gini coefficient of white incomes—was greatest. An even higher correlation of the same type among states was computed by S. Bowles.[6]

Reich puts the political factor in the most general way...that racism helps to legitimize inequality, alienation and powerlessness, providing a legitimacy for these characteristics that is necessary for the stability of the capitalist system as a whole.[7]

But the damage is also concrete and immediate. Racism facilitates anti-labor legislation. It isn't an accident that so-called "right-to-work" laws are nearly universal in the southern states, the traditional stronghold of racism. Racism favors militarism and aggression. Again, the role of the South as the political center of militarism is quite clear. Racism and anti-Communism have been the *main* political weapons used by reaction to divert, weaken, or wholly eliminate the positive social directions charted by the New Deal reform policies. These include the right to work, in the genuine, not the union-busting sense; the right to escape from poverty; the right to equality regardless of race, sex or creed; the right to education and medical service; the right to decent housing; the right to freedom from governmental repression; the right to own and operate small farm and non-farm enterprises; the right to freedom from fear of war.

On the other hand, the very struggle for Black equality provides a dynamic force for every one of these progressive directions which, given the cooperation of the majority of white working people, can become absolutely decisive in winning a positive course of policy in all of these domains.

As shown in Chapter 3, since the 1970's peak in relative African American income gains won in the post-civil rights era, white/Black income differentials have spread until virtually all of the progress made since World War II has been lost.

Was the correlation of these two trends—widening economic racial discrimination and loss of real wages—merely coincidental? Hardly. The 1970s initiated a period of rapid increase in the share of racially oppressed workers in the total labor force—especially Latino workers. And obviously, intensified discrimination against any sector of the working class had a sharp divisive effect on the working class as a whole—and significantly undermined its power.

The South

The South remains the region where slightly more than 50% of the African American people live and where discrimination against Blacks is most severe.

The South is also the region where incomes of white workers are lowest and where poverty among whites is highest. This remains true despite the rapid growth of industry and the overall economic and financial importance of the area.

The South is also the region where the rights of labor, white and Black, have been most trampled; where trade union membership and influence has been most drastically curtailed; where the organization of unions faces the highest obstacles. The "right-to-work" laws have almost completely smashed unions in states with the fastest growing industry—North and South Carolina. Table 10:2 shows the percentage of manufacturing workers in trade unions in each of the southern states. All have right-to-work laws. The border states, which do not have such laws, are not listed.

In the South as a whole, the percentage of unionization is less than half that in the North. Racism, not systematically combatted by unions, fostered the passage of anti-labor legislation and the election of right-wing politicians—usually extremists in both their racism and their servitude to their greedy, anti-labor sponsors.

TABLE 10:2. UNION MEMBERSHIP IN MANUFACTURING INDUSTRIES
Percent of Total Employment, U.S. Total and Southern States, 1989

United States	23.8%	Mississippi	7.6%
Alabama	14.3	North Carolina	4.4
Arkansas	11.2	South Carolina	2.9
Florida	9.0	Tennessee	12.7
Georgia	11.7	Texas	13.8
Louisiana	19.4	Virginia	11.9

(Source: *Stat. Abst.* 1993, No. 688, p.435.) See also p. 298.

Do White Workers Gain or Lose From Racism?

On this question there is a divergence of opinion, not only among sociologists, economists, trade unionists, etc., but also ambiguity on the part of some researchers, including Tidwell.

Basically, the choice is between two concepts:

a) White people as a whole, and white workers in particular, are the gainers from discrimination; the income differential against Black workers is an income differential in favor of whites.

b) White people as a whole, and white workers in particular, are losers from discrimination; the income differential against Black people exerts downward leverage on the incomes of whites, and splits and weakens the working class in its conflict with capital.

Andrew Hacker, expressing concern and even outrage at the conditions of Blacks, seems to accept the first view while implying criticism of whites for holding that view. He writes, for example: "...few white Americans feel obliged to ponder how membership in the major race gives them powers and privileges."[8]

Hacker opines that white people as a whole benefit from their whiteness, but in a negative sense: they are not subject to the penalties of being Black, a fact that has vast economic value to them. In a way, he acknowledges a possible psychological feeling of gain with a reality of not sharing someone else's loss. He writes:

America has always been the most competitive of societies. It poses its citizens against one another, with the warning that they must make it on their own. Hence the stress on moving past others, driven by a fear of falling behind. No other nation so rates its residents as winners or losers.

If white America orchestrates this arena, it cannot guarantee full security to every member of its own race. Still, while some of its members may fail, there is a limit to how far they can fall. For white America has agreed to provide a consolation prize: no matter to what depths one descends, no white person can ever become black.

Hacker poses a hypothetical question to students: "If an official visits you and informs you, a white person, that new records disclose that you are actually black, and will live for another 50 years as a black person, ...How much financial recompense would you request?"

> When this parable has been put to white students, most seemed to feel that it would not be out of place to ask for $50 million, or $1 million for each coming black year. And this calculation conveys, as well as anything, the value that white people place on their own skins.[9]

Actually, this is not the most scientific approach: e.g. how large was the sample and from what social strata were respondents drawn? Moreover, the formulation of the question was designed to elicit an answer such as that cited. A neutral question, such as, "What would be your response to this information about your race?" instead of specifying financial remuneration would surely bring forth a wide and revealing range of answers. Not all would think to give primacy to financial remuneration.

A struggle goes on for the soul of white Americans. Yes, most are nurtured with prejudices. But it is a fact that, before being taught otherwise, white and Black children play together without prejudice. Which precept will predominate? The KKK racist type who break windows or burn crosses on the lawns of Black families moving into a neighborhood? Or the white workers who stand side by side with their Black co-workers on the picket lines, and the Black and white workers, professionals and students who acted together in the civil rights actions in the South?

Hacker's view is that there is just one side, as indicated by the title of his book: *Two Nations: Black and White, Separate, Hostile, Unequal.*

He writes:

> In the eyes of white Americans, being black encapsulates your identity. No other racial or national origin is seen as having so pervasive a personality or character. [Being black] you early learn that this nation feels no need or desire for your physical presence...While few openly propose that you return to Africa, they would be greatly pleased were you to make that decision for yourself.[10]

There are material bases for both attitudes among white workers. Racism is encouraged by the real estate sharks who tell them that the value of their homes will diminish if Black families move into the neighborhood. And ultimately these profiteers make their predictions a fact: by stimulating white flight, they are able to buy up the homes at a bargain—and then re-sell them to Black families at inflated prices.

But white workers learn that Black workers, by reason of their own knowledge of class oppression, are the most reliable and most resolute in building their unions. Unfortunately, it is not generally recognized that the 1950s-1960s—the period of the most significant gains for Blacks—was also the time of important all-around gains for the working class as a whole. Nor that the past two decades of intensified discrimination, accompanied by the anti-labor offensive, has also been a period of union busting and of losses in real wages afflicting the majority of all workers.

There are a number of academics who espouse the concept that whites gain from racist discrimination. Norval D. Glenn's article, "Occupational Benefits to Whites from the Subordination of Negroes," is a case in point.[11]

The national Urban League's Billy Tidwell, a staunch advocate of united action for racial equality, at first endorsed the view that white people as a whole, and white workers in particular, are gainers form racism. He posed the issue with unusual clarity:

> With respect to economic gains, the dispute largely revolves around which segments of white America have benefited as opposed to whether or not benefits have accrued. One school of thought holds that racial discrimination in the labor market has mainly benefited white workers by influencing employers to bid up the wages of the artificially circumscribed supply of labor. This so-called neoclassical theory is associated most prominently with Gary Becker. The opposing view argues that capitalists and high income whites are the prime beneficiaries, as discrimination weakens the solidarity and bargaining strength of workers as a group. African American and white workers are seen as having common class interests that are undermined by the existence of racism...
>
> Despite such disagreements, our own position concurs with Glenn's conclusion that "discrimination and its supporting prejudice persist mainly because majority people gain from them." The point holds whether or not the degree of benefit varies among segments of the majority population. As a general proposition, there is no question that racism has, on the aggregate level, afforded white Americans predominant control over economic resources and access to economic opportunities largely at the expense of the African American minority.[12]

He further argues that whites experience important, "albeit perverse," psychic rewards from their collective dominance over African Americans.

However, later in his work, Tidwell contradicts his earlier position:

> The second objective of our analysis, then, is to examine how the economic conditions of African Americans impact the nation's economy and, thus, the individual economic self-interests of the white majority. There is some indication that a more enlightened perspective on this topic is beginning to take hold. For instance, MONEY magazine, the highly respected periodical on financial affairs with a predominantly white readership, recently published a major article on "Race and

Money." One of the most cogent assertions of the article is that " while blacks bear the brunt of racism, their resulting inequalities cost all Americans enormously."[13]

More specifically, Tidwell asserts:

As to the economic dysfunction's of discrimination against African Americans, in particular, Perlo's conclusion accords with our own judgment:
"...Economic discrimination against Blacks is the nation's number one economic problem. No economic problem affecting the majority of the population can be solved or significantly eased unless the solution includes a vast improvement in the economic situation of Black people and substantial reduction of the discrimination against them."[14]

Tidwell makes the point that improving the incomes of Blacks would strengthen "the economy" and, by implication, all sectors of society—while in his previous, converse argument, noting the benefits to whites from discrimination, he specifically says "The point holds whether or not the degree of benefit varies among subgroups of the majority population."[15] It is important to stress a class position in order to counter the harmful effects of programs influenced by capitalist goals, which objectively stand in the way of the needs of oppressed peoples.

Realistically, the only way white workers—the majority of the white population—can gain from racist discrimination is by becoming employers and themselves, in turn, exploiting African Americans; obviously an impossibility for most workers. White workers who resist affirmative action employment programs, or the integration of housing, schools, etc., do so because they have been convinced that minorities threaten their jobs, that neighborhood integration will reduce the value of their homes, etc.

Trade unions, by and large, support affirmative action—albeit not firmly enough, and there have been instances of their sabotage of that program. But the main line on union propaganda is positive: that all workers gain, not lose, from elimination of racist discrimination.

It cannot be emphasized too strongly that the decades of major gains of the Black people in reducing discrimination—the 1950s and 1960s—were also the decades of the most significant gains of the entire working class: in real wages, in formation and consolidation of unions, in achieving a degree of social security and humane working conditions.

And the subsequent decades of increasing racist discrimination were also the period of serious losses for all workers: in relative and absolute wages; in the smashing of unions; in the destruction or non-enforcement of labor-protective legislation and the enactment of anti-union "right-to-work" laws; in the flagrant overt use of racially oppressed workers in other countries to worsen conditions and increase the exploitation of all workers in the United States.

In the 1950s and 1960s, when workers gained most, the profits of the capitalists were most restricted; the tax structure of the country was more progressive; and financial-industrial monopoly complexes were subject to controls. Since 1970, the decades of heightened racism have seen regressive social policy; a shift to a regressive pattern of taxation; extravagance and a blatant ostentatious lifestyle of the tycoons; financial excesses by the capitalist class on a unprecedented scale; financial crimes involving enormous sums, for which the whole population have been forced to pay through government bailouts financed by our taxes.

White Workers Lose Heavily From Racism

White workers do not gain materially from racism; they do not profit because minorities lose. In fact, *white workers are major losers from racism.*

It is the objective of capitalist propaganda to convince white workers that they are better off, materially and psychologically, because they are not Black—especially those whites who live in predominantly white neighborhoods. This persistent ideological campaign does influence white workers, and too often whites either accept the status quo or do not actively contest it. A fringe group may even be recruited by racist outfits; likewise only a minority of class-conscious white workers actively participate in struggles against racism.

It is unfortunate that there has been little publicized emphasis on the fact that white workers lose from racism, except by Communists and progressive academicians, e.g., those quoted in this chapter.

A fundamental reason for the loss white workers bear is the fact that a racist environment leads to divisions in the working class, preventing unity and thus strengthens capital in each enterprise. Even more critical, it gives capital the advantage on the legislative front, in law enforcement and judicial decisions. This has been devastatingly brought home to labor during the last quarter of the 20th century, with the weakening of all labor-protective legislation, the decline of 5 million in trade union membership, the reduction in real minimum wages, increased taxation on workers, etc.

A major political compaign of the AFL-CIO and the entire trade union movement was against NAFTA, correctly warning that the action would facilitate the ability of employers to move jobs from the United States to Mexico. And the operation of NAFTA has validated the unionists' fears. The movement of those jobs from the United States to enterprises south of the border, with wages one-tenth of those in the United States, takes advantage of racial differentials, of the colonial and neo-colonial regimes imposed on Latin American countries by U.S. imperialism. Racially oppressed Hispanics in the United States are subjected to even harsher racial discrimination in their own countries.

American labor also protests the movement of jobs to low-wage Asian countries, an increasing problem. But again, the Asian workers are victims of imperialist racial oppression, just as are the Asian immigrants who are exploited in U.S. sweatshops.

There is less concern about the export of jobs to Africa simply because the plunder of Africa has been mainly by European-owned transnationals, not American. But that is also analogous to discrimination against Blacks in the United States.

On the other hand, although there has been more export of U.S. capital to Canada, Western Europe, Japan and Australia than to any other areas, there is little objection to that: (a) wages and conditions are, on the whole, equal to those in the United States; and (b) European and Japanese transnationals invest as much here and provide as many jobs for U.S. workers. Thus, what is involved is a transfer of ownership not necessarily affecting total employment.

On the whole, U.S. labor, its majority white, loses far more from racism within the United States than from the loss of jobs to low-wage countries abroad.

Of course, the motivation for the movement of facilities to the South—as well as to the developing countries—is the low level of wages. And, in the case of the South, the weakness of trade unions, the "right-to-work" laws, and the general lack of workers' rights. This is possible because, while legally segregation and Jim Crowism have been excised, the same cabal of racist bankers, manufacturers and landowners holds sway economically, politically and socially. They have inherited the ideology of the slave owners—and often are the direct descendants of slave-owning families. Their selfish, greedy and racist domination creates devastating conditions for African Americans and fosters a low living standard for the entire working class.

Of course, workers are very aware that the level of immigration has soared in recent years, bringing in from Latin America and Asia nearly a million legal immigrants per year, plus another half-million net—after deportations—of undocumented workers. The government's immigration policy is sponsored by the capitalists: by using racist discrimination against these incomers, it is possible to drag down the U.S. wage level of all workers, white, black, Latino, etc. Whether the racially oppressed workers are oppressed over the border in Mexico, or as an immigrant to the United States, the impact on the U.S. workers is similar.

Until recently there were some white workers who were not unduly affected by the anti-labor offensive, with its special racist impact, mainly because of the exclusionary policies of the skilled craft unions. But those sectors have been hit hard by the downsizing of corporate payrolls, as union contracts are broken in the construction, printing and other specialized "labor aristocracy" trades.

When, in compliance with affirmative action programs, some minority workers are hired, there are some protests, cries of "reverse discrimination." But the employment of the non-union Black workers—who are not organized because of the unions' racist membership policies—is not what is taking their jobs: unemployment among African Americans has been rising more rapidly than among whites. What is happening is that the anti-labor campaign of capital is directed toward these high-wage sectors, and the hiring of Blacks—at substantially lower wages than the union rate—fosters much-to-be-desired divisions among workers instead of unity that would foil the superprofit goal.

Another loss—for whites, and Blacks.

What About the Economy and the Capitalists?

The main concern of many economists and politicians is that, as they see it, "the economy" loses because of the shortage of consumer purchasing power due to the lower income of African Americans and other minorities.

For example, John Roosevelt's principal concern, in 1956, was that "...discrimination cost $30,000,000,000 a year in lost purchasing power."[15] His concern, as expressed, was not with the hardships of the minorities, but with the losses to the entrepreneurs whose sales were reduced by lower purchasing power. That is in tune with the then-prominent proposal of Leon Keyserling and other liberals that financial concessions to the working class would improve consumers' purchases and so increase business activity.

Billy J. Tidwell elaborated on this theme. After paying tribute to the great accomplishments of American capitalism, "...the envy of the western world," he worries that its leadership "...has been seriously challenged" by such countries as Japan, West Germany and South Korea.[16]

Claiming that the central issue is to raise productivity so as to be more competitive, he argues that racism is a constraint on economic progress. "This is the context in which the issue of the economic costs of racism takes on far-reaching significance."

He quotes various authors to this effect:

Discrimination on the basis of gender or race is not only harmful to its victim, it wastes important resources. When talented people are denied access to jobs commensurate with their potential, productivity and economic competitiveness suffer.[17]

Tidwell's ideological commitment to capitalism is very strong, and his expression of it is relevant to the issue:

> In American society, where the free enterprise system reigns supreme, the general welfare is defined and pursued in terms of economic interests. This in not intended to be an indictment. Free enterprise is most compatible with our democratic precepts and, for the most part, has afforded Americans an exceptionally high standard of living. Hence, the primacy of economics is not in dispute here. To the contrary, our aim is to demonstrate that racism has been a serious hindrance on economic performance and well-being. In this sense, there is little question that we can no longer afford the price.
>
> The analysis addresses two interrelated concerns—the economic price that African Americans themselves have had to pay and the price that racism has cost the general economy.[18]

Tidwell calculates that if Black incomes had been raised to the level of white, the gross national product would have been increased by 1.8%, or $74 billion, in 1988.[19]

Productivity and competitiveness have been major topics of consideration in Washington, especially with the advent of Bill Clinton to the Presidency: his desire to accelerate labor productivity and to better the competitive position of U.S. goods on world markets. But that approach has a fatal flaw, as did the analysis of an earlier generation of liberals whose main argument for improving labor conditions was that "it" would be "good for the economy."

The fallacy, of course, is the deliberate concealment of the class nature of our capitalist society. In reality, a very small coterie of very rich, very powerful capitalists not only own the main means of production but indisputably control the government and dictate its economic, political and social policies.

To these monopoly capitalists the prime function of economic policy and action is to assure the maximization of their profits. Read any corporate annual report to investors or the speeches of corporation CEOs and the primacy of profit is clear.

During the economic depression of the early 1990s, corporation executives fell like nine-pins, on the decision of boards of directors representing the owners of capital—because they were not producing enough profits, not because of some calculations of their personal "productivity." And their replacements were sufficiently ruthless and capable of raising profits by throwing thousands of workers onto the waste heap and forcing the remainder to work longer hours under more onerous and unsafe conditions. The lower wages paid to African Americans, Hispanics, etc. meant so much more profits right away.

Certainly, in the long run, the resulting curtailment of consumer spending could hurt their business—and their profits. But that downtrend—in the future and theoretical—was problematical and could possibly be controlled, while the gain was immediate, tangible, and huge.

Establishment propaganda, regardless of the political party at the helm, is designed to glorify capitalism: by calling it "free enterprise"—when there is nothing free about enterprise under capitalism; by extolling "our democratic precepts," implying commitment to governance by the people when, actually, elections are brazenly purchased for many millions of dollars. U.S. capitalism supports, with taxpayers' money, the so-called "democratic," but actually murderous regimes of Guatemala and El Salvador, which protect the U.S. corporations that employ workers at a fraction of what even Black labor gets in the United States.

So there is no question but that U.S. capitalists gain exorbitantly from racism.

Now let us consider the possibility that capitalists would really gain by ending racist discrimination—even if their gains might be less than workers' gains.

Raising Black incomes to the level of whites' would require a number of steps—by far the most important would be to raise the wages and salaries of Black workers to match those paid white workers. Obviously the immediate impact would be to reduce employers' profits, since the wage income of workers is a cost of production to employers.

Liberals argue that Black workers will spend more money, providing more profits to the capitalists selling them more consumers goods and services. There will then be more demand for goods and more workers will be required to produce the more goods and services. This argument may not be spelled out in development of the thesis that "it" would be "good for the economy," but the supposed advantage to capitalists is implied.

How valid is it? In the first place, capitalists would typically consider the obvious immediate negative effect on their profits. To them, longer term gains from more spending by African Americans would be speculative. And they would be conscious—if the liberal academic theorists are not—that raising wages of Blacks and Latinos to the level of whites would inevitably strengthen the bargaining position of *all* their workers and might lead to higher overall labor costs far greater than the cost of equalizing wage rates. Further, they might not be able to offset this by raising prices because of international competition.

As with any major reform, the long-term actual impact on economic activity, profits, etc., would depend on a complex of economic and political factors not necessarily predictable in advance. But the main factor is that capitalists are not going to make the estimate; they oppose the reform because of the immediate adverse effect on their profits. That's the bottom line.

Are there any capitalists who favor reducing discrimination? Yes. But their motive is not expectation of economic gain but the fear of the social consequences of maintaining existing discrimination. The broader, more united and militant the struggles of the forces against discrimination, the more the capitalist class will feel impelled to grant concessions, regardless of the impact on their profits.

Extra Profits From Racism

I calculate that the direct *extra* profits of the capitalist class from racism are approximately equal to the wage differentials against African Americans, Hispanics, etc., multiplied by the number of workers employed in private enterprises.

But isn't part of the overall differential due to the lower level of jobs performed by Blacks? Shouldn't one measure the extra profits as equal to the differential for the same kind of work?

True. However, in practical terms, the overall differential comes close to that. Most of the overall differential applies to minorities at the same general occupational level.

For example, in 1991, the *median* differential against Black workers over all was 32%, while the differential against Black skilled craft workers was 25%. Moreover, within each general skill level, Black workers tend to be consigned to the worst jobs—such as the dangerous and unhealthy foundry and paint-handling jobs in steel and auto; washing dishes rather than waiting on tables in restaurants, etc.

This factor is sufficiently important, in my judgment, to call for taking the *median* differential among all workers and applying it to the number of Black, Hispanic, etc., workers affected rather than summing up the reported differentials within each broad occupational group.

Within each broad occupational group the particular jobs to which Black and Latino workers are consigned are underpaid for all workers, compared to jobs requiring comparable skill that are largely limited to white workers. The analogous situation, widely recognized, is in respect to "women's jobs," and the movement for pay equalization to remove this form of discrimination has achieved some successes.

A case in point: I know a young African American who is employed to inspect various factories to measure the extent of nuclear radiation. He is classified as a laborer and gets a laborer's wage. But his counterpart, usually white, employed to determine nuclear safety in a power plant or a nuclear weapons plant, is classified as an inspector or engineer and paid three times as much. Yet the skills required are essentially identical, and the danger faced by the African American is greater because he inspects smaller plants that have little or no background of inspections or security standards.

I have limited the calculation of extra profits from racism to those obtained directly by private employers through underpaying minority workers. Actually, however, the profits are much greater, for two reasons. They do not take into account the extra profits made by employers as a result of the downward pull of discrimination on wages of white workers. Since there are so many more white workers than minority workers, this factor alone may equal or exceed the amounts cited here as extra profits from racism. Moreover, the estimates do not take into account wage differentials against minorities in government employment. While private employers do not directly profit from these differentials, they gain in two ways: first, the capitalist class is the major beneficiary of government expenditures gotten by the exploitation of workers and, second, because the working class pays most of the taxes used for workers wages.

Table 10:3 and Chart 10B show the extra profits from racism against all minorities growing from $56 billion in 1947 to $197 billion in 1992, (expressed in 1995 dollars), a multiplication of 3.5 times. This amount considerably exceeds the rate of increase in the size of the minority working class population. Of course, these figures are approximations, based on assumptions others may question, since a case could be made, within the framework of the analysis, for data up to 20% lower or higher than my estimates. On the other hand, however, the data in Table 10:3 do not take into account the extra profits resulting from the downward pull on white workers; wages as a result of employers making use of the Black/white differential. Trends indicate that by 1995 losses of minority workers due to super-exploitation reached $250 billion. Because there are so many more white workers, this indirect form of extra profits probably at least equals the direct extra profits from racism.

The extra profits from the super-exploitation of Black workers alone, in 1992 dollars, went up from $48 billion in 1947, shortly after World War II, to $107 billion in 1992. The extra profits from super-exploitation of Latino, Native American and Asian workers rose tenfold, reflecting the rapid growth in the Latino and Asian working class population, so that by now they yield, together, nearly as much extra profits as do Black workers.

As of 1995, taking into account extra profits of the capitalist class due to racism directly at expense of minority workers and indirectly at expense of white workers, came to $500 billion, or a half a trillion dollars.

TABLE 10:3. SUPERPROFITS FROM EXPLOITATION OF MINORITY
            WORKERS SELECTED YEARS, 1947-1992
            (Billions 1995 $)

Year	Black	Hispanic	Other	Total
1947	48	8*		56
1972	60	28*		88
1980	74	34	4	112
1992	107	84	6	197

* Includes "Other"
SOURCES:
1947: Perlo, *American Imperialism*, p.89 ($4 billion raised to $7 billion for conceptual consistency with later figures, and addition of 15% for estimated relative size of Hispanic, Asian and Native American workers, then raised to 1992 dollars.
1972: *Economics of Racism*, 1975 edition, p.148
1980: Calculated from P-60, No. 132, T 53, p.101, with adjustment explained in appendix.
1992: Calculated from P-60, No. 184, T 34, p.174, with adjustment explained in appendix.
Consumer price index for urban consumers (CPI-U) used to adjust figures to 1992 prices to 1995 prices.

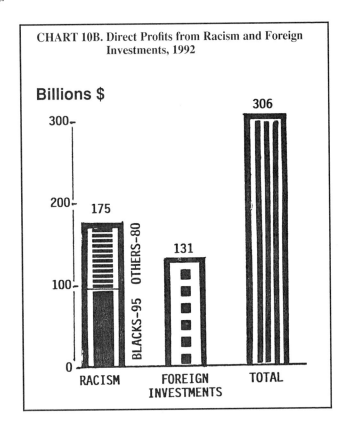

CHART 10B. Direct Profits from Racism and Foreign
          Investments, 1992

This, of course, does not include the much larger amount of profits derived from the basic exploitation of all workers, Black, white, and brown.

Earlier calculations, which I and others made shortly after World War II, were limited to measuring the differentials in pay for industrial workers, the direct producers of value and surplus value. However, now it is appropriate to consider differentials against all minority workers from whom employers make a profit as part of the total, regardless of the sector of the economy. A number of Marxist economists consider that value is created in areas beyond industry, as narrowly defined.

More importantly, a distinction has to be made between the creation of surplus value and how it is distributed and used. Values created in the productive sectors of the economy are distributed throughout the economy, including the non-productive sectors. Large profits made by huge corporations in the burgeoning gambling industry, in advertising—which has captured most of the broadcast time—and by such entertainment giants as Time Warner and Disney enterprises, create no value. But they employ and exploit hundreds of thousands of workers. They also plunder their customers, e.g., those who lost an estimated $9 billion to the large-scale gambling enterprises of Nevada and Atlantic City in 1993.

And even these industries, to the extent that they employ and pay low wages to Black, Latino and Native American workers, are making extra profits from racism.

Profits From Racism and From Foreign Investments

Profits from racism and from foreign investments are both features of U.S. imperialism that have escalated in importance. In the recent period, domestic profits from racism have gone up more rapidly, and definitely exceed profits from the export of capital. Total profits from foreign investments of all types peaked in 1990 at $161 billion, and declined during the subsequent cyclical crisis to $131 billion in 1992, with little change in 1993. This is considerably less than the $200 billion of *extra* profits received from the super-exploitation of minority workers in the United States.

One can look at it another way. U.S.-owned transnationals employ 2.2 million workers in their Latin American plants compared with about 9.5 million Hispanic workers in the United States. Some 600,000 Asians—other than from highly industrialized Japan—are employed by U.S.-owned companies located in Asian countries compared to 4 million in the United States.[20] Barely 100,000 Africans in Africa are employed by U.S. corporations in comparison with the employment of 12.5 million African Americans in this country. These statistics do not take into consideration the plunder of the nations' natural resources, the draining of wealth and the extortionate debts to the money center banks.

But with all of these qualifications, it is necessary to conclude that under present conditions, racism in the United States is quantitatively a more important source of monopoly superprofits than foreign investment.

However, the balance in not overwhelming. And since the destruction of socialist societies in the USSR and Eastern Europe, there has been a rapid surge of foreign investment by U.S. transnationals, which are taking advantage of the strengthened U.S. military-political position. Thus there is a possibility that superprofits from foreign investments will catch up to and surpass superprofits from domestic racism--an eventuality that would be of little consolation to U.S. workers, white and Black.

Conclusion

With a historical perspective, few would deny that it was specifically the slave owners who profited from slavery, and that the white workers and farmers were exploited and were losers from that form of society. Furthermore, little could be done to alleviate the condition of the slaves other than by abolishing the system of slavery and the slave-owning class.

The analysis presented here explains why—after decades of struggle, civil rights laws, efforts of millions of African Americans to obtain higher education, to establish businesses, to purchase homes wherever they desire—the evils of economic discrimination, of social exclusion and confinement to ghettoes remain essentially unchanged. Yes, the country would gain enormously by raising the incomes of minority people to those of whites, but that is not the intention of employers who pay the wages and salaries. On the contrary, the capitalist class offers stubborn resistance to whatever slight and temporary gains have been won after bitter mass struggles.

Racism, domestically and internationally, is so interwoven in the system of capitalism, especially in its modern, imperialist phase, that the complete eradication of racist discrimination will require its replacement by socialism. Yet major gains toward significant reductions in discrimination can be won within the confines of capitalism—so long as struggles are not based on the assumption that it is necessary to conform to the concept that profits of capitalists must increase.

11. Housing

EAST ST. LOUIS, ILL.—A river and a world away from the glass towers and pre-occupied hum of St. Louis lies a charred skeleton of a town...East St. Louis, with its acre upon acre of burnt-out hulks that were once houses, its sad tales of backed-up sewers and of police cars that run out of gas, of garbage piled so deep that entire streets are rendered impassable...has become a textbook case of everything that can go wrong in an American city.[1]

East St. Louis, once a major rail and river traffic center, is now one of the most tragic ghettoes in the United States. The city is broke and deeply in debt, despite the highest tax rate in the state of Illinois, because the property has such small value. Ninety-eight percent of its inhabitants are Black; fully half of the adults are unemployed; about 75% of the population receives some form of welfare. It has been forced to lay off 1,170 of 1,400 city employees; its city hall was foreclosed. Since 1987 there have been no garbage pickups.[2] At the time of the 1993 Mississippi floods, not a word was carried in the mass media about what happened to East St. Louis—in the very eye of the storm.

The city is surrounded by major chemical and pharmaceutical plants whose tax dollars could support the city. But these corporations pay no taxes to East St. Louis as, by arrangement, they are in separate legal districts. Nevertheless, their plants poison the residents with concentrated noxious fumes and spills from chemical-laden trains that pass through the city. Monsanto, Big River Zinc, Cerro Copper, American Bottoms Sewage, Trade Waste Incineration, Pfizer—all contaminate East St. Louis, but contribute no revenue and very few jobs.

Even if they could afford it, East St. Louis residents would not be permitted to move to nearby, healthier communities because of the racist and segregationist policies of the banks and real estate interests that make and enforce the restrictive directives. Virulent racism is very much alive there. Police even close the one bridge across the Mississippi River open to pedestrians to prevent African American mothers, with their children, from attending the Fourth of July street fair and annual festivities.

---

*Similar forced physical separation of Blacks and whites is not limited to the poorest African Americans. The majority of the city of Mount Vernon, just north of New York City is Black, better off than most Black communities. But to the East across a many-laned parkway, is Pelham Manor and Pelham, rich white peoples' preserves. The city and the Pelhams are connected by a footbridge over the parkway. In the racist offensive of 1995, the Mayor of Pelham is striving to have the footpath destroyed to keep Mount Vernon residents out, an attempt meeting serious resistance from the people of Mount Vernon.

According to a journalist of the *St. Louis Post- Dispatch*, within East St. Louis:

> The decimation of men within the population is quite nearly total. Four of five births in East St. Louis are to single mothers. Where do the men go? Some to prison. Some to the military. Many to an early death. Dozens of men are living in the streets or sleeping in small, isolated camps out behind the burnt-out buildings.[3]

And, from the *New York Times*:

> ...economists can think of few if any places outside perhaps rural Appalachia or the Deep South where the problems are so pervasive and extreme.[4]

But there are, of course, places in the North that are nearly as bad. In Camden, New Jersey—a largely Black, ghettoized suburb of Philadelphia—a major municipal effort to involve the population (there were 1,200 volunteer firefighters) succeeded in reducing the number of fires, many arson-instigated, to four per night from an average of 20 each night![5]

Sections of large cities are prey to similar conditions of deterioration—e.g. the South Bronx of New York City. As for the South, where slightly more than half the African American population lives:

DEEP SOUTH AND DOWN HOME, BUT IT'S A GHETTO ALL THE SAME

> Jonestown, Miss.—This forlorn little town of rickety shotgun shacks and 1,467 people, surrounded by the table-top-flat cotton fields of northwest Mississippi, has the spent air of a place that history has passed by.
>
> But throughout this forgotten corner of America and in the other poorest parts of the South, hamlets like Jonestown are writing a bitter epilogue to integration. Small towns that were once economically stable and racially mixed are becoming pockets of poverty and overwhelmingly black—75 to 100 percent so.

As in northern cities, white families have left and white capitalists have taken business with them. Jonestown's ex-mayor, Bobbie Walker, said: "We have 1,476 people, but we may have 100 who actually work. Almost all the stores have closed. The town is basically broke."

Sociologist Bruce Williams commented:

> There's racism all over the United States, but it's not as systematically oriented and as ideologically grounded in religion and Southern tradition as it is here in Mississippi ...The rural elite is interested in maintaining the status quo, and that's it.

The author of the article, journalist Peter Applebome, wrote:

...except for the general decay, the economic hierarchy in Jonestown is not much different from what it was during segregation . The only major business...is the Delta Oil Mill...that produces $22 million in cottonseed oil a year. All the clerical and supervisory jobs are held by whites, and many of the laboring jobs are held by blacks. There are still blacks working in the cotton fields, but none at the small Jonestown branch of the Sunburst Bank.

To many blacks, the rural ghetto is the racism of the Old South in a new form, now employing economic deprivation instead of Jim Crow laws.[6]

Segregation

The overwhelming majority of African Americans live in conditions of segregation, and that means not only a kind of semi-quarantine but also an inferior lifestyle:

- Poor housing, poorly maintained.
- Poor shopping facilities.
- Poor transportation, non-maintenance of roads, few parking facilities in large cities for even the minority of Blacks who own cars.
- Inferior schools.
- Removal of industrial plants from the communities, and scarcity of new employment opportunities. Lack of access to employment outside the ghettoes.
- Unsanitary conditions: inadequate or no collections of garbage; infestation by rodents and roaches; faulty sewage disposal.
- Impermissible environmental pollution.
- Prevalence of crime; exposure to murder, hostile police forces, target of drug dealers.

In almost all cases, these appalling conditions are the norm. They are dramatically worse than the circumstances of the majority of the white population, although not quite as extreme, yet, as the *faellas,* the shantytowns of Latin American countries. Most U.S. Blacks live in dwellings that at least provide elementary protection from the weather—although this situation is changing as homelessness rises.

Segregation greatly compounds inequality of income: a Black family with a poverty-level income living in a ghetto is far worse off than a white family with an equally low income living in a community with better-off whites.

Segregation has been the lot of Blacks from the time of slavery. Little has changed in the South, except that it has become more urbanized, although rural segregation remains important, and more absolute.

In the North, segregation was less rigid and not as strictly enforced as long as the Black population was small, and later when the militant actions of the

1930s-1960s brought limited material and social progress. By the 1970s, the situation deteriorated in the North as well as in the South, along with the worsening economic status of African Americans. The acceleration of segregation and racism has been one of the vilest by-products of the 20th century corruption and decay of capitalism in the United States.

> There was a time, before 1900, when blacks and whites lived side by side in American cities. In the north, a small native black population was scattered widely throughout white neighborhoods. Even Chicago, Detroit, Cleveland, and Philadelphia—cities now well known for their large black ghettoes—were not segregated then...
>
> ...No matter what other disadvantages urban blacks suffered in the aftermath of the Civil War, they were not residentially segregated from whites. The two racial groups moved in a common social world, spoke a common language, shared a common culture, and interacted personally on a regular basis. In the north, especially, leading African American citizens often enjoyed relations of considerable trust, respect, and friendship with whites of similar social standing.
>
> Of course, most blacks did not live in northern cities, and didn't experience these benign conditions. In 1870, 80% of black Americans still lived in the rural south, where they were exploited by a sharecropping system that was created by white landowners to replace slavery; they were terrorized by physical violence and mired in an institutionalized cycle of ignorance and poverty...[7]

In 1890 only 6.7% of northern city Blacks were segregated. By 1910 this index was up to 9.7%. Then the process of segregation began in earnest so that the index was 29.9% in 1929, including 70.4% in Chicago, 51.0% in Cleveland, and 41.8% in New York.[8] By 1940 the formation of Black ghettoes in U.S. cities was essentially complete, and persists to this day.

Moreover, in many cases, ghetto conditions worsened as accelerated immigration of Blacks from the South to the North during the 1940s and 1950s resulted in overcrowding in the restricted ghetto communities, leading to severe deterioration of housing structures.

In the post-World War II boom years, millions of new homes were built—but in most places exclusively for whites. In January 1994, the media eulogized the newly deceased William Levitt, whose company had built 17,000 nearly identical, inexpensive houses in Nassau County, New York, in 1947-1950. These affordable homes were provided for working class and middle class *white* families. Levitt specifically excluded African Americans, ignoring the protests of progressive forces. He imposed restrictive covenants on purchasers, whereby they agreed not to sell to Blacks—covenants that were of dubious legality but not successfully challenged.

At the time of Levitt's death, the *New York Times* commented: "The community is more diverse, too... Levittown today is racially mixed."[9] But actually of 53,286 inhabitants in 1990, exactly 137 were African Americans. The

Levitt company has been very selective as to what "mixing" it has permitted. There are nearly 1,000 Asians and 2,000 Latinos in the community, a mere 5%.

Also in Nassau County, one of New York City's wealthy suburbs, small Black ghettoes have been created, such as the poverty stricken community of Roosevelt. Of its 15,030 inhabitants, only 676 are non-Hispanic whites; 13,331 are African Americans.[10]

Nassau County is a shocking example of the "hypersegregation" organized by landlords against tenants. A considerable majority of Blacks in the New York metropolitan area are tenants. This applies also to a large proportion of white working class families: only very highly paid workers can now afford to buy a house in the area's overpriced marketplace.

Most apartment rentals are not advertised, sometimes because the apartments are "illegal"—carved out of basements or garages; sometimes because it's cheaper and easier to rent through brokers or apartment rental services, which also screen applicants. Brokers habitually charge prospective tenants $100-$125 for lists of available apartments—the only way for many workers to find a place to live.

The Places to Live agency asks landlords what their preferences are for "race, age, national origin and gender," and it programs its computer accordingly. This practice, which has been going on for years, was exposed—and some State action taken—only because two victims, an African American man and a Native American woman, filed lawsuits against the agency with the help of a non-profit housing organization.

The Black man, Zephania Bennett, a machinist, asked for listings in the mainly white area where he already lived, Rockville Center. Agency owner John McDermott refused and would give him listings only for Black sections of Hempstead—which proved to be false. When Bennett asked for his $125 back, McDermott called him an "ignorant Black bas—d." The Native American woman was refused listings in Levittown although many apartments were available.

The State's assistant attorney general in charge of the case referred to this practice of real estate agencies as leading to the "hypersegregation" of Long Island.[11] McDermott blatantly vocalized his racism, as well as anti-Semitism and male chauvinism. But his policies and actions are typical of agency directors who may be more cautious, publicly at least.

What is most disturbing is that these cases highlight the fact that no government agency enforces fair housing laws; that action was taken against this particular racist only because two of his victims, indignant and determined to fight back, filed personal lawsuits. If they eventually receive some monetary recompense, it will probably not be publicized. McDermott and his ilk will not be driven out of business, "reformed," or sentenced to the long prison terms they deserve.

Overall, on Long Island, segregation is more severe than in New York City:

> ...95 percent of black residents are concentrated in 5 percent of the census tracts...the likelihood of a white resident of Nassau living in the same census tract as a black or Hispanic person is only 8 percent, and the chance that white children will find black youngsters in school with them is just 9 percent.

In the segregated communities, [African Americans] not only receive markedly inferior educational, library, etc. facilities, but are more heavily taxed on homes of comparable or less value. While minority residents are 14% of the Nassau total, gerrymandering prevents their election to local office and none has ever been elected to a countywide office.[12]

The discrimination and racism against African Americans in Nassau cannot be rationalized by the usual disparagements: broken families, welfare burdens, high crime, drugs, etc. The Black families who made it to Nassau were mainly professionals, highly paid blue and white collar workers, administrators. The median family income of Black households in Nassau in 1980 was just short of $45,000, 50% *above the median* household income of all households in the United States; higher than the median for all 50 states; and 36% above the median for New York State.[13] But Nassau's Black residents are forced to a quality of life not much better than that of the lower-income Black working class families in the central city ghettoes.

These examples provide proof, if such is necessary, that it is the racism of white segregationist bigots and real estate opportunists that is responsible for the discriminatory housing codes imposed on African Americans! And it is clear, also, that economic status—as determined by capitalist standards—does not prevent Black families from racist reprisals.

In the early 1960s, after the limited civil rights gains and before the accelerated resurgence of segregation, I saw streets in Detroit with well-kept homes and lawns on alternate streets, Black families on one block and white families on the next. Black and white workers had good jobs in the auto plants and other industrial establishments, and decent homes in the same neighborhood. But 30 years later that was all gone, due to the combination of the "white flight," massive unemployment, deterioration of services in a city now preponderately Black.

Massey and Denton made extensive statistical studies of segregation in the 30 largest metropolitan areas in the country. They found that in the North the index of segregation averaged 80.1% in 1980, and in the South, 68.3%.[14]

These figures represent the percentage of Blacks who would have to move into white areas to achieve an overall balance.

A comparative analysis of 1990 Census data shows little change. The intensification of racist propaganda by the ruling class, as expressed by their dominant Republican Party politicians, plus the racism of incumbent administrations in opposing affirmative action in the courts, have prevented significant relief from supersegregation.

Poverty is brutal in many ghettoes less notorious than East St. Louis, especially where basic industry has declined. An Ohio research organization measured poverty by census tracts in Cuyahoga County, which includes Cleveland and its major suburbs, year by year since 1970. For 1970, maps show a handful of tracts with more than 50% poverty—involving not more than 1%-2% of the county's area. By 1980 the 50%-plus poverty area had extended; there was a heavy concentration of tracts in the East-Central part of the county, with about 20% of Cuyahoga's area. By 1991 the poverty zones had more than doubled and now included close to 50% of Cleveland City proper. Overwhelmingly, these spheres of super-poverty incorporated Cleveland's Black ghetto.[15]

Various ethnic groups, especially new immigrants to the United States, tend to settle "among their own kind." However, these people have never been as isolated from the life of the community as were Blacks and, after a time— through intermarriage and social/economic/community integration—they have become an integral part of the overall white population, a status not shared by African Americans.

There remain remnants of snobbish white Anglo-Saxon exclusivity, formally or informally barring Jews, for example, as well as African Americans. But these exceptions are, for the most part, limited to select resorts, golf clubs, perhaps a few exclusive residential enclaves. By and large, Jews, Italians, Poles, Greeks—as well as all other European ethnic groups—are free to live where they please.

Massey and Denton define five features of segregation. By their definition, any metropolitan area whose index of segregation is above 60% for four or all five of the indicators is regarded as *hypersegregated*,

> According to these criteria, blacks in sixteen metropolitan areas were hypersegregated in 1980...These sixteen metropolitan areas are among the most important in the country, containing six of the ten largest metropolitan areas in the United States. Together they house 35% of the nation's black population, and 41% of all blacks living in urban areas.[16]

The rural Blacks are almost all in the South, where they are segregated in special hamlets.

Blacks and Hispanics

According to many measures, there is not much difference between the economic status of African Americans and Latinos. However, there is one crucial difference: segregation of Latinos is much less stringent than that of Blacks. And analysis of 1980 data shows that the average index of Hispanic segregation is decidedly lower than that of Blacks, in each of Massey-Denton's five categories. For example, in the key index of concentration of the population in a small area, the index for Hispanics typically averaged two-thirds that of Blacks in 1980.[17]

In fact, a similar spread prevails in the Los Angeles area, where the Latino people are the largest sector of the population, and might therefore be expected to be more segregated.

The reason for this differential between African Americans and Hispanics is that segregation is primarily *racist* in character. In annual Census Bureau surveys, 95% of all Hispanics classify themselves as white.

Massey and Denton analyzed the race factor for cities with a predominance of Latinos of Caribbean origin: although a larger proportion are of mixed racial heritage, a very substantial majority consider themselves white.

The indexes of segregation for 10 metropolitan areas in the Northeast show that the degree of segregation sharply rises according to the color of the person: least for white Hispanics—51.9; most for Black Hispanics—80.0; with mixed-race Hispanics in between—71.9.[18]

Whether or not all white people have some degree of racial prejudice, as has been claimed, I believe that the majority of whites are as willing to accept African Americans as any other ethnic group as neighbors and to welcome their participation in community affairs. It is the small minority of fanatic bigots whose scare tactics too often succeed in stirring up home owners when African Americans move into a neighborhood, in infecting the community with fears of declining property values, crime on the streets, etc.

Suburbanization

As industry and other forms of economic activity moved from the central cities to the suburbs between 1970 and 1980, the percentage of whites living in northern metropolitan suburbs rose from 64.3% to 70.8%. The percentage of African Americans living in the suburbs went up from 17.2% to 23.1%, so the disparity remained essentially unchanged.[19] Moreover, as noted for Blacks, moving to suburbs often meant simply moving to another ghetto, although the degree of their isolation was less.

Ghettoization, whether in cities or suburbs, enables landlords, mortgage lenders, etc., to impose harsh terms that lead to deteriorating housing conditions. Added to that, mass unemployment makes it impossible for many African Americans to keep their homes.

Racism in suburbia—in economic and residential areas—intensifies job discrimination. As long as industry was concentrated in or near cities where both Blacks and whites lived, even if there were ghettoes, employment discrimination was not compounded, in a major way, by geographic considerations. But with suburbanization, most economic and housing opportunities move out of reach of Black workers, who are herded into inner cities, adding a major dimension to the overall pattern of job discrimination.

So the struggle against segregation and discrimination in housing—in all its aspects, including in suburbanization—is a vital element on the agenda of Black workers for equality in employment.

Home Ownership

The goal of most families is to own their own home. It gives a certain minimum of security, control over their own lives. However, nominal home ownership is often illusory. Generally, only 5-10% of the purchase price is paid in cash—the down payment share has shrunk markedly—the rest is under the thumb of the mortgage lender. The banks and related financial companies have thereby gotten control over the bulk of the country's housing supply, either through direct lending to residents, or to landlords who rent out homes.

During the first two decades after World War II there was a marked improvement in the nation's housing supply, associated with a sharp rise in home ownership.

Finance capital thereby controls trillions of dollars of property, a large share of the nation's wealth. Concentration of financial capital has led to concentration of mortgages in the hands of giant banks, which buy up mortgages or "servicing," i.e.—collection rights—from original lenders. As the scale of outstanding mortgages became far larger than the resources of the banks, basically limited to deposits made in them, the federal government came in as a partner, in one of the most important aspects of state monopoly capitalism, in which the lines between public property and giant corporate private property becomes increasingly blurred.

Today the great bulk of home mortgages outstanding are held by government sponsored corporations—Federal National Mortgage Association ("Fannie Mae"), Federal Home Loan Mortgage Corporation ("Freddie Mac"), and Student Loan Marketing Association ("Sallie Mae"), which includes mortgages in its loans to students.

Originally set up and financed by the federal government out of taxes, they have been privatized. That is, turned over to the complex of giant financial corporations, as private corporations making big profits, listed on the New York Stock Exchange, but with one-third of their directors appointed by the President of the United States, retaining the tax exemption privileges of federal borrowers, and with implicit federal guarantees of payment to investors. The banks make the mortgage loans with big profit from fees and other charges, sell them to these state-private corporations on profitable terms, and to a considerable extent retain "servicing rights" as well as direct connection with the borrowers as customers of their banks.

And it is this combination of financial power which directly dominates enforcement and intensification of housing segregation and discrimination in every respect.

More, industrial giant corporations, tied in with financial capital in myriad ways, are also directly involved in the housing situation. GE, General Motors, and Sears are among the industrial combines that have financial subsidiaries with large mortgage portfolios. They are also involved through their placement of plants so as to contribute to the overall pattern of housing and employment discrimination, as in the example of Monsanto, Pfizer, and others surrounding and financially starving East St. Louis.

This financial-industrial-government monopoly web dominates enforcement and intensification of housing segregation and discrimination in every respect.

The Widening Gap

During the postwar housing boom, from 1940 to 1960, home ownership among white households rose from 45.7% to 64.6%; minority home ownership from 23.6% to 38.4%— no equalization there. Later home ownership growth continued at a slow pace.[20]

After1980, Black and Latino home ownership declined, and by 1992 were 42-43%, somewhat lower than in 1980; while non-Hispanic white home ownership reached a record, exceeding 70%.[21]

Problems faced by Black and Latino tenants were magnified as construction of new public housing units virtually stopped and in many places maintenance of existing homes deteriorated. As tenants, the majority are barred from participating in the $250 billion per year in deductions from taxable income for interest on housing mortgages and from real estate taxes.[22] Relatively few of the minority homeowners can participate in this benefit, owing to the smaller size and composition of their incomes, which make itemized deductions impractical.

The Role of the Banks, Insurance Companies, Realty Brokers

Confronting the would-be home buyer are the agents who sell and rent housing; who will not sell a home to an African American in some parts of cities and in some suburbs; who "steer" prospective Black buyers to areas that are already segregated or that may be "turning." The key factor here is not the personal racism of the realtors, although doubtless most of them have the strong racial prejudices that are required for the discriminatory practices they follow in order to stay in business.

It is the bankers and insurance companies that call the shots that, directly or indirectly, give the segregationist orders to realtors. To close a sale usually requires a mortgage and insurance, and as bankers "redline" areas that are closed to African Americans and will not approve mortgage loans to them in the restricted areas, realtors knuckle under.

These agents also play a prominent role in converting integrated areas into ghettoes. Accepting the "wisdom" of sociologists that whites will, for example, tolerate a Black population percentage of 10% but not 30% in a given neighborhood, they start rumors that Black entry—which has reached a "critical" level—will drive down property values. Racist organizations fan the flame. Sometimes a panic is started among white homeowners, who sell their homes at bargain prices to move out of the "threatened" areas. Then, guess what! Real estate agents and developer-owners resell the properties to Black families—at escalated prices.

The *Wall Street Journal* published a blockbuster exposé detailing the results of a Boston Federal Reserve Bank survey of how U.S. bankers handle millions of mortgage applications. Of 2.7 million mortgage applications accepted for consideration in 1991, only 5.9% of those considered and 4.8% of those approved were for Blacks; 5.6% of those considered and 5.2% of those approved were for Hispanics. The figures for Blacks were considerably less than half their share of the population. Lending to Hispanics and Native Americans was also well below their population shares. Note that gross discrimination begins even before consideration is given to lending to minorities.

Among applications considered, the rejection rates for Blacks was 2.27 times that of whites in 1990 and 1.91% in 1991; Hispanic rejection rates about 1.4% that of whites. This pattern of discrimination was across the board for almost all lenders and all major metropolitan areas. The highest discrimination ratios, more than 3 times, were reported by Chicago institutions, characteristic of the exceptionally intense racism pervading that city in many other respects. Citibank, the nation's largest, reported high ratios of Black to white rejection rates for California; Chase Manhattan and Chemical Banks for New York. General Motors, through its large mortgage subsidiary, had a discrimination ratio of 3.39% in Pennsylvania, nearly 3 times in Michigan, its home state, and in New York. Add this to the bill of charges against GM for minimizing Black auto dealerships or coverage of Black areas in salesrooms; one can only assume similar discrimination in car lending by General Motors Acceptance Corp.

Discrimination was extreme regardless of credit records or income levels. Among applicants in the affluent income range of $50,000 to $100,000, Blacks were rejected 2.5 times more than whites. Typically, bankers base refusal on some trivial item on the Black application form that would be overlooked in the case of whites. Ghetto residents, lacking convenient banking services, often hoard their savings, and offer this "mattress money" as down payment, which the lenders use as an excuse to turn the prospective borrowers down. One application was refused because of a 38-cent debit on a ten-year old account that had been paid but not entered in the computer!

The state-private giants, which now play a vital role in housing finance, directly intensify housing discrimination and segregation. In 1991 only 1.7% of the loans bought by Fannie Mae and 1.9% of those bought by Freddie Mac were in predominantly minority areas.

The Federal Housing Administration and the Veterans Administration, which provide directly guaranteed mortgage loans, exercise similar discrimination[23]

Lawsuits by Black homeowners in Atlanta exposed a shocking example of usury by Fleet Financial, which started in Rhode Island to become a $50 billion colossus operating nationwide.

The legal action revealed that Fleet Finance, the Atlanta mortgage lending subsidiary, selected "Black neighborhoods for mortgage loans at annual rates that sometimes exceeded 30 percent." In settlement of the suits, Fleet agreed, in addition to cash repayments to its victims, not to charge future borrowers more than 12% above the prime rate, which meant, as of the end of 1993, not more than 18%. Further, it agreed to reduce prepaid finance charges to 5% or less. This at a time when average mortgage rates were close to 8% and initial fees and charges about 1.5%.[24]

In other words, Fleet agreed to reduce, somewhat, the scale of its rip-off of African Americans.

The lawsuits alleged that these usurious rates were meant to bankrupt the borrowers quickly so that the finance company "could foreclose them later and sell the property at a profit."[25]

Thus, a Black homeowner with a typical mortgage of $50,000 has to pay more than $5,000 a year over and above "normal" financial charges. In effect, these excessive extra charges, added to the superexploitation of African Americans on the job, are a further factor that markedly increases the stake of the capitalist class, and finance capital in particular, in racism.

Racist Violence Against Black Residents

In some places, whites and African Americans mobilize to foster integration, to counter panic selling, and to welcome Blacks to a neighborhood. But all too often the racist strategy is successful. Although in some areas where exclusion of Blacks is not a live issue supported by the local residents, there may be many racially mixed couples and, in recent years, a growing number of non-segregated African American families.

In the case of a mixed couple, the white husband or wife negotiates the home purchase, procures the mortgage, insurance, etc. Black families usually arrange purchase directly from the homeowners, without the intercession of agents.

However, too often, especially in metropolitan areas, racist forces—with the connivance of police and other local authorities, and with support from a significant part of the white population—forcibly prevent Black families from settlement. Those few who brave such barriers face social isolation, ostracism of their children, physical attacks, KKK cross burnings, and even arson. Major suburbs of Detroit and Chicago—Dearborn and Cicero—are notorious examples.

For 20 years, the ruling circles, politicians, and racists of Yonkers—largest city in New York's Westchester County—have succeeded in defying repeated court orders to open the eastern part of the city to African Americans.

YEARS AFTER BIAS RULING, YONKERS STILL IS A HOUSE DIVIDED, headlined a *New York Times* feature:

> Mary Munson is weary from the din in the streets, the filth in the elevators, and the ever-present threat of drugs and violence that stalks her son and daughter as they travel to and from school. After 10 years of living in this rundown west side neighborhood, Ms. Munson...hopes the next phase of a court-ordered housing desegregation plan will mean an opportunity to finally better her family's circumstances...On the east side of this city, in a mostly white neighborhood known as Mohegan Heights, Anthony C. Romero, a retired paint salesman, moved here from the Bronx 39 years ago. He purchased his four-bedroom house [for] $28,000. [It] is worth about $285,000 in today's market. But Mr. Romero and his wife, Mary, who are white, fear that a federal judge's order to build subsidized housing in their neighborhood for west side residents...could cause the value of their home to plummet.[26]

A handful of "affordable" housing units have been built and occupied. But the order to improve the situation with 800 additional units continues to be blocked: private builders refuse to contract to build the dwellings, and there is no public housing program.[27]

A shocking case of unbridled racism occurred in Vidor, a suburb of Beaumont, Texas—a known Ku Klux Klan stronghold. Vidor has 11,000 whites, no Blacks; Beaumont's population of 114,000 is 41% Black. The Black median income is 47% that of whites in Jefferson County, where Beaumont is the main city; and in Orange County, where Vidor is located, 44% that of whites. The Orange County Blacks all live outside Vidor.

In 1992 a federal judge ordered Vidor to desegregate its all-white 70-unit public housing complex, and a half dozen African Americans moved in. But an aggressive campaign of threats, obscenities and insults became so onerous that by August they all left. The first man to move in, and the last to leave, was William Simpson. He was quoted as saying: "There are good people here, don't get me wrong. But it's overshadowed by the negativity, the hostility, the bigotry of this town." Three days after the interview, Simpson was murdered on the streets of Beaumont.[28]

Vidor was not alone. The desegregation order covered 170 federal housing projects in 36 East Texas counties. The Federal Housing Administration, under contract since 1957 to operate the Vidor, and other, projects, has done nothing about their segregated structure.

The Vidor expulsionary tactics and Simpson's murder pressured Housing Secretary Henry G. Cisneros so that he "took control of the Orange County Housing Authority in Vidor and said 10 to 12 Black families would be moved into the all-white community near the Louisiana border."

The mayor of Vidor, Ruth Woods, who said she supports integration, was pleased at the action.[29] But does Mayor Woods have enough support among the white population to eliminate Klan activities in the future? And, more important, can this be more than a token action?

To make real progress against segregation, the Justice Department would have to collaborate with the NAACP and all organizations fighting segregation, to enforce, vigorously, tough measures to desegregate all areas. Such a program would require legal authorization; determined commitment and a large, trained staff; allocation of millions in funding; the illegalization of racist organizations, with rigorous punishment for infringements—e.g., imprisonment for threats, violence, cross burning, etc. Further, progress would require active mobilization by local trade unions in support of desegregation struggles which, up to now, has been lacking in most cases.

Role of the Government

Federal policy makers, regardless of the party in power, have fostered segregation. Challenges by African Americans and progressive organizations, including the Communist Party, have forced some moderation in the official position: periodically there has been limited support for desegregation and for other steps to reduce racial inequality and discrimination.

During the long, bitter civil rights struggles in the South, FBI agents were on hand, but only as "observers"! They never gave protection to Black or white protesters, never exposed or stopped pogrom-like outrages of the police, KKK or other racist forces.

At that time the Kennedy and then Johnson administrations intervened in some court cases and sponsored civil rights legislation that assisted in the struggle. However, succeeding administrations, notably those of Nixon and Reagan-Bush, increased overtly racist policies: they even intervened in court cases to undermine the civil rights legislation of the 1960s, and used vicious racist propaganda as their main electoral weapon.

The Supreme Court has exerted a powerful influence. Its 1954 ruling against segregated schools helped create the environment for the civil rights gains of the following decade.

Twenty years later, the Supreme Court decision in "Bradley vs. Milliken" was, in the words of dissenting Justice Thurgood Marshall, "...a giant step backward... guaranteeing that Negro children in Detroit will receive the same separate and inherently unequal education in the future as they have been unconstitutionally afforded in the past."

And Judge J. Skelly Wright of the United States Court of Appeals stated that "...the national trend toward residential, political and educational apartheid will not only be greatly accelerated, it will also be rendered legitimate and virtually irreversible by force of law."[30]

During the Reagan-Bush years the Supreme Court was converted, essentially, into a reactionary private club. Most of its decisions, supported by the administration in power, further undermined the supposed intent of the civil rights legislation.

The public response to revelation of the systematic discrimination by banks forced government and FRB officials to threaten "tough action." Lawrence Lindsey, a governor of the FRB, started a campaign to deny banks with racist lending records authority to go through with proposed takeovers of other banks. He was repeatedly overruled until November 1993. By then he had persuaded enough other members of the Board to join him, and a proposed takeover by Shawmut Corporation of Boston was quashed because of its racist lending record. Lindsey, a conservative, was shocked into his position after tours of inner cities and talks with the residents.[31]

Simultaneously, President Clinton proposed "tough new rules" to put added pressure on banks to lend to African Americans. According to press accounts, the rules would require more accounting of actual market shares for minorities, but "...they would not set fixed quotas"—the absence of which is the decisive loophole against effective enforcement.[32]

The outcome, finally, will depend on lengthy negotiations within the Administration and with the bankers and insurance companies that are the main perpetrators of housing segregation and discrimination. Typically, Clinton said that the new rules would take effect more than a year after the announcement—and, if his program for health reform is any indication, that deadline will be further postponed!

The real power in this situation was revealed when the FRB immediately and unequivocally denounced Clinton's proposal. In consonance with the complex bureaucracy involved in finance, the proposals "will be put out for public comment by the Office of the Comptroller of the Currency, the Office of Thrift Supervision, the Federal Deposit Insurance Corporation, and the Fed."[33]

Any illusions that the Democratic Party and President Clinton might be a progressive force in housing policy must have been shattered by his proposals shortly after the Republican Congressional victories in 1994. He announced his intention to radically slash or eliminate a whole series of government housing programs that offered even minimal assistance to moderate and low income families. In this, as in other areas, he raced to compete with the Republicans in destroying what was left of the "social safety net," rather than taking a principled stand and at the very minimum announcing his intention to veto any slashes imposed by the new rightwing-dominated Congress.

Furthermore, the Supreme Court, by a 5 to 4 vote in 1995, decreed exceptionally severe restrictions against affirmative action measures, in a case about legislative districting, threatening to sharply reduce the inadequate Black representation in Congress.

State and local governments compound the racist housing policies of the federal government. Public housing projects, mainly financed by the federal government, are turned over to local "authorities" to operate and control. Like so many of the "authorities" that dominate city finances, transportation, bridges and other key facilities, they are not elected but appointed—leaving the elected city officials powerless to run major sectors of urban affairs.

New York City's public housing authority operates 324 projects with 180,000 apartments housing 600,000 people. It received $800 million in 1992 to operate, renovate and build houses (very little was for new construction).

Blacks and Hispanics comprise more than half New York City's population, and a much greater percentage of them are in the low income bracket. They are most eligible for access to the public housing projects, with their comparatively moderate rents. However, in most projects, a substantial majority of the apartments are allotted to white families. Significantly, the housing authority violated the Fair Housing Act of 1968 by subverting the imposition of racial quotas—to keep Blacks and Latinos out rather than to assure them their fair share of apartments. Moreover, secret codes were used to designate projects to which only white families should be referred. *Mind you, the authority members, of the same social strata that cries bloody murder at mention of quotas to overcome discrimination and segregation, have for years been using quotas to impose segregation!* One method has been to give preference to white families in areas where whites already predominate, and to Black families in ghetto areas, a practice clearly designed to perpetuate housing segregation.

A lawsuit attacking the racist practices was filed in 1990 on behalf of more than 100,000 families. A proposed settlement, covering 31 projects, agreed to reserve 1,991 units for Black and Latino families "...who can show they were excluded...because of the city's selection process. Three out of every four apartments that become vacant at these projects will go to those families until the 1,991 units are filled."[34]

Thus, caught using quotas against oppressed peoples, the authority had to agree to specific numerical goals—i.e. quotas—to counteract its previous racist practices. But as is typical of such legal settlements, only a tiny fraction of the victims will benefit and, at that, it will take a long time to carry out. Turnover is very slow in the public housing projects.

> Evidence in the case showed that the Federal Housing Department knew about some of the city's racial practices and did nothing to correct them.[35]

Partly as a result of such struggles, nonetheless, public housing in New York City was a little less segregated than in most cities. In fact, Massey and Denton found that in 7 of 15 major metropolitan areas, the degree of segregation in public housing exceeded the degree of segregation in private housing.[36]

Obviously patchwork solutions squeezed out locally after years of struggle are not going to change racial housing segregation. Obviously, also, private builders and banking institutions are not going to do it. What will solve the problem is a vast federal public housing program, administered with deliberate use of quotas and location of projects to ensure racial integration in order to eliminate all facets of segregation. See the final program chapter for details.

12. Racism in Education

by David Eisenhower, Ph.D.

Advanced education has become increasingly a requirement for economic well-being. Government officials, employer organizations, and academics stress that modern technology requires brains, not brawn. Secretary of Labor Robert Reich has provided college graduates with the cachet of economic royalty with the cognomen "symbolic analysts."

The gap between earnings of college graduates and high school graduates has widened considerably. Increases in steady employment are concentrated in college graduates and those with advanced degrees obtaining professional and managerial jobs. Permanent employment of basic blue collar workers has declined alarmingly, while employers demand far more in labor, skill and inventiveness from those remaining. Meanwhile, the cost of a full college education soars, barring large segments of the population, especially among minority peoples with their lower average incomes. The entire education system is characterized by the headline, "More separate and less equal."[1]

There was no denying the reality of racist education prior to the Supreme Court's 1954 *Brown vs. Board of Education* decision that ended "Jim Crow" schooling.

Subsequently, conventional wisdom has held that the state has been genuinely committed to educational equality, a belief supported by instances of court-ordered integration and well-publicized affirmative action programs.

However, the educational results since *Brown* reveal otherwise. The policy of inferior education for students of color has remained, although the means became more covert and the coverup more determined.

Over the decade, 1981 to 1991, for example, the high school completion rate of African American and Latino students remained low and changed little.

HIGH SCHOOL COMPLETION RATES

	White	Black	Hispanic
1991	87%	72.5%	55.4%
1981	84%	71.8%	56.8%

SOURCE: The Condition of Education:1993. National Center for Educational Statistics, June 1993. U.S. GPO, p.58

According to NCES, adult literacy, another measure of educational equity, shows a sharp disparity between whites and people of color. Based on a literacy test taken by a national sample, the majority of whites scored average or above, while the majority of African Americans and Hispanics scored below average.[2]

Another measure of the unequal nature of education is the percent of advanced degrees conferred upon African Americans and Hispanics compared to whites. (Note that the percent of bachelor and doctoral degrees awarded to African Americans declined between 1977 and 1989.)

DEGREES CONFERRED (Bachelors/Doctorates)

	Blacks	Hispanics	Whites
1977	6.5%/4.3%	2.1%/2.9%	89.5%/91.4%
1989	5.7%/3.5%	1.8%/2.4%	84.5%/89.3%

SOURCE: Andrew Hacker, *Two Nations*. New York, 1992, p.234.

Scholastic Aptitude Tests (SAT) scores are yet another indicator of the inferior preparatory education available to students of color.

STUDENTS TAKING THE SAT (1990-AVERAGE SCORE)

Black	Hispanic	Whites
737	803	933

SOURCE: Hacker, op. cit., p. 142

Academic circles have engaged in endless theoretical debates over the causes of unequal education. They've also produced countless, narrowly-defined studies focusing on student study habits, the teacher-student relationship, pedagogy, the family background of students, student discipline, student health, student language skills, etc., in pursuit of the "variables" contributing to unequal school achievement.[3] Taken together, the theoretical and empirical work by academics and their popularization by the corporate media have tended to divert attention from the system of educational apartheid administered through state policy.

How do government policies guarantee racist educational outcomes? By:

* promoting a high degree of segregation in education, corresponding to patterns of housing segregation;

* operating overcrowded, underfunded, segregated city schools, with far too many students per teacher and inadequate supplies and facilities;

* allocating unequal funds per student depending upon where the student resides; i.e. in the suburbs or in cities;

* pursuing the "politics of race" and mobilizing opposition to the equalization of funding;

* concentrating poverty and accelerating economic polarization, leaving inner-city youth, in particular, with few opportunities;

* resisting changes from a Eurocentric curriculum; and

* failing to insure that teachers are representative of the student body.

State-sponsored patterns of housing discrimination, discussed in Chapter 11, reinforce the segregation of schools. As Douglas Massey and Nancy Denton write:

> Residential segregation is the institutional apparatus that supports the racially discriminatory processes and binds them into a coherent, uniquely effective system of racial subordination.[4]

According to the Harvard Project on School Desegregation, 74.3% of Hispanic students—or 3.7 million out of 5 million—attended predominately minority schools. The figure for African American students is 66%—or 4.6 million out of 6.9 million attending predominately minority schools.

These figures reflect the re-segregation of schools, with the nation's largest cities having the highest concentration of Black and Hispanic students. For larger inner cities, "15 out of every 16 African American and Latino students are in schools where most of the students are non-white." The story is the same for smaller city and suburban schools. There is a clustering and concentration of students of color.[5]

The table below shows the trend of segregation.

% OF BLACK AND HISPANIC STUDENTS IN PREDOMINANTLY MINORITY SCHOOLS, BY YEAR

Year	Black Students	Hispanic Students
1968	77%	55%
1972	64%	57%
1980	63%	66%
1986	63%	72%
1991	66%	73%

SOURCE: Harvard University School of Education

The intensification of school segregation is the direct result of influential Republican and Democratic politicians openly pandering to the racist prejudices of many white voters. As a feature of a governing strategy, politicians permeate politics with race in order to consolidate, in Andrew Hacker's words, "a self-conscious racial majority"[6] opposed (even at its own expense) to governmental programs promoting socio-economic justice.

President Clinton's comments to those assembled for the NAACP Legal Defense and Education Fund's observance of the 40th anniversary of *Brown vs. Board of Education* are a good example of the race-baiting and scapegoating which has again come to mark ruling-class politics. In his prepared remarks, Clinton attacked the "new segregation" he saw taking root in America. For Clinton, however, the "new segregation" had nothing to do with patterns of residential and educational segregation. Rather the "new segregation" Clinton warned about came from African Americans. According to the President, Black extremists rather than white racists and public policy dominated by racism, were responsible for the resurgence of racial polarization.[7]

School segregation also results from Supreme Court rulings, such as the 1974 *Milliken vs. Bradley* decision and the 1992 *DeKalb County, Georgia* decision. The former exempted suburban areas adjacent to Detroit from an area-wide desegregation plan that would have merged urban and suburban school systems. The latter removed federal court oversight of desegregation efforts once local school districts made "good faith" efforts to achieve equity, even in the face of unequal resource allocations.

Systematic underfunding of segregated schools and political resistance to equalization guarantees the unequal outcomes of education. Thomas Sobol, the beleaguered New York State Education Commissioner, recently observed that N.Y. State runs two distinct school systems—one urban, minority, poor and failing—and the other suburban, white, affluent and successful. Sobol's comments could be repeated by every Commissioner of Education who yearly reviews data on the expenditures per student for each school district.

Urban school districts are particularly underfunded, victimized by:
• a politics of white, suburban privilege;
• a fiscal "crisis" caused by tax breaks granted the rich and corporations, depriving states and cities of revenues and short-changing urban school districts (bringing school districts like Los Angeles to the verge of insolvency);
• a system of funding schools based on local real estate taxes which gives wealthier districts an advantage over poorer, urban districts;
• a state school aid formula that falls short in equalizing spending per student across school districts; and
• drastic cuts in federal urban assistance, forcing cuts in city budgets.

Following is a table indicating spending for three New York districts.

District	Percent of Population		Median Family Income	Pct. Poverty	Spending per Student	
	non-Hispanic white	Black & Latino			Total	State Aid
Wading River (Suffolk)	95%	5%	$58,947	4.1%	$17,435	$1,087
Greenburgh (Westchester)	74%	19%*	57,838	1.3	15,128	2,643
Mount Vernon (Westchester)	36%	63%	34,830	11.8	9,112	3,651

SOURCE: NY State Department of Education and 1990 Census of Population. *There is also a substantial Asian population

New York is not exceptional in providing separate and unequal education. While school funding varies greatly from state to state, there are distinct racist patterns described in compelling detail by Jonathan Kozol in his aptly named book, *Savage Inequalities.* [8]

Data from school districts in the Chicago area and from districts in New Jersey reveal the racist, anti-workingclass nature of education in the U.S.

CHICAGO AREA 1988-1989

School District	Spending per Pupil
Niles Township High School	$9,371 capitalist and middle class, white
Glancoe (Elementary and Jr. High)	$7,363 mixed socially, mainly white
Wilmette (Elementary and Jr. High)	$6,009 mainly working class, white
Chicago (all grades)	$5,265 mainly working class, Black and Latino

NEW JERSEY 1988-1989 SCHOOL YEAR

School District	Spending per Pupil
Princeton	$7,725 high income, overwhelmingly white
Summit	$7,275 high and middle income, white
Jersey City	$4,566 working class, mixture of races
Camden	$3,538 working class, almost all Black

(Source: Kozol, p.236)

In March, 1993, New York City filed suit in State Supreme Court charging that the State's school aid formula was discriminatory, arguing that New York schools were "severely split between urban and suburban areas, between one world that is largely African American, Latino, Asian American and poor and another that is largely white and prosperous."[9]

New York City's legal action is being repeated in at least 29 states. In ten states the way schools are funded has been declared unconstitutional. Some of the states' school financial systems have been held illegal more than once.[10]

Effort to achieve educational equity, however, have met with intense political opposition across the country, attacked as "Robin Hood" formulas. As journalist Nicholas Lemann observed:

> ...spending-based remedies to the inferiority of all-minority public schools...attract such intense political opposition—having recently [contributed to the defeat of Governor Jim Florio of New Jersey... that they are often assumed to be impossible.[11]

In July 1994, for the third time since 1973, the New Jersey Supreme Court ruled that the state's system of funding public education was unconstitutional because it provided an "inferior education to predominantly African American and Latino urban students." Just as in prior court rulings, opposition to changing the status quo immediately appeared. Robert Boose, executive director of the New Jersey School Board Association, "whose power," according to one news report, "rests squarely in the heart of Gov. Whitman's core constituency, the suburban [white] school districts," is one opponent determined to extend suburban education privileges into the 21st century. He is reported as saying, "This is going to be a 24-round fight and right now we're only in the 18th."[12]

For 25 years ruling circles in Texas have also successfully resisted court orders to partially redistribute tax funds to provide a more equitable distribution. Spending on the 5% of school children in Texas' richest districts averaged $11,801 per child; spending on schools of the 5% in the poorest districts averaged $3,190 per child.

Under court order, a trivial reform authorizing reallocation of 2.75% of school revenues to poorer districts was beaten by 63% of voters in an election in which only 25% of the eligible voters participated. The racist, anti-labor forces, financed by Texas billionaires and millionaires, conducted a vicious campaign, and successfully mobilized the right-wing, racist voters of the state. Supporters of the amendment did not unite to mobilize the overwhelming majority who certainly would have voted for the amendment had they been adequately informed about the issue.

Under instructions from the State Supreme Court, a judge threatened to withhold funds from schools if there was no compliance with the policy of more equitable funding. Since, in fact, this would have merely closed the schools a couple of weeks early, the stage was set for another round in the quarter-century maneuvering of the rich to maintain their privileges through racist discrimination.[13]

The journalist reporting on the Texan school battle, Sam Howe Verhovek, commented:

> ...proposals to do away with local school taxes altogether, replacing them with a state tax that could be apportioned equally among the schools, are almost uniformly dismissed around the country as undermining local control.[14]

Of course, the slogan of "local control" is misleading. What is meant is capitalist class control. No matter how democratic the procedures of local school boards, the wealth in the rich districts give them the funds to run the schools for their children lavishly, while local efforts of school boards in poor districts simply cannot overcome the lack of funding to which they are doomed because of their poverty.

Thus a large portion of the residents of suburban school districts pay a heavy price for the adequate schools in their districts. Middle-income employees, skilled workers and retirees are faced with soaring property taxes while their real incomes stagnate or decline. The allocation of property taxes is determined by a wealthy minority, by real estate and banking interests, by those with political pull able to benefit from loopholes and exemptions.

The most severe racist discrimination is in the South, as is the most severe discrimination against the working class as a whole.

In Alabama, a state judge has ruled that the state's schools violate the Constitution by failing to provide adequate education.

In Sardia, AL:

> At the Shiloh Elementary and Middle School the library has not bought any books in 20 years. There are no science labs, no band, no music, no art, no foreign language courses. The roof leaks and the dingy 43-year old building is about worn out.[15]
> There are worse schools in Alabama, like the one in adjacent Wilcox County where raw sewage seeped for years onto a playground and termites ate through books...[16]

In the cities and counties that are 99% white, conditions are not as bad; but they are not good anywhere in the state. Wealthy people send their children to private school but that is becoming more expensive and—contrary to popular belief—nationally the proportion of children in private schools has been declining.

In March 1994, Michigan became the first state to adopt a centralized state tax to fund education, replacing the local real estate tax approach. The features of the Michigan school-funding plan are being reviewed by a number of other states, many of whom are in state courts over constitutional problems with the way their schools are currently funded. As a result Michigan could serve as a model for "reforming" the way schools are funded around the country. This is unfortunate because Michigan's plan replaces the property tax with an unreliable and regressive sales tax, a hike in cigarette taxes and a larger take from state Keno games.

Furthermore, the state plan would *maintain* the spending gap between rich and poor districts by allowing richer districts to raise additional taxes to augment the basic state's spending-per-student grant. In five years all districts would receive $4,200 per student, an amount that represents merely a floor. Wealthy districts would be permitted to spend more than twice that amount.

The class and racial nature of educational politics and policy is obvious around the country. The state *insures* that students in wealthy, predominately white districts receive preferential education, providing advantages to some while denying them to others. The state, in other words, operates an educational system that applies racial and class criteria to establish who is "qualified" and who is "disqualified." Rationed education is the mechanism to ration opportunities.

Who gets to be a full-time faculty member in higher education is but one implication of the rationing of education, in this case the regulation of advanced degrees. According to the U.S. EEOC, Blacks and Hispanics hold a tiny percent of full-time teaching positions in our colleges and universities.

	Male			Female		
	White	Black	Hispanic	White	Black	Hispanic
%Full-time faculty (1991)	68.2	2.5	1.4	31.8	2.2	0.8

(SOURCE: "Higher Educational State Information Report #EEO-6." EEOC, Washington, D.C.: GPO, 1993)

A similar picture emerges from U.S. EEOC data with respect to secondary school teachers:

	Male		Female	
% of total	Black	Hispanic	Black	Hispanic
Secondary Teachers (1992-1993)	3	1.5	6.3	1.7

(SOURCE: "Elementary Secondary Staff Information Report." #EEO-5, Washington, D.C.: GPO, 1993)

It is, furthermore, a truism that education is crucial for financial success.

However, racism systematically denies Black and Hispanic students an adequate education. On graduation from high school, therefore, Black youth are less likely to have the standard qualifications for jobs requiring a high-school education, and less likely to have the qualifications for college admissions, or at least to the better ranking colleges and to the most promising of educational specialties within college. And the benefits of education are much less for people of color than for whites.

The average (mean) income of Black males, e.g., as a percentage of the average for white males with a corresponding amount of education, tells a dramatic story.

EDUCATION AND INCOME, MALES 25 YEARS OR OLDER, 1991

Amount of Education	Percent Black of White Mean Income	
	1991	1971
Less than 9 years	87.0%	77%
High School	75.3	69
Incomplete College	75.6	67
College Degree	68.1	70

(SOURCE: P-60 No.180 Table 29, and P-60, No.85, T 49, shown in *Economics of Racism*, Table 9, p.43)

In 1971, there was a wide gap between the incomes of Black and white males, no matter what the degree of education. The gap was about 30% for high school or more education. But by 1991 the situation had worsened, in that the more education, the wider the gap. For high school and partial college education, the gap was about 25%, but for those with a college degree it was a full 32%! The significance of this is increased when one considers that the importance of a college education has grown significantly over the past two decades. By 1991, one-fourth of white males 25 years or older had obtained a college degree, as compared with less than one-eighth of African American men (11.9%).

Periodically, there are federal reports and initiatives announced with much fanfare and hand-wringing. The 1983 "Nation at Risk" report and the "Goals 2000" initiative adopted by the nation's governors in 1990 are two recent examples.

However, such interest shouldn't be taken seriously. While rich in slogans, adequate money is never provided to achieve the goal of building a "nation of learners." Under self-imposed financial constraints, federal resources for improving education in grades one through twelve actually declined from $12.1 billion in FY 1992 to $11.6 billion in FY 1993.[17]

When George Bush was president, he cautioned that more spending on public education was not the best answer. He even admonished parents of poor children who see money as a cure for educational problems as symptomatic of a society that has come to "worship money."[18] For the Bush administration, "school choice" vouchers for private schools and the privatization of education became the responses to preempt any drive to provide any genuine equal education.

Current educational policies have been developed to prepare and allocate the various grades of labor, to determine who gets a well-paying job assignment and who is consigned to the growing number of unskilled, low-wage jobs, and to make it appear that "individual merit" or cultural factors were responsible for it all.

Furthermore, the unequal outcomes of education are part of a comprehensive strategy of the ruling class to preserve its power through the maintenance of white skin privilege and prevent unity of Black, white and Latino not only in education, but in all areas of everyday life.

A really equitable system, so long as residential segregation persists, would have each state set roughly equal standards of spending per pupil, and of pupils per teacher, to be financed out of revenue. For majority Black and Hispanic districts, funding and staffing should be raised to somewhat above state average levels, to help compensate for educational disadvantages imposed by ghetto conditions.This should be accomplished without reducing funds for most school districts, aside from a few districts of the very rich, where school funding and staffing are way above average. A further improvement would be for large-scale federal aid distributions that reduce differences in funding and staffing resulting from wide dispersions of average income levels and potential tax sources among the states.

13. Racism in Health Care

by Lawrence D. Weiss, Ph.D.

Pervasive racism is one of the hallmarks of American history. The theft of the land and all its resources was accomplished with the racist justification that Native Americans were no better and were often worse than the beasts found in the untamed wilderness. Their lot was to be hunted down and destroyed in a genocidal fury that accompanied the expropriation of North America by small and big-time capitalists. Racism justified the immeasurably brutal destruction of whole nations in Africa by the slave trade, and the creation of a slave economy in much of North America. Racism has since justified the exploitation of Asian labor gangs to build the great railroads in America's West, the theft of the vast Southwest from Mexico and the subsequent exploitation of Mexicans and other Latin American workers in industry and agriculture throughout the United States. Given the fundamental centrality of racism to the building of the world's premier capitalist nation, it should come as no surprise that public health, personal health, and the institution of medical care all continue to bear the heavy, ugly burden of racism.

Brief History

Until the 1960s there was overt discrimination against African American physicians and patients by white-dominated hospitals and associated white physicians. While the most extreme discrimination predominated in the southern and border states, there was significant discrimination in health care institutions across the nation. African American physicians could not admit their patients to "white" hospitals, nor could they gain hospital privileges in these hospitals. As a result they were effectively barred from practicing medicine in white hospitals. In addition, white hospitals for the most part simply ignored African American communities by locating elsewhere. Under these adverse conditions, African Americans and some white entrepreneurs founded at least 200 hospitals since the 1800s, featuring African American physicians and support people serving African American patients in their own communities. The historical importance of these institutions can hardly be overstated. They provided health care for African Americans who could get it nowhere else. They provided training grounds and facilities in which to practice medicine for African American physicians who could not practice elsewhere. They

This Chapter is excerpted with permission from the manuscript of a medical sociology textbook prepared by Lawrence D. Weiss.

trained and gave experience to many African American workers, professionals and entrepreneurs who could not have found comparable employment elsewhere (Taravella 1990). Nevertheless, the relatively few Black physicians and the underfinanced Black hospitals could adequately serve only a fraction of the Black population in need. African Americans isolated in rural areas found it particularly difficult to gain access to health care.

Ironically, as a result of civil rights victories eliminating overt discrimination in many health care facilities in the 1960s, formerly Black hospitals faced an extremely difficult situation. In effect, one of their main historical reasons for existence appeared to have evaporated. Black hospitals lost the struggle for Black physicians and patients as these streamed to the wealthier formerly all-white hospitals. In addition Black hospitals were increasingly financially squeezed by the growing poverty of the inner-city patients they served. In 1944 there were at least 124 Black hospitals, but only eight remained by the end of 1989. All the rest had been closed or had been merged with formerly all-white institutions (McBride 1993).

From the mid-1940s to the mid-1960s Federal Hill-Burton grants disbursed about $2 billion to establish a network of acute-care hospitals across America. While the federal program prohibited discrimination in facilities by Hill-Burton on the basis of "race, creed, or color," there was a widely used provision which allowed for the construction of separate health care facilities for African Americans if such facilities were "of like quality." In reality, however, facilities for African Americans were often separate but were rarely equal to those of whites. By the end of 1962, 89 "racially exclusive" facilities in 14 southern and border states had received $37 million in Hill-Burton for construction or remodeling. In North Carolina, for example, in the mid-1960s Hill-Burton funds had constructed 27 hospitals exclusively for whites, and only four for Blacks. In Charlotte, the state's largest city, the major hospital reserved 437 beds for whites and only 30 for Blacks despite the fact that nearly a quarter of the city's population was Black (Smith 1990).

Segregation of hospitals and nursing homes was extensive in the North as well. A mid-1950s study of hospital segregation in Chicago found that over half of all patients in the county public hospital were Black, but less than one percent of the patients in area private hospitals were Black, despite the fact that nearly half of the city's Black population had hospital insurance. A mid-1960s study of hospitals in Buffalo found rampant discrimination:

Hospital A: Concentration of Negro patients in one wing; Negro maternity cases are restricted to one particular floor; Negro doctors are excluded from both the active and courtesy staff; Negro applicants have been denied admission to the nursing school.

Hospital B: Negro patients are excluded from two floors; Negro patients experience continual difficulty in obtaining requested accommodations.
Hospital C: Negro patients excluded from new wing of the hospital.
Hospital D: Color matching segregation by rooms and areas in maternity.
Hospital E: Negro patients are excluded from the new section of the hospital.
Hospital F: Color matching in maternity area.
Hospital G: Negro employees excluded from dietary department.
(New York State Advisory Committee 1964, 10, quoted in Smith 1990, 594.)

The Civil Rights Struggle for Access

Smith (1990, 567) identifies five social processes he considers primarily responsible for largely eliminating segregation in health care facilities by the end of the 1960s:

1. World War II, which weakened Jim Crow ideology in the United States because it was similar to Nazi ideology of racial superiority;

2. The Cold War with the Soviet Union which heightened the international awareness of racist discrimination in the U.S., embarrassing the federal government;

3. The Civil Rights movement;

4. The expansion of health care programs at the federal level after World War II;

5. The strong growth of the national economy in the 1950s and 1960s.

Of all these factors, the civil rights movement was the only one that specifically mobilized organizations and large groups of people to fight racism and discrimination in medical facilities. One of the key organizations in this struggle was the National Medical Association (NMA), founded just before the turn of the century when jim crow racism had reached its peak in the South. The NMA was composed of about 60 medical societies scattered across the nation. These societies were started by African American physicians who had been excluded from white-dominated state medical societies that made up the national constituency of the American Medical Association (AMA). During the 1930s and 1940s NMA's struggle against discrimination focused on the racist exclusion of African Americans from AMA-affiliated state medical societies and from most segregated hospitals:

> The medical-staff by-laws of most hospitals stipulated that appointments would be made only from members in good standing with the local medical societies. Exclusion from these local medical societies blocked any chance of gaining staff privileges at white hospitals. Black physicians were thus far more likely than black patients to face restrictions in access to hospitals. As the practice of medicine became increasingly hospital-dependent, access to hospitals became an increasingly critical problem (Smith 1990, 568-9).

The NMA Good Will Committee was formed in 1938 to try to fight racism in the AMA and its constituent state societies by friendly persuasion. The Committee's first significant victory came a couple of years later when it convinced the AMA to leave off the special notation "(Col.)" after every "colored" physician in the AMA directory. A decade later the Committee influenced the AMA to pass a weak resolution requesting AMA-affiliated state medical societies to "study" the question of racist exclusionary practices. This watered-down concession was probably a political move to try to wean the NMA away from supporting the Truman administration's proposal for a national health insurance program, adamantly opposed by the AMA. During the late 1940s the NMA urged the Association of American Medical Colleges (AAMC) to adopt a resolution against racist discrimination in medical school admissions. In its annual meetings the AAMC repeatedly refused to do so; however, about this same time the Legal Defense Fund of the National Association for the Advancement of Colored People (NAACP) took a couple of cases to the Supreme Court which resulted in the admission of African Americans into medical schools in Arkansas and Texas.

In 1953 the NMA and the NAACP formally joined forces to establish the NAACP National Health Program. The Program's strategy had two components: the first was to try to convince hospitals to voluntarily eliminate segregation and exclusion of African American physicians, and the second was to build legal cases against those hospitals that refused. A series of annual national conferences beginning in the late 1950s jointly held by NMA and NAACP focused on the issue of ending segregation in medical facilities. These goals were adopted by the Kennedy and Johnson administrations, "due in part to the strong support that the NMA, in contrast to the AMA, had provided in the early 1960s to pending Medicare legislation" (Smith 1990, 573). A series of suits brought by the NAACP and NMA in the late 1950s and early 1960s against hospitals made the case that, since they accepted Hill-Burton funds, they could not discriminate under the "due-process, equal-protection provisions of the U.S. Constitution." A 1963 victory in the U.S. Court of Appeals for one of those cases resulted in the issuance of new, more stringent anti-discrimination language by the Surgeon General for health care facilities receiving Hill-Burton funds. A year later the historic Civil Rights Act passed which prohibited discrimination based on "race" for any entity receiving federal financial assistance—which included most hospitals in the U.S. In 1964 the Johnson administration held a widely attended conference to encourage the private health care facilities to desegregate according to the law. The following year Medicare and Medicaid legislation passed which required any facility accepting money from either program to comply with civil rights legislation prohibiting discrimination based on "race." This tied both physician and hospital revenue to the elimination of discriminatory practices—an important carrot along with the punitive legal stick.

By the end of 1966 the staff of the Office of Equal Health Opportunity in the Public Health Service had grown to 600 persons. Thousands of hospitals had been reviewed for compliance with the Medicare anti-discrimination provisions. A couple of years later the acting director of the Office for Civil Rights reported that 97 percent of all hospitals in the U.S. were committed to provide nondiscriminatory services. Civil rights groups argued that the federal government was glossing over its duty to enforce the law, and should withhold funds from many certified hospitals to comply with the civil rights provisions. However, on the whole, most hospitals eliminated overt discriminatory practices to comply with federal regulations. On another front, discriminatory practices in nursing homes were barely affected by the civil rights advances of the 1960s:

> Although many southern communities focused on integrating their nursing homes, in part due to their smaller size, larger proportion of private ownership, and lack of active medical staff involvement. While the new Medicare and Medicaid regulations closed many older wood-frame facilities for life-safety violations, no homes were closed because of competition for patients from newly integrated white facilities. Many of the closed black hospitals were converted to nursing homes and continued to provide care to a predominantly black clientele (Smith 1990, 581).

In the mid-1980s an elderly white person was 1.36 times more likely than an elderly African American to be a resident of a nursing home. Over half of all nursing home payments came from Medicaid. African Americans accounted for 31 percent of Medicaid recipients, but only 8 percent of the recipients of Medicaid in skilled nursing homes. Across the nation there is a geographic pattern in the distribution of long-term care facilities. States and counties with higher proportions of white residents have higher proportions of nursing home beds. Various studies tend to point to discrimination as the principal cause of these gross discrepancies:

> The effect of these patterns of discrimination in geographic access and the economic barriers that help create them, while exacerbating their consequences, is racial discrimination in access. As a result, a large proportion of the Medicaid dollars for nursing-home care, intended to provide access to the poor without regard to race, actually provides a catastrophic long-term insurance benefit to the white middle class. (Smith 1990, 586).

The NMA remained very active through the latter half of the 1960s and into the 1970s. It continued to work with the NAACP as well as with many of the newer activist civil rights organizations such as the Southern Christian Leadership Conference (SCLC) and the Student Nonviolent Coordinating Committee (SNCC). In addition the NMA became extremely active as a lobbying organization for civil rights legislation and for progressive health care reforms, often at odds with the AMA. After the murder of three civil rights workers in 1964, NMA provided dozens of medical workers to serve in the South with civil rights organizations. Many of these medical professionals joined the Medical Committee for Human Rights (MCHR), which by 1966 had various health workers established in branches in 30 northern and southern cities. In the late 1960s MCHR expanded its mission to include exposing discrimination in health care facilities in northern facilities as well as in the South. By the early 1970s MCHR had ceased to have much of a national political presence, but in its heyday it "managed significant initiatives in the North that included establishing child health programs for ghetto neighborhoods, protest marches against discrimination in local hospitals, and support for recruiting black and Hispanic youth into medical work fields" (McBride 1993, 323). On another front in the late 1960s African American physicians of the NMA in conjunction with progressive whites used funds from the Office of Economic Opportunity (OEO) to establish over 100 neighborhood comprehensive health centers targeting public health and individual medical needs of low-income minority communities.

Despite some successes in the areas of civil rights and health care, and the delivery of better health care services in some minority communities, the health of African Americans as a people began to enter a critical stage. As a result, in 1976 Atlanta University convened the W.E.B. DuBois Conference, a national meeting of scholars from various fields to address the serious and growing problem of the health status of African Americans and the lack of adequate health care facilities in their communities. NMA physicians warned against health care reform in the shape of a monolithic health insurance bureaucracy, arguing that such a system would not serve the needs of the poor and the inner-city ghettoes. Instead, NMA members argued for an expansion of Medicaid which was more directly pertinent to low-income communities.

In the 1980s, under the conservative Reagan administration, free-market health care emerged as the ideology buttressing the medical-industrial complex. NMA African American physicians and other progressive health care activists argued that market medicine responds to well-insured individuals rather than groups of people (such as African Americans) with shorter life spans, higher rates of chronic diseases and incapacitating disabilities, and minimal protection from infectious diseases.

Other developments included cuts in medical care for urban neighborhood residents. Federal and employment-based medical benefits were declining, community health centers were underfinanced, and municipalities were decreasing subsidies for free medical services for the poor at city hospitals...For example, in 1982 federal funding for the nation's 872 community health centers was decreased by an average of 30 to 45 percent. This revenue decline resulted in service cutbacks or closings at 238 (28 percent) of health centers. A study of 5 health centers in Boston attributed a 14 percent reduction in obstetrics visits, a 13 percent drop in pediatric visits, and a significant increase in local infant mortality to the federal aid reductions...(McBride 1993, 327).

In 1984 the NMA published a series of studies documenting serious problems with the health care system as a whole, and specific health problems among African Americans focusing on the "wide disparity in the health of black and white Americans: black Americans show higher maternal and infant mortality rates, lower life expectancy, and higher death rates linked to cardiovascular disease and cancer" (McBride 1993, 330). The following year the Department of Health and Human Services released a report compiled by a task force of high-ranking federal officials. The *Report of the Secretary's Task Force on Black and Minority Health* documented the failure of the health care system to eliminate differences in mortality and illness based on skin color and ethnicity. The report noted that African Americans were experiencing nearly 60,000 preventable deaths annually compared to the white population, due in large part to "cancer, cardiovascular disease and stroke, substance abuse, diabetes, homicides and accidents and infant mortality" (McBride 1993, 331). A couple of years later, the AIDS epidemic hit African American communities with a vengeance. A massively inadequate health care system was entirely unprepared for yet another health care crisis in minority communities. Dr. Louis W. Sullivan, Secretary of Health and Human Services in the Bush administration, summarized the situation in a brief article published in the *Journal of the American Medical Association* (1991):

> I contend that there is clear, demonstrable, undeniable evidence of discrimination and racism in our health care system. For example, each year since 1984, while the health status of the general population has increased, black health status has actually declined. This decline is not in one or two categories, it is across the board...

Even the conservative AMA admits that racism continues to play a significant role in explaining persistent differences in health care access and treatment between whites and minorities. According to a report published by AMA's Council on Ethical and Judicial Affairs:

> Disparities in treatment decisions may reflect the existence of subconscious bias. This is a serious and troubling problem. Despite the progress of the past 25 years,

racial prejudice has not been entirely eliminated in this country. The health care system, like all other elements of society, has not fully eradicated this prejudice (Council on Ethical and Judicial Affairs 1990, 2346).

Minorities and Access to Health Care

The issue of access to health care among minorities is inextricably tied to the fact that minorities are vastly underrepresented in the higher-level health professions. In 1991, for example, only 3.2 percent of all physicians were Black, 3.4 percent of pharmacists were Black and a mere 1.5 percent of all dentists were Black despite the fact that African Americans represent well over 12 percent of the total population (Bureau of the Census 1992, 392-4). A history of overt racism and institutional discrimination are responsible for both discrimination in access and in the health professions. Moreover, since minority physicians tend to practice in minority communities, there is a direct relationship between lack of access and the underrepresentation of minorities in the upper tiers of the health professions.

African Americans are nearly twice as likely as non-Hispanic whites to lack health insurance, and Hispanics are nearly two and one-half times as likely not to have health insurance (Short, et al. 1989). Moreover, these minorities are losing their health insurance coverage at a faster rate than non-Hispanic whites. Despite the fact that African Americans and Hispanics together accounted for a bit more than 20 percent of the total population, between 1977 and 1987 these minorities accounted for over half the increase in the number of uninsured Americans. In the ten-year period beginning with 1977, the percent of uninsured whites climbed from 12 percent to 15 percent, but uninsured African Americans grew from 18 percent to 25 percent, and Hispanics from 20 percent to a shocking 35 percent. A national survey found that 86 percent of those in fair or poor health who were covered by health insurance saw a physician in a one-year period, while only 63 percent of those not insured but in fair or poor health saw a physician. The uninsured have significantly less access, and minorities are much more likely to be uninsured (Cornelius 1993, 16, 18, 22, 24).

Bill Clinton, in his campaign for the Presidency in 1992, promised universal health insurance coverage. His administration set up a bureaucracy to draft appropriate legislation, which became bogged down by pressures from and attempts to satisfy various sectors of the private health industry, its providers and financial intermediaries. The experience of Canada and various European countries providing centrally financed universal coverage was ignored, as were progressive United States groups urging a "single payer" system for our country.

Prolonged deal-making between the White House and Congressional leaders in 1994 gutted the inadequate Clinton proposals and ended up with no live proposal for significant reform. However, the struggle for a single payer system continues on a state-by-state basis, with prospects for significant breakthroughs in some states.

While Blacks, Latinos and Native Americans would benefit from government financed health coverage, none of the existing proposals, including single-payer formulas, specifically provide for the elimination of the existing many-sided racial discrimination. Meanwhile, under the guise of "budget balancing," government benefits through Medicaid, Medicare and other health programs through which sections of the minority population benefit are being slashed.

When seeking health care, Hispanics are more than twice as likely as non-Hispanic whites to use hospital outpatient clinics or emergency rooms, and African Americans are more than three times as likely. As these minorities progressively lose health insurance coverage, they often have nowhere else to turn but the emergency room for health care. While their acute care needs are more or less met in this manner, emergency rooms and clinics cannot provide the continuity of care necessary for adequate, comprehensive health care, particularly for the chronically ill. On average, under 10 percent of non-Hispanic whites wait more than an hour to be seen by a health care provider, but proportionally twice as many Hispanics and African Americans wait at least one hour. Long waits act as a deterrent to seeking needed care, and put these patients at higher risk for leaving the health care facility before receiving care. Long waits may also be one of the factors which have contributed to a serious decline in recent years of physician visits by African Americans. In 1982, 80 percent of all African Americans saw a physician at least once during the year. By 1987 only 63 percent had seen a physician in that year. Even after waiting for long periods of time, language barriers may put Hispanics and other minorities who may speak little or no English at a serious disadvantage in the physician's office. A study of Medicaid sites in seven states that represent nearly 85 percent of the total Hispanic population in the United States found that a third of these sites had no special services to help monolingual Hispanic patients (Cornelius 1993, 16, 20).

Commenting on differences in mammography use according to income and education, Lawrence Bergner of the National Cancer Institute has expressed concern that simply expanding mammography programs (and by implication any health care service) without specifically targeting the underserved population simply results in larger gaps based on income and education. In addition he critiques the pejorative "blame the victim" implication made by some health planners and educators who fail to reach their target populations. He notes that despite the expected expansion of mammography programs nationwide,

> [i]t is not unlikely that the differences between groups will still persist. Women in the medical care mainstream—those who have an ongoing relationship with a health care professional, who are native English speakers, who have no significant cultural taboos or skepticism about medical care, and who are able to deal with copayment or other marginal costs—will have gotten the message and obtained the service. Women who are disadvantaged in these or other categories will be reported to have "failed" to obtain mammography. They will probably be referred to as "hard to reach." Would "underserved" be more accurate? (Bergner 1993, 940).

African American and White Differential Access to Health Care: Selected Studies

Elderly African Americans Receive Fewer Medical Services

Dr. Escarce and colleagues (1993) looked at a 5 percent national sample of Medicare enrollees aged 65 and older in order to examine Black-white differences in the use of 32 medical procedures and diagnostic tests by the elderly. Altogether they examined the records of 1,200,000 enrollees. They were interested in studying this question because

> Elderly Blacks generally score lower than elderly Whites on self-ratings of health status. Blacks also have a shorter life expectancy than Whites, and the difference in life expectancy between Blacks and Whites who reach age 65 is increasing. Substantial differences in the type of care that Blacks and Whites receive have been documented in the non-Medicare population, and recent studies suggest that similar patterns may occur among the elderly (Escarce et al. 1993, 948).

The 32 procedures included diagnostic services such as exercise stress test, mammogram and chest radiograph; and restorative medical procedures such as coronary bypass surgery, cataract extraction with lens insertion, and total hip replacement. Overall,

> Whites...were more likely than Blacks to receive 23 of the 32 study services...and for many of these services the racial differences in use were substantial. Whites were between 1.5 and 2.0 times as likely as Blacks to receive eight of the study services, between 2.0 and 3.0 times as likely to receive three of the services, and more than 3.0 times as likely to receive [a variety of vascular procedures]. In contrast, Blacks were more likely than Whites... to receive only seven of the study services, and for four of these services, the differences in use were small (Escarce et al. 1993, 949-50).

The researchers also looked at the question of the use of newer or higher technology services compared to older or lower technology services. They found that whites were more likely to receive the newer, high-tech services compared to Blacks. For example, whites were more likely to receive a high-tech magnetic resonance imagery scan of the brain, but less likely than Blacks to receive a technologically passe computerized tomographic scan.

African Americans Less Likely to Have Cardiac Procedures

Whittle and colleagues found that a number of medical procedures to diagnose or treat heart disease were used much more frequently on white patients than on African American patients in Veterans Administration hospitals. The researchers noted that "[w]hite race was a statistically significant predictor of the use of each of the procedures, regardless of which independent variables were included" (Whittle, et al. 1993, 623). Moreover, when the analysis was restricted to veterans with limited income, the white/Black differences remained. The authors conclude by noting that

> The extent to which subtle or overt racism underlies racial differences in the use of cardiac procedures is unclear. We believe that inadequate health education, differences in patients' preferences for invasive management, delivery systems that are unfriendly to members of certain cultures, and overt racism may all play a part. Allocating responsibility more precisely will require studies that control for angiographic data and directly examine interactions between patients and medical professionals. Debating how much "blame" should be allocated to which factor should not delay efforts to clarify and remedy each of these deficiencies in our medical care system (Whittle, et al. 1993, 626).

Black/White Differences in Reported Prenatal Care Advice from Health Care Providers

Kogan and colleagues (1994) were interested in the question of Black/white differentials in the content of health education offered by the providers of women's health care. The question is important given well-documented higher rates of infant mortality and prematurity among African American babies. The researchers looked at a sample of 8,310 women from the 1988 National Maternal and Infant Health Survey. Here's what they found:

> The present study suggests that large numbers of women of all races do not receive sufficient health behavior modification information as part of the content of their prenatal care. In particular, Black women are more likely not to receive health behavior advice that could reduce their chances of having an adverse pregnancy outcome. Specifically, they are less likely to report smoking and alcohol cessation advice (Kogan, et al. 1994, 87-8).

Black/White Differences in Health and Health Care Service Utilization Among the Elderly

Researchers Mutchler and Burr (1991) were interested in looking at the hypothesis that health differences in later life between African Americans and whites are a function of socioeconomic status. Their sample included most African Americans and whites over 55 years of age in the 1984 national Survey of Income and Program Participation (SIPP), totalling 848 African Americans and 8,955 whites. A simple description of the health status and health care utilization by African Americans and whites in this study indicates that African Americans fare worse on every measure. For example, on the more subjective measures, such as the self-rating of current health, nearly 60 percent of African American respondents rate their health fair or poor, whereas a bit more than a third of the whites rated their health fair or poor. On more objective or quantifiable measures, such as days spent in bed due to health problems in the last four months, nearly 79 percent of the whites spent no days in bed, whereas fewer than 71 percent of African Americans spent no days in bed:

> ...[E]ven after socioeconomic characteristics are considered, Blacks report significantly poorer self-rated health than whites. Consistent to this result, Blacks report more visits to a health professional during the year prior to interview, even after controlling for socioeconomic status. These indicators, perhaps more than the others, suggest that above and beyond the socioeconomic costs of being Black, the *stress* associated with minority group status may take a toll on perceived health among older Blacks. (Mutchler and Burr 1991, 352-3; emphasis in original.)

Access to Long-Term Care Facilities

Belgrave and colleagues (1993) reviewed the literature concerning long-term care institutionalization rates among African Americans and whites. They were particularly interested in determining which of three theories contributed the most to understanding patterns of institutionalization among African Americans. The "double jeopardy" theory explains the greater poverty, morbidity, and mortality among African American elderly who also face cumulative adverse effects of a lifetime of racism. The "age as leveler" theory focuses on the concept that differences between African American and white elderly narrow compared to prior times in the life cycle due to income supports and public insurance such as social security and Medicare. The third theory involves alleged cultural differences which lead African Americans to shun long-term care in favor of care by friends and family.

The available evidence indicates that African Americans are much less likely than non-Hispanic whites to be institutionalized in long-term care facilities. In 1963 African American elderly were only 37 percent as likely as whites to be institutionalized. The corresponding figure climbed to 46 percent in 1969 and 65 percent in 1985. The big spurt after the early 1960s was the result of Medicare legislation passed at that time, which pays for long-term care for the indigent elderly. Studies show that nursing homes serving African Americans are more likely to be segregated, and more likely to be of lower quality than those serving the white elderly. Despite the fact that numerous studies indicate that African American elderly are sicker and more disabled than white elderly. African American elderly are less likely to be institutionalized in a skilled nursing facility, and more likely to be to be in an intermediate care facility than whites. The authors of this study make a crucial observation regarding the frequently observed poorer health status of the African American elderly:

> The poorer health status of African Americans relative to whites is often attributed to the greater likelihood of living in poverty, lower occupational status, lower educational levels, etc. The implication of this, explicitly or implicitly, is that if it were not for such factors, there would be no health differences between the two populations..., that race and racism per se are not the major issues. However, it is important when holding such variables constant in racial comparisons to remember they are anything but equal in the population. Similarities within income categories or education levels cannot be allowed to obscure that it is precisely through inequalities in attaining income and education that some of the strongest effects of racism are felt (Belgrave et al. 1993, 382).

Between 1959 and 1985 poverty rates have been dropping for the elderly as a whole, but the gap between African Americans and whites has grown. In 1966, 55 percent of elderly African Americans—compared to 26 percent of elderly whites—lived in poverty, a ratio of two to one. By the end of the 1980s, the percentage of all elderly poor had dropped, but the ratio between African American and white elderly had climbed to over three to one. Fully 80 percent of single African American elderly women live below 125 percent of the poverty level. The authors point out that the consequences of pervasive poverty have a negative impact on health and quality of life. They note that a person's ability to make use of Medicare benefits is "...dependent upon one's ability to pay premiums and co-payments. For poor and near-poor aged, this can mean being deprived of the right to use Medicare benefits" (Belgrave et al. 1993, 382).

Turning to the topic of cultural issues as possible determining factors for Black/white differences in institutionalization, the authors summarize several studies indicating that African Americans have developed extensive kinship networks where eating meals, residences and even child rearing is shifted around among friends and family to meet various needs. This pattern is pervasive among many low-income and minority ethnic groups, and results from common environments of poverty and exploitation. In addition, elderly African American women are more likely to be heads of households compared to elderly white women, and therefore are more likely to be providing needed care and putting off receiving needed care for themselves. The authors sound a note of caution about how to interpret these realities:

> [These cultural practices] should be recognized by social scientists. However, if the cultural response to deprivation is not viewed in a historical and structural context, it can hamper our ability to understand such things as disparities in the use of institutionalization. By examining cultural patterns of living in the inner city in a vacuum, and neglecting the factors behind the creation of these patterns, it is easy to conclude that African Americans are doing just fine.
>
> The hypothesis that culture explains differential use of institutional care might be comforting to white academics but it cannot be simply accepted at face value. A valid assessment of the effects of culture cannot be done solely from census and similar data but will require information on the nature of possible support roles themselves (Belgrave et, al. 1993, 384).

In other words, the cultural differences noted by the authors may be consequences of obstacles *rather than a preferred cultural substitute* for institutionalized long-term care, Finally, in concluding the article, the authors believe that the double jeopardy hypothesis has more utility in explaining Black/white institutionalization differences in long term care facilities than the other two theories. Despite this, the authors are quite critical of the double jeopardy theory because, among other deficits, it assumes but does not seek to understand the social consequences of racism per se.

Hispanic Access to Health Care

Socioeconomic factors play a major role in limiting Hispanic access to health care; however, there are important differences among various Hispanic peoples. Mexicans comprise about 62 percent of the roughly 20 million Hispanics in the United States. Puerto Ricans comprise 13 percent, Cubans 5 percent, Central and South Americans 12 percent, and other Hispanics 8 percent. As a group, Hispanics are overrepresented in low-income inner-city urban areas. All Hispanic groups suffer from lower average levels of education compared to non-Hispanic whites. For example, 15.4 percent of Mexican-Americans over 25 years of age, and 10.3 percent of Puerto Ricans, have had less than five years of schooling compared to non-Hispanic whites, with only two percent. All Hispanic groups except for Cubans are significantly underrepresented among occupations such as managerial/professional and technical/sales. Mexicans are particularly disadvantaged because nine percent are employed in the seasonal, low-income, hazardous farming sector. In the late 1980s the median Hispanic family income was 36 percent less than the median income of non-Hispanic whites, and Hispanics were 2.5 times as likely as non-Hispanic whites to lack either private or public health insurance (Ginzberg 1991, 238-9).

The underrepresentation of Hispanic health care providers is a contributing obstacle to health care access. While Hispanics comprise about ten percent of the total population, between 2.2 and 3.0 percent of dentists, registered nurses, therapists and pharmacists are of Hispanic origin. Interestingly, about 5.4 percent of all physicians are Hispanics, but many of these trained outside the United States and subsequently immigrated. Hispanic students, particularly Mexican students, are still very underrepresented in American medical schools (Ginzberg 1991, 240).

Mexicans are not only the most numerous of the Hispanics, but also suffer from some of the most onerous access difficulties. A significant number of Mexicans live along the U.S.-Mexico border. There they suffer disproportionately from hazardous waste contamination, air and water pollution as well as a serious paucity of affordable and available health care facilities.. Over 110,000 Mexicans live in *colonias* in Texas, unincorporated areas lacking basic sanitation facilities and running water. California has legislated particularly draconian measures for limiting access to need-based services such as Medicaid for Mexican immigrants (Ginzberg 1991, 239-40).

Focus on Migrant Farm Workers

Perhaps Mexican migrant farm workers as a group suffer more than any other significant Hispanic sub-group from a combination of an unhealthy environment plus serious obstacles to health care access. There are an estimated 1.5–2.5 million hired farm workers in the United States. Migrant farm workers are a subpopulation of these, characterized by seasonal travel and temporary residenc as they harvest the nation's fruits and vegetables. Typical migrant farm workers are young married Mexican couples and their children. Estimates of the total number of migrant farmworkers range from one to four million people, with some of the estimates including entire families instead of just adult workers. For well over a century migrant farmworkers have suffered a host of deprivations and abuses, largely outside the view and attention of the public. Graphic investigative journalism and monographs were published in the 1940s and periodically thereafter, exposing the plight of migrant farmworkers. Beginning in the 1960s a smattering of laws and programs were established to address some of the most serious social problems faced by migrant farmworkers, but they have had minimal impact in the fields where migrants work, and in the shacks where they live (U.S. General Accounting Office 1992, 2-8). Struggles of the United Farm Workers Union (not coincidentally also dating back to the 1960s) for better working and living conditions, improved occupational safety and health, and adequate compensation have resulted in some victories and a nationwide struggle in unity with them. However, results have been insufficient and in some cases relatively short-lived due to massive, ongoing corporate resistance.

The socioeconomic profile of migrant farmworkers represents the first of a series of obstacles to health care access. A 1990 nationwide survey of migrant farmworkers found that median family income ranged from $7,500 to $10,000 annually, with the result that half the families had incomes below the poverty level. In addition, Social Security Administration (SSA) studies show that agricultural employers are three times as likely as other employers to underreport, or not report employee earnings at all. The result is that migrant farmworkers do not receive Social Security benefits including retirement, disability, and survivors insurance; or receive lower benefit amounts than those to which they are entitled. Supplemental Security Income (SSI) provides financial support to eligible low-income persons who are aged, blind or disabled. Rural non-English speaking persons, such as migrant farmworkers, are at particularly high risk for not knowing about SSI benefits and eligibility, and underutilizing this source of financial support. Only 20 percent of migrant farmworkers surveyed had any health insurance coverage whatsoever from employers. The average adult migrant farmworker has completed eight or fewer years of formal education, and their children may fare little better. The typical migrant child is two or more years below grade level in reading and mathematics skills, and suffers a dropout rate 50 percent higher than the local population (U.S. General Accounting Office 1992, 8, 25-6, 37).

The working and living environments of migrant farmworker families are inordinately hazardous. The most recent nationwide study of migrant farmworker housing, done in 1980, estimated that there was enough housing for only about one-third of the migrant workers. A more recent study looking at Washington, Oregon and California came up with a similar conclusion, but did not include dependents who travel with the migrant farmworkers. Researchers from the General Accounting Office (GAO) reported:

> In 1989, deficient and overcrowded housing conditions appeared to be common for hired farmworkers, especially migrants. Numerous studies tell of migrant farmworkers living in shacks, barns, old school buses, and other seriously substandard dwellings. A family may have to sleep on a dirt floor in a 1-room house with no furniture, running water or electricity (U.S. General Accounting Offices 1992, 28-9).

Exposure to poisonous pesticides is probably the most significant single health hazard faced by migrant farmworkers and their families. After innumerable repeated pesticide poisoning suffered by farmworkers, the Environmental Protection Agency (EPA) in 1983 finally acknowledged that its worker protection standards were entirely inadequate. Nearly a decade later, the Agency began to update its standards, but to date the situation has not improved very much. During 1990, EPA found 633 violations of pesticide regulations, but levied only 42 fines. The Occupational Safety and Health Administration (OSHA) has enacted important regulations requiring supervisors to give farmworkers training, information and protection relating to pesticide safety. OSHA, however, has deferred jurisdiction to EPA over worker exposure to agricultural chemicals, so OSHA's ability to protect farmworkers is moot. As a result,

> Hired farmworkers go into fields sprayed with pesticides, but many have no knowledge of the specific chemicals they are exposed to or the potential health risks. A 1988 study of 460 hired farmworkers in Washington found that 89 percent did not know the name of a single pesticide they had been exposed to, and 76 percent had never received any information on appropriate measures for protection (U.S. General Accounting Office 1992, 17).

Most importantly, EPA itself does not itself know if thousands of widely used pesticides are safe even if used with "appropriate measures for protection." They are currently gathering safety data on thousands of older types of pesticides which were never carefully tested, but estimate that their research will last into the next millennium. Exposures to pesticide can cause permanent damage or death from acute exposure, but also may lead to cancer, birth defects, neuropsychological conditions, and a host of lesser irritations and medical problems. The EPA estimates that there are 300,000 acute illnesses each year due to pesticide exposure (U.S. General Accounting Office 1992, 12-3, 18).

Migrant farmworkers are commonly deprived of the most rudimentary personal hygiene facilities. OSHA regulations require farms with 11 or more workers to provide uncontaminated drinking water, hand-washing facilities and toilets. Nevertheless, a 1990 national survey found nearly one-third of all the farmworkers lacked one or more basic sanitation facilities. A few states such as North Carolina also legally require basic sanitation facilities on farms employing ten or fewer workers, but a 1990 study of small farms in North Carolina found only four percent of the farmworkers had access to drinking water, hand-washing facilities and toilets (U.S. General Accounting Office 1992 19-20).

The children of migrant farmworkers are at particular risk for a variety of health problems, in large part because children frequently work or play in dangerous, pesticide-sprayed fields. In most sectors of industry, hazardous work may not be done by adolescents under the age of 18, but dangerous farm work such as operating a tractor or hay baler can be done by a 16-year-old. Nonhazardous work on farms can legally be done by children as young as 12, but in the rest of industry the typical age is 14 or 16. Despite the lax regulations for child labor on farms, an estimated 100,000 minors a year are illegally employed on American farms. Federal regulators who enforce child labor laws inspect less than two percent of workplaces annually, and fines levied average a bit over $200 per incident. All agree that these token fines do not deter employers from illegally employing minors. As a practical matter about one-third of farmworkers surveyed in a multistate survey had children working in the fields. Many children have to work to help the family survive, others are in the fields because no affordable day care is available. In a 1990 study in western New York, one-third of all the migrant children working on farms had been injured during the year. Nationally 300 children and adolescents are known to have died in the course of farm work between 1979 and 1983 (U.S. General Accounting Office 1992, 20-23).

Children in the fields, whether they work or not, are more susceptible to pesticide poisonings because they absorb proportionally more of the toxins, they are biologically at a more sensitive stage of development, and they are less likely to observe even the most rudimentary safety precautions. "A 1990 study of migrant children working on farms in western New York found that over 40 percent of the children interviewed had worked in fields still wet with pesticides, and 40 percent had been sprayed while in the fields" (U.S. General Accounting Office 1992, 12-3).

Finally, migrant farmworkers and their families suffer from some very direct barriers to health care access. Only a fraction of them have private health insurance, as mentioned earlier. As many as 50 percent of all migrant farmworkers are undocumented workers; i.e., they cannot work legally in this country. As a result they are also prohibited from using Medicaid. Those who qualify for Medicaid are often blocked from using it due to 45-day processing periods imposed by many states. By the time the migrant is eligible, he or she is long gone from the state. A study in the early 1980s found that only 12 percent of migrant farmworkers in New York had Medicaid coverage. If migrants do have Medicaid coverage from another state, physicians are unlikely to accept it. States are free to agree to reciprocally accept one and another's Medicaid coverage, but those states with substantial migrant labor forces generally choose not to. A federally funded network of migrant health clinics are a primary source of health care for migrant farmworkers and their families, but due to Department of Health and Human Services budget constraints (or perhaps budget priorities), the clinics actually serve less than 15 percent of the nation's migrant farmworkers (U.S. General Accounting Office 1992, 24-5).

Summary and Discussion

Due to limitations of space, some important issues were only touched upon, and others were left out completely. Some minorities, Native Americans for example, and some Asian minorities, such as Cambodian or Vietnamese, suffer serious lack of access to health care as well as a host of other socioeconomic problems exacerbated by racism and institutional discrimination. The question of environmental racism has not been addressed in this discussion, but it is crucial to a full understanding of the health status of minorities. A number of studies in recent years find that hazardous waste dumps and seriously polluting industries tend to be concentrated in minority communities. During the early 1990s, the Department of Energy targeted Native American reservations as sites for burial of nuclear wastes, offered large sums of cash, employment, and perks to desperately poor communities. This chapter is able to touch on only a few of the important issues concerning the economics of racism and healthcare.

Sociologists make the distinction between institutionalized discrimination and prejudice. Prejudice involves beliefs that people of color, women, Catholics, etc. are inherently inferior in one or more ways. Prejudice often leads to discriminatory behavior, singling out people by race, for example, in order to deprive them of jobs, promotions, the right to live in a particular neighborhood or to deprive them of life itself. Prejudiced racists are generally obvious, but institutionalized discrimination is much more difficult to perceive. Institutional discrimination involves the everyday functioning of a social institution with the consequences of racial (or other) discrimination, but without the apparent intent of prejudice. For example, a hospital located in an urban center may close the emergency room because too many uninsured minorities are using it without reimbursing the hospital. Hospital administrators would claim they closed the emergency room because they were losing too much money, not because of prejudice. The result, however, is the further decline of health care accessibility for minorities. Another very important aspect of racism: its deliberate ideological use in the struggle against labor. Hospital administrators use racism to break nursing strikes, and politicians shilling for big business use racism to win cuts in Medicaid funding. The struggle against racism is often simultaneous with the struggle against capital.

Personal health status, public health and medical care in the United States all suffer from widespread institutionalized discrimination, personal prejudice and the ideological uses of racism. The long struggle against racism and institutionalized discrimination in health care has been bravely fought and successfully waged by civil rights activists of all colors, organized labor and minority health professionals who have suffered discrimination by white-dominated health care institutions. The struggle, which dates back well into the last century, has borne some fruit but cannot rest. Racism in all its forms is intensifying as the structural crisis of advanced capitalism wreaks havoc among the social institutions upon which wage earners, the unemployed, and the retired rely. Health care is central to life itself. Future struggles against racism are certain to organize around this most important social institution.

14. The Police-Judicial Assault on the African American People

In 1959, driving through the Florida Keys, I saw one of the infamous southern chain gangs of Black prisoners, a prevalent mode of torture by the racist authorities of the Jim Crow South. Ironically I was on my way to Cuba, where a liberated people were still celebrating their freedom from this kind of police terror.

Within a decade or so, the civil rights struggles in the U.S. South put an end to the barbaric chain gangs here. But the growing racist offensive reached a point by the mid–1990s where the press showed photographs of revived chain gangs. The mainly Black prisoners were equipped with mallets to smash rocks, a torturous exercise in the broiling sun. The caption admitted the rocks were not used: the exercise was strictly a punitive occupation.

By now, several states have joined Alabama in this barbaric practice. Moreover, they are "proud" of it; they invite journalists to witness this stench of fascism that is spreading over the land without censure by the leaders of the U.S. Congress.

The legal code applied against African Americans is much more stringent than against the rest of the population, a degree of discrimination more extreme than in any other aspect of life.

For example: researchers find that 13% of Blacks, like 13% of whites, are regular users of narcotic drugs. But a Black user is four times more likely to be arrested than a white; eight times more likely to be convicted; and 19 times more likely to be imprisoned!

Imprisonment for drug use has been rising at astronomical rates.

But if Black users were imprisoned at the same rate as other users, total imprisonment for drug use would be slashed 70%, and most of the new prisons being built at breakneck speed would not be needed.

Now non-Blacks—whites and others, who are 87% of the population—are only 26% of those imprisoned for drugs.

Details are discussed later in the chapter.

New York:

The corruption scandal surrounding the 30th Precinct of Harlem grew yesterday as the authorities announced the arrest of 14 more police officers, including two sergeants.

So far 29 officers have been implicated, including supervisors. More arrests are expected, raising the total to nearly one out of six of the officers in the precinct.

> The ring of officers, who were assigned to take guns and drugs off the streets, operated throughout 1992 and 1993, breaking down doors of apartments in northwest Harlem in order to steal drugs, guns and cash...
>
> Investigators said the band, which called itself "Nannery's Raiders" (after Sgt. Kevin P. Nannery, of Newburgh, NY—VP), faked police radio and 911 emergency calls to make their raids on narcotics dealers, most of whom were Dominicans they thought were unlikely to report their operations to higher police authorities.

The Police committed repeated perjury, causing the dismissal of many criminal cases. Taking advantage of a breakdown of the Police Department's internal policing system "where several independent rings of officers numbering from 2 to 10, some of which evidently worked closely with narcotics rings dealing in one of the prime wholesale cocaine-dealing centers in the metropolitan area."[1]

Operating in an area that is overwhelmingly Black, the 14 arrested cops are all white.

The same day's paper, on the same page, showed the picture of a African American boy shot and killed by a cop because he was holding a plastic rifle. A month earlier a Black cop chasing a youth who had fired a gun on a subway platform was shot in the back four times, while lying face down on the ground, by a white cop. The police chief and the Mayor absolved the shooter of blame.[2] Shortly thereafter a fake scene was staged at the semi-conscious victim cop's bedside and the story given out that the victim had forgiven his attacker. Fortunately the victim, officer Desmond Robinson, recovered and exposed the incident as a fraud.

Harlem resident Jill Nelson writes of the gauntlet of heavily armed drug dealers and police who stand idly by, through which adults going to work and children going to school must pass. The people know:

> That drugs and crime unchecked sap the lifeblood of any community. That when they are allowed to flourish with the active or tacit approval of the police, the devastation is that much greater.

A mayoral commission, in a two-year investigation, found that "New York City police officers often make false arrests, tamper with evidence and commit perjury on the witness stand."[3]

The practice, often condoned by supervisors, "is prevalent enough in the department that it is known by its nick name: 'testilying'."

At least 140 cases of corruption involving high-ranking officers were buried in a special file and never pursued or prosecuted.[4]

Almost everywhere calls for independent control over police forces are strongly resisted, and even organized, hard-fought struggles rarely succeed in overcoming the resistance.

In 1993, a year before the corruption scandal broke, the police had been active, and perhaps decisive, in the election victory of a veteran prosecutor known for his racist bias, Rudolph W. Giuliani, over the African American incumbent, David Dinkins. During the campaign thousands of police demonstrated against Dinkins at City Hall, with racist gibes. Giuliani joined in this demonstration.

As mayor, Giuliani promptly proceeded to slash city services across the board, and followed a hard-line get-tough policy against city workers, including firing many and freezing wages. He was carrying out the budgetary demands of the ruling Wall Street establishment. The ruling big business groups had heavily financed the election campaigns of Giuliani and earlier Mayors who had connived with corrupt, racist police forces. The inference is justified that police forces constituted under their control amounted to a praetorian guard of the ruling class and its interests, acting on a local scale with the brutality and corruption characteristic of police states worldwide.

Philadelphia

The case of the Philadelphia police revealed a horror for the Black community even more than that of Harlem...It concerns "a group of officers so corrupt, callous to the rights and welfare of residents, that the details have shaken this city to its roots.

Mrs. Patterson is one of dozens, perhaps even hundreds of victims of a band of five renegade officers who for at least three years haunted her predominantly poor and black North Philadelphia's neighborhood, beating, robbing, lying and planting phony evidence...

"She went to jail for three years for something she was apparently completely innocent of " said Lynne Abraham, the Philadelphia District Attorney. "This whole thing has made me physically ill. This is the ultimate betrayal of the public trust, and it has some very destructive consequences. It justifies people's suspicions of the police."

But the question remains: why didn't the District Attorney stop the police gangsters, whose activities were not really a secret? And why did the Mayor, Edward G. Rendell, not do anything to stop it; but who now worries that the city might have to shell out millions of dollars in lawsuits by victims— "money we desperately need for human needs and basic services."[5]

It is this police force, judiciary and city government that kept a Black political activist, Mumia Abu-Jamal imprisoned for 13 years, and only days from execution, when worldwide mass pressure forced a stay of execution.

Crime and Imperialism

In the 20th century, the century of monopoly capitalism and imperialism, the United States became the crime capital of the world of developed capitalism. Along with the marauding, murdering marines, naval forces, and armies in victim countries in Latin America and Asia, the internal armies of repression—police and FBI, together with their judges and prosecutors, carried out an increasingly intense assault on the working class as a whole. From the very beginning, this assault had an extraordinarily sharp edge against the African American people.

Criminal gangs, often in collaboration with police, became major plunderers in the country's cities, extracting heavy tribute from small business, serving the more powerful capitalists by strikebreaking, imposing their agents in controlling positions in many trade unions, gaining influence in the capitalist political parties, while engaging in murderous warfare over the division and redivision of territory for plunder. They became the major agencies for the import and distribution of narcotic drugs and organizers of prostitution. White collar crime became endemic in the financial world, plundering billions, with only occasional token arrests and fines, more rarely imprisonment. Corruption in government became general, highlighted in recent decades by the involvement of presidents and their immediate entourage.

Crime rose and fell inversely with the business cycle, as people desperate for food and other basic needs, not organized for political struggle, engaged in criminal activities. The rate of homicides jumped from 0.5 per 100,00 people in 1900 to 9.7 per 100,000 in 1933, the nadir of the great depression; receded to 4.5 per 100,000 with economic recovery, before rising again during the structural crisis of capitalism to 10.7 per 100,000 in 1980. And it has remained in that range since, even during years of economic upsurge and boom, signifying a deterioration in the situation.[6]

Arrests, Trials, Imprisonment of Blacks

Of course, there are criminals as happens with every race or ethnic group plunged into the deepest miseries of extreme poverty, unemployment, hunger and homelessness. But Black crime, for the most part, is small stuff, involving tens or hundreds of dollars, as against the millions stolen by the important thieves.

Some Black crime involves violence, usually against other African American people. Crime can be explained, but not justified. But the main crime is the police repression against the Black people, applied against many who have taken no part in criminal activity.

White working class youth may drive to the local bar, where they gather with their friends, who often include policemen. Black youth, having no jobs and no cars, congregate on the street to talk and socialize. And all too often racist policemen will order them to disperse, and on defiance or delay, club, handcuff and arrest the victims for "disorderly conduct," resisting arrest, etc.

The number of arrests in the United States—320,000 in 1933—leaped to 6,250,000 in 1970 and to 10,500,000 in 1991. Throughout this period, the number of white people arrested equaled 2.5 to 3 times the number of Black people arrested.

Typically, in 1991, 69% of those arrested were white, 29% were Black.[7] Since a Black is much more likely than a white to be arrested, regardless of criminality, the percentage of actual criminals who are Black must be far less than that.

I refer here to the kinds of crimes for which arrests are normally made. That *excludes* the systematic bribing of officials for contracts, the forced pay-offs to inspectors to prevent condemnation of buildings, the Mafia-organized collection of tribute from proprietors in a wide range of businesses as a condition of avoiding arson, bombings, or murder, the notorious widespread corruption of police forces. It also *excludes* white collar crime, peaking at such outrages as the savings and loan bailout, which cost taxpayers at least 150 billion. It also *excludes* crime among government officials, elected and appointed: the Watergate crimes, leading to the impeachment of President Nixon; the Bush Administration, during which the President's relatives were involved in savings and loan swindles; the Clinton Administration, which brought the entire sewer of Arkansas politics to Washington.

African Americans have a very small part in these areas because they are so excluded from the decisive positions of power in the private economy, and in government; i.e., from the capitalist class and its leading circles.

Through the combination of lying police witnesses, racist judges and prosecutors, incompetent or venal "public defenders" on whom Black prisoners are usually forced to rely, a Black arrestee is more than twice as likely to end up in prison as a white arrestee. As a result, the inmate population of the country's jails and prisons consists 47% of African Americans,—roughly 4 times their share in the population, 14% Hispanics 1.5-2 times their share in the population, and 37% non-Hispanic whites, roughly one-half their share in the population.[8] This means that a Black individual is eight times more likely than a non-Hispanic white individual to be in jail. Thus the impact of mass imprisonment on the Black communities—and also, but less sharply, on Hispanic communities—is of a qualitatively higher order of magnitude than the impact on white communities. And that impact has grown in severity with the surge in imprisonment of the past two decades.

The anti-labor, racist offensive of the past two decades has led to a sharp increase in imprisonment of working class people, most intensely affecting Black and Latino communities. Between 1970 and 1991 the number of people confined to state prisons multiplied four times, with the rate of increase accelerating after 1980, when the Reagan Administration came to power.[9]

During this period the number of Black inmates increased much faster than white inmates. Between 1983 and 1991 the number of white inmates of jails increased 46%, of Black inmates 114%, and Latino inmates 94%.[10]

Table 14:1 shows the percentage distribution of the inmate population, at 20 year intervals:

TABLE 14:1. PRISON INMATES, 1930-1991

| | Percent of Total | | | |
	White	Black	Other	Hispanics
1930	76.7	22.4	0.9	
1950	69.1	29.7	1.2	
1970	60.5	35.8	3.7	
1991	49.1	47.3	3.5	
1991 (Hispanics separated)	37.1	45.3	3.5	14.0

SOURCE: 1930-1970, Hacker, P.197
1991 *Stat. Abst.* 1993, No. 344, p.210

In 1930, Blacks were less than one-fourth of the prison population. The proportion increased steadily, but most rapidly after 1970. While the overall prison population increased about four times during those 21 years, the Black prison population multiplied 5.3 times. The rate of imprisonment of Blacks accelerated qualitatively, from very heavy, to mass imprisonment, as might apply to a people resisting an invading army. The intensity of imprisonment of African Americans in the United States exceeds that of Africans in South Africa, or Palestinians in territories seized by Israel.

Ruling class propaganda tries to convince the public that the mass imprisonment of people, especially young men, is in response to a soaring crime wave. That is far from the truth. Between 1975 and 1991, the rate of reported crime, in relation to population and households, *declined* by 30 percent.[11]

The jamming of prisons resulted from a marked increase in severity of sentencing, including laws enacted on a state and federal level. "In the 1980s, draconian sentencing laws were used to combat the drug problem...Currently, 60% of inmates in federal prisons and 20% of inmates in state prisons are there on drug charges."[12] A young Black arrested with a small amount of narcotics in his or her possession, many end up with a many-year prison term—while the large-scale use of narcotics by the upper classes is generally ignored by the police and the courts.

During 1994 President Clinton gave top priority to passage of a far more rigorous "crime package," which Congress passed after the President exerted exceptional personal pressure on individual members of Congress. A number of crimes were added to which the death penalty applied, funds for 100,000 more members of police forces, and rejection of a provision that would have given opportunities for combatting the extreme discrimination against Black prisoners in application of the death penalty.

As proposed by the President, the bill included modest provisions for social programs in high-crime areas, but these were mainly deleted from the law as adopted.

Meanwhile, successive Administrations and Congresses were engaged in ruthlessly slashing social and economic programs that would provide needed—services and above all, employment at decent wages, to young working class people. Furthermore, by 1993 it became official policy to maintain unemployment at a high level.

Business Week ran a special feature on "The Economics of Crime" in 1993, which emphasized the tough approach. But there's the admission:

> New prisons are being built, but the number of police has barely kept pace with the growing population. *Meanwhile, economic and social programs that could quickly bring down crime are largely ignored...job prospects for young adults and teenagers have soured, lowering the economic rewards for staying straight...its crucial that the U.S. boost spending for job training and other programs in order to give teenagers and young adults better alternatives to crime* (My emphasis—VP).[13]

Estimates have been published of very high percentages of young Black men in prison; and under probation or parole. Andrew Hacker writes "After all, one in five Black men ultimately spends some time behind bars, almost seven times the rate for whites" [and the white rate is even lower, if Hispanics are excluded].[14]

My estimates are, updating published data, that as of 1994, of 1,500,000 people in prisons or jails, some 700,000 were Black. Of 5.3 million Black men in the 15-35 year age range, 1,475,000, or 28% of the total, were imprisoned, under probation or parole.

The criminalization of young workingclass men of all races has become very severe, but of Blacks it is terrible. *Business Week* estimates (1993) that 6.2% of white men aged 20-29 are in prison, probation or parole, 10.4% of Latino men in that age range, but a shocking 23% of Black men aged 20-29.[15]

The Sentencing Project, an advocacy group based in Washington, estimates that in 1990 one out of four Black men in their twenties were under police jurisdiction, but that with the rapid rise in imprisonment and sentencing, that as of 1995 that proportion had risen to nearly one-third in the criminal justice system, a result verified as essentially correct by Dr. Allen J. Beck, an expert of the Justice Department's statistics division.

The Sentencing Project also found that while Blacks were 13% of monthly drug users, roughly comparable to their share in the population, they were 35% of those arrested for drug possession, 55% of the convictions, and 74% of the prison sentences.[15a]

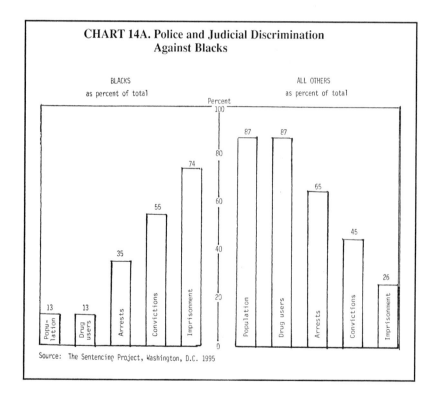

CHART 14A. Police and Judicial Discrimination Against Blacks

BLACKS as percent of total

ALL OTHERS as percent of total

Source: The Sentencing Project, Washington, D.C. 1995

This is one of the clearest exposes of the blatant racist discrimination involved at each stage of the police-judicial-prison systems of the United States.

Carrying the calculation a step further, these figures mean that a Black user is 19 times more likely to end up in prison. By the same type of measurement, on the way to prison, he is 4 times more likely to be arrested, and 8 times more likely to be convicted. Thus the discrimination intensifies at every stage of the judicial-legal system.

Profits and Losses from Crime

Government spending—federal, state and local—for police, prisons, courts, etc. has multiplied even more spectacularly than the number of its captives. In 1954, $2.1 billion was spent, in 1970, $8.6 billion, in 1990, $74.2 billion![16] Certainly it is much more by now (1996). President Clinton's Budget for fiscal year 1995 included a 21% increase over 1994, and much "get tough on crime" rhetoric. The increase over 1990 was 48 percent. If state and local spending has increased in like proportion, a reasonable assumption, overall spending in 1995 will go well above $100 billion.[17] Under congressional mandate, overall "discretionary spending" by the federal government is held unchanged at just under $550 billion per year as far out as 1999. But among the cabinet agencies, spending by the Justice Department, in which most anti-crime activity is centered, is called on to increase 86 percent.[18]

Along with the increase in dollar spending, has come a rapid increase in the number of policemen and an even faster rise in the overall anti-crime bureaucracy, with employment—at all levels of government—reaching 1,722,000 by 1990.[19]

This figure, as of 1990, represented full-time equivalent employment, so total anti-crime personnel, including part-timers, were certainly more, and there has been a considerable increase since. The total may safely be estimated, as of 1995, at 2 million or more. This approximates the active duty military and civilian personnel of the armed forces. Thus the U.S. government employs about as many people to suppress the working class and poor at home as it does to police the rest of the world on behalf of reactionary regimes and U.S. transnational corporations.

The increase in law enforcement spending is providing a profit bonanza to the capitalist class. A *Wall Street Journal* lead feature in 1994 was headed:

TRIANGLE OF INTERESTS CREATES INFRASTRUCTURE TO FIGHT LAWLESSNESS—CITIES SEE JOBS; POLITICIANS SENSE A POPULAR ISSUE—AND BUSINESSES CASH IN.

Despite declining Pentagon orders, armament manufacturers were reaping rising profits through accelerated munitions exports and, especially, "conversion" to weapons of internal repression: "Westinghouse Electric, Minnesota Mining & Manufacturing Co., General Dynamics...have created special divisions to retool their defense technology for America's streets."

Sandia National Laboratories, a major research and development center for nuclear weapons, is experimenting with blinding and deafening sprays.

Goldman Sachs, Prudential Insurance, Merrill Lynch are "competing to underwrite prison construction with private, tax-exempt bonds—no voter approval required."[20]

In addition to the profits from government contracts related to crime, private companies are making profits from soaring spending on anti-burglar devices for homes and cars, private guards, etc. As of 1993 *Business Week* estimated such spending at $65 billion per year. It is stimulated by the intense media and governmental campaign arousing fear in the population.

Costs to Workers, African American People

Working people bear the main burden of rising taxation, including that resulting from soaring crime control costs. Workers, blue collar and white collar, are the main victims of crime, and direct losers from its impact. Business Week estimates the annual costs to crime victims from property loss, medical care and shattered lives at $220 billion.[21]

The losses of Black people especially, but also Latino people from crime are disproportional by a wide margin. The victimization rate from crime, per 1,000 persons, in 1991, was 44 for Blacks, 30 for whites. Among males, the rate for Blacks was a record 61, for whites 38. Blacks were the victims of approximately one-half of all homicides, for a rate of being killed roughly 7 times that suffered by whites.[22]

In addition, *Business Week* estimates a cost of $50 billion from urban decay, the cost of lost jobs and fleeing residents,[23] accelerated by crime. Blacks and Latinos, the main residents of central cities, have to absorb the bulk of this $50 billion loss.

As nearly half of all prisoners, Blacks suffer terribly from the obvious economic losses from imprisonment. In 1991, 69% of all prisoners were employed at the time of arrest.[24] Presumably at least half of the Black prisoners were employed at time of arrest. Besides their loss of income, the much larger number of Blacks who have been in prison, who have arrest and conviction records, are greatly handicapped in seeking employment. More, the wave of racist propaganda criminalizing the entire African American people is used by racist employers to justify their discrimination against Blacks in employment and pay, inflicted on all Blacks, including the majority who are completely law-abiding. While unmeasurable, such losses account for a significant share of the huge overall losses sustained by Blacks and Latinos from the adverse income differentials against them.

New specialist corporations have been formed to carry out construction contracts, and contracts to operate privatized prisons. An example, is Corrections Corporation of America, whose stock is listed on the New York stock exchange. According to the *Wall Street Journal*: "Its founders and officers include major contributors to both major parties." Included among the officers are a former commissioner of corrections for Arkansas, Clinton's bailiwick, and a former director of the Federal Bureau of Prisons.

The cynicism and greed of capitalists is highlighted by the following incident:

> ...businessmen stood up and cheered in Massachusetts when...Sen. Edward Kennedy announced that Fort Devens, slated for closure, would be converted to a federal prison.[25]

Police State

The United States imposes upon African Americans many features of a police state: police forces riddled by racism and brutality; arbitrary arrest and imprisonment on a massive scale—as of the early 1990s 3.1% of U.S. Black males were imprisoned, more than four times the rate of 0.7% among South African Black males (before the formal ending of Apartheid). When a business man or politician is arrested, a courteous procedure is followed. Often he is advised in advance, and agreement, is made as to when he will appear, with legal assistance. Bail is granted immediately, so that he does not spend time in jail prior to conviction.

The arrest of a Black man resembles an attack by thugs...thugs protected by their uniforms, guns, clubs, high-powered vehicles and equipment. The arrest is likely to include beatings, use of life-threatening choke holds at the whim of the policemen, without evidence of the victim's wrongdoing.

Terrible police beatings and killings are occasionally reported, but these are a small fraction of those that take place. The videotaped beating of Rodney King, with 20 cops participating or looking on approvingly, led to a mass uprising in Los Angeles during which cops killed many more. Police killings in Texas, New York, and other states have led to protest demonstrations.

In the South, during the 1880s and 1890s over a hundred lynchings were *reported* yearly, by gangs of the Ku Klux Klan and other vigilante groups. At first, white workers and Blacks were murdered in equal numbers, but by the 20th century, the scores of annual lynchings were almost exclusively against Blacks.[26] Now the lynchings are carried out by policemen in jails. A federal inquiry revealed 46 hangings of prisoners by police in Mississippi jails over the period 1987-1992.[27] Protected by a racist judicial system, systematically lying in court without fear of punishment for perjury, policemen know that they can get away with unrestrained brutality without fear of imprisonment or of losing their jobs.

The first African American was appointed a federal judge in 1949. Beginning in the 1960s occasional Blacks were appointed. During the 12 years ending in 1992, only 2 of the 115 Reagan-Bush appointees were Black, while a number appointed earlier retired, and by 1993, six more were eligible for retirement. A. Leon Higginbotham Jr. Senior Judge and former Chief Judge of the U.S. Court of Appeals for the Third Circuit, wrote:

> I am forced to conclude that the record of appointments of African Americans to the Courts of Appeals during the past 12 years demonstrates that, by intentional Presidential action, African American judges have been turned into an endangered species, soon to become extinct.[28]

Sgt. Don Jackson, a Black police officer on leave from the Hawthorne, Cal. police department, drove into Long Beach, Cal. followed by an unmarked KNBC-TV van. He was on a personal sting operation to investigate police racism. He was stopped by white police officers from Long Beach, one of whom shoved his head through a window during the arrest. He wrote:

> Some people wonder how I have the audacity to challenge the police. I have the audacity because I know who I am and I know what the police have represented to my people.
> It is the police that tracked us as we fled the plantation. It is the police that took Rosa Parks off the bus in Montgomery, Ala. It was police chief 'Bull' Conner who set dogs and fire hoses on Black men, women and children protesting for their civil rights in Birmingham, Ala.
> Operating free of constitutional limitations, the police have long been the greatest nemesis of Blacks irrespective of whether we are complying with the law or not. We have learned that there are cars we are not supposed to drive, streets we are not supposed to walk. We may still be stopped and asked 'Where are you going, boy?' Whether we're in a Mercedes or a Volkswagen.[29]

Two years after Jackson wrote the above words in a *New York Times* op ed the police chief in nearby Los Angeles, Daryl F. Gates, refused to fire, no less arrange the prosecution, of the guilty cops in the notorious Rodney King case. The Mayor, Tom Bradley, an African American, called for Gates' resignation. He refused. Instead, the police union discussed a drive to recall Bradley. In this case, as in so many others, the armed power of the police made mock of the formal trappings of capitalist democracy.

In the large cities of the United States the police force plays much the same role as an invading army in an occupied city. The officers are mainly white, they almost all live outside of the ghetto area or the city itself, and they are often commanded by crudely racist chiefs. In every one of the 22 largest cities, the percentage of Blacks in the police force is less than the percentage of Blacks in the population, with a median of about one-half as much.[30] In Philadelphia, for example, 19% of the police, 38% of the population, were Black. But the same 19%, *at most* likely applied to the police actively patrolling the ghetto areas, which are nearly 100% Black.

Moreover, that applies to the rank and file cops. The higher ranking officers, who give orders, set policy, give ideological guidance to the rank and file, are much more exclusively white. In New York City, where Blacks were 28.4% of the population, in 1994, Blacks were 11.6% of all members of the police force, and 12.5% of the plain cops and detectives. But they were 7.3% of the sergeants, 5.9% of the lieutenants, and absolutely none of the 310 captains. 7 out of 163, or 4% of those in the very top ranks, are Black. These are apt to be in staff jobs. Domination of the precincts, where police action takes place, is, wholly white.

Two thirds of the white cops live either in suburbs outside the city or in Staten Island, the borough which is formally a part of the city, but entirely different in ethnic and economic composition. 21% of the Black cops are also outside residents. The fact is that white policemen and ranking officers, from outside of New York City, unsympathetic to the problems of city residents, act as an occupying army.[31]

An inevitable conclusion follows from the detailed evidence compiled by the Mollen Commission: Corruption and brutality are not evils of individual "rogue cops." These are features of the entire Police Department, from top to bottom. While not every member of the police department steals or blackmails for bribes; and not every member brutalizes minority people...a large proportion of the cops on patrol do, and those who do not, cover up for them; while the superior ranking officers condone this criminal activity. Moreover the top ranks of the Police Department, in their training and disciplining of the police force, instill anti-labor, racist ideology, directly or indirectly; emphasizing personal characteristics in accepting or rejecting applicants for officers' jobs, they evidently find favorable racist, anti-labor attitudes. The "old boys" network of top ranking officers—all male and white; creates a powerful apparatus of enforcement and repression on behalf of the all male and white members of the social clubs of the top circles of capital.

Journalist Jim Genova gives these details of the Mollen Commission report:

> The most shocking finding of the investigation was the level of organization of these police gangs. Police "crews"—groups of a dozen or more cops—would meet in secret locations within a given precinct (usually a drug-infested neighborhood with a predominantly Black or Latino population) and "identify" drug sites, plan

raids, share proceeds according to regular and agreed-upon principles...drink, avoid patrol duties, meet girlfriends and use cocaine.

The crews used police equipment to "forcibly enter and loot drug trafficking locations. They use the police radio network, and code names, to mount and coordinate operation...

...a number of supervisors knew...about corruption within their commands and did nothing to stop it...

The Commission was unable to obtain sufficient evidence concerning the corruption of the high command, because the department would not turn over some records and others were either "lost" or destroyed...

The report concluded that corruption and brutality went hand in hand. The crew would "terrorize minority neighborhoods." Officers would "routinely beat local residents as well as suspected criminals. The Mollen Commission found these patterns of brutality, corruption and premeditated criminal activity...part of a "20-year cycle of corruption."

The report showed a trend towards large-scale organized crime with rigid command structures and intense loyalty among its members, along the lines of street gangs.

The report concluded that many people in minority neighborhoods fear the police more than the criminals. "Who do you call when you need help," one woman asked, "You can't call the police".[32]

The Commission recommended establishment of a body to oversee the Police Department independent of the city government. Mayor Giuliani not only blocked that, but even opposed an oversight body whose members he would appoint.

In the immediate wake of the Mollen Commission report, only one New York City cop was arrested and sentenced to 14 years in prison—but that was despite refusal of the New York City authorities to prosecute. He was arrested and prosecuted by Nassau County police, where the particular officer, Michael Dowd, lived. It was evident from the attitudes of Mayor Giuliani and his police chief William Bratton that if they have their way there will be no criminal trials and punishments of the large number of police and supervisors guilty of these crimes; which means that the crimes will continue or be increased, this after the Knapp Commission report twenty years earlier.

Victims of police brutality and their families, unable to get the guilty cops punished in criminal court, are left only to sue for damages in civil court. Often these are settled with the stipulation that the terms and the very existence of a settlement be kept secret. For example, it is common knowledge among African American residents of Peekskill, New York, that such payments are made by the city of Peekskill on behalf of the Peekskill police, notorious for their racism and brutality.

Gannett News Service reporter Rochelle Sharpe investigated 10 cases— out of a total of more than 500 considered—where juries ruled that the police must pay the victims—or their survivors—$100,000 or more. With some verdicts running to more than a million dollars, the total paid by city governments on just these 100 cases came to $92 million. But of the 185 officers involved, only 8 were disciplined, 17 were promoted, and no action was taken in the case of the other 160 officers.

While African Americans are most frequently victimized by brutal cops, whites are also at risk from the police. In San Diego, a jury awarded a white former priest, Jim Butler, $1.1 million after a sheriff's deputy "pushed Butler to the ground, kneed him in the back, then slammed a car door on his legs—all because he wanted to help victims of a car crash."[33]

By 1994, federal and many local governments were intensifying police-state measures. President Clinton sought ways to promote warrantless police sweeps of public housing projects, where Blacks were the major residents, after a Federal Judge halted an effort by the Chicago Housing Authority to conduct such searches without warrants. Clinton said that his Attorney General and Housing Secretary had devised a "constitutionally effective way" to carry out such searches. He appealed for tenants to aid the cops...[34]

A *Wall Street Journal* headline: POLICE TEACH GETTING ARRESTED SAFELY 101, was over an article by Brett Pulley described a two-hour course inflicted on 200 students in an overwhelmingly Black school in Suitland, Maryland by a group of officers from the County Police Department.

> They told the students to speak when spoken to and not to strain against handcuffs...during the forums students aren't giving any information regarding their Miranda rights, or how they should protect themselves if taken into custody...

The officers are making the rounds of many of the predominantly Black public high schools in the county.

> After dividing the students into groups, police officers explain why they often stop and question them. Because the students live in an inner-city area, they're more likely to fit the description of crime suspects...
>
> Cpl. Tony Avendorph, a police-force veteran, explain how something as innocent as popular clothing can draw instant suspicion.

This man and another cop illustrate brutal methods they use against arrested people, and attempt to justify them.

> A few students are visibly angered by the demonstrations. One young female student snaps, "I don't like any police." Cpl. Anita Rosser responds "Okay, you said you don't like police. Wouldn't I be wrong to say I don't like all young Black men?"[35]

She would be wrong, in that the very conduct of the police before the students reveals their profound racist insensitivity, and their feeling that they are justified in using special repressive measures against the Black population. How this practice of mass terrorization and intimidation of Black youth can be permitted is evidence of the degree to which systematic police brutality has become a normal part of exercise of state power in the United States.

Thomas L. Friedman writes in a *New York Times* lead story:

The Agency for International Development, which spent the cold war fighting Communism with foreign aid and helping poor countries like Bangladesh immunize children, has found a new customer for its services: America's inner cities. The good news is that the A.I.D. has something to offer. The bad news is that parts of Los Angeles, Boston and Baltimore now need it as much as Bangladesh.[36]

The A.I.D.'s main function was and is to combat not only communism, but all national liberation movements, to destabilize all governments that did not knuckle under to the orders of U.S. imperialism. The social assistance was a trivial sugar-coating. The *New York Times* discusses only the intention of A.I.D. to dispense advice and expertise for do-good programs. However, it is reasonable to assume that A.I.D. is involved in order to transfer part of its expertise to disorganizing, disorienting, splitting and in the final analysis suppressing all liberation struggles and movements in the cities, all actions aimed to end discrimination and inequality, to empower the city residents to rebuild the cities, to combat police repression. It is possible that A.I.D. efforts will fail, but the danger of this new form of racist intervention against the African American and Latino peoples must be taken seriously.

Human Rights

The terrible crimes of fascism against peoples of many countries brought the issue of human rights to the fore. It has been a frequent subject of international negotiations, United Nations debates and resolutions, United Nations documents, the International Declaration of Human Rights, and the more important and detailed Covenants on Human Rights, dealing respectively with economic and social rights; and with Civil and Political Rights. Having been ratified by the governments of a sufficient number of countries, they are regarded as part of international law.

The United States Government has never ratified the covenants, and understandably, because they include many items that, while they are broadly acceptable to the American people, are contrary to the political line of the majority of members of the U.S. Congress.

Indeed, the United States has one of the world's most vulnerable records

on human rights, comparable to the record in the many countries run by pup-
pet governments and the local exploiting classes with extreme brutality, mass
repression and killings.

Yet, the U.S. condemns alleged human rights violations in other countries
as a major propaganda weapon, used to justify its economic, political, and military warfare against its targets.

One such target has been the Chinese Peoples Republic. For years, economic discrimination against China was excused as a reprisal for that country's supposed violation of human rights. While most favored nation status
was finally granted to China in 1993, the political pressure on China continues, with the constant threat of new discriminatory actions, if China does not
change certain internal practices.

A Chinese writer responds on this issue, referring to a report of U.S. Assistant Secretary of State John Shattuck noting shortcomings in our own human
rights record, and stating, "it is of little use to proclaim principles of human
rights protection at the international level unless they can be meaningfully
realized and enforced domestically."

The writer goes on to cite cruel violations of human rights "through the
enslavement of African Americans and the following discrimination against
them, destruction of the culture and society of native Americans and maltreatment of immigrants. In addition, women in the United States do not share
equal rights with men."

Conceding that "China's human rights conditions are far from satisfactory," the writer claims that it is doing better than we are in indicators relevant
to this chapter:

> In 1990, 9.37 out of every 100,000 people were murdered in the United States,
> while in China the figure was less than 2 in 100,000...More than 70 women in
> every 100,000 in the United States were raped, while the figure was 4 in 100,000
> in China...The United States has 1.1 million people serving jail terms, 455 out of
> every 100,000, which is a world record. Yet in China the ratio was only 99 to
> 100,000 in 1990, less than one fourth that in the United States.

He claims a much lower death rate among Chinese than among United
States prisoners, indicating a more humanitarian prison regime, and a repeat
rate among released prisoners of only 8%, compared with 41% in the United
States."[37]

The issues discussed in this chapter should be considered in the light of
this basic correlation—between the status of social and economic rights and
the status of political and personal rights.

Capitalism proclaims its adherence to personal and political freedoms—

indeed that's the whole emphasis of the United States Bill of Rights, but in the economic and social field considers valid only the rights of property.

The working people of the United States struggle for their most elementary economic and social rights, against determined and recently sharpened capitalist opposition. And inevitably, the attack on the economic and social rights of the masses of Americans carries over to a further limitation of their political and personal rights. The increase in crime and in imprisonment of violators, alleged or real, is directly connected with the increase in the sections of the population facing dead ends economically, and unable to survive within legal bounds.

Thus the campaign of reaction to deprive the masses of all public alleviation of social and economic hardships contributes directly to the growth of crime which the capitalist politicians have raised into primacy as political issue.

In joining in the campaign for President Clinton's crime bill, the reactionary forces insisted on removal of the section providing minimal funding for programs designed to ease the economic conditions spawning crime. Enforcement of the new act on crime will increase the deprivation of human rights of masses of the people, while accompanying measures will inevitably tend to increase and worsen criminal activity.

In both areas, economic and social, and political and personal, Blacks especially, and other "minority" peoples, are the main targets and victims of this two-sided assault. And to make matters worse, it accompanies the reactionary drive for elimination of restrictions against racist ideology and its implementation in racial discrimination all along the line.

15. Labor Union Influences

Unions represent the collective power of workers in dealings with their employers. They promote the economic interests, and within limits, the political interests of workers, including those of Black workers. Operating under the slogans of "an injury to one is an injury to all," and "unity of all workers regardless of race and creed" unions have a moderately egalitarian philosophy, which favors reducing discrimination against the most exploited groups of workers.

However, U.S. unions, by and large, do not carry on an active struggle to overcome discrimination against African Americans, nor do their leaders understand the need for such a struggle. Moreover, a number of unions, notably craft unions, actively discriminate against Black workers, and a degree of racism is reflected in the policies of most of the large unions, including relative exclusion of Black members from leadership.

Trade unions uphold the interests of workers in struggle with employers, provide the organized base that makes it possible for workers to conduct strikes over economic issues, health and safety issues, etc. Politically, for the most part, the unions oppose the capitalists on local issues, and on domestic national economic and social issues. But throughout the past half century, the period when organized labor became a significant force in the basic industries of the country, they have been chained by their leaders to the Democratic Party, a party of the capitalist class, and have resisted attempts to form an independent labor-based political party.

The main leaders of the AFL-CIO have supported the capitalist system and key policies of the capitalist class. Increasingly, during recent decades of weakening union power, they have gone in for collaboration with employers in campaigns to increase productivity, to strengthen "their" employers in competition with non-union rivals, but ultimately at the expense of their own members and their jobs.

Moreover, through U.S. government-financed institutes, the main labor leaders have provided agents and propaganda materials for splitting the trade unions in foreign countries, to undermine socialist governments, and prevent Communist and progressive-led forces that had led the labor movements from obtaining political power. In Latin America and other "third world" areas, these agents, sometimes in direct collaboration with U.S. investors plundering the countries, have carried out such splitting and wrecking activities against labor and anti-imperialist movements striving to break away from the chains of neocolonialism and establish independent courses of development. Since much of the population of these countries are people of color, this pro-imperialist policy is distinctly racist in its impact.

Yet, on the whole, the unions are a positive force in the struggle for equality. Without them, there would be no perspective for victory in the struggle. But to win, it will be necessary to overcome weaknesses in the unions, to transform them into more consistent instruments of class struggle, and to convince their white members, especially, that an active struggle against racism is in their own self-interest.

The general program of the trade unions is favorable to gains by Black working people. But the African American people have their *own* programs, to meet *their* special needs, to end *their* extra exploitation and achieve real equality. What is needed is an alliance of the whole working class with the African American people around the overall program of labor and the special program of the Black people. The same principle applies to relations between the unions and movements of Latino peoples, Native American peoples, and other racially or ethnically discriminated against sectors.

The labor-Black alliance requires renewing the leadership and broadening the perspective of the trade union movement, in which the recognition of the need for an important role for Black leadership in the unions, and a high priority for a special program for Black equality, are prominent features.

The victory of the more progressive slate in 1995 elections that changed the leadership of the AFL-CIO has already had some positive results: the increase in the share of the budget devoted to organizing from 5% to 25%; improved involvement of African Americans, Latinos, and women in leadership; and a more militant tone in strike support. However, this has to be seen as the beginning of a process, with a potential--not yet assured--for a decisive turn. Much more is required to effect a major change in the balance of forces in favor of the working class and minorities. This new situation is discussed further at the end of the chapter.

Historical Development

The trade unions remain the best organized, and potentially the decisive section of the American working class. They arose through a long period of bitter, heroic struggles of millions of workers against arrogant, ruthless employers, the police and armed forces under their control, as well as hired armies of thugs. Many workers were killed in the battles to consolidate newly organized unions.

Unions became a major factor in the 20th century, following the establishment of monopolies in the basic industries, involving great concentration of workers in single factories and mines. A vital factor was the spread of Marxist socialist ideology and organization. Eugene Debs, Socialist candidate for President, obtained 900,000 counted votes, 6% of the total, in 1912, and slightly surpassed that total in 1920, despite the beginnings of anti-Communist, anti-socialist, anti-labor terror that had put Debs in prison.

The October revolution in Russia stimulated the growth of revolutionary Communist ideology and organization in the United States and other countries. Left-wing leaders, such as William Z. Foster and Jack Johnstone organized hundreds of thousands of workers in the steel, meat packing, mining and other basic industries. Union membership, less than a million and equal to only 6% of non-agricultural employment in 1900, multiplied to 5 million, or 18%, in 1920.

The defeat of the great steel strike by the combined forces of the employers and their armies of scabs, the armed forces and police, and the press, combined with the Palmer Raids and the deportation of thousands of militant workers, was followed by a rapid decline in union membership.

But the Communists and allied left forces came back with renewed vigor during the Great Depression. For the first time, after severe struggles, the citadels of basic industry were stably organized, and monopoly corporations were forced to sign contracts with industrial unions of the newly formed Congress of Industrial Organizations (CIO).

Union membership soared from 2.7 million, or 11%, in 1933 to 14 million, or 35% of total employment, and a majority of blue collar workers in manufacturing industry, in 1945. This was a peak.

The McCarthyite anti-Communist witch hunt after World War II weakened the unions. Government intervention forced Communists and other leftists out of leadership positions in most industrial unions. Tens of thousands of militant workers were thrown out of factories. The AFL and CIO merged into the AFL-CIO, but within this united trade union movement, the conservative AFL leaders retained the major power positions. Leaders of the main industrial unions, purged of Communists, adopted anti-Communist policies, tended to focus on narrow trade union issues, and retreated from former emphasis on major progressive national policy issues, such as the struggle for full employment.

Still, the rapid growth of the U.S. economy, stimulated by the Korean and Vietnam Wars, created conditions for the growth of trade union membership, although this lagged behind the growth in employment. Numerical membership peaked at 20 million in 1974. But then, with the structural crisis of U.S. capitalism, notably the relative weakening of basic industry, union membership declined numerically, and the percentage drop in union membership accelerated. By 1993, union membership was down to 16.6 million, or 15.8%

of wage and salary employment (see Table 15:1 and Chart 15A). That's less than half the percentage of workers in unions at the end of World War II.

TABLE 15:1. UNION MEMBERSHIP, TOTAL AND PERCENTAGE OF NON-AGRICULTURAL WAGE AND SALARY EMPLOYEES SELECTED YEARS, 1900-1993 (IN THOUSANDS)

Year	Membership	Percent of total employees *(non-farm)*
1900	868	5.7%
1910	2,140	9.9
1920	5,048	18.4
1930	3,393	11.6
1933	2,689	11.3
1940	8,717	26.9
1945	14,322	35.5
1960	17,049	31.4
1974	20,199	25.8
1983	17,717	20.1
1993	16,598	15.5

SOURCES: Hist. Stat. of the U.S., Vol. I, pages 137, 178; Stat. Abst., 1982-3, no. 680, p.408; Stat. Abst., 1993, no. 689, p.436; Employment and Earnings, January 1994, Table 57, p.248, Economic Report of the President, 1994, T B44, p.318;
Note: Excludes Canadian members of U.S. unions. Excludes 2-3 million members, in later years, of employee associations, mainly of government workers.

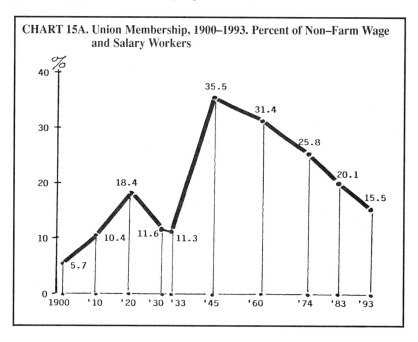

CHART 15A. Union Membership, 1900–1993. Percent of Non–Farm Wage and Salary Workers

Black Workers and the Unions

For over two centuries, U.S. unions have been a battleground of two ideologies—a narrow guild ideology of winning favors for a selected small group of workers by exclusion of others, and even at their expense; and a one-for-all, all-for-one, ideology of unity of the entire class against employers. Racism has been a main ingredient of the narrow ideology, and along with it political capitulation to employers on all general issues concerning the people. The class unity stance has been associated with progressive gains and must ultimately prevail.

Black-white relations have been a major theme in the history of American unionism, with ups and downs associated with the economic and ideological struggle. The main development of trade unionism dates from the end of the Civil War, and in the first decades the overall trend was positive. The National Labor Union, emerging in the late 1860s, favored unity of Black and white workers, but lacked a specific program to that end. It was paralleled by a cooperating Colored National Labor Union. The Marxist-led International Workingmen's Association had a more conscious policy of white-Black unity. The Knights of Labor reached its peak in the 1890s as the largest labor organization in the world, with 600,000 members, including 10-15% Black workers. It represented a high point of an approach to industrial unionism and of Black-white labor unity.

However, it was replaced by the American Federation of Labor, which came to the fore late in the century as a federation of craft organizations, with a practical approach of winning relative security for some white workers and removing Blacks from traditional areas of work. Many AFL unions formally excluded Blacks. By 1902 only 3% of its more than a million members were Black.

The Industrial Workers of the World (IWW) challenged the AFL early in the 20th Century. Blacks were prominent in its leadership, and it organized Blacks and whites jointly, even in the Jim Crow South. But the IWW did not understand the need for special demands to end discrimination in industry, incorrectly believing that there was "no race problem...only a class problem. The economic interests of all workers, be they white, Black, Brown or Yellow are identical, and all are included in the program of the I.W.W."[1]

Its notable that the sociologist William Julius Wilson, who would be horrified to be identified with the I.W.W., reflects, superficially, that approach in his *Declining Significance of Race* (see next chapter). But there's a basic difference. The I.W.W., while overestimating the understanding of the need for such unity on the part of white workers, *fought for it*, while Wilson uses the formula to combat understanding of the need for such unity.

The southern Brotherhood of Timber Workers extended this tradition in several years of militant struggle against the open-shop employers and the entire weight of the National Association of Manufacturers. This union, organized by Socialists, maintained Black-white unity against brazen attempts of employers to use race divisions to break the union.

During World War I Black workers obtained a substantial number of industrial jobs. The first really successful organized drive conducted on an all-industry rather than craft basis, was that of the packinghouse workers, led by left-wingers Foster and Johnstone. About 20,000 of the 200,000 unionized packinghouse workers were Black, and Black-white unity was a major factor in their wartime victories.

The founding of the Communist Party in 1919 brought into the labor movement for the first time a political grouping which made a major issue out of the fight for equality of Black people in every sphere of life, and against all forms of racist practices and ideology. In 1929 the left forces formed the Trade Union Unity League as a grouping of small left-led unions in previously unorganized industries. At its convention 64 of the 690 delegates were Black, an unprecedented proportion for a national trade union gathering.[2]

Throughout the 1930s and 1940s the Communists and other left-wing forces contributed substantially to the rapidly growing strength of Black workers in the trade union movement. This was particularly important in the CIO unions established in auto, steel, chemical, rubber, electrical and other machinery, and other major industries.

Black membership in labor unions increased from about 60,000 in 1930 to more than 700,000, and from a little more than 2% to 5% of total membership. The number and proportion of Black workers was higher in the CIO than in the older, craft-oriented AFL, although some of the AFL unions were now organized on an industrial basis, and were more like the CIO unions in policy.[3]

The new industrial unions set up fair employment committees, and were instrumental in establishment of the government Fair Employment Practices Committee in World War II, after Black trade union leader A. Philip Randolph organized a march of 50,000 on Washington to protest employment discrimination. The Communists and other left elements led the campaign for hiring of Black workers in the burgeoning aircraft, shipyard, textile and other industries primarily serving or greatly stimulated by wartime demands.

At the end of World War II, the Communists raised the demand for special measures to preserve the jobs of Black workers, in order to prevent operation of the customary last-to-be-hired, first-to-be-fired rule as postwar layoffs occurred. However, this was thwarted by the cold war McCarthyite expulsion of Communists from unions. For a decade there was virtually no progress against discrimination in unions, and discrimination in industry increased, with a resulting deterioration of the relative economic position of African Americans.

The civil rights struggles in the mid-1950s were accompanied by a revival of action within the unions for equal employment. This affected the terms of the merger of the two labor federations into the AFL-CIO in 1956. A Civil Rights Department was set up, and strong statements were put into the merged federation's constitution, but there was little practical implementation.

Randolph and other Black unionists organized the Negro-American Labor Council to exert pressure on the AFL-CIO and to combat its organizational discrimination.

Under the impact of the broad civil rights movement and corresponding legislation, the Vietnam War boom in industry, and the revival of progressive currents within the labor movement, Black membership in trade unions expanded.

African American workers proved most ready to join unions and to carry out militant struggles. By the 1970s the percentage of Black workers in trade unions exceeded their share in the number of workers employed. So Black union membership expanded longer and held up better than white membership. In 1977 Black trade union membership reached 2.4 million, or 12.5% of total union membership.[4]

That number held, so that with the decline in overall union membership, the proportion of African Americans in total union membership reached 14% by 1983 and 15% by 1993. Hispanic, Asian and Native American union membership also increased, so that by 1993 minority union membership reached 4.3 million, or 26% of total union membership. Of all white wage and salary workers in 1993, 15% were members of unions; while Black union members totaled 21% of all employed Black wage and salary workers. However, Black workers, along with white, lost ground in the relative extent of union membership during the 1980s, even though the number of Black union members remained unchanged.[5]

The higher union representation of Black workers in correlated with two other relationships: Black workers are more represented among Government employees than among private employees, and more represented among blue collar than among white collar workers. Overall trade union representation among government workers is much higher than among private workers; and much higher among blue collar workers than among white collar workers. The growth of unionization among government employees is partly due to the relatively large representation of Black workers, who are in the forefront of organizing efforts.

The same applies to the role of women in the trade unions. In recent decades, organization of women has proceeded rapidly, and again Black women have been in the forefront. In 1993, when 15% of all Black employed wage and salary workers were union members, the figure for African American males was 13%, for females 17%! Also important has been the rapid growth in organization of service workers, a large proportion of whom are minorities and women.

Role of Unofficial Labor Groups and Progressive Peoples Organizations

In the late 1960s and 1970s there emerged a number of Black caucuses devoted to overcoming the discrimination against Black workers by employers and union officials. In 1972 the Coalition of Black Trade Unionists (CBTU) was organized on a national scale. It was formed in a sharp break with AFL-CIO President George Meany, over his failure to oppose the racist President Nixon in the 1972 election. It focused on national political action, as well as questions of discrimination in local situations. It continues to function in the 1990s.[6]

Broader rank and file caucuses, involving white and Black workers, gave major attention to this issue in campaigns to invigorate the trade unions and change them from class collaborationist to class struggle policies. Some of these groups, notably the National Steelworkers Rank and File Committee, gave much prominence to the struggle for Black equality. New and more progressive leaderships were chosen by the Teamsters, the United Mineworkers of America, and the Steelworkers. The more democratic manner of operation and a class struggle outlook inevitably helped struggles for equality. Communist workers are prominent in this new rank and file movement, as in earlier stages of union progress. Professor Ray Marshall writes:

> The CIO's equalitarian racial policies stemmed directly from the ideological positions held by many of its leaders, who were young, idealistic people with broad social outlooks. Some of them were Communists, a group which has almost always adopted equalitarian racial positions...there can be little question that, by emphasizing the race issue to get Negro support, the Communists forced white union leaders into paying more attention to racial matters.[7]

While Marshall was writing of an earlier period, the same holds true today. But his phrase "to get Negro support" calls for comment. Of course, any movement seeks the support of those it assists. But any implication that building support supplants in importance the object itself, equality, is unfounded.

The NAACP, the largest non-religious membership organization of Black people—but with some white membership—has a long history of legal struggle for equal employment, with significant victories since the Civil Rights laws of the 1960s. Corresponding groups among Puerto Rican and Mexican American people are becoming more active. The National Organization of Women carries out lawsuits and other forms of struggle for equality in employment for women. The struggles of women and African Americans for equal employment and economic gains tend to be mutually reinforcing.

There were significant indications of intensified class struggle and fight-back among unions in the mid-1990s, analyzed as follows by Scott Marshall:

> New dynamics of class unity are coming to the fore among workers. The most visible and active coalitions of Black, Latino and white workers are based in the organized sectors of the working class. In strike struggles, in the fight for a public works jobs program, in voter registration drives, and in the course of battling anti-immigrant laws, labor/community coalitions are emerging in force. Organizations like the Coalition of Black Trade Unionists (CBTU), Coalition of Labor Union Women (CLUW) and Labor Council for Latin American Advancement (LACLA) are playing a more dynamic role—not only in labor but in working class communities.[8]

Union membership has brought major improvements to all workers, and somewhat reduced discrimination against Black and Latino men (Table 15:2).

TABLE 15:2. MEDIAN WEEKLY EARNINGS OF FULL TIME
            WORKERS, 1994

		Union	% of White	Non-Union	% of White	% Extra Wages of Union members
Men	White*	$640	100%	$513	100%	25%
	Black	524	82%	359	70%	46%
	Latino	506	79%	316	62%	60%
Women	White	546	100%	386	100%	41%
	Black	452	83%	323	84%	40%
	Latino	402	74%	289	75%	39%

SOURCE: E & E. January 1995, T. 41, p.215
* Data for white workers *not* adjusted to eliminate Hispanic white workers.

Among men in 1994, white union members with full-time jobs got 25% more than non-union members; while African American union members got 46% more than non-union members, and Latino union members 60% more than non-union members. The white/Black differential, 30% among non-union members, was reduced to 18% among union members. Among women of all races, union membership brought gains of about 40% in wages. The wider gains of Latino men may be associated with successful organizing drives in very low wage service industries, which employ many Hispanic people. Still, even among union members, weekly earnings of Latino workers remain quite low.

Still, certain features are troublesome. The $116 per week dollar differential in white/Black weekly earnings of union members is certainly serious, and represents an increase over a $92 differential just three years earlier. In fact, whether organized or unorganized, Black and Latino workers have recovered less from the depression year 1991 than white workers. In the three years 1991-1994, white male union members gained 10.2%, Black male union members 7.2%, and Hispanic male union members 5.2%, half as much as white male union members. Even in that recovery period, Black and Latino male union members lost ground in comparison with the 8.8% rise in the consumer price index. The situation among women union members is even sharper—whites gained 14.5%, Blacks 7.6%, and Hispanics 7.5%, a marked widening of differentials.

While sex discrimination remains severe, it is noteworthy that both among union and non-union members, Black and Latino men earned less than white women.

Furthermore, among male union members, the ratio of Black to white fulltime earnings was slightly lower in 1994 than a quarter of a century earlier, in 1970. Among women union members, there was a definite deterioration—the differential against Black women widening from 9% in 1970 to 17% in 1994.[9] The data in Table 15:2 shows that the 1994 differentials against Black and Latino women were just as severe among union members as among nonmembers.

With those qualifications, the table does indicate the substantial positive contribution of unionization to higher wages, and among men in reducing racial discrimination. But why did progress stop in the early 1970s? In the main the answer must be attributed to the stepped up anti-labor, racist offensive of the capitalist class.

Part of the answer must be attributed to a general shortcoming of the trade union movement. The unions favor equality, oppose discrimination. But with few exceptions, they do not initiate or support special measures to obtain equality—i.e., decisive affirmative action programs, including the use of quotas, goals and timetables.

Moreover, when affirmative action measures conflict with seniority systems, or civil service rules, the unions generally uphold the seniority systems or tests provided in civil service jobs and some private industries to govern promotions or hiring for better jobs. These systems are important union gains, limiting employer favoritism in promotion, hiring and firing, but they evolved historically before the civil rights struggles brought the issue of achieving racial equality to the fore. Strict application of many seniority procedures, for example, ignore the employer practice of "last to be hired, first to be fired," which put Black workers at a disadvantage in seniority ratings. Tests used, often with little or no relation to the job involved and oriented to the backgrounds of white people, put workers who grew up in segregated Black areas at a disadvantage.

The example of New York City school custodians (discussed in Chapter 6) illustrates the problem, even in a union local with progressive traditions.

Adjustment of seniority systems and test procedures to give priority to affirmative action programs would actually strengthen the effectiveness of seniority systems for all union members.

Here are some examples of failure on the part of major unions to carry out priority affirmative action programs:

The Teamsters Union is the largest in the country. Racist practices in the industry have kept Black workers out of the better-paying long distance trucking jobs. In 1974 the Civil Rights Division of the Justice Department won a consent decree with 7 large trucking firms, providing for quotas of one-third to one-half of new hires for Black and Latino drivers. The then reactionary, gang-connected leadership of the Teamsters Union has since been replaced by a relatively progressive and honest leadership. However, the union has not carried out an active struggle to overcome past racist practices. The share of Black workers in truck driver jobs declined from 14.4 % in 1972 to 13.9% in 1981 and 12.3% in 1993. The 1972 and 1981 figures include other non-white workers with Black workers; however, even if the other non-white drivers were excluded from the figures for the earlier years, there would be a definite decline by 1993 in that share. The 12.3 % share of Blacks among truck drivers is far less than their 20-25% shares in comparable occupations—bus drivers, taxi drivers, industrial truck and tractor drivers.[10] This is very important, because truck driving is one of the relatively few blue collar occupations that has enjoyed a long-term upward trend.

The situation remains better in the industrial unions formed in the 1930s and 1940s with Left leadership. Despite expulsion of the Left leadership from most of these unions, enough of the older tradition remains to make a substantial difference from the situation in the older craft unions.

Yet serious discrimination persists against Black workers in the basic industries. The union leaders do little to counter the continued exclusion of Black workers from the highest paying skilled jobs, and their concentration in the lowest paying, most unhealthy jobs. They tend to exclude Black members from top leadership positions. The United Automobile Workers has a relatively good record. Its Fair Practices and Anti-Discrimination Department carries on significant educational activity. Its contracts provide a basis for grievance action against the many cases of discrimination in the plants. And yet, discrimination remains sufficiently severe to bring about the self-organization of Black members into special caucuses, and Blacks are leaders in the militant rank-and-file groups developing in this, as in other, unions. Black presidents have been elected in many locals in the Detroit area, and are prominent in the local leadership generally.

In the early postwar period, the Social Democratic sections of the UAW leadership, with the help of FBI raids against, and firings of Communists and other progressive workers and leaders, obtained full control, broke their former coalition with left-progressive forces, and gradually moved towards policies with large components of class collaboration.

Basic demands of rank and file workers, such as for a shorter workweek without reduction in pay, were abandoned by the leadership in negotiations with the companies. Nor was an active struggle against racism in the industry carried out on the broad scale necessary. One result is brought out by the following table, concerning the distribution of blue collar jobs in plants of the Ford Motor Company, operating under union contract.

TABLE 15:3. BLACKS AND WHITES IN BLUE COLLAR JOB CATEGORIES, FORD MOTOR CO. 1993

	Black	White	Ratio White to Black
Craft workers	9.0%	89.4%	9.9
Operatives	25.4	71.7	2.8
Laborers	28.1	69.2	2.5
Service Workers	26.5	71.9	2.7

(SOURCE: Ford Motor Company, Annual Report to Stockholders, 1993.)

A crucial aspect of job discrimination is in exclusion from skilled craft jobs. Different degrees of training are needed for each skilled craft. For some jobs, the training can be obtained outside of Ford. Other crafts are special to the automobile industry, so training by Ford, on the job, is necessary. In any case, training for all or nearly all skills can be provided on the job, or during special preparatory classes, in a comparatively brief period.

For 25 years Ford Motor Co. has been under provisions of civil rights law calling for non-discrimination in employment, and action to remove past discrimination. Still, ten times as many white workers as Black have skilled craft jobs at Ford, while only 2.5 to 3 times as many white workers as Black are employed in the other blue collar and service categories. For not having come much closer to equality in distribution of blue collar and service fobs, Ford Motor Company is guilty of racist employment practices.

But what about the UAW? For 50 years the union has had solid contractual relations with Ford Motor Co. It has the power to influence hiring and promotion of workers. Under basic trade union principles, it has the duty to overcome company discrimination in employment, and it has had Civil Rights law and the EEOC as extra weapons to use in ending discrimination. It has not done so, nor, to my knowledge, has it attempted to do so.

The very existence of the union, with its representatives who deal with the company, with its elected shop stewards in the plant to uphold the workers' interests, has certainly created an environment which reduces or eliminates the most crude forms of racial discrimination by the employer. The occupational distribution of Black workers is probably less discriminatory against them than it would be without the union. But that is not enough. Failure of the union to positively fight for job equality has weakened the union in this period of company downsizing and plant closings—overtime hours that can kill for some, permanent layoffs for others.

The monthly publication of the UAW, *Solidarity*, in a 1993 article featured "The National Negro Labor Council...Civil Rights Trailblazers." Formed in 1951 at a meeting of over 1,000 Black unionists, The National Negro Labor Council (NNLC) "blazed a trail for the civil rights struggles that followed, fighting job discrimination and winning new rights for Black workers."

Owing to its influence, and the pressure of the left-led UAW local 600 in Detroit, General Electric and Ford were forced to hire Black workers at their new Louisville, Kentucky plants. The article names former local 600 leaders, Detroit Mayor Coleman Young and former Illinois Congressman Charles Hayes, one of the few trade unionists elected to Congress. The NNLC

> was forced to disband in 1956 under relentless Cold War attacks. Because it took the federal government to task on job discrimination and because it refused to bow to the anti-Communist hysteria of the times, the NNLC was relentlessly hounded by the government. The Justice Department labeled it "subversive"...and in April 1956 the NNLC was dissolved. However, its leaders continued the struggle.[11]

Not stated, but implied, is the fact that Communists were prominent in organizing and in the work of the NNLC, as they had been in organizing and winning contracts by the UAW. However, the article is rather hypocritical in failing to reveal that its social democratic leadership, having expelled Communists, and put through a Constitutional provision barring them from union office, directly participated in the "relentless cold war attacks." Nor has it moved to correct that period by welcoming Communists and other progressives back into participation in leadership, along with the militant policies and active struggle against racism that they espouse.

Aside from the major unions, positive contributions have been made by some of the smaller, left-led unions, in fighting for equality. Thus, the left-led International Longshoremen's and Warehousemen's Union has been the leading trade union force in the San Francisco Bay area and on Hawaii. It not only established practices minimizing discrimination among its members on account of race, but has influenced the entire labor situation in this respect. Local 1199 of the Drug and Hospital Workers Union has helped tens of thousands of Black and other minority workers to win decent working and wage conditions, in combat against managers and owners of hospitals, and state governments which helped employers with injunctions, jailing and fines of the union leaders. District 65 of the National Distributive Workers (AFL-CIO), The United Electrical workers (UE-Ind), and the Transport Workers Union (TWU-Ind) are other unions with a background of continuing progressive leadership, which have made significant overall contributions to reducing discrimination and combating racism in industry. Rank and file movements and some locals of major unions have similarly good records.

With all the shortcomings, on balance the trade unions have been a major assistance in the struggle for equality, against discrimination in employment and labor conditions. Nowhere has this been more important than in the political role of the unions.

Political Role of the Trade Unions

As the civil rights struggle developed during the 1950s and 1960s, the political front became increasingly important in the struggle of the African American people for social and economic emancipation. There was a clear differentiation in the position of the working class and that of the capitalist class on this issue. The civil rights organizations and the trade union centers formed a united front on most legislative and electoral issues, nationally and in a number of states. Major unions gave active support in personnel and funds to the civil rights campaigns in the South. A white women worker of the UAW was killed by racist deputies in a famous Alabama civil rights march. In turn, the civil rights struggles proved a stimulant to trade union organization of white as well as Black workers, and helped overcome repression against trade union organizers.

Trade union pressure was important in winning enactment of key civil rights legislation of the mid-1960s. An NAACP legislative leader said "organized labor gave unfailing consistent and massive support where it counted most" in the drive for this legislation. At the same time, the civil rights organizations supported trade union legislative objectives.[12]

The unions provided the main political force behind the enactment of periodic improvement and broadened coverage of minimum wage legislation.

Precisely because of the traditional consignment of Black workers to the worst paid jobs, such legislation is of particular importance. Opposition to this legislation always comes from employer groups. Regardless of the racist ideology and practices of many officials in their own unions, when the class interests of the workers force them into conflict with employers, as in the case of labor legislation, Black workers gain, not only as workers in general, but in the reduction of prevailing discrimination against them.

Similar considerations apply to many other types of welfare and labor legislation. Moreover a comparable alignment of forces has operated in the state and municipal political arena. In states with strong unions, minimum wage legislation, unemployment insurance benefits, workmens' compensation laws, and other labor and social welfare provisions are considerably superior to the federal standard—this is of particular value to Black and Latino workers.

Trade unions have an uneven record in relation to the campaigns of the growing number of Black elected officials. But more often than not, when a Black candidate has run against a racist white candidate, the trade union influence has been mainly on the side of the Black, while the business establishment has been mainly on the side of the racist.

The overwhelming majority of Black officials have been elected on the Democratic Party ticket, which has the support of most unions. The shift of the Black vote from the Republicans to the Democrats coincided with the emergence of the new militant, industrial trade unions and the allegiance of these unions to the Democratic Party. At the same time, the unions have been significant in opposing ultra-right and fascist tendencies in politics.

The beneficial influence of trade unions in the struggle for equality has been significantly decreased by the weakening of trade union power during the 1980s and early 1990s. The savage attack by President Reagan against the Airline Controllers in 1981, crushing their strike, destroying their union, and throwing the entire membership out of work, signaled a major anti-labor, anti-union offensive by the capitalist class. The unions are subjected to increasing legal restrictions, structured to forbid cooperation between unions and solidarity among workers in the face of mounting consolidation of financial and industrial control of hundreds or thousands of units scattered around the country so that a strike by workers in one factory often is but a pinprick to the corporate monopoly.

The spread of "right-to-work" laws, which confront unions and their organizing campaigns with formidable obstacles are concentrated in the southern states, where half the African American population lives, and hence has a marked racist impact. The Wagner Act, the basic "Magna Carta" of labor, won during the New Deal period, has been largely stripped of its positive content, and other progressive labor legislation is at best weakly enforced.

Particularly serious has been the failure of the trade union movement to mount a sufficient campaign to prevent the long-term deterioration of the federal minimum wage law, through failure of Congress and the President to enact increases matching rising living costs. Black and Hispanic workers bear the brunt of this blow.

The leadership of the AFL-CIO and the most influential industrial unions have fallen short of the firmness and vision needed to face this anti-labor challenge. One weakness is the extremely limited scale and scope of labor political-economic demands, which generally remain within the bounds of capitalist debate, and are unable to inspire membership enthusiasm. More important is the general failure to organize mass mobilization and activity in support of demands, or to fully support independently organized progressive mass mobilizations. An example of the weakness of AFL-CIO politicians was their support in 1993 of President Clinton's abortive "health reform" proposal, which failed to conform to his campaign promise of universal coverage; and rejection of the single-payer proposal, which had been won by Canadian labor, and enjoys broad support in the United States. African American and Latino workers, especially, are in need of this or equivalent reform which would help provide them with the medical care now lacking.

However, the most basic shortcoming of trade union political policy is their marriage to the Democratic Party, one of the twin parties of U.S. monopoly capital. Along with that goes opposition to construction of a labor party or a broadly based anti-monopoly party in which labor has a major voice. One result is that there is rarely, if ever, a trade unionist Senator, never more than one or two trade unionists in the House of Representatives, and no trade unionist member of the cabinet or other high-ranking administrative position or judicial post. Thus, while the function of the Commerce Department is to advance the interests of business, that of the Labor Department is to supervise and record labor, not to be its advocate. As a result, the United States lags far behind all other advanced industrial countries in labor legislation, social support legislation, and other requirements of elementary modern civilization. Again, "minority" workers are the most serious losers from this shortcoming.

Black Contribution to Labor

If the Black struggle for equality has gained, on balance, from the activities and policies of the organized labor movement, the working class as a whole and the trade union movement in particular have gained even more from the struggles of Black working people.

During the 1980s the growing Black Caucus in Congress emerged as the most consistent progressive grouping. Increasing in size in the 1990s, it also became part of a forming progressive caucus. However, the unity and effectiveness of the Black Caucus was diluted by its members' dependence on financial campaign contributions from capitalists, Black and white, and by their ties to the Democratic Party machines. Yet the overall positive impact of Black membership in Congress was emphasized by the nationwide campaign of reactionary forces during the 1990s to defeat Black candidates for Congress, including changes in boundaries of Congressional districts to undermine majorities for Black officials.

During the 1980s and early 1990s Black mayors were elected in a number of the largest cities. They exerted a progressive influence for working people generally as well as for Blacks, but their power was severely limited by financial restrictions imposed by State Constitutions. Nevertheless, concerted campaigns have succeeded in getting key Black mayors defeated.

In recent years, most Black judges have played a progressive role on a national and local level. Black voters have supported pro-labor candidates for office by a wider majority than any other sector of the population.

The contributions of African Americans to the entire U.S., working class has been felt even more distinctly in the factories and on picket lines. Black workers, to an extent beyond their proportion numerically, have participated actively and with special militancy in organizing campaigns, strike struggles, and day-to-day lesser conflicts of labor and management. Black workers are prominent among rank and file forces striving to remedy the conservatism and class collaboration tendencies of some key industrial union leaderships.

Establishment propagandists, and some progressive writers who come out against racism, convey the impression of Black strike breaking as a general phenomenon, and of a widespread hostility of Black people to unions as such. William Julius Wilson has been particularly influential in spreading this line. Prominence has been given to the use of Black strikebreakers in the steel strike of 1920, and William Z. Foster has been misquoted in this respect. In the last century Black workers strove continually to get into unions. Foster wrote:

> Unfortunately, however, there were white chauvinist prejudices among the white workers and their leaders to bar the Negro from the unions, to keep him out of the skilled trades, and to force him into the role of strikebreaker if he wanted to work in industry—all of which errors dovetailed neatly with the employers' plans for the Negro in industry. Early American labor history is replete with the tragic experience of white workers striking to bar Negroes from skilled jobs and unions. Wesley lists 50 such strikes against Negro workers between 1882 and 1900. On more than one occasion white workers also broke the strikes of Negro workers...

By their anti-Black policies, the AFL leaders "drove a wedge between the labor movement and the Negro people." This...

> tended to force Negro workers to the conclusion that if they wanted...work in industry, their only way to get it was by acting as strikebreakers, as the employers wanted them to do. And in fact, this sometimes happened...the matter of Negro strike-breaking, however, had been grossly overstated. The fact is that for every Negro who took a striker's job there were dozens of white strikebreakers."[13]

Thus, the number of Blacks among strikebreakers has been disproportionately small. The historical development of the Black role in labor unions is governed, in the final analysis, by the objective community of interests of Black and white workers. Within that overriding community, Blacks have special interests—the need to overcome age-old discrimination and extra exploitation. To the extent that white workers and their leaders do not recognize these special needs, the community of interests of Black and white workers is disrupted.

It is in the self-interest of white workers to recognize that their general needs as workers can be met with any degree of sufficiency and security only to the extent that the special needs of Black workers are met simultaneously.

One of the keys to the revival and strengthening of labor, the majority of the population, to achieving its proper weight in the affairs of the country, is the recognition by its membership of *the centrality* of the fight for full equality for Black workers within the general objectives of the working class as a whole. Labor needs to elect a leadership that will see and act on this central struggle in a similar manner. Also vital is to support aspirations for equality of Latino workers, while emphasizing unity of Black and Latino workers and opposing employer attempts to utilize Hispanic workers as a means of isolating African American workers from employment.

In 1995, three major industrial unions with a combined membership of about two million announced plans to merge over the next several years. This, and other mergers by smaller unions, partly counters the record merger wave among corporations, which are directed sharply and often explicitly against labor, with the most serious impact on minority workers.

The election of John Sweeney as the new president of the AFL-CIO reflects both changes that are taking place within the labor movement and the urgency of further growth with increased unity of white, Black and all workers. The new executive council of 54, 27 percent of whom are women and minorities, also reflects a recognition of the need for wider representation. President Sweeney promised a new level of labor activism and militancy, and the organization of unorganized workers, the majority of whom are minority and/or women.

The fight for affirmative action is one of the crucial questions facing the leaders and members of the merging unions and the new leadership of the AFL-CIO. This fight, along with militant struggle in the economic, social and political arenas can produce a united, broad forward movement in the interests of all workers.

16. From Racist Ideology to Violent Repression

Racist ideology follows two main lines:

A. The crude theory of Black genetic inferiority, dehumanizing the African American people. It includes claims of reduced mental capacity, cultural backwardness, inborn criminality. This is the main line of the overt racists, practitioners of crude discrimination, racist violence.

B. The "sophisticated" theory that the inferior situation of Blacks is due to "objective" economic and social factors, not to intentional racism. This theory is meant to appeal to the majority of white people who consider themselves as relatively free of racial prejudice and, it is hoped by its purveyors, will be dissuaded from the need to act jointly with oppressed peoples in ending discrimination and for social progress.

Most ideologists of racism peddle various blends of these two approaches in their arguments. In this chapter we will examine the views of the most prominent advocates of racist ideologies during the last third of the 20th century, people whose works are generally academic in format, but have been repackaged to gain as wide mass currency as possible.

Racist ideology has emphasized a variety of doctrines at different stages of U.S. history. These themes have been connected with the main thrusts of racist attacks and exploitation at each stage. However, no theory of racist ideology ever vanishes, but remains as backup for each new concoction.

No one is born a racist. It is the insidious indoctrination, instilled from earliest years, that propagates and perpetuates the phony "theory" of the superiority of the white race. That the motive for this "theory" is based on amassing profits for the few by the exploitation of the rest is not widely understood, nor publicized by the media that controls mass information. And never mind the fact that the overwhelming majority of the world's population are people of color!

The most vicious fabrication is the thesis that African Americans are biologically inferior, are primate-related rather than human. This obscenity corresponds to the centuries-long enslavement of Black people. It was a precept used to rationalize the contradiction between the practice of slavery and the proclamations of freedom and equality in the Bill of Rights, and it prevailed throughout the country, in the North as well as in the South—as did slavery.

This thesis flourished after the Civil War. It was a contributing factor in the defeat of Black struggles for real freedom during the Reconstruction period and was used to justify rigorous Jim Crow laws in the South, where the over-whelming majority of African Americans lived. Segregation was strictly enforced: Blacks were forbidden to eat where whites ate, to drink from the same fountains, or to use the same public toilet or other facilities. To some extent, there was partial application of these dicta in the North.

In the 20th century, when the United States joined the European powers in sharing out colonial possessions, the theme of biological inferiority was used as justification for the inhuman status assigned to the colonized peoples, especially those of Africa and Asia. Also, the slogan "deport Blacks 'back to Africa'" was used by racist movements. The idea also had some support among a section of the Black population—the Garvey movement—who did not accept the ideology of racial inferiority but looked to the lands of their forefathers for an escape from oppression.

With the increasing sophistication of the working class, bigots sought to put over pseudo-scientific fabrications as vindication for continuing the lie of Black inferiority: speculations about genetic deficiency; claims of smaller brain cavities, etc. And even by the second half of the 20th Century when new racist concepts were pushed forward, biological inferiority was subordinated, but far from eliminated—despite scientific disproof. That canard remains imbedded in the ideology of racists, criminals and neo-fascist organizations, which have been growing again in number and influence as the structural crises of U.S. society deepens. City police, brutalizing Black communities, freely shout obscenities—e.g., likening Blacks to chimpanzees. The capital-ist ideological roots of such outrages are occasionally exposed when some prominent college president or professor, a politician or business tycoon is caught making a similar statement publicly.

The tendency got a renewed "literary" launching with publication of *The Bell Curve* by Charles Murray, in collaboration with Richard Herrnstein. The book argues that IQ scores are determined in large part by the genetic makeup of people who take the tests, a long-disproved fraudulent theory. The fascist orientation of Murray's garbage is indicated by Jason DeParle's summation:

> The authors say the country is witnessing the rise of a cognitive elite, people who are intermarrying and passing on to their children their genetic advantages. They see an underclass operating in reverse, with unemployed men and welfare moth-ers passing on genetic disadvantages in communities rife with disorder. As the gap widens between the mental haves and have-nots, the authors predict the rise of a new conservatism, "along Latin American lines," with the cognitive elite employ-ing repressive, police-state tactics to protect themselves from the growing danger.[1]

Because IQ tests are constructed to refer to information which is not widely available in ghettoized communities, as well as projecting cultural norms different from those prevailing among Black people, it is a fact that African Americans normally obtain lower average marks in these tests.

The *Boston Globe* quoted scientists denouncing the book as "pseudo-science" and editorially attacked the book's "high energy quotient." The *New York Times* featured DeParle's article with the cover head: "The Most Dangerous Conservative." But the general repudiation of Murray's line by academic researchers does not apply to highly placed capitalists, without whose support Murray would never have been heard. Dropped by one think tank for his fraudulent ideas, he was taken in tow by the American Enterprise Institute. Murray spends much of his time on the high-paid corporate-executive lecture circuit, and is a guest at the vacation retreats of the super-rich.

Earlier Murray first gained such support with a book advocating the abolition of welfare, which emerged during the 1990s as a major drive of big business and their politicians in both political parties.

> Murray's influence is still on the rise, both as the enemy of social programs and the champion of the two-parent family. His prophecy last year of a coming white underclass touched a national nerve, and it brought a flurry of proposals to deny welfare to young mothers. It also brought a respectful comment from President Clinton. While he did not agree with Murray's solutions, the President said, the warning about out-of-wedlock births "did the country a great service."[2]

A more sophisticated aspect of propaganda is directed at people who oppose racism. An extremely important feature of modern capitalist class propaganda emphasizes the growing size of the Black "middle class," by which is meant Blacks with higher incomes, government and corporate officials and managers, television announcers, highly paid athletes. They, along with the still small and weak capitalist sector of direct labor exploiters, do constitute an increase in their numbers. The reasoning, expressed or implied, is that through this route problems of discrimination are being eased and will be more or less automatically solved. Thus there is no need for people to be concerned, to unite to combat racism.

But the reality is quite different. The increase in the number of better-off Blacks, *still relatively small*, is accompanied by a worsening of the situation of the Black members of the working class. Increased inequality among the Black people, mirroring the same phenomenon among whites, is particularly marked. It masks an intensification of the overall weight of racism against the African American people as a whole.

Morality and the Family

The charge of alleged amorality—even immorality—of Black people has gained credence and become a main subject of American racists. Family structure, sex relations, and personal habits have been attacked from all directions, and accusations of drug abuse, violence and criminal actions have been used to instill fear of Black men. One specific aim was to reinforce the campaigns for compulsory sterilization to reduce the Black population.

The Civil Rights gains of the 1950s and 1960s—principally the Voting Rights Act of 1966—did give impetus to the struggles for restitution and equality. Under President Lyndon Johnson, with his demagogic "Great Society" program of minor domestic concessions, the most ruthless large-scale racist war of conquest in the history of U.S. imperialism—the war against Vietnam—was accelerated. Johnson talked of the increasing discrimination, the poverty and segregation imposed on the African American people. True, he talked of the need for jobs, for decent housing, education, health care. But he offered nothing concrete to provide for any of these. Instead, he called for a conference of scholars and experts—government and private. But the core of his speech at Howard University on June 4, 1965, was a contradiction:

Family Breakdown

Perhaps most important—its influence radiating to every part of life—is the breakdown of the Negro family structure...It flows from centuries of oppression and persecution of the Negro man. It flows from long years of degradation and discrimination, which have attacked his dignity and assaulted his ability to provide for his family...

The family is the cornerstone of our society...When the family collapses it is the children that are usually damaged. When it happens on a massive scale the community itself is crippled.

So...unless we work to strengthen the family—all the rest, schools and playgrounds, public assistance and private concern—will never be enough to cut completely the circle of despair and deprivation.[3]

Johnson's speech was written by Assistant Secretary of Labor Daniel Patrick Moynihan and presidential assistant Richard N. Goodwin. It was based on a 125-page report written by Moynihan: "The Negro Family: The Case for Political Action." With politically expedient duplicity, the report was interspersed with factual material about the deteriorating conditions of the African American people, the rise in unemployment, segregation, poverty, etc. But its main thrust was the all-out attack against African Americans, blaming them for their plight. Going beyond the crude racism of the southern Bourbons, Moynihan directed his venom against the sexual mores and family life of Black people, alleging their self-destruction of the male-dominated family—that sexist "cornerstone" of American life. There were also attacks against the alleged mass criminal activities of Blacks, as he attributed to them "sub-standard" intelligence, as evidenced by failures on Army "mental tests."!

The press—and columnists guided by Johnson personally—took on the task of popularizing the details of the Moynihan report's assault. The report itself, soon made public, became a powerful implement for inculcating racist prejudices among the masses of the white population, while providing official sanction for racist employment, housing, education, etc. policies.

And Moynihan, who turned to electoral politics, has been rewarded for his "contributions" by a prolonged tenure in the U.S. Senate.

The basic message of the report was that "we"—the capitalist establishment—will tell "you"—the African Americans—how to conduct your personal lives, including even the most intimate details: e.g., even how many children you may have. But concerning the overwhelming economic and social problems imposed by racism, it's hands off! The solutions are up to "you"—as long as "you" cope as individuals. No mass action, please! or due procedures will be followed to restore order.

As for state and local governments in the South, where the majority of "you" live, their overwhelming, crude racism is no concern of "ours," the federal government. And that also holds true for the many northern state and local governments whose policies differ in degree from "ours." Nor is it up to "us" to interfere with employers who discriminate against African Americans, or real estate and banking interests that foster segregation and scare whites from living next to Blacks, or even to step in to rectify the underfinanced and ill-equipped schools Black children attend.

Sure, Congress passed some laws and set up some new agencies that will collect statistics and write reports. And now "you" will be able to file complaints! But as for action to promote equality, forget it. That's up to Black private enterprise. And meanwhile, work on straightening out "your" paranoid personalities.

Of course the report did not spell out these particulars in those terms, but that is precisely what happened. Since then, all of the components of suffering and inequality and instability have been aggravated and in some respects multiplied.

Consider Moynihan's imputation that African American men weren't willing to work. During the early 1960s the proportion of Black men in the labor force was only slightly less than that of white men—and even higher if self-employed are discounted and consideration is limited to wage and salary workers.

But under the propaganda barrage of the report, and the corresponding actions, and inactions, of the government, the proportion of Black men counted in the labor force and, even worse, the proportion with jobs, dropped disastrously.

With the deterioration of the economy, a similar downtrend afflicted white men, but not nearly so severely.

The alleged criminality of African Americans was highlighted by Moynihan:

> It is probable that at present, a majority of crimes against the person, such as rape murder...are committed by Negroes...There is, of course, no absolute evidence.[4]

In fact, there is decisive evidence that is not the case. But the charge of criminality against Blacks has been used to justify racist discrimination in all aspects of life. It was made a primary political weapon of the Republican Party in the 1980s and 1990s. And the Democratic president, Bill Clinton, campaigned for the tough "anti-crime" legislation that, enforced by the racist police forces, will impact most directly against Black people and Latinos.

In the introduction to his report, Moynihan avers:

> A [Black] middle-class group has managed to save itself, but for the vast numbers of the unskilled, poorly educated city working class, the fabric of conventional social relationships has all but disintegrated.

Elsewhere in the document, Moynihan suggests that this "middle class" represents about half the total of the Black population and, when based on family structure, as much as three quarters. The Senator thus classifies as "middle class" those Black workers who manage to get decent jobs—both husbands and wives—and are therefore able to support a family. In actuality, however, the accepted concept of "middle class"—either considered in social class terms or in the upper middle-income concept (today above $50,000 in family income)—would be a small part of Moynihan's "middle class." In his report, Moynihan posed as a scientific researcher with racist conclusions "objectively" obtained. But, like other academic and political racists, Moynihan wore—and wears—two hats. Away from the lingo of officialdom, he reveals himself as a tout for the overt racist ideology of the slave owners. He claimed that there are genetic "strains" in the Blacks that "produced high rates of divorce and illiteracy"—thus contributing to the campaigns of the southern troglodyte politicians to thwart the movement for integration.

Nearly 30 years later, as an influential, powerful U.S. Senator, Moynihan was still maneuvering to guide legislation in an anti-labor, racist direction. By 1994 he had sunk more deeply into the racist cesspool. He claimed that the rising number of children born out of wedlock provides "evidence" that a "new type of human being" is evolving. These children, he asserted, would constitute a "new species" biologically unable to "interbreed" with Homo Sapiens. This he said, was "ominous" for the very survival of the species Homo Sapiens.[5]

To back up his iniquitous assertions, Moynihan affronts Black children born to unmarried parents, using the pejorative term "illegitimate." Although in 1950 almost 10 times as many Black infants as white (proportionate to population) were born to unmarried parents, by 1988 four times as many babies were born to unmarried Black parents as to unmarried whites (proportionately), showing the sharper rise among whites.

The burden on working class women required to head a household is severe, especially when compounded by racist discrimination. But the policies of government and the capitalist class have multiplied the number of women placed in such conditions. In 1950, 17.2% of African American households and 5.3% of white households were headed by women—the Black percentage was 3.2 times greater. In 1990, 56.2% of Black households and 17.3% of white households were headed by women. The ratio was still 3.2 times; for both Black and white families the proportion had tripled. And for white families it was as high in 1990 as it had been for Black families in 1950.[6]

Moynihan's slanders were in support of President Clinton's welfare reform bill, an overt racist proposal directed against the tens of millions, white and Black, receiving aid to dependent children, food stamps, and other of the miserly relief measures the U.S. government provides for the most poverty stricken.

Not surprisingly, Senator Jay Rockefeller of West Virginia, fourth generation "liberal" political representative of the Rockefeller family, said, "You (Moynihan) were right then (in 1965) and you are right now."[7] Thus the Rockefeller family of multi-billionaires continues its long-standing leadership in the racist campaign to limit population growth of African Americans through forced sterilization and discriminatory lack of medical care.

Under the right-wing Republican Administration of Richard Nixon, and his successor Gerald Ford, racist propaganda as well as action intensified.

Emphasis was placed on lack of education as an explanation of poorer jobs and higher unemployment among African Americans, but in such a way as to cover up the racism which resulted in the inferior education of Blacks, and to create the impression that Black people were responsible for their inferior education. That has continued to be a theme of official propaganda, despite the fact that struggles for better educational opportunities are a leading part of African American campaigns in the present period. Moreover, the argument that a college degree is needed for a decent job has become a major theme, taking advantage of the fact that the supply of people with college degrees far exceeds the number of jobs that actually require B.A. or higher skills.

Until not so long ago, in sections of the country separate and grossly unequal education was enforced by law. And to this day de facto segregation and inferior education are imposed by school authorities, by housing segregation, by establishment of whites-only private schools, and other devices.

Clearly the inferior education of Black youth is part of racist discrimination, and not an independent causal factor. William Ryan, in his powerful and passionate book, *Blaming the Victim*, wrote:

> What is wrong with the victim? In pursuing this logic, no one remembers to ask questions about the collapsing buildings and torn textbooks, the frightened, insensitive teachers, the six additional desks in the room, the blustering, frightened principals, the relentless segregation, the callous administration, the irrelevant curriculum, the bigoted or cowardly members of the school board, the insulting history book, the stingy taxpayers, the fairy-tale readers, or the self-serving faculty of the local teachers' college. We are encouraged to confine our attention to the child and to dwell on all his alleged defects. Cultural deprivation becomes an omnibus explanation for the educational disaster area known as the inner-city school.[8]

Indeed, in addition to being subjected to qualitatively inferior education, African Americans are deliberately educated for lower-income, dead end jobs through the notorious tracking system.

It is said that part of the reason why many of the Jewish people in the United States have "made it" is because of their tradition of being "people of the book"—their striving and self-sacrifice for education. But Ryan shows that sociological studies reveal the same traits among Black people, the same extra striving, extra sacrifice for education. Clearly, the real trouble is that they are deliberately barred both from high quality education and from enjoying its fruits. The discrimination is more determined, more persistent, more absolute, than that which Jewish people faced in anti-Semitic discrimination in the educational system in the past, and still face to a limited degree.

In 1974 the President's Council of Economic Advisors admitted that actual discrimination against Blacks continued regardless of the degree of education they obtained. With remarkable twists of logic, they conceded that past racist discrimination might account for part of this, but not present racism; and in the process, utilized standard racist stereotypes:

> Several factors can be mentioned to explain why Black males still receive lower earnings than white males after adjustment for schooling, age, region and marital status. Prior investments made in the child at home are important in determining the extent to which a student benefits from schooling. Black youths are more likely to come from poorer homes where the parents have less schooling, to have poorer diets, and to be less healthy. They are likely to start school with fewer advantages and skills than the typical white youth. Moreover, at least in the past, there was dis-

crimination against Black youths in public school expenditures. Later on, as adults, Blacks have poorer health, and may have poorer information about better jobs. Some of the current wage differences may thus be a consequence of past discrimination.[9]

Since, according to the authors, many of these factors are difficult to measure, "one cannot reliably measure the extent of...discrimination that now exists," or its effects on earnings.

This agnostic conclusion, as well as the tenor of the entire discussion, aims to convey the impression that discrimination today is either negligible or non-existent. Note the overt expressions of racial prejudice, such as the claim that Black parents do not "invest" enough in their children, and that Black children start school with less "skill" than white six-year olds. The main thing however, is that insofar as some of these "factors" are accurate descriptions of reality, they merely describe *aspects of discrimination*, rather than independent circumstances.

A year later, the President's economists tried to justify the terrible crisis increase in Black unemployment. Their attempts to "factor out" unemployment differentials according to various alleged causes left a significant residual due to racist discrimination. Like the damned spot on Lady Macbeth's hand, they couldn't get rid of the differential. In fact, they admitted that the spot is spreading, the differential widening. So they turned to a new line of argument, blaming it on equal employment legislation! Here is the tortuous reasoning paraphrased:

The employers would like to discriminate more against Black workers in wages, and keep the extra profits. However, equal opportunity legislation, minimum wage laws, etc., make it more difficult to profiteer from lower wages. It is easier to prove discrimination in wages than discrimination in employment. So employers discriminate against Blacks in employment, causing higher rates of unemployment.[10]

This has no logical or factual basis. Equal opportunities legislation is supposed to apply to employment and wages equally. To explain violation of the former requirement by compliance with the latter is to tacitly condone the violation. Moreover, as shown in Chapter 3, the legislation has not brought about equal wages for equal work, while discrimination in hiring has been more often and more easily proved to the satisfaction of establishment judges than discrimination in wages.

The intent of all this is to convince employers and white workers that Black workers should be forced to work for substandard wages, "in their own interest." Heavy unemployment among Blacks is their own fault for pressing for equal opportunity legislation. To remove any doubt of their intent, the presidential economists add this crudely racist sentence: "Moreover, the prospect of equal pay may encourage Blacks to quit jobs with low pay and search longer for more promising positions."[11]

This is the modernized version of the southern plantation owner complaining about his "uppity" field hands.

Banfield

Academic propaganda in the 1960s seeking to justify economic discrimination against Blacks avoided, for the most part, overt racism.

The 1970s, with the political rise of racist Governor George Wallace, and the accession to the presidency of Richard Nixon, created a marketplace for a more sinister scholar who would use a flimsy veneer of socio-economic analysis to barely disguise blatant racism and incitation to anti-Black repression. Professor Edward C. Banfield, who served in 1970 as head of President Nixon's task force on model cities, was the leader of this trend. He admits that racial prejudices are a factor in the inferior economic situation of Blacks, but gives them only a marginal role in comparison with the most vile racist explanations:

> Cultural differences—and conceivably even biological ones as well—also account in some degree for the special position of the Negro, as they do for that of every ethnic group.[12]

Here Banfield, whose works are still published, pays his respects to the outright racist theories of the innate inferiority of Blacks, but with a veneer of scholarship.

He implies scientific impartiality by saying there are cultural and ideological differences among other ethnic groups. However, when he gets down to brass tacks, all the differences ascribed to Blacks are negative; to others they are generally positive. Here is an example of his slander against African American people. Referring to areas vacated by whites, and occupied by Blacks:

> Looking at the neighborhoods they had left a decade or two before, suburbanites were often dismayed at what they saw—lawns and shrubbery trampled out, houses unpainted, porches sagging, vacant lots filled with broken bottles and junk..." The people moving in "cared little or nothing for lawns and had no objections to broken bottles."[13]

Banfield's book *The Unheavenly City*, was published in 1970, before the devastation of Detroit, or the "rust-bowl" slashing of midwestern industry. About then I was in Detroit, and

...I spent some time in a working class area of Detroit, with street after street of separate two-story houses, inhabited by the "block-busting" system: solid Black blocks sandwiched in between solid white blocks. Conscious of the Banfield-type slander, I walked from block to block to study the relative cleanliness, neatness, etc. In every respect the Black blocks were as good or better. And in more cases, Black householders were improving their homes. I also drove through Cleveland, not long after vast areas had been bulldozed by "urban renewal" programs which turned out to be "Negro removal" programs—areas looking as if bombed out by war. To a Banfield, the damage was done not by avaricious landlords and their governmental collaborators, but by their Black victims.[13a]

Under the guise of citing a sociologist's description of what "the community" thinks of "the scum of the city," Banfield characterizes typical Blacks as criminals with no self-respect, given to "delinquency, sexual promiscuity," "perversion," "incestual relations," as "loud," "vulgar," "lazy" belligerent alcoholics. But again there is a cover-up. The quoted description is of an all-white community. So, asks Banfield, if this is true of lower class whites, why is it racist to use it as a description of lower class Blacks?[14]

This "class" characterization of the Black masses is the cornerstone of Banfield's "scholarly" contribution. His social classes have little in common with the Marxist social classes, which are determined by the relation of the people to the means of production, by their role in the country's economic life. No, his classes are defined by cultural-ethical-psychological qualities. He defines four classes, from the best to the worst. If it just happens that the description of the best class clearly refers to the big tycoon's image of himself; and of the next-to-the-worst class to the capitalists' image of the worker he exploits; and the worst class to the racists' view of the majority of Blacks, so be it. It's the tycoons, with their class and racial prejudices, who endow his professorial chair and promote his books.

The upper class individual is most "future-oriented," not only for his family, but for the community, the nation, for all mankind. This paragon is "self-respecting, self-confident, self-sufficient...tolerant." He places "great value on independence, curiosity, creativity...consideration of others." And it's clear from details given that he is also rich.

The "middle class" has less of these good qualities, and is more interested in "getting ahead" personally, in being a conformist.

The "working class" man lives for the present. He emphasizes "cleanliness, neatness, obedience." He cares naught for world affairs, for culture. He is family-centered, has few friends, only companions. He likes crowds, noise, smells, has no use for privacy. In brief, a useful, if vulgar, robot.

The "lower class" individual "lives from moment to moment." He lacks self-discipline, works "only to stay alive and drifts from one unskilled job to another." He's a sex maniac, "suspicious and hostile, aggressive yet dependent," without any loyalty to group or mate.[15]

According to estimates favored by Banfield, 58% of all Blacks are "lower class," 37% "working class," 4% "middle class," and only 1% "upper class." But among whites 17% are lower class, 50% working class, 21% middle class, and 12% upper class.[16]

This fits in with his blaming Black people themselves for their lives in miserable ghettoes, and the working class majority among whites—with their supposedly crude narrow-mindedness—as responsible for what little racism he is willing to concede as part of the picture.

Banfield also hits on other themes, like the old chestnut that discrimination against Blacks is due to their being the "latest wave" of immigrants to the North, a crude untruth when he wrote it, and obviously ridiculous 25 years later when waves of other immigrants have followed, with no easing of the situation of African Americans.

But he uses this to excuse residential segregation, as due in part to "his having cultural characteristics that make him an undesirable neighbor," with which any Ku Klux Klan member would agree.

Banfield opposes all governmental programs against racism, or directed to providing better conditions for the poor. He sees no end to segregation, and blithely justifies it:

> The increasing isolation of the lower class is a problem, to be sure, but it is hard to see what can be done about it. The upper classes will continue to want to separate themselves physically from the lower, and in a free country they probably cannot be prevented from doing so.

As for the lower classes, his program is:

1. Encourage the Black to realize that he himself, and not society or racism is responsible for his ills.
2. Get them out of school at 14, and put those unable to get jobs in the army or a "youth corps."
3. Give cash subsidies to the "competent" poor, but only goods to the "incompetents" and encourage or force them to reside in an institution or a semi-institution, such as a "supervised public housing project."
4. "Intensive" birth control "guidance."
5. Increased police powers against Black areas and people, more "stop and frisk" and the like, including jailing those "likely" to commit violent crimes.[17]

In short, a sinister, cynical, Apartheid program for the United States. Banfield's "scholarship" may no longer be in major direct use, but it is reflected, in muted form, in the academic apologetics of the 1980s and 1990s.

The Theory of the Underclass

Ideologists of the "blame the victim" school came up with a new concept. Led by scholars such as William Julius Wilson, they have changed the term for those who do not "make it" from "working class" or, as in the Moynihan report, "lower class," to "underclass."

In the 1980s and 1990s, Wilson, an African American professor at the University of Chicago, rose to prominence in academic circles and beyond—in the mass media, among politicians, etc. His central thesis is that racism no longer accounts for the sufferings of African Americans, but has been displaced by class differences. Although Wilson's definitions of classes, for the most part, are not race-specific, he develops the idea of "the underclass," consisting decisively of poor African Americans and other minorities living in the urban ghettoes. The underclass is defined as people who are totally excluded from society, do not work, are unwilling to work, exist by criminal activities, etc. This is the sector that Marx called the lumpen proletariat.

The term "underclass" is not only inaccurate—most of those so labeled are clearly part of the working class, employed or unemployed—but it is an ugly racist epithet. Its aim is to exile from society tens of millions of poor people—a major portion of African Americans, Latinos, immigrants and other racially oppressed peoples. As well as the poorest whites—the homeless; those living in the states with the lowest living standards, such as Mississippi and West Virginia.

By stressing the alleged role of the underclass, Wilsonites tend to "blame the victims" of racism, rather than the racist ruling class, for the discrimination and inequality that pervades all aspects of American life.

Wilson's scholarship is poor—key to his arguments are alleged "facts" that are controverted by any serious research. But his influence and theories are effective. Establishment sociologists who, unlike Wilson, concur that the factor of racism is crucial in discrimination, do not fault Wilson but use his term "underclass," although without his pejorative significance.

This theory is used, also, to justify racist ideology and discriminatory actions among sections of the white population, especially those with high incomes living in all-white areas. And these are the people who have so much clout when it involves keeping Blacks, especially, from neighborhoods; who veto appropriations for schools in low-income areas, etc.

Since 1978 Wilson has been chairman of the sociology department at the University of Chicago and, since 1979, a member of the board of directors of the Social Science Research Council. Also, from 1975-79 he was a member of the board of University Publications of the University of Chicago Press.

Evidently Wilson has been of considerable influence in academic appointments and in the choice of publications in the field of race relations.

Wilson's main thesis is set forth at the very start of his 1978 book: *The Declining Significance of Race:*

> ...through the first half of the twentieth century, the continuous and explicit efforts of whites to construct racial barriers profoundly affected the lives of black Americans. Racial oppression was deliberate, overt, and is easily documented...As the nation has entered the latter half of the twentieth century, however, many of the traditional barriers have crumbled under the weight of the political, social and economic changes of the civil rights era. A new set of obstacles has emerged from basic structural shifts in the economy. These obstacles are therefore impersonal but may prove to be even more formidable for certain segments of the black population. Specifically, whereas the previous barriers were usually designed to control and restrict the entire black population, the new barriers create hardships essentially for the black underclass;
>
> The technological and economic shifts of the post-World War II period precipitated the movement toward decentralization and residential development in the suburbs... The flight of the more affluent families to the suburbs has meant that the central cities are becoming increasingly the domain of the poor and the stable working class. Thus in major cities...not only have public schools become overwhelmingly populated with minority students, but the background of both minority and white students is primarily working or lower class... The more affluent white and minority families are increasingly opting to send their children to parochial or private schools if they remain in the central city or to suburban schools if they move to the metropolitan fringe.[18]

In his later book *The Truly Disadvantaged* Wilson examines the economic shifts which harm Blacks. Prominent is the shift of industry from inner cities to suburbs. The "more affluent" whites and Blacks move with industry, but the "underclass" remains behind.[19] The racism that forces most Blacks to remain in central cities and handicaps those who do move is analyzed in Chapter 11, dealing with housing.

Wilson himself cites data establishing the effective role of employer racism in the move of industry to the suburbs:

> For example, a recent study by the Illinois Advisory Committee to the United States Commission on Civil Rights reported that among the 2,380 firms in their statewide sample that had left the central cities and relocated in the suburbs between 1975 and 1979, black employment decreased by 24.3 percent compared to a white employment drop of only 9.8 percent. This study also found that although minorities were 14.1 percent of the statewide work force between 1975 and 1978, they were 20 percent of the formerly employed workers in the firms that shut down."[20]

Wilson's definition of social classes is an artificial construct that ignores the real class distinctions in society. He describes three classes: a) the "middle class," consisting of all white-collar workers and skilled craft blue-collar workers; b) the "working class," consisting of the statistical category of "operatives" or semi-skilled workers; and c) the "lower class," consisting of service workers, laborers, and farmworkers. The "underclass" is discussed as a section of the "lower class," and in some of Wilson's discourse is equated with the "lower class."[21]

But there is no upper class in Wilson's hierarchy. Aside from that, his three classes are exactly those of Banfield. His omission of an upper class is not a trivial matter. It's as if the multi-millionaires—who own controlling shares in U.S. corporations, who figure so prominently in the publicity about prominent personalities, who occupy the key positions in government and by their financing determine most of candidates who win elections—as if they do not exist. The omission makes a mockery of his claim of substituting a class analysis for a racial analysis. Omission of the capitalist class leaves the field clear for any and all irrelevant explanations for racial differentials.

Exclusion of the capitalist class evades the central conflict that has to dominate any analysis of classes that is socially meaningful—the class or classes of exploiters and the class or classes of the exploited: slave owners and slaves; feudal lords and serfs, capitalists and wage workers.

As defined by Wilson, "classes" are simply ranks or castes within the working class. Calling these categories basic social classes conforms to the capitalist objective of splitting the working class—exemplified, for example, in attempts to assure separate bargaining by craft unions; to foster the feeling of superiority among white collar workers, even those with lower earnings and poorer conditions than many blue-collar workers.

Wilson writes: "The social problems of urban life in the United States are, in large measure, the problems of racial inequality."[22] But turning reality on its head, he attributes the inequality, not to racism, but to the shortcomings of Blacks themselves.

However, he does give a major role to supposed antagonism between white and Black workers. Grossly distorting the works of Karl Marx and the conclusions of the leader of the Great Steel Strike of 1919, William Z. Foster, he blames this on Marx's theory of labor and value, and on Black scabbing—not mentioning the much more frequent scabbing of whites on strikes involving Blacks.

Wilson's treatment strengthens the positions of those who oppose or sabotage efforts necessary to achieve strong unity between Black and white workers. Unified actions have been the trend at all stages of successful forward movements of the U.S. working class.

Further, in a really incredible fiction about the role of the federal government, Wilson wrote:

> However, because the government not only adopted and resolutely implemented antidiscrimination legislation to enhance minority individual rights but also mandated and purposefully enforced affirmative action and related programs to promote minority group rights, it was clear that by 1980 many thoughtful American citizens, including civil rights supporters, were puzzled by recent developments in the black community.[23]

By "recent developments" he referred to the bitter struggles that erupted during the 1980s. These, Wilson judged, were unnecessary because of what had been accomplished!

Only amazing ignorance or a deliberate attempt to deceive could explain Wilson's claim of "purposeful enforcement" of affirmative action programs to effect the objectives of civil rights legislation. Unfortunately, publicly supported affirmative action programs were scattered, involving at most thousands of workers and resulting from lawsuits and other forms of struggle. These were all too often thrown out by courts. Moreover, government reports showed no overall change in the extreme economic differentials against African Americans since enactment of the Civil Rights laws of the 1960s.

In *The Truly Disadvantaged* Wilson emphasizes another theme as reinforcement of his thesis that racism is not a significant factor in the plight of African Americans. He argues that affirmative action cannot work when there is a slack labor market, but only when the labor market is tight:

> Thus, the necessary factor for minority mobility is the availability of positions. For example, affirmative action programs have had little impact in a slack labor market where the labor supply is greater than the labor demand... On the other hand, the impact of anti-bias programs to enhance minority jobs tends to be greater in a tight labor market...
> Not only are there sufficient positions for many qualified workers, but also employers faced with a labor shortage are not as resistant to affirmative action.[24]

However, labor shortages appear only rarely, and in limited areas, in the United States. An overall surplus of labor is chronic, and the federal government, at the bidding of the capitalist class, follows policies that ensure high unemployment to keep the balance in the labor market favorable to employers. So only rarely and in special locations, is there any economic obstacle to prevent employers from carrying out discrimination against Blacks. Note that Wilson, as if unconsciously, admits that employers generally are racist when he notes that they are normally "resistant to affirmative action."

In the 1980s, during the rapid growth of high-tech industries along Rte.

128 semicircling Boston, Massachusetts, a local labor shortage did occur. At its peak, perhaps a hundred thousand workers were employed—but very few African Americans. The employer excuse was that they were "not qualified." Nor were employers willing to provide training to Black workers. In fact, however, a goodly proportion of the need was for clerical and semi-skilled blue-collar jobs for which plenty of unemployed Black workers were qualified.

The only labor shortage was during World War II. Then there were significant gains in Black employment and income—albeit far from sufficient to eliminate the persistent inequalities, and many of the gains were lost after the war. Again, the relatively low unemployment during the Vietnam War was accompanied by minor Black economic gains, which were, however, at least equally attributable to the peaking of Civil Rights struggles.

Wilson's writing is meant to foster a liberal image, a factor that has contributed to his influence. E.g., in *The Truly Disadvantaged* he argues that welfare is not the cause of greater African American family instability, etc. The main problem, he says, is that of unemployment, especially hitting young Black males. He presents statistical data and concludes:

> ...a compelling case for once again placing the problem of black joblessness as a top priority item in public policy agendas designed to enhance the status of poor black families.[25]

True enough! But this is a deviation from his main thrust—the innate inferiority of most Blacks. He argues that aside from "the talented tenth," the overwhelming majority cannot benefit from equal individual opportunity and, as a result, over a 20-year period the civil rights movement had shifted to equal rights for groups. But, he says, this can't work either because most individuals in the groups haven't the qualifications, or ability. He quotes the columnist William Raspberry:

> There are some blacks for whom it is enough to remove the artificial barriers of race. After that, their entry into the American mainstream is virtually automatic. There are others for whom hardly anything would change if, by some magical stroke, racism disappeared from America.

And Raspberry adds this whopper: "Everyone knows this, of course."[26]

In approving Raspberry's line, Wilson again confirms his acceptance of the vicious racist concept of Black inferiority—except for a select minority, a modern perversion of the post-Civil War slogan of the "talented tenth," which was applied in a different historical context.

In his closing address as President of the American Sociological Society, in 1990, Wilson expressed his concern about the wave of criticism by researchers of the term "underclass" as pejorative to the African American people. He presented arguments, pro and con, for abandoning the term. He was fearful that a substitute phrase would not reflect his position on the cultural problems of the Black community. Nevertheless, as a matter of expediency with regard to the liberal research community, he decided to substitute the term "ghetto poor." But, he asserted, it would mean the same thing.

> I will substitute the term "ghetto poor" for the term "underclass" and hope that I will not lose any of the subtle theoretical meaning that the latter term has had in my writings.[27]

He need not have feared! As he himself noted, the term "underclass" has gone beyond the academic fraternity to common use by the media. Thus it must be exposed for its "blame the victim" derogation of African Americans. More important, the *concept* has to be exposed, even where a substitute term is used.

Several top leaders of major civil rights organizations have accepted the main theses of Wilson—and Moynihan. For example, in his keynote address as incoming president of the National Urban League, Hugh P. Price claimed that "the global realignment of work and wealth" has become a "bigger culprit" than racism in accounting for poverty among inner-city African Americans. He emphasized the problems of the urban poor and urged affluent African Americans to contribute $500 to $1,000 each to finance the hiring of counselors for inner-city youth programs.

Although Price guardedly conceded that racism remains a factor, the essence of his remarks led to the *New York Times* headline A RIGHTS LEADER MINIMIZES RACISM AS A POVERTY FACTOR.[28]

It's not without relevance that Price is a former vice president of the Rockefeller Foundation, an important, key component in the formation of the ideology of the dominant circles of finance capital.

To establish his loyalty to such sponsors, Price gloats over "the collapse of Communism" and praises the "marvelous" capitalist economy "for most Americans." He urges that employers reserve "...training slots and real jobs for residents of neighborhoods or census tracts with high unemployment rates."

> The way I see it, this wouldn't be a politically contentious race-based approach. Instead, it's a more palatable alternative which recognizes that poor people of all races need decent jobs.[29]

This is an evasion of reality. Racist discrimination singles out African

Americans for special subjection to unemployment, poor housing and education, low incomes—regardless of where they live. What is required now as much as ever—in addition to programs for jobs for all unemployed—is special affirmative action priorities that reduce and aim to ultimately eliminate the marked discrimination against Blacks in all fields of life.

If the Urban League follows the line of Dr. Price, it will studiously avoid making any contribution to the broadening ongoing struggles against racist employers, bankers, police and politicians. It will become an ingrown charity organization—a false substitute for dealing with real world problems.

The theory of the "underclass" is central to modern versions of racist ideology, attacking as intrinsically inferior a significant section of the African American people and, by extension, all people of color—the majority of the world's population, in fact.

President Clinton has visited Black churches and has spoken to conferences of Black ministers and other influential African American groups. He aims to win African American support for his legislative program—including the racist crime bill. Plus, he is trying, determinably, to ensure Black votes for his reelection in 1996, as well as to reinforce the diversionary ideological lines of Moynihan, Wilson, et al.

Clinton's racist ideology stood out in his November 1993 speech to Black ministers. There was literally no mention of the acute economic and social problems faced by the African American community, or of the racism that still pervades American society. Instead he spouted the acme of ruling class apologetics: "Yes, without regard to race, if you work hard, play by the rules, you get into a service academy or a good college, you'll do just great."

And he attributed this, slanderously, to what Rev. Martin Luther King, Jr. would say were he alive today!

For the most part, this was an all-out, racist "blame the victim" speech, devoted to typical distorted declamations about crime, drugs, and broken families in the ghettoes, garnished with chauvinistic boasting about defeating Communism.

Perhaps a *New York Times* editor, consciously and ironically, put in a corner of the page dominated by Clinton's speech the account of an all-white jury that cheated a Black couple who sued an insurance company after jury members compared Blacks to chimpanzees and told racist jokes. Two years later an appeals court tentatively ordered a new trial![30]

But let's not forget that Clinton wants the Black vote. So, on vacation, he arranged for the press to carry a photo of him sharing a golf cart with big business favorite Vernon Jordan, African American lawyer and political maven.[31]

Democrats and Republicans

The main lines of intellectual rationalization of racism since the period of Civil Rights struggles have used the more sophisticated versions of racist lies and distortions analyzed in this chapter. They have been the meat of major Democratic Party politicians and heavily influence the leadership of trade unions tied to these politicians. But their "milder," concealed racism paves the way for the most vicious actions of racism—from the accelerating police persecution of blacks to the rise of heavily armed all-white "militias" and revivals of the KKK, to the radio racists and anti-Semites with their audiences of tens of millions.

And it is the Republican Party, the most favored party of big business, that engineers, supports, and provides fuel for the extremist neofascist tendencies among racists. It was Ronald Reagan and his allied media monopolists who gave decisive publicity to the vile racist slander that contributed so significantly to his election to the Presidency. His successor, George Bush, followed suit. It was through such methods that the Republican Party won control of the Congress in 1994. It has mainly been under Republican Administrations that the economic gaps between whites, Blacks and Hispanics have widened. By the mid 1990s the Republicans had led an all-out attack on affirmative action.

The object is to destroy what is left of affirmative action, and give free reign to open application of racist discrimination in all walks of life, enforced by terror and violence—that of police, and that of private groups—both closely affiliated with the Republican Party. This action is supported by the lying propaganda slogan that affirmative action has been "reverse discrimination" against white men—with no basis in fact—thereby to inflame a section of the white working class population with racist prejudices and drastically weaken the working class, under attack from all sides by corporate employers.

Characteristic of the new breed of Republican racists is Mayor Rudolf Giuliani of New York, who openly participated in the racist riot of several thousand policemen at City Hall. Also California governor Pete Wilson, the major sponsor of the infamous anti-Latino anti-immigrant Proposition 187, and leading campaigner to abolish the affirmative action program at the University of California. A program that looked good on paper, but under control of racist officials, was successfully squelched of real content, so that the proportion of Black students, 4%, in 1984, was still 4% in 1993!

The liberals, the Democrats, have failed to offer effective resistance to this offensive. President Clinton, after a long period of waffling, finally concluded that his political future was doomed if he completely capitulated to the Republicans on this issue. He made a major speech in favor of affirmative action. But what kind of affirmative action?—affirmative action without quotas and preferences! But in most areas, quotas and preferences are the only, the necessary and practical component of affirmative action.

True, Clinton qualified his opposition by stating that he is against preferences for "unqualified" persons. But in the eyes of the racist employers who do the hiring, Blacks and Latinos are never "qualified." The whole purpose of affirmative action formulas is to take this determination out of the hands of racist employers—to assume that Blacks are qualified for decent jobs—which they are; that Blacks are qualified to live where they want in decent housing— which they are, and qualified to be elected to public office without being blocked through gerrymandered electoral districts.

An affirmative action policy without the use of its necessary tools is mere rhetoric, and effective surrender to the racist forces. And, unfortunately, such disclaimers are common among trade union leaders, such as those of the United Auto Workers, who, providing strong argument in favor of effective action, assure readers of their intention to avoid "preferences" and "quotas," a policy which has left Black workers in inferior employment situations in the auto industry decades after the UAW, with strong Black support, won exclusive bargaining rights against the Big Three automotive employers.

17. A Program for Equality, Progress and Justice

What, if anything, can be done, NOW, to counter the virulent racism and discrimination against oppressed peoples? Taking into account the capitalist political domination in the United States and accepting the premise that eradication of racism and the achievement of equality can be achieved only under socialism, can the lot of African Americans, Latinos, Native Americans and other victims of discrimination be significantly reduced?

In fact, an example of how radically racism can be diminished even under capitalism is provided by the case of immigrant Asians. Through much of the last century and well into the 20th century, racist prejudice and discrimination against people of Asian origin, especially Chinese at that time, was extreme. They were cruelly exploited as farm laborers, railroad workers, and in other capacities. As with African Americans, prejudice linked to skin color and other physical characteristics was fomented by those who were in a position to reap extra profits by exploiting them.

During World War II, the United States fought Japan, Germany, and Italy. Japanese residents, citizens and aliens alike, were herded into concentration camps. Germans and Italians were not persecuted.

However, since World War II discrimination against Asians has largely disappeared. And this phenomenon is rooted in economic changes: the rise of a powerful capitalist class in Asian countries, especially Japan. And despite its emergence as an economic rival, it is a close political-military ally of U.S. imperialism. There has been substantial immigration of Asian capitalists, large and small, as well as of trained professionals whose services are in demand by U.S. corporations, colleges, hospitals, etc. Clearly there is no similar surge of capitalist economic development in African countries, but the fact that economic gains can be the basis for radical reduction of racial prejudice does apply, nonetheless, to Black people as well as Asians.

Some Asian immigrants—mainly Vietnamese and Filipino—are subject to the racism and discrimination of the oppressed. They are employed in sweatshops and as dishwashers and busboys, etc. and live in appalling conditions.

Japanese-Americans who were unjustly sequestered during World War II, and their heirs, have received about $20,000 each from the U.S. government as compensation. Appropriate reparations to African Americans for their two centuries of barbaric treatment would have to be many times more, at least in the hundreds of thousands each, a sum sufficient to lift them out of poverty.

However, this is not at present the main direction toward which struggles are directed.

A Progressive Program

Programs advanced during the 1990s by progressives—members of Congress, African American groups and other organizations—tended to offer programs for U.S. government spending of roughly $50 billion per year for projects that would generate jobs. These proposals covered education, housing, health, etc. as well as construction and other structural projects. But that budget is less than 1% of the gross domestic product (GDP) and could bring about no more than marginal and temporary improvement in employment.

In 1993 the GDP of the United States approached *$6.4 trillion!* A peaceful government program amounting to 13% of GDP would have to approximate $800 billion. (The 13% is explained below.) This is the scope of the "People's Economic Program" published by the Communist Party, USA in 1993. In addition to direct creation of jobs, this program also includes measures to raise wages and salaries radically and to reduce the workweek without reduction in pay. It also specifies major affirmative action measures.

This combination, if accompanied by suitable price limitations, would sharply raise effective mass consuming power. Overall, there would probably be a greater stimulation to private employment than the Korean War. Thus it would be consistent with requiring government provision of enough jobs for full employment. Of course, experience might indicate a total program moderately larger or smaller than $800 billion, and naturally expenditures would rise with rising prices.

The net financial cost would actually be less than $800 billion annually; $200 billion or more could be saved by reducing military and related spending to the level now required for the defense of the United States, which is threatened by nobody. About as much could be saved by ending so-called "tax expenditures"—exclusions in tax laws, essentially legal loopholes—mainly benefiting the rich and their corporations.

A program to achieve economic equality has two main requirements:

1. Affirmative action; that is, specific measures to improve the economic conditions of African Americans, Hispanics, Native Americans and sections of the Asian population;

2. Measures to advance the conditions of the entire working class.

In the struggle against racism, affirmative action must be primary—as discussed in Chapter Eight.

The affirmative action provisions of the program would result in African Americans, Latinos, and Native Americans getting 6-7 million of the estimated 16 million jobs that would be generated. Thus white workers would get 9–10 million additional jobs. In this way joblessness for both white and minority workers would be ended, with progress for minority workers being faster because they have much further to go.

Doubling minimum wages, restoring effective trade union rights, radically increasing social security and health benefits, combined with the near elimination of joblessness, would essentially end poverty in the United States.

Table 17:1 shows the proposed distribution of government expenditure and employment generated for the several major components of the program. Amounts are in addition to 1992 government programs, and are calculated in terms of 1992 costs and requirements. The jobs generated are figured at the rate of one job for every $50,000 of expenditure. This is conservative, since it is intended to include not only the jobs required for final production, as well as for components and materials, but also those generated by workers spending most of the increases in their incomes. It is within the range used by the AFL-CIO in its program for additional infrastructure outlays.

TABLE 17:1. PEOPLE'S FULL EMPLOYMENT PROGRAM

Component	Annual Outlays ($ billions)	Jobs (millions)
Infrastructure	$120	2.4
Housing	$250	5.0
Education	$200	4.0
Health	$200	4.0
Child Care	$40	0.8
Environment, Culture & Recreation	$40	0.8
TOTAL	$800 billion	16.0 million

SOURCE: Economics Commission, CPUSA, "A People's Economic Program," 1993.

The size of the program was determined by the amount necessary to provide jobs for 16 million additional people, approximately double the average number of officially counted unemployed, over the three years 1993–1995.

Other parts of the program, not including government spending, would create millions of additional jobs. Especially important in this respect is the reduction of the workweek to 35 hours without reduction in pay, accompanied by elimination of enforced overtime. Also, doubling the minimum wage and ending the anti-labor legislation that hampers trade union organizing and struggles would result in greater mass consuming power. In turn, this would require more workers to produce and distribute consumer goods and services.

Of course, these figures are indicative. The actual amount to effectuate full employment would depend on a variety of economic and political factors, and could be determined only in the course of struggle for enactment and enforcement of the program.

Full Employment at Decent Wages

The closest the United States has come to the full employment of all who want to work was during World Wars I and II, when many millions were inducted into the armed services and, in addition, millions were employed in war industries. The scale of government spending involved is indicated by the fact that in 1944, when officially measured unemployment was reduced to 1.2%, national defense expenditures absorbed 42% of the gross national product.

It is true that the scale of spending needed to approach full employment was exceedingly great partly because at the start of World War II the United States was in the grip of the deepest, most prolonged depression in its history. During the Korean War, which did not start from so low a base of economic activity, national defense outlays of 13% of GNP did not quite generate full employment: in its peak year, 1953, overall unemployment was 2.9%; Black unemployment was 4.5%; youth—7.6%.

The AFL-CIO expresses labor's view on full employment:

> Full employment must be a top priority of economic policy. Jobs at fair and decent pay must be available for every person who needs a job and wants a job... If there are not enough jobs in the private and public sectors for all who want jobs, the federal government must be the employer of last resort.[1]

I would amend this statement in one respect. The federal government must be the employer of *first resort* in order to achieve full employment or come close to it, regardless of what is done by private employers. This is so because the capitalist class is opposed to full employment, and will not cooperate with a program designed to achieve it. Also, capitalist employers are opposed to affirmative action and other measures that are necessary for full employment and that aim to eliminate poverty.

The value of preferential employment, housing and educational programs for oppressed minorities will be enhanced enormously if accompanied by programs providing for improvements in these areas for all working people. *But concessions to workers in general cannot be a substitute for preferential treatments for African Americans.* A rising tide may raise all boats, but in the sea of a racist society, the boats of African Americans are raised only marginally in the absence of simultaneous affirmative action programs. For example, the

AFL-CIO and the building trades unions advocate large infrastructure projects, a desirable program. But in the past many building trades unions, government agencies and private employers have collaborated to retain a near monopoly of employment for white workers, and a near monopoly of contracts and sub-contracts for white contractors.

Still, affirmative action programs are greatly handicapped in periods of high unemployment, and especially of rising overall unemployment. And exclusionary practices will be easier to change when massive public projects bring about a drastic decline in unemployment and a rapid rise in total employment. The combination of high employment and affirmative action programs is the guarantee that whites will gain along with Blacks. It will tend to overcome the fears that racists try to instill in white workers—that equality for Blacks means losses for them. It is the basis for uniting the whole working class and African Americans in the political struggle that is needed to obtain both the affirmative action measures and the measures designed to benefit all working people: employment, education, public and social services.

Progressive programs aiming at major improvements in these living conditions are often supported partly with the argument that they are "good for the economy", create "consumer buying power" and hence are "good for business"—so are beneficial to everybody, to all social classes. This rationalization represents wishful thinking. Such programs actually change the balance against capital and for labor; through unionization, raising minimum wages, etc., they directly increase workers' incomes at the expense of profits.

Thus, while liberal elements of the capitalist class may support minor aspects of such programs, capitalists as a whole strongly oppose them and continually plot to turn back and destroy what partial progress has been made. That, indeed, has been happening during the last quarter of the 20th century as the political balance has shifted, strengthening capital against labor.

Full Employment

The objective here is to end the severe unemployment among Blacks and Latinos in part by moving towards ending unemployment among all workers. The decisive principle is that Congress should put the "full" into what is often inaccurately referred to as the Full Employment Act of 1946, and provide the necessary means for accomplishing it. A real full employment law would guarantee the right to work to every individual 16 and over wanting and able to work. To guarantee implementation it would be the responsibility of the federal government to organize productive and other useful activities on a sufficient scale to employ all those lacking jobs.

This would call for a number of corollary provisions, of undoubted value in themselves and, at the same time, serving as the objectives of labor activity sponsored under this law. For example, a huge network of well-staffed, well-equipped child care facilities would be required to make real the possibility of work to millions and millions of mothers who want to work, but are now barred from it for lack of such facilities. And special provisions would have to be made for the health needs of those millions with health problems who are currently barred from employment because employers refuse the necessary adjustments and facilities.

A very major and important part of the program would concern employment of youth, and in part, provide services and facilities of particular interest to youth. The problem of unemployment is most serious, and most damaging, among the youth of the country, and especially among the Black youth.

Obviously, *a larger percentage* of the Black population than of the white population would benefit from a full employment program, but *a larger absolute number* of white people than Black would benefit. And this would be true of most of the proposals discussed in this chapter. However, owing to the special severity of unemployment among Black people, they would be entitled to a significant degree of priority in employment as the new government and government-sponsored jobs were organized.

Infrastructure

The AFL-CIO calls for $60 billion yearly for rebuilding the nation's infrastructure, with the main focus on roads, bridges and similar transportation requirements. It estimates that this would generate 1.3 million jobs. But much more is needed for the accumulated backlog of essential work on bridges and roads, public transit, water works, etc., especially considering that current requirements are increasing at an estimated rate of $40 billion yearly. The People's Program contemplates doubling the amount suggested by the AFL-CIO, to $120 billion yearly, generating 2.4 million jobs.

At least half would be allocated for central cities and other run-down urban areas, such as Camden, New Jersey; East St. Louis, Illinois; and Gary, Indiana. Racist patterns would be reversed, so that communities in which African Americans, Hispanic peoples, and Native Americans live would no longer be deprived of decent schools, well-surfaced roads, garbage collection and other public services.

Rapid transit rail lines and other public transit systems would be a major part of the program, relatively much more than their present meager share. This is necessary not only to provide rapid transportation to those without private automobiles, but also to provide ready access to jobs in suburban areas and to city centers.

Affirmative action provisions would be enforced in hiring for all construction and maintenance of infrastructure facilities.

The difference in location of projects and greater emphasis on urban rapid transportation mark an important qualitative difference from the AFL-CIO program. Presently, infrastructure projects tend to be concentrated in wealthier suburbs and "exurbs," as well as in the countryside, where few Blacks reside. Thus an increase in projects without changing the emphasis tends to fully maintain existing discrimination against Blacks and Hispanics on such projects.

Housing

The $250 billion yearly proposed for public housing would finance construction of 2.5 million housing units yearly. Over several years this would provide for the roughly 10 million people now living in doubled up conditions or actually homeless, and begin to make a dent in providing decent housing for the number, at least as large, now living in substandard housing conditions, urban and rural. The total includes up to $50 billion yearly for maintenance and reconstruction of existing public housing. Rents would not exceed 20% of tenants' incomes.

The program would at least permit the United States to catch up to other advanced industrialized countries in public housing facilities. Integrated occupancy would be required, with priority to minority people, whose housing needs are by far the greatest.

Education

The proposed addition of $150 billion yearly to educational spending would increase total government educational outlays by about one-third. However, as contemplated in the program, it would be focused on the areas now so badly short-changed, for which total outlays would be doubled.

During the 1990s reactionary forces opened a significant campaign to destroy public education through "privatization"; i.e., turning the schools over to private companies operating for profit. This has already been done in some places. Inevitably, if not stopped, it will reach a stage where free public education at the elementary and secondary level will be destroyed, and parents forced to pay profiteering companies for their children's education. More than ever, school curricula will be shaped to promote the ideological offensive of capital. Teachers, to obtain and keep their jobs, will be forced to act as mouthpieces for anti-labor and racist ideologies.

Instead, progressive reform requires ending existing government subsidies to private education at the elementary and secondary levels, and raising the government share of higher education to the leading position. Subsidies to private schools are in effect subsidies to parents who wish to take their children out of integrated educational environments, and inevitably are accompanied with reductions in government funding for the already under-financed schools in ghettoized urban and rural areas.

The additional funding should have the following purposes:

Support free, federally funded, integrated, multi-lingual and multi-cultural education; radically reduce class size in the overcrowded areas of the city poor; construct additional school buildings; raise salaries of teachers in such schools sharply, to compensate for the additional difficulties where pupils are ill-prepared for school.

Health

The additional funding for health would be sufficient to provide health coverage for those currently without health insurance. (Other objectives discussed in Chapter 13.)

Financing

Financing of the Communist Party's Program would be from the following sources:

- Radical reduction in military and international outlays, as well as for the vast interventionist intelligence and covert action apparatus.
- Reduction of interest rates and of interest payments on the national debt.
- Increase of corporate and top bracket individual income tax rates to previous high levels.
- There will be savings in outlays for unemployment compensation and for programs to relieve poverty, as unemployment and poverty are progressively eliminated.
- Additional tax revenues will accrue corresponding to the rise in mass incomes and expenditures resulting from application of the program.

Struggle

This program, both its positive proposals and its financing, requires unremitting struggles on the part of the working class and all racially oppressed peoples.

Every aspect of the program is opposed by the capitalist class, and each part of it even by sections of the class directly affected,

Proposals for financing directly counter drives of the power elite. In particular, regardless of conditions, capitalists generally, and specific sectors especially, want to maintain military spending, to increase it when possible, and to prevent its reduction even when no obvious need for "national security" can be rationalized.

Struggles over taxation are continuous at all levels. Capitalists seek to prevent increases and to force the lowering or even complete abolition of the progressive income tax, as by the right-wing-supported "flat tax" proposal.

The struggles require mass mobilization and action in all forms. Very important is the political aspect, including electoral activity. This requires going beyond the confines of the two-party, Republican and Democratic, system. These two parties are completely controlled by the capitalist class. There are slight differences: the Republican Party is always overtly reactionary on all issues; the Democratic Party uses more demagogy to maintain a voter base within the working class and Black communities. But in practice, it always ends up in the same general camp as the Republicans—often by retreats before a Republican offensive.

In the crucial field of international affairs, there is even less superficial difference. Indeed, Democratic administrations, during the last half of the 20th century, have guided the aggressive expansion of U.S. imperialism as much as Republican administrations. Given the crucial importance of international affairs, increasing with the internationalization of capital and the intensification of its worldwide activity, the interests of American workers are more than ever concerned with confronting capital on the international as well as the domestic front.

Thus what is called for is a political party of all workers: of the Black, Hispanic, and other oppressed peoples, of progressive whites of all classes. So long as labor remains—through its leadership—subject to a party of its exploiters, the tendency will be for those African American people's organizations that see the unconstructive character of the Democratic Party to go in the direction of nationalist movements, away from a united labor front.

Decisive labor participation in a political movement with a really independent program and opposed to the parties of capitalism is an important requirement for the struggle against racism in its economic as well as all other aspects of life.

Socialism and Equality

National and racial equality is not a pipe dream. Experience shows that it can be approached by replacing capitalism with socialism. The Soviet Union, during its 70 years of existence, went far towards ending economic and cultural inequalities among its 87 nationalities. With the destruction of socialism, national rivalries and conflicts reappeared. Socialist Cuba, even under extreme pressure from the United States, has moved far to equalizing the situation of its white and Black people.

Socialism, by eliminating the possibility of private profit from the labor of others, eliminates the material basis of racism. It doesn't eliminate national differences nor does it eliminate national economic differentials overnight. Neither does it automatically eliminate national and racial prejudices among people. However, the basis exists for the rapid reduction of prejudices, assisted by the whole weight of official propaganda, literature and the practical integration of peoples. National economic differentials are speedily eliminated because a central plan for the entire country can provide for the development of natural resources and industry at a faster pace in the less developed areas, and ensure a faster rise in the living standards of the peoples who live there, while simultaneously benefiting the entire country.

Certainly the establishment of a socialist-oriented society in the United States will be a decisive step towards the elimination of racial inequalities in our country.

But the campaign for such elimination is *here and now*, in a capitalist United States, and must be jointly conducted by those who favor or take for granted continuation of the capitalist social structure and those who already see socialism as organically connected with the achievement of the basic equality of peoples. The important factor is to prevent ideological differences from being used to divide the activities of those tens of millions who must actively work together to make equality a reality in the United States.

Appendix

TABLE 3A. BLACK HISPANIC PERCENTAGES OF NON-HISPANIC WHITE
MEDIAN FAMILY INCOME

Year	Black	Hispanic	Years	Averages Black	Hispanic
1939	40.0				
1945	55.3				
1946	51.4				
1947	49.9				
1948	52.2				
1949	49.8		1946–49	50.8	
1950	53.0				
1951	51.4				
1952	55.4				
1954	54.1				
1955	53.9		1950–55	53.7	
1956	51.3				
1957	52.1				
1958	49.8				
1959	52.2				
1960	53.8				
1961	51.8				
1962	51.8				
1963	51.3		1956–1963	51.8	
1964	54.3				
1965	53.6				
1966	57.8				
1967	58.7				
1968	59.9				
1969	60.7				
1970	60.7	70.2			
1971	59.6		1968–71	60.1	70.2
1972	58.7	70.0			
1973	57.4	68.8			
1974	58.7	69.9			
1975	60.5	65.8			
1976	58.4	64.8	1972–76	58.7	67.8
1977	56.1	67.0			
1978	58.1	67.1			
1979	55.7	68.1			
1980	56.7	65.9			
1981	55.2	68.2	1977–81	56.4	67.3
1982	54.0	64.5			
1983	55.0	63.9			
1984	54.2	66.2			
1985	55.8	63.3			
1986	55.6	63.1	1982–86	54.9	64.2
1987	54.9	60.6			
1988	55.0	62.0			
1989	54.5	63.3			
1990	56.0	61.3			
1991	54.9	60.9	1987–91	55.1	61.6

3A (cont'd)

Year	Black	Hispanic	Years	Averages Black	Averages Hispanic
1992	52.4	53.4			
1993	52.4	57.5	1992–93	52.4	58.0

Sources: 1939, Author's rough estimate.
1945–1966: *Economics of Racism*, USA, 1975 Ed., Table II, p. 53
1967–1993: Calculated from P60-188, Table D-2, pages D5–D7
Medians for non-Hispanic white families, as given for 1972-1993. Not given for 1967-1971; Calculated by author assuming consistent trend of relationship between medians of all white and non-Hispanic white families. No adjustment to non-Hispanic white basis made for years earlier than 1967.

Chapter 3: Note on car insurance costs. *
The study, based on data collected by the State of Connecticut Insurance Department, averaged rates charged by three major insurance companies, Allstate, Travelers, and Hartford Accident and Indemnity. The insurance covers personal liability, collision and comprehensive, in identical amounts. It applies to the same model of vehicle, 3 years old and driven 10,000 miles per year. The driver is 40 years old, drives to work, and has had no significant accident.
The annual costs are as follows:

District 32, (City of New Haven):	$1,557
District 33, nearby suburbs:	$1,162
District 21, distant suburbs (exurbs):	$1,063

*Analysis prepared by Arthur Perlo.

TABLE 3B. MEDIAN FAMILY INCOMES OF WHITE, BLACKS, AND HISPANICS, 1967–1993, IN ADJUSTED* 1992 DOLLARS

Year	CPI adjust.	Median Family Incomes non-Hisp. white	Black	Hispanic	Index 1972 = 100 non-Hisp. white	Black	Hispanic
1967	108.7	34892	20841		88.8	90.4	
1968	108.3	36306	21603		92.4	93.7	
1969	107.4	37797	22943		96.2	99.5	
1970	106.4	37389	22695		95.2	99.6	
1971	106.4	37425	22306		95.3	96.7	
1972	106.2	39280	23056	27488	100.0	100.0	100.0
1973	106.3	39999	22968	27537	101.8	99.6	100.2
1974	105.3	38849	22789	27156	98.9	98.8	98.8
1975	104.5	37861	22902	24917	96.4	99.3	90.6
1976	104.4	39021	22789	25297	99.3	98.8	92.0
1977	104.3	39472	22142	26444	100.5	96.0	96.2
1978	103.5	40310	23403	27033	102.6	101.3	98.3
1979	101.9	40179	22361	27374	102.3	96.9	99.6
1980	99.9	38039	21584	25062	96.8	93.6	91.2
1981	99.1	37116	20471	25309	94.5	88.8	92.1
1982	99.1	36612	19776	23600	93.2	85.8	85.9
1983	100.0	37340	20551	23848	95.1	89.0	86.8
1984		38420	20837	25430	97.8	90.4	92.5
1985		39191	21887	24809	99.8	94.9	90.3
1986		40540	22535	25596	103.2	97.7	93.1
1987		41385	22732	25071	105.4	98.6	91.2

3B (cont'd)

Year CPI adjust.	Median Family Incomes			Index 1972 = 100		
	non-Hisp. white	Black	Hispanic	non-Hisp. white	Black	Hispanic
1988	41646	22924	25817	106.0	99.4	93.9
1989	41934	22866	26528	106.8	99.2	96.5
1990	41048	22997	25152	104.5	99.7	91.5
1991	40421	22197	24614	102.9	96.3	89.5
1992	41541	21735	24260	105.8	94.3	88.3
1993	39913	20487	22965	101.6	88.9	83.5

Sources: P60-174 Appendix Table B-1. p. 196
P60-188, Table D-2, pp. D-6-D-7
Consumer Price Index for 1993 on 1992 base = 103.0
Col. 2 Source: calculated from P60-172, Table B-1, p. 352.
Explanation: Historically, long-term comparisons of consumer income were based on the consumer price index (CPI) to measure real changes.
Since the late 1980s the U.S. Commerce Department, in its annual consumer income studies (P-60 series), gave alternative calculations using another index (CPI-XI).
This index goes up more slowly than the CPI for the period 1967-1984, for which it was calculated. As a result, real incomes, for periods starting in the 1970s or earlier, are made to look as if they improve more, (or decline less) than using the official CPI. The rationalization is to recompute housing costs as they are now computed, by rental equivalence. However, nobody knows the internal details of what they did and, in any case, the official CPI, according to labor estimates, doesn't go up fast as the real cost of living, so this would only make it worse.
Wherever required, I have adjusted given figures to the official CPI-U, using the factors in the above table. Politically, sneaking in CPIXI is part of the ongoing campaign of right-wing forces to adjust downward col adjustments in wages, social security benefits, etc.

TABLE 3C. WHITE/BLACK HOUSEHOLD INCOME DIFFERENTIALS IN THE DETROIT AREA, 1989

Area	White Households			Black Households			
	Number (000)	Household Median $	Incomes "Total" $MM	Number (000)	Household Median $	Incomes "Total" $MM	Percent Black of White Median
Suburbs:							
Counties							
Macomb	258	39115	10,092	4	25,244	101	65%
Oakland	373	43,801	16,338	27	38,650	1,044	88
Washtenaw	90	38,322	3,449	10	24,590	246	64
Wayne ex Detroit	375	37,600	14,100	25	18,000	480	48
Total Suburbs	1,096	40,127	43,979	66	27,894	1,841	70
Detroit City Main Metro.	95	21,000	1,995	270	17,800	4,806	85
Area Totals	1,191	38,601	45,974	336	19,783	6,647	51

For calculating "totals," medians are treated as if they were means. Actual totals would be higher, as means are always larger than medians. However, this method yields a reasonably close approximation of the actual medians for the totality of suburbs and for the area as a whole.
The area covered does not exactly coincide with the official metropolitan area, but provides a more useful analysis of the comparative income situation.
Source: Census of Population, 1990, County and City, Census Bureau.

TABLE 3D. PER CAPITA INCOMES, U.S. AND 7 CENTRAL CITIES, 1989

| City | Per Capita Income $ | | | | Percent of white | |
	Total	White	Black	Hispanic	Black	Hispanic
U.S.	14420	16074	8859	8400	55	52
New York	16281	25955	10505	8420	40	32
Los Angeles	16188	27897	11257	7111	40	25
Houston	24261	23435	8366	7021	36	30
Chicago	12899	20440	8559	7438	42	36
New Orleans	11372	20804	6539	11483	31	55
Birmingham	10127	15353	7188	13763	47	89
Detroit	9443	12113	8809	7518	73	62

Data provided by Census Bureau, including that needed to estimate per capita incomes of non-Hispanic whites from data on per capita incomes of whites, Hispanic people, and numbers of white and other Hispanic people.

TABLE 4A. HOUSEHOLDS WITH VERY LOW AND WITH VERY HIGH INCOMES, 1989 (NUMBERS IN THOUSANDS)

| | Households Total Number | Incomes under $5,000 | | Incomes above $100,000 | |
		Number	% of Total	Number	% of Total
Total	91,994	5,685	6.2%	4,037	4.4%
White	73,532	3,437	4.7	3,638	4.9
Black	9,942	1,514	15.2	127	1.3
Hispanic	5,872	520	8.9	114	1.9
Native American	625	78	12.5	9	1.4
Asian	2,020	136	6.7	151	7.5
"Other"	2,497	230	9.2	29	1.2

Source: Census Bureau Tabulations, 1990 CPH-L-94 Household Income in 1989, for the United States, Regions, Divisions, and States, by Race. (Figures differ from those in Chart 4-1, partly because these figures are for households, while the chart deals with families). According to Table 4:1, the number of rich white households slightly exceeds the number of very poor white households; but the number of very poor Black households is 12 times the number of rich Black households. The differences are in the same direction among Hispanic and Native American families; while the data for "Asian" households is roughly similar to that for white families.

TABLE 5A. PEOPLE LIVING IN POVERTY, 1973–1993 OFFICIAL DATA
(NUMBERS IN MILLIONS)

Year	Total	White	Black	Hispanic
1973	23.0	12.9	7.4	2.2
1974	23.4	13.3	7.2	2.4
1975	25.9	14.9	7.5	3.0
1976	25.0	14.1	7.6	2.8
1977	24.7	13.9	7.7	2.7
1978	24.5	13.8	7.6	2.6
1979	26.1	14.4	8.0	2.9
1980	29.3	16.4	8.6	3.5
1981	31.8	18.0	9.2	3.7
1982	34.4	19.4	9.7	4.3
1983	35.3	19.5	9.9	4.6
1984	33.7	18.3	9.5	4.8
1985	33.1	17.8	8.9	5.2
1986	32.4	17.2	9.0	5.1
1987	32.2	16.0	9.5	5.4
1988	31.7	15.6	9.4	5.4
1989	32.4	15.5	9.5	6.1
1990	34.6	16.4	10.0	6.8
1991	36.7	17.4	10.4	7.1
1992	38.0	18.2	10.8	7.6
1993	39.3	18.9	10.9	8.1

Source: P60-185, Table D-2, page D-5; Census Bureau Preliminary Release on Poverty for 1993. Numbers are for non-Hispanic white, calculated by author for years 1973-1978. Numbers for 1989-1993 are preliminary, subject to revision. Calculations of non-Hispanic whites living in poverty for years earlier than 1989 are shown in Table 5B.

TABLE 5B. NON-HISPANIC WHITE POOR CALCULATED FOR YEARS
1973-88 (IN THOUSANDS)

Year	Hispanic poor	.95 Hisp. poor	white poor	non-Hisp. white poor
1973	3,366	2,248	15,142	12,894
1974	2,575	2,446	14,736	13,290
1975	2,991	2,841	17,770	14,929
1976	2,783	2,644	16,713	14,069
1977	2,700	2,565	16,416	13,851
1978	2,607	2,477	16,259	13,782
1979	2,921	2,775	17,214	14,439
1980	3,491	3,316	19,699	16,383
1981	3,713	3,527	21,553	17,006
1982	4,301	4,086	23,517	19,431
1983	4,633	4,401	23,984	19,583
1984	4,806	4,566	22,955	18,389
1985	5,236	4,974	22,860	17,886
1986	5,117	4,861	22,183	17,322
1987	5,422	5,151	21,195	16,044
1988	5,357	5,061	20,715	15,654
1989	5,430			15,599
1990	6,006			16,622
1991	6,339			17,741
1992	6,655			18,308

TABLE 6A. DISTRIBUTION OF WORKING CLASS POPULATION AND
EMPLOYMENT BY RACE, CHANGES NEEDED TO ELIMINATE
DISCRIMINATION AGAINST MINORITIES, 1992, (PERCENT IN
THOUSANDS)

	Total	White*	Black	Hispanic	Other
Population Ages 16–64	100.0	75.8	12.0	8.7	3.5
Potential Wage & Salary Workers (Total less Self-)	100.0	75.1	12.5	8.9	3.5
Employed Wage & Salary Workers	100.0	78.2	10.7	7.9	3.2
Percent Change to Achieve Equality Without Reducing White Employment	4.1	0	21.7	17.2	14.7
Number Employed (thousands)	107,236	83,906	11,474	8,472	3,384
Resulting Employment From Needed Changes (thousands)	111,684	83,906	13,965	9,933	3,880
Numerical Change (thousands)	4,448	0	2,491	1,461	496

Sources: *E & E*, Jan 1993, Table 3, p. 174-177, Table 39, p. 218. *Stat. Abst.* 1993, Table 23, p.
22.
*Non-Hispanic white taken as total of white less 95% of Hispanics, as per data in annual Current
Population Surveys.

TABLE 6B. JOB DISCRIMINATION AGAINST BLACKS AND HISPANICS, MALE AND FEMALE, SELECTED YEARS, LARGE COMPANIES REPORTING TO THE EEOC.

Year	Discrimination Indexes*			
	Male		Female	
	Black	Hispanic	Black	Hispanic
1967	28.72	10.10	6.89	6.12
1975	12.18	8.84	4.69	4.69
1980	9.09	8.32	4.16	4.54
1985	8.80	8.80	4.41	4.71
1992	7.70	8.68	4.24	5.35

*Discrimination Indexes: The complete absence of discrimination would be reflected by 1. The lower the index, the less discrimination exists.
Source: *EEOC*: Job Patterns for Minorities and Women in Private Industry, for respective years, U.S. Summary page.
Explanation of Appendix Table 6B; discussed on p. 88 of text.
For 1992, about 32% of white males were in the top two categories, and only 10.4% of Black males, so the discrimination is about 3 times or 33%. At the other end, one-third of Black males were in the bottom two job categories and 13% of white males, or the Black figure 2.5 times that for white. The overall discrimination is taken as the multiple of the 3 times at the top and the negative 2.5 times at the bottom, which comes out to 7.70% as shown in 6B. The improved index for Black males, 1992 compared to 1985, is probably due to less EEOC reports filed by large companies and less accurate reports, plus an even higher percentage of Black males relative to white in the lowest job categories. The main point of the Index is to indicate the persistence of discrimination against Black and Hispanic workers, male and female, in large companies. As we explain in the text, it is much worse in small companies.

APPENDIX TABLE 6C. MINORITY SHARES OF TOTAL EMPLOYMENT, LARGER PRIVATE COMPANIES, SELECTED YEARS, 1975–1992

Minority Group	Percentage Share of Total Employment				
	1975	1980	1985	1990	1992
All minorities	16.2	18.9	20.3	22.6	23.0
Men	9.6	10.5	10.5	11.5	11.8
Women	6.6	8.5	9.7	11.1	11.3
Black	10.7	11.6	12.1	12.7	12.5
Men	6.2	6.1	5.9	6.0	5.9
Women	4.5	5.4	6.2	6.7	6.7
Hispanic	4.3	5.4	5.7	6.7	7.0
Men	2.8	3.3	3.3	3.9	4.1
Women	1.6	2.1	2.4	2.8	2.9
Asian	0.9	1.5	2.1	2.8	3.0
Men	0.4	0.8	1.1	1.4	1.5
Women	0.4	0.7	1.0	1.3	1.5
Indian	0.3	0.4	0.4	0.5	0.5

6C (cont'd)

Minority Group	Percentage Share of Total Employment				
	1975	1980	1985	1990	1992
Men	0.2	0.3	0.2	0.3	0.3
Women	0.1	0.1	0.2	0.2	0.2

Source: *EEOC* Reports* for respective years.
*Table 6C does not include data for 1966 and 1967, the first two years of the reports. Evidence indicates that the data still had considerable inconsistencies and, in any case, did not include employment of Asians and Native Americans.

TABLE 6D. POPULATION AND EMPLOYMENT OF MEN AND WOMEN, 1994 *(THOUSANDS)*

	Population	Employment		Percent Women of Men	
		Number	Percent	Population	Employment
Male					
White	80,059	57,542	71.9	106.8	83.0
Black	10,258	6,241	60.3	123.0	105.7
Hispanic	9,104	6,530	71.7	99.3	64.5
Other	4,038	2,667	66.0	107.6	85.4
Female					
White	85,496	47,738	55.8		
Black	12,621	6,595	52.3		
Hispanic	9,014	4,258	47.2		
Other	4,343	2,277	52.4		

Note: The data for whites in this table are not corrected to eliminate Hispanic whites. The relevant ratios are sufficiently similar that correction would not significantly change results.
Source: *E&E*, Jan., 1995, T.5, p. 168. Population refers to non-institutionalized persons aged 16 and over.

Appendix to Table 7:4
Calculation of Discrimination indexes in craft employment against male Black and Hispanic workers for 1992: The principle is that without discrimination, Blacks and Hispanics would have the same percentage of their total blue collar employment in craft jobs as did white blue collar workers.
In fact, according to EEOC reports, while 34.93% of white blue collar workers had craft jobs, only 16.97% of Black blue collar workers and 17.98% of Hispanic blue collar workers had craft jobs. The Black percentage was 48.6% of the white percentage, and the Hispanic percentage 51.5% of the white percentage. The same procedure was followed for earlier years.

With reference to Table 9:1, page 141
In later publications, the Census Bureau has reduced the reported value of sales of Black-owned firms for 1982 by 22%, supposedly to make the figure comparable with that for 1987, which omitted corporations not using "subchapter S," a provision lowering taxes for corporations with

fewer than 35 shareholders. But by 1987 virtually all privately held corporations were taking advantage of this provision, which had not come into such general use by 1982. In 1987 there was only one "publicly owned" company with a majority of Black shareholdings. Thus, a more reliable comparison is between the 1987 results with the originally published 1982 results.

Table 10:2, p. 161. Adjustments to calculations:
Extra profits from racism, initial calculation, equals excess of mean wage and salary of non-Hispanic white worker over mean income of Black, Hispanic, and other worker, respectively, multiplied by numbers of such workers.
Adjustments:
1. To take out differentials in government employment, from which no *direct* profit is made by capitalist class. This adjustment is taken as a reduction of 8%, resulting from government employment amounting to 15% of Black employment, but wage differential in government employment being half as much as in private employment.
2. To allow for additional profits of employers, from lower payment of pensions, bonuses, vacation time, health coverage, etc. to black, Hispanic, etc., workers—added extra profit of 10%.
3. Allowance for unreported workers—add extra profit of 3%.
4. Combination of these three adjustments, an increase of 5%.
The same overall adjustment was used for all three categories of oppressed peoples, although the government correction for Hispanic workers, taken by itself, would be less than that for African American workers.
This adjustment was applied to both the 1980 and the 1992 statistics.

Reference Notes

Chapter 1 pp. 1 to 6

1. Douglas S. Massey and Nancy A. Denton, *American Apartheid: Segregation and the Making of the Underclass*, Cambridge MA., 1993
2. Jonathan Kozol, *Savage Inequalities: Children in America's Schools*, New York, 1991
3. Gerald Horne, *Reversing Discrimination: The Case for Affirmative Action*, New York, 1992
4. Andrew Hacker, *Two Nations: Black and White, Separate, Hostile, Unequal*, New York, 1992
5. Billy Tidwell, *The Price: A Study of the Costs of Racism in America*, National Urban League, 1990

Chapter 2, pp. 7 to 24

1. Felicity Barringer in *NYT*, 7/16–17/91
2. *Stat. Abst.*, 1992, Table 8, p. 11
3. Ibid., 1993, #20, p. 19
4. Barringer, op. cit
5. *NYT*, 7-26-91
6. *Stat. Abst.*, 1991, Tables 15, 16, pp. 14-15
7. *WSJ*, 3-8-94
8. Special Analyses: Budget of the U.S. Government, FY 1975, pp. 154-155
9. *NYT*, 3-16-74
10. Herbert Aptheker, *Political Affairs*, 1/74

Chapter 3, pp. 25 to 40

1. Kozol, *Savage Inequalities*, pp. 41-42
2. P60-184, Table 34, p. 34, and Table C-1, page C-12;
3. Hacker, *Two Nations*: p. 68; P60, No. 180, Table 1, pp. 2-3
4. Ibid., pp. 68-69
5. *The Economist*, London, 3-12-94
6. 1990 Census of Population and Housing, 1990 CPH-5-34, New York, Table 9

Chapter 4, pp. 41 to 58

1. P60-180, T.B-6, pp. B9, B10
2. U.S. Census Bureau, PINC-08, "Details of Earnings by Occupation and Race, 1991," unpublished data
3. U.S. Census Bureau 1990 CPH-L-94,

"Tabulations of 1989 Household Income Data by Race and by State," from 1990 Census of Population and Housing
4. *Economics of Racism*, 1975, pp. 37, 39, 73
5. *Stat. Abst.*, 1994, No. 19, p. 19
6. EEOC, "Job Patterns for Minorities and Women in Private Industry," 1992, T. 1, p. 1
7. U.S. Census Bureau, 1990 CPH-L-92, "Educational Attainment of Persons 25 Years and Over, by Race and by State: 1990"
8. N.Y.S. Dept. of Econ. Development, compilations of 1990 census data
9. *NYT*, 10-30-94
10. *NYT*, 10-30-94; 11-18-94
11. U.S. Census Bureau P70-34, "Household Wealth and Asset Ownership: 1991," T. 1, p. 2
12. Ibid. T. 1., p. xiv
13. Ibid. T. 2, p. 5
14. Ibid.
15. Arthur Kennickell and Janice Shack-Marquez, *Changes in Family Finances from 1983 to 1989*, in *FRB*, Jan. 1992, T. 2, p. 3
16. Ibid., pp. 4-5
17. Census Bureau, P70-34, T. H, p. xiii
18. Barry Johnson and Marvin Schwartz, in "Statistics of Income Bulletin," Spring 1993, pp. 105-113
19. Census Bureau P-70-34, T. H, p. xiii
20. Ibid, T. 4, p. 7

Chapter 5 pp. 59 to 78

1. *Ossining Citizen Register*, 4-20-91
2. *NYT*, 12-12-92
3. Ibid., 12-23-92
4. U.S. Census Bureau, P60-185, *Poverty in the United States*: 1992, Table 2, p. 2; Preliminary release on 1993 poverty statistics
5. P60-185, Tables, 14, 15, 16, pp. 84-96
6. Ibid., Table 14, p. 14
7. *NYT*, 9-2-94
8. *Survey of Current Business*, July 1994, Table 1.1, p. 54; 3.12, p. 77
9. P60-185, Table 6, pp. 16-19
10. Ibid., Table 2, pp. 2-3
11. Joint Center for Political and Economic

Studies, Washington, D.C., "The Declining Economic Status of Black Children, Examining the Change: Summary of Findings"

12. P60-185, Table 6, pp. 16-19
13. *NYT* 8-7-94
14. *Stat. Abst.*, 1994, No. 752, p. 493; 1993, No. 763, p. 488
15. P20-477, "Household and Family Characteristics," March 1993, Table 2, pp. 8-10
16. P60-185, pp. A6-A 7, Table A-2, page A-6
17. *Stat. Abst.*, 1993, No. 708, p. 454
18. *Stat. Abst.*, 1994, No. 703, p. 460
19. P60-188, Table 8, p. 22
20. Ibid., p. A-7
21. P60-185, Table F, page xviii
22. P60-188, Table 8, p. 22
23. Ibid., Table G, p. xix
24. *NYT*, 11-24-94
25. *WSJ*, 11-8-94
26. *NYT*, 11-23-94
27. *PWW*, 11-12-94

Chapter 6 pp. 79 to 100

1. *NYT*, 12-1-94
2. P60-184, T. 26, pp. 100-102
3. Ibid.
4. *Stat. Abst.*, 1993 T. 539, p. 346
5. *NYT*, 5-14-94
6. EEOC, EEO-1 Report, 1975, p. iii
7. EEOC, EEO-1 Report, 1967, p. vii
8. Ibid., p. ix
9. J. Kirschenman and K.M. Neckerman in *The Urban Underclass*, Brookings Inst., 1991, pp. 202-232
10. Ibid., p. 210
11. Ibid., p. 217
12. Ibid., pp. 230-231
13. E & E, Jan. 1944., T. 22, p. 208
14. U.S. Census Bureau, P. 23, No. 42, T. 51. p. 67; P 20, No. 488, Table E, p. 9
15. *WSJ*, 9-14-93

Chapter 7 pp. 101 to 121

1. *EROP* 1993, pp. 59-60
2. BLS: *Work Experience of the Population in 1991*, USDL 92-644
3. BLS: *Worker Displacement in the Early 1990's*, USDL 94-434
4. John Maynard Keynes, *General Theory of Employment, Interest and Money*, N.Y., 1935, p. 162
5. *Business Week*, 9-16-85

6. *E & E*, Jan., 1993, T. 39, p. 218
7. *E & E*, Jan., 1995, T. 5, p. 168
8. *E & E*, Jan., 1993, T. 6, pp. 179-80
9. *E & E*, Jan., 1995, T. 11, pp. 175-76
10. BLS: *Work and Family; Employer-Provided Training Among Young Adults, Report No. 838*, Feb. 1993
11. Census: P60-184, T B-17 and T B-18, pp. B35 and B 37
12. Peter Kilborn in *NYT*, 11-26-94
13. EEOC Combined Annual Report 1991-1992, p. 9
14. Ibid.
15. Kilborn, op. cit.
16. EEOC: Laws Enforced by the EEOC, pp. 3-4
17. *WSJ*, 9-14-93
18. Perlo, *Economics of Racism*, 1975, p. 134
19. EEOC: "A Unique Competence: A Study of Employment Opportunities in the Bell System," from *Congressional Record*, 2-17-72, pp. 1260-61
20. *NYT*, 1-25-94

Chapter 8 pp. 122 to 135

1. Gertrude Ezorsky, *Racism and Justice: the Case for Affirmative Action*, Ithaca and London, 1991, p. 1
2. Melvin J. Urofsky, *A Conflict of Rights: The Supreme Court and Affirmative Action*, N.Y., 1991, pp. 16-17
3. Ibid., p. 18
4. *WSJ*, 8-2-74
6. Horne, *Reversing Discrimination: ...*p. 2
7. *NYT*, 12-15-94
8. "U.A.W. Putting Together the Affirmative Action Puzzle," in *Solidarity*, May 1995

Chapter 9 pp. 136 to 152

1. *Stat. Abst.*, 1972, No. 965, p. 585; 1991, No. 1075, p. 543
2. *Hist. Stats.*, series K 109-153, p. 465; *Stat. Abst.*, 1993, No. 195, p. 653
3. W.E.B. DuBois, *The Autobiography of W.E.B. DuBois*, New York, 1968, p. 290
4. Special Analyses, Budget of the United States, FY 1975, T. L-1, p. 183, E-8, p. 89, D-3, p. 63
5. *Stat. Abst.*, 1982-83, T. 877, p. 518; 1993, T. 856, p. 541
6. *Stat. Abst.*, 1993, No. 868, p. 542
7. Andrew F. Brimmer, in *Black Enterprise*, May 1992, pp. 43-44

8. Ibid.
9. Marcus Alexis and Geraldine R. Henderson, "The Economic Base of African-American Communities: A Study of Consumption Patterns," in National Urban League, *The State of Black America*, 1994, New York, 1994, p. 81
10. *Survey of Current Business*, May and July 1993
11. *Black Enterprise*, Sept., 1991, p. 67
12. Ibid., June 1995, p. 91
13. Ibid., and *Stat. Abst.*, 1994, No. 1281, p. 476
14. *WSJ*, 2-13-91
15. *Black Enterprise*, June 1993, p. 82
16. Sears Roebuck Co., *Annual Report* 1992, p. 82
17. Andrew Brimmer in *Economics of Racism* (Perlo), 1975, p. 194
18. Marjorie Whigham-Desir: "Set Back for Set-Asides", *Black Enterprise*, June 1995, pp. 190-196
19. Gracian Mack in *Black Enterprise*, June 1995, pp. 157-158

Chapter 10 pp. 153 to 174

1. *EROP* 1955
2. John Roosevelt, speech to Commonwealth Club of San Francisco, *NYT* 7-7-56
3. *WSJ*, 2-28-74
4. *Daily World*, 3-7-74
5. Michael Reich: "The Economics of Racism," in Edward, Reich, and Weisskopf: *The Capitalist System*, Englewood Cliffs, N.J., 1972, pp. 316, 318
6. Ibid., pp. 317-318
7. Ibid., p. 320
8. Andrew Hacker, *Two Nations*: ...p. 4
9. Ibid., pp. 31-33
10. Ibid., pp. 32-33
11. Norval D. Glenn, "Occupational Benefits to Whites from the Subordination of Negroes," *American Sociological Review*, Vol. 28, June 1963, pp. 447-448
12. Billy J. Tidwell, *The Price*: ...,pp. 18-19
13. Walter L. Updegrave, "Race and Money," *Money Magazine*, December 1989, in Tidwell
14. Perlo, *Economics of Racism*, 1975, in Tidwell
15. John Roosevelt, op. cit.
16. Tidwell, op. cit. pp. 70-74
17. Joseph Duffey, *California Management Review*, 1988, in Tidwell, p. 72
18. Tidwell, op. cit., p. 60
19. Ibid, p. 74
20. *Survey of Current Business*, May, December 1993; *EROP* 1993, T. B-19, p. 369; BLS, "The Employment Situation," January 1944

Chapter 11 pp. 175 to 191

1. Isabel Wilkerson, in *NYT*, 4-4-91
2. Ibid.
3. Quoted in Kozol, *Savage Inequalities*, p. 15
4. Wilkerson, op. cit.
5. The *NYT*, 11-2-93
6. The *NYT*, 8-21-93
7. Massey and Denton, *American Apartheid*: ...pp. 17-18
8. Ibid., p. 24
9. *NYT*, 1-31-94
10. 1990 Census of Population and Housing, CPH-1-34, New York, "Summary Population and Hoiusing Characteristics," T. 3, p. 72
11. Diana Jean Schemo, The *NYT*, 2-15-94
12. *NYT*, 3-17-94
13. Census Bureau special tabulations; *Stat. Abst.* 1993, No. 719, p. 461
14. Massey & Denton, op. cit., T. 3.1, p. 64
15. Council for Greater Opportunities in Greater Cleveland, "Poverty Indicators, Cuyahoga County, Ohio, Trend, 1970-1991"
16. Massey & Denton, op. cit., pp. 75-77
17. Massey & Denton "Hypersegregation in the United States" in *Demography*, Vol. 26, No. 3, Aug., 1989, pp. 379-385
18. *American Apartheid*, p. 113
19. Ibid., Table 3.2, p. 68
20. *Stat. Abst.* 1993, No. 1235, p. 724
21. Ibid., No. 1236, p. 724
22. IRS *SOI Bulletin*, Spring 1993, figure H, p. 11; *Stat. Abst.* 1993, No. 527 p. 340
23. *WSJ*, 1-31-92; 11-30-92
24. *Stat. Abst.* 1993, No. 811, p. 515
25. *NYT*, 12-17-93
26. *NYT*, 8-15-91
27. Ibid.
28. Shreveport, La., *Times*, 9-3-93
29. *NYT*, 9-15-93
30. *NYT*, 7-26-74
31. *WSJ*, 12-8-93
32. *NYT*, 12-9-93
33. *NYT*, 12-11-93

34. *NYT*, 12-7-92
35. Ibid.
36. *American Apartheid*, T. 7.1, p. 201

Chapter 12 pp. 192 to 201

1. Gannett Suburban Newspapers, 10-23-91
2. U.S. Government Printing Office, "Adult Literacy in America," Sept. 1993, p. 32
3. Christopher J. Hurn, *The Limits nd Possibilities of Schooling*, Needham Heights, MA, 1993; Caroline H. Perse'l, *Education and Inequality*, N.Y., 1977
4. Massey & Denton, op. cit., p. 8
5. William Celis, "Study Finds Rising Concentration of Black and Hispanic Students," *NYT*, 12-14-93
6. Hacker, op. cit., p. 201
7. Gwen Ifill: "President Urges Building on School Desegregation," *NYT*, 5-18-94
8. Kozol, op. cit.
9. Sam Dillion: "School Board Challenges Aid Formula," *NYT*, 3-16-93
10. Jorjanna Price: "Squeeze Play: 28 States Join Texas in School Finance Skirmishes," Texas Comptroller of Public Accounts, *Fiscal Notes*, Nov. 1992
11. Nicholas Lemann: "Brown Now," *NYT*, 5-18-94
12. Iver Peterson: "Court's Decision Gives Whitman Some Breathing Space," *NYT*, 7-13-94
13. *NYT*, 5-3-93
14. Ibid.
15. *NYT*, 6-9-91
16. Alabama Education Department, Annual Report, 1990-91, p. 30
17. Government Printing Office, *The National Education Goals Report: Building a Nation of Learners*, Washington D.C. 1993
18 Kozol, op. cit., p. 205

Chapter 13 pp. 202 to 221

Belgrave, Linda L., May L. Wykle, and Jung M. Choi. 1993. Health, "Double Jeopardy, and Culture: The Use of Institutionalization by African Americans." *The Gerontologist* 33(3):379-385

Bergner, Lawrence. 1993. "Race, Health, and Health Services." *American Journal of Public Health* 83(7):939-41

Bureau of Census. 1992. *Stat. Abst. of the United States*, 1992

Cornelius, Llewellyn J. 1993. Ethnic Minorities and Access to Medical Care: Where Do They Stand? *Journal of the Association for Academic Minority Physicians* 4(1):16:-25

Council on Ethical and Judicial Affairs, AMA. 1990. "Black-White Disparities in Health Care." *Journal of the American Medical Association* 263(17):2344-6

Escarce, Jose J., Kenneth R. Epstein, David C. Colby, and J.Sanford Schwartz. 1993. "Racial Differences in the Elderly's Use of Medical Procedures and Diagnostic Tests." *American Journal of Public Health* 83(7):948-954

Ginzberg, Eli 1991. "Access to Health Care for Hispanics." *Journal of the American Medical Association* 265(2):238-241

Kogan, Michael D., Milton Kotelchuck, Greg R. Alexander, and Wayne E. Johnson. 1994. "Racial Disparities in Reported Prenatal Care Advice from Health Care Providers." *American Journal of Public Health* 84(1):82-88

McBride, David. 1993. "Black America: from Community Health Care to Crisis Medicine." *Journal of Health Politics, Policy and Law* 18(2):319-337

Mutchler, Jan E., and Jeffrey A. Burr. 1991. "Racial Differences in Health and Health Care Service Utilization in Later Life: The Effect of Socioeconomic Status." *Journal of Health and Social Behavior* 32(December):342-356

New York State Advisory Committee To the United States Commission on Civil Rights. 1964. *Report on the Buffalo Health Facilities*. Washington: U.S. Civil Rights Commission

Short, P., A. Monheit, and K. Beauregard. 1989. *A Profile of Uninsured Americans*. National Medical Expenditure Survey Research Findings 1, National Center for Health Services Research and Health Care Technology Assessment. Rockville, Md.: Public Health Service

Smith, David B. 1991. "Population Ecology and the Racial Integration of Hospitals and Nursing Homes in the United States." *The Milbank Quarterly* 68(4):561-596

Taravella, Steve. 1990. "Black Hospitals: Struggling to Survive." *The Washington Post* (Sept. 11):WH12, 13, 14

U.S. General Accounting Office. 1992. "Hired Farmworkers: Health and Well-

Being at Risk." Report to Congressional Requesters. Feb

Whittle, Jeff, Joseph Conigliaro, C.B. Good, and Richard P. Lofgren. 1993. "Racial Differences in the Use of Invasive Cardio-vascualr Procedures in the Department of Veterans Affairs Medical System." *The New England Journal of Medicine* 329(9):621-658

Chapter 14 pp. 222 to 239

1. *NYT*, 9-29-94
2. Ibid., 8-24-94
3. Ibid., 5-20-94
4. Ibid., 4-22-94
5. Ibid., 8-28-94
6. *Hist. Stat.*, pp. 414–415; *Stat. Abst.* 1993, No. 305, p. 195
7. *Stat. Abst.* 1993, No. 313, p. 198
8. Ibid., Nos. 342, 343, p. 210
9. Ibid., No. 343, p. 210
10. Ibid., No. 342, p. 210
11. Ibid., No. 308, p. 196
12. *Business Week.*, 12-13-93, p. 78
13. Ibid., pp. 72–73
14. Hacker, *Two Systems*, p. 196
15. *Business Week*, 12-13-93, pp. 72–78
15a. Fox Butterfield in *NYT*, 10-5-95, *NYT* editorial, 10-7-95
16. *Hist. Stat.*, p. 416, Stat. Abst., 1993, No. 322, p. 202
17. *Budget of the U.S. Government, Fiscal Year 1995*, p. 197
18. Ibid., Table 7-4, p. 238
19. *Stat. Abst.*, 1993, No. 322, p. 202
20. *WSJ*, 5-12-94
21. *Business Week*, 12-13-93
22. *Stat. Abst.*, 1993, No. 309, p. 197, No. 305, p. 195
23. *Business Week*, 12-13-93
24. *Stat. Abst.*, 1993, No. 344, p. 210
25. *WSJ*, 5-12-94
26. *Hist. Stat.*, p. 422
27. *NYT*, 3-18-93
28. Ibid., 7-29-92
29. Ibid., 4-20-91
30. Hacker, op.cit., p. 236
31. *NYT*, 7-17-94
32. *Peoples Weekly World*, 7-16-94
33. Gannett News Service, *How Cops Beat the Rap*, Series reprint, 1992
34. *NYT*, 4-17-94
35. *WSJ*, 6-16-94
36. *NYT*, 6-26-94
37. Yu Quanyu in *Beijing Review*, Oct. 3-9 1994, p. 24

Chapter15 pp. 240 to 258

1. Philip S. Foner, *History of the Labor Movement in the United States*, Vol. 4, New York, 1965, p. 127
2. William Z. Foster, *History of the Communist Party*, New York, 1952, p. 257
3. Ray Marshall, *The Negro Workers*, N.Y., 1967, p. 29
4. BLS Report 558, "Earnings and Other Characteristics of Organized Workers," 1977, T. 2, p. 1
5. *Stat. Abst.* 1993, No. 689, p. 436; E&E., Jan, 1944. T. 57, p. 248
6. *NYT*, 5-6-74
7. Marshall, op. cit., p. 24
8. Scott Marshall in *PWW*, 7-9-94
9. P 23, No. 46, T. 43; E&E, Jan. 1995, T. 41, p. 215
10. *Stat. Abst.*, 1982-83, No. 651, p. 389; E&E., 1/94, T. 22, p. 209
11. *UAW*, Solidarity 9, 1993
12. Ray Marshall, op.cit., pp. 40-41
13. Foster, *The Negro People in American History*, NY, 1954, pp. 367, 374

Chapter16 pp. 259 to 279

1. *NYT Magazine*, 10-9-94
2. Ibid.
3. Lee Rainwater and William L. Yancey, *The Moynihan Report and the Politics of Controversy: The Negro Family: The Case for National Action*, 1967, p. 130
4. Ibid., P. 88
5. Jim Genova in *PWW*, 7-23-94
6. Andrew Hacker, op. cit. p. 68
7. Ibid., p. 80
8. William Ryan, *Blaming the Victim*, N.Y., 1971, p. 4
9. *ERP, 1974*, pp. 153-154
10. Ibid. 1975, pp. 112-113
11. Ibid.
12. Edward C. Banfield, *The Unheavenly City*, Boston, 1970, p. 73
13. Ibid., pp. 32-33
13a. Perlo, *Economics of Racism*, 1975 p. 122
14. Banfield, pp. 76-77
15. Ibid., pp. 48-54
16. Ibid., p. 266
17. Ibid., pp. 245-246
18. William Julius Wilson: *The Declining*

Significance of Race, Chicago, 1978, pp
1-2

19. Wilson, *The Truly Disadvantaged*,
Chicago, 1987, pp. 135-6
20. Ibid., p. 136
21. *The Declining Significance of Race*, p
127
22. *The Truly Disadvantaged*, p. 20
23. Ibid., p. 128
24. Ibid., pp. 122-123
25. Ibid., p. 92
26. Ibid., p. 113
27. Wilson: "Studying Inner-City Social Dis-
locations: The Challenge of Public
Agenda Research," *1990 Presidential
Address*, reprinted in *American Sociological Review, Vol. 56*, Feb., 1991
28. *NYT*, 7-24-94
29. Hugh B. Price, Keynote Address,
National Urban League Convention, Indi-
anapolis, IN., 7-24-94
30. *NYT*, 11-14-93
31. Ibid., 8-18-94

Chapter 17 pp. 280 to 289

1 AFL-CIO, The Pocketbook Issues,
November 1991, p. 28

Index